Philosophy of Comics

ALSO AVAILABLE FROM BLOOMSBURY

Aesthetics: The Key Thinkers, edited by Alessandro Giovannelli
Problems in Value Theory, edited by Steven B. Cowan
The Political Power of Visual Art, by Daniel Herwitz
The Visual Language of Comics, by Neil Cohn

Philosophy of Comics

An Introduction

**Sam Cowling and
Wesley D. Cray**

BLOOMSBURY ACADEMIC
LONDON • NEW YORK • OXFORD • NEW DELHI • SYDNEY

BLOOMSBURY ACADEMIC
Bloomsbury Publishing Plc
50 Bedford Square, London, WC1B 3DP, UK
1385 Broadway, New York, NY 10018, USA
29 Earlsfort Terrace, Dublin 2, Ireland

BLOOMSBURY, BLOOMSBURY ACADEMIC and the Diana logo are trademarks of
Bloomsbury Publishing Plc

First published in Great Britain 2022

Cover design by Louise Dugdale
Cover image: *Little Sammy Sneeze*, 1905, by Winsor McCay

A catalogue record for this book is available from the British Library.

A catalog record for this book is available from the Library of Congress.

ISBN: HB: 978-1-3500-9844-2
PB: 978-1-3500-9845-9
ePDF: 978-1-3500-9846-6
eBook: 978-1-3500-9848-0

Typeset by Deanta Global Publishing Services, Chennai, India
Printed and bound in Great Britain

To find out more about our authors and books visit www.bloomsbury.com and
sign up for our newsletters.

To Harriet and Stephanie.

—Sam

To Ronnie James, Foot Foot, and Luke the Drifter.

—Ley

Contents

Figures

Preface

Philosophy is big. And if you know where to look, you can find philosophy about almost anything. For that reason, it's a peculiar fact that despite the sheer vastness of philosophy, the philosophy of comics has only just barely gotten underway. We're grateful to the philosophers who first started writing on comics, and we're hopeful that this book is evidence of how sprawling, weird, and exciting the philosophy of comics can be. We also hope that our engagement with their ideas and arguments is evidence of how many good questions in the philosophy of comics remain to be asked (or answered).

Ley (she/they) sends unyielding gratitude to their colleague pals, quaran-team, and therapist. Big hugs to Agatha Switchblade, Mistress Lady Una Booma Butterfly, and Cosey Fanni Kitty. Much love to the family and to Huel. High-fives to Sam all day, every day.

Sam (he) is enormously grateful to his family for putting up with the comics strewn around the house all the dang time and to his colleagues for graciously suffering through his (never funny and rarely relevant) comics references. He recommends everyone write a book with Ley.

Thanks to Island Fantasy (Nanaimo, British Columbia), World's Greatest Comics (Westerville, Ohio), Vault of Midnight (Grand Rapids, Michigan), and Collected (Fort Worth, Texas) for their generous research assistance. Support your local comic book shop.

Sam would like to thank the R.C. Good Foundation for a fellowship that made the writing of this book possible. Ley thanks TCU for an AddRan Summer Faculty Research Grant in 2019 that did the same. Thanks also to the Billy Ireland Cartoon Library and Museum at Ohio State as well as the Ray and Pat Browne Pop Culture Library at Bowling Green State University. Much gratitude to audiences at the 2018 Canadian Philosophical Association meeting, Denison University, Texas Christian University, the University of Manitoba, the 2018 meeting of the American Society for Aesthetics Rocky Mountain Division, the Batman and Popular Culture Conference in 2019, the 2018 Cartoon Crossroads Columbus, as well as to Bryan Conn and John

McHugh, for helpful feedback on various things that went on to become chunks of various chapters.

This book wouldn't exist without our students and the discussions we've had with them about philosophy, comics, and the philosophy of comics over the past several years. Thanks to each of you.

Introduction

1. Philosophy through Comics

A young girl runs into the longing arms of her parents while a statuesque man in a suit and hat stares on, beholding his success in saving her. While these characters might as well be standing on a city sidewalk, this action

Figure 1.1 *Mr. A* (1973), Steve Ditko. Mr. A looks at reunited family while criminals plummet into the abyss of text.

unfolds on a featureless white rectangle that seems to hover in space. The rectangle is surrounded by massive bands of text including words and phrases like "reason," "justice," and "retaliatory force." At the degrading edge of the rectangle, two figures, drawn in heavy blacks, desperately hang on for dear life. In the next panel, they beg for mercy and forgiveness while plummeting into a cluster of words like "injustice" and "corruption" which are piled up like a kind of typesetting car crash. The man in the suit and hat stands above, looking in the opposite direction, indifferent to their cries. Pages earlier, he shot one of their gang and ignored their pleas for help while saving the young girl from their kidnapping and ransom attempt.

This is one of many remarkable moments in Steve Ditko's uncompromising superhero comic *Mr. A* (1973), and the moral questions it raises are difficult ones. What do we owe to evil doers? When and to what extent is punishment rational? What actions are permitted when we attempt to save someone's life? Historically, addressing these and other fundamental ethical questions has been a central concern of philosophers. It's easy, too, to see why philosophers would have much to say about the moral principles implicit in Ditko's heroic depiction of Mr. A. They're not exactly uncontroversial, after all.

One intellectual project at the intersection of philosophy and comics— call it *philosophy through comics*—uses comics like *Mr. A* to present, understand, and answer philosophical questions. Philosophy through comics takes seriously the possibility that comics can provide us with tools or insights useful for tackling ethical, epistemological, and other issues within philosophy. Apart from its distinctive focus on the medium of comics, philosophy through comics is therefore quite similar to other projects like philosophy through film or philosophy through science fiction that use works within a specific medium or an entire genre as a launching point for philosophical inquiry.

An importantly different project at the intersection of philosophy and comics—the one with which this book is concerned—is the *philosophy of comics*, which applies philosophical methods in order to better understand the medium of comics. Where philosophy *through* comics uses comics as a means toward more general philosophical ends, philosophy *of* comics seeks to provide a philosophical theory of what comics are, what is distinctive about how comics work, and why comics matter. Just as other areas of philosophy take aim at specific topics like law, love, commerce, the environment, and pretty much any other subject, the philosophy of comics takes comics and the practices surrounding them as central objects of inquiry. As we'll see, this project requires delving into a wide variety of philosophical issues and areas, but the main aim is clear: to provide philosophically sound answers to the complex and diverse questions that might be raised about comics.

With this distinction between projects in mind, someone doing *philosophy through comics* might look at *Mr. A* and pose questions like the following:

- What account of rationality would vindicate Mr. A's view that reason requires him to kill the kidnappers?
- Does our willingness or reluctance to view Mr. A as a hero indicate that his methods are morally objectionable?
- Is the implicit premise of *Mr. A* that criminals are beyond redemption remotely plausible?

Tackling such questions is one of several ways we might hope to make progress in assessing philosophical theories about topics like reason, justice, and punishment. In contrast, when doing the *philosophy of comics*, quite different questions—ones specific to comics—are front and center:

- How are text and image related in these bizarre panels? For example, is it *true* in Ditko's story that there are huge words floating behind Mr. A?
- Is a comic with these sorts of moral commitments rightly classified as a *superhero* comic or does it belong to a different genre?
- How much should Ditko's own views and intentions affect our interpretation of comics like *Mr. A*?

Questions of these sorts, if properly addressed, promise to shed much light on the comics medium.

Although philosophy through comics and philosophy of comics can and do overlap, appreciating the difference between the two is an important part of understanding each. But we also need answers to two further questions: Where does the philosophy of comics fit within the discipline of philosophy? And what is the connection between the philosophy of comics and the field of comics studies? We take up these two questions in the next couple of sections. Along the way, we'll introduce some key concepts and some of the methodological commitments that will play an important role throughout this book.

2. Philosophy of Comics

As a discipline or field of study, philosophy is notoriously difficult to define. Perhaps the most famous definition owes to Wilfrid Sellars: "The aim of philosophy, abstractly formulated, is to understand how things in the broadest possible sense of the term hang together in the broadest possible sense of the term" (1962: 35). While this might be accurate, it also might not be terribly informative. What, for example, does it mean for things to "hang together" and how should we go about the pursuit of understanding? Does, say, scientific experiment or writing poetry count?

However we might define philosophy as a discipline, it remains fairly standard practice to divide it into subdisciplines on the basis of subject matter. Different subdisciplines like ethics, epistemology, and logic are therefore driven by questions concerned with different subjects. So, for example, ethics is concerned with goodness, moral value, right action, and other moral notions and therefore addresses questions about how we ought to act and what kinds of things are morally valuable. Similarly, epistemology, a different sub-discipline, is concerned with knowledge, justification, evidence, and so on. It therefore tackles questions regarding what, if anything, we are justified in believing and where the limits of human knowledge lie. Subdisciplines of philosophy are numerous and for almost any subject matter you might think up, there is some portion of philosophy that addresses it directly or indirectly. Despite this, there is no universally accepted way of dividing up all of philosophy and no matter how one might hope to do so, overlaps and intersections are unavoidable. Some of these are obvious. For example, when we investigate the epistemology of ethics, which asks how we acquire moral knowledge, we will find ourselves engaged in epistemology and, to at least some degree, ethics. Some overlaps and intersections are less obvious. It is, for instance, all but impossible to do political philosophy without, at the same time, doing ethics—for example, by accepting or rejecting claims about how citizens and states ought to treat one another.

One of the broad conclusions of this book is that the philosophy of comics has substantial intersections across much of philosophy—more, we think, than has yet been acknowledged by the vast majority of philosophers. Despite this, it remains commonplace to view the philosophy of comics as falling within the philosophy of art, which is the subdiscipline of philosophy concerned with—well, art. According to some, it would be more apt to say that the philosophy of comics falls within the subdiscipline of *aesthetics*, but this is a point of philosophical controversy. (On the aesthetics versus philosophy of art distinction, see Hick (2012: 3–4).) Depending upon one's philosophical views, aesthetics might be narrower than, broader than, or just the same thing as the philosophy of art. If that seems a bit puzzling to you, you're not alone. Here, however, we will simply sidestep this controversy and mark our preference for talking about the philosophy of art rather than aesthetics (though we'll sometimes talk about aesthetic *properties*; more on that later).

There are good reasons for questioning whether the philosophy of comics is most naturally viewed as a part of the philosophy of art. Some of these reasons are straightforward: it is unclear whether all comics are works of art. Some comics are advertising, instruction manuals, or pornography that arguably fall short of being art. And, if the philosophy of comics is taken to be a part of the philosophy of art, then there would be some comics—namely, those comics that are *not* artworks—that the philosophy of comics would not be concerned with understanding. But, of course, the philosophy of comics *is* concerned with those comics and any other ones regardless of whether or not one counts them as art. So the philosophy of comics seems at once narrower and broader than the philosophy of art, in that it focuses primarily not on artworks but on a class of things that happen to be art, sometimes.

Other reasons to deny that the philosophy of comics is a part of the philosophy of art are a bit more complex and perhaps more controversial. Suppose, for example, you believe that the key philosophical questions about comics revolve around how, as a hybrid medium—one that brings together written text and (typically) drawn images—comics represent information. So understood, the philosophy of comics stands alongside other subdisciplines like the philosophy of language and the philosophy of images, which seek to understand linguistic representation (how words represent things) and pictorial representation (how pictures represent things). And, together, these three subdisciplines *really* fall not within the philosophy of art but in a different and rarely labeled subdiscipline that we might call the *philosophy of representation*.

Despite these issues in philosophical taxonomy, it is clear that holding the philosophy of comics to be a part of philosophy of art comes with certain theoretical and practical benefits. It explains and makes clear its commonalities with parallel philosophical projects like the philosophy of film and the philosophy of music—both of which share the same complicated relationship, discussed earlier, with the philosophy of art more generally. It also serves as a continuing reminder that perennial questions in the philosophy of art regarding context, interpretation, and value can and should be asked of those comics that happen to be artworks. And, more often than not, when philosophers have been interested in comics, it has been because those comics are artworks of an interesting or important variety. Depending upon the future of the philosophy of comics, there might eventually be reason to resist situating it within the philosophy of art, but, for our purposes, it is a helpful space within which to envision the work undertaken in this book.

Once we have found a place for philosophy of comics in the sprawling field of philosophy, we are still left with a looming methodological question: How should we go about doing the philosophy of comics? In trying to answer this question, the first thing to note is that there is no easy answer to the much broader question: How should we go about doing philosophy? This is due, in part, to the fact that there is no such thing as *the* philosophical method. There are, of course, better and worse ways to do philosophy. Everyone should agree that the method of unreflective guesswork is inferior to the provision of clear and careful arguments. But, beyond this, one finds nothing but controversy. Since it would take an entirely different book to mount a comprehensive case for the philosophical methodology we'll rely upon here, we'll have to settle for briefly describing *our* preferred way of doing philosophy and, in particular, doing the philosophy of comics.

In keeping with the contemporary analytic tradition, our focus is on explaining phenomena as clearly as we can and then offering arguments for and against competing theories that seek to explain these phenomena. We avoid, as best we can, concepts and distinctions that cannot be drawn through clear examples or, better yet, given explanations or analyses in something like everyday language. While it might be exciting or enlivening to be presented with provocative but opaque claims about comics (*everything is a comic! nothing is a comic!*), we believe that there are more and less plausible views about comics and that rigor and clarity in argument offer the best way to discern them. Throughout, our hope is to make genuine philosophical progress in understanding comics, but progress only occurs as part of a philosophical and intellectual community. For that reason, we're more interested in being clear and proven wrong than being vague and immune to refutation—in part, that's because the former option is something from which all of us might learn. We're also quite sympathetic with cartoonist Ivan Brunetti's observation, "Just when I think I've stumbled upon some philosophical truth, I remember at least one favorite cartoonist whose work violates whatever blustery principle I may have just posited" (2006: 7).

This description of philosophical methodology might be surprising for those who've only seen philosophy from afar, if at all. It's easy (and kind of fun) to caricature philosophy as a discipline based upon cryptic defenses of wild theses that are philosophically attractive precisely because they're so provocative and incredible. That is, of course, a way that *someone* might do philosophy, but it's a bad way to attempt to improve our collective understanding. Moreover, we don't deny that there might be good philosophical reasons to believe certain striking or surprising theses about comics or anything else, for that matter. For example, it is famously difficult to rebut arguments for external world skepticism—roughly, the view that we are ignorant about almost all of what we take ourselves to know. There are also powerful philosophical arguments for exotic metaphysical views that, if accepted, would likely require us to radically revise our worldview—for example by seeking to show that are no ordinary objects like tables, chairs, or even people.

For those committed to what we might call "first philosophy," philosophical reasoning is absolutely foundational. This is because philosophical arguments can, in principle, overrule what science, common sense, and other sources of belief lead us to accept about the world. So, for those committed to first philosophy, pretty much every philosophical issue is a live one and, if we find ourselves unable to rebut the arguments on the table, we might well be rationally obligated to radically revise our worldview. Are there any physical objects? Has any object ever really moved? Is any action really morally permissible? For those engaged in first philosophy, assessing the balance of philosophical arguments is of paramount importance, since we cannot rely merely upon our familiar assumptions about topics like matter, motion, and morality.

This book isn't an exercise in first philosophy. That's not because we don't think first philosophy is without merit. It's because first philosophy has little place within the philosophy of comics. If we don't know anything about the external world, then of course we don't know anything about comics. And, if there are no physical objects, then, of course, there are no comic books or comics creators. For this reason, making progress in the philosophy of comics requires that we take on a wide range of working assumptions about a surprising number of philosophical issues. In effect, by narrowing our philosophical focus to comics, we thereby set aside various big-ticket philosophical questions for another time.

As a consequence, philosophy of comics is a kind of "second philosophy." It proceeds on assumptions, not only that there are comics, but also that it makes sense to talk as if there are people who make and read them, and as if much of what we (and they) believe about comics is more or less correct. Now, this doesn't mean that people—indeed, even exceptionally knowledgeable people—can't be mistaken about comics. We ought not take anyone's beliefs about comics (or most anything else) as sacrosanct. To the contrary, the philosophy of comics is especially interested in actively interrogating the beliefs of those engaged in the practices that involve comics and doing our best to systematically think through them.

In much the same way that the philosophies of music and mathematics seek to understand the practices of music and mathematics by examining what happens within these fields, the philosophy of comics seeks to understand comics by carefully attending to comics practice. We'll draw upon this term—"comics practice"—throughout this book, so it will be useful to clarify it a bit here. At its most general, it refers to any of the things that people do that involve comics, including social activities like the comics burnings of the 1950s, economic activities like increasing the price of comics in the 1990s, and political activities like using the Punisher logo as an ideological symbol in the 2010s. Of course, when our concerns are philosophical, it makes sense to focus on those activities that might shed the most light on the nature of comics. The obvious place to look is to what comics creators, readers, and critics as well as printers, publishers, librarians, archivists, and many others say about comics. This, in turn, requires that we scrutinize, along with many other practices, activities like the creation of comics in studios, discussions of comics production at comic conventions, interviews with comic creators on podcasts, the archiving of comic strips in museums, the development of collection policies about comics in libraries, and, most obviously, the reading of comics pretty much anywhere and everywhere.

In addition to comics themselves, comics practice reveals itself through a wide range of texts and sources. These include comics reviews in magazines or on websites, historical retrospectives in exhibits or books, and fan opinions published in letter columns. These are only a very partial list of things that constitute comics practice but, taken together, these and other sources serve as a central guide for understanding what comics are and how they work. But, as rich and interesting as these sources are, they are also an incomplete and often inconsistent guide. Like most human affairs, comics practice is a messy, vague, and confusing thing, and one regularly finds contradictory, ambiguous, or wildly implausible views expressed. (Shockingly, folks talking about comics don't always seem to be striving for philosophical coherence.)

So, when pursuing answers to philosophical questions about comics, we can and should draw upon some additional resources. These include the critical practices that surround other mediums like film and printmaking as well as general philosophical considerations like logical consistency and coherence with our best philosophical theories. For this reason, the philosophy of comics does not seek to simply aggregate and summarize comics practice but to use it just as Sellars's definition suggests: as a tool for understanding how comics and the world hang together in the broadest possible sense.

Just as the philosophy of music might help us understand practices like music criticism, it is by no means a replacement for music criticism. Similarly, the philosophy of comics is not a replacement for comics criticism, which Darren Hudson Hick (2016: 330) characterizes as "the interpretation, analysis, and evaluation of one or more given works." While some forms of comics criticism overlap with scholarly work on comics, most of it does not. As Hick notes, comics criticism is rightly viewed as a spectrum that ranges from "comics reviews intended primarily to advise the comics-buying public" to "scholarly works of criticism usually detached from any commercial considerations." So, while the philosophy of comics is far from a guide to which comics one ought to read, it does aim to illuminate the concepts, assumptions, and commitments that underpin the practice of comics criticism in its various forms.

Consider, for example, certain kinds of critical disagreement that emerge regarding specific comics. In a 1989 letter to *The Comics Journal* (#130), comics creator Harvey Pekar famously complained about the central conceit of Art Spiegelman's *Maus* (originally serialized from 1980 to 1991), saying "Spiegelman could've used the drawing style he used in 'Prisoner from the Hell Planet' [1972] in *Maus*, but that would not have been as arty as employing animals, and he has difficulty distinguishing between arty and artful, and between gimmickry and genuine innovation, as do many comics fans." Understanding the core of Pekar's critique—whether or not we agree with it—requires unpacking a range of complex notions including what "drawing style" amounts to in the context of Pekar's criticism and, in addition, what it means for a drawing style to be "arty." The philosophical projects that flow from this therefore involve spelling out the distinction between style and genre in comics, the typical relationships between them, and what Pekar might mean when he attempts to distinguish "gimmickry" and "genuine innovation." Importantly, this work of unpacking and understanding Pekar's criticism is a philosophical enterprise that need not aim at settling the merits of *Maus* but, instead, on understanding how the practice of comics criticism sometimes works.

3. Philosophy and Comics Studies

A recurring theme in comics criticism, whether in popular histories of comics or interviews with comics creators, is the cultural status and artistic prestige of the medium. That story is a complicated one, tracing through the celebrity of cartoonists like Alex Raymond and Al Capp in the forties, the outright vilification of comics and comics creators in the fifties, the oscillating neglect and celebration of creators like Frank King and Will Eisner over the last eighty years, and the current esteem afforded cartoonists like Chris Ware and Alison Bechdel. We are more than content to leave the work of charting this complex history to comics historians. (Indeed, a recurring problem within comics studies—one we'll try our best to avoid in this book—is non-historians repeating claims founded upon uncertain or incomplete historical records.) That said, there is a different history, that of the philosophy of comics, which warrants special attention here.[1]

The history of the philosophy of comics—in the sense under discussion here—is exceptionally short. Within analytic philosophy in particular, comics have received remarkably little attention when compared to musical traditions like opera and the so-called classical tradition, literary forms like plays and novels, and visual arts like painting and sculpture. Even film and television, which share certain historical and cultural affinities with comics, have received swifter, smoother receptions. Aaron Meskin (2011: 855) considers a range of possible explanations: low cultural status, a lack of philosophical problems distinctive to the medium, and the absence of a canon of inarguable comics masterpieces. But, whatever its cause, philosophical engagement with comics, in the form of either philosophy through comics or philosophy of comics, has been a long time coming. And, if we set aside pop culture volumes like *X-Men and Philosophy* (2009), which are intended for popular audiences and typically (and by design) meet only the loosest of academic standards, it is rare for comics to make an appearance in the analytic philosophy of art, even as brief examples, prior to 2000. Perhaps the main exception is a discussion of the medium as one among many in Noël Carroll's *A Philosophy of Mass Art* in 1998.

Things changed, slowly, after the publication of the first book-length work of philosophy focused on comics, David Carrier's *The Aesthetics of Comics*, in 2000. Jeff McLaughlin's edited volume, *Comics as Philosophy*, was another early contribution in 2005. Despite these steps forward, it wasn't until almost a decade later that a substantial body of related philosophical work on comics emerged, driven by the efforts of philosophers including Roy Cook, Darren Hudson Hick, Aaron Meskin, Christy Mag Uidhir, and Henry Pratt. Perhaps the best indicator of when the philosophy of comics established itself is the publication of *The Art of Comics: A Philosophical Approach* (2012), edited by Cook and Meskin. That book brought together leading contributors to the philosophy of comics and offered extended engagements with many of the questions that have been at the forefront of the philosophy of comics. And, in many ways, that work serves as a partial blueprint for where and how to deepen philosophy's engagement with comics. Our book aims to build upon it while extending it outwards and upwards in a variety of different ways.

Explaining how the philosophy of comics relates to philosophy is a simple matter when compared to the task of explaining how the philosophy of comics relates to the field of comics studies. Let's start with the obvious: comics studies is an interdisciplinary academic and scholarly field that studies comics. There are conferences, journals, societies, courses, and even a few departments and programs. So described, this provides us with no insight into the methods, priorities, structure, and tendencies of comics studies. After all, there is, in principle, a vast range of potential ways to undertake systematic academic or scholarly inquiry into comics. As a matter of historical fact, however, (Anglo-American) comics studies has been largely dominated by scholars with academic backgrounds in English and departments like Communication and Media Studies. So, while artists, historians, art historians, linguists, and philosophers have made contributions to comics studies, they are dwarfed in number by comics studies researchers who find their academic home in English or nearby departments. (The exception that proves the rule: *The Seduction of the Innocent* (1954) by Fredric Wertham is almost certainly the most influential book on comics and his background is in the psychological sciences.)

Although comics studies is, in principle, unlimited in its diversity of methods, it has, in practice, typically functioned as a kind of cognate area for English (and English-adjacent) departments. This has yielded mixed results. There has been a wealth of interesting work, sensitive to narrative considerations as well as contexts of production and reception. At the same time, there has also been a widespread derogation of the pictorial aspect of comics in critical discussions. (Philosophers, ourselves included, are no less guilty, and, in what follows, we leave aside careful formal analysis, pointing where we can to the contributions of others.) A popular explanation for why text has been prioritized over image in comics studies has been the disposition of literary theorists to engage comics primarily as texts rather than as a hybrid of image and text. Commenting on this trend, Charles Hatfield, a comics scholar who teaches in an English department, says, "the disciplinary fit has not been easy, or seamless. For one thing, I can now see that the refusal (or mistrust) of images has been one of the basic ideological moves of literary studies" (2017: xi). Similarly, as critic R. C. Harvey puts it, "Too often . . . consideration concentrates on the essentially literary aspect of the work, the narrative and its implications" and ignores the "visual" while privileging "the verbal" (2005: 23). These issues aside, comics studies has clearly benefited from the pioneering work by those in English departments and throughout this book we will discuss a range of exemplary contributions. (We point toward some in the "Recommended Readings" section.) It is unlikely that any other academic discipline would have fared better than English had it been disproportionately influential in shaping comics studies. But, even so, it is only alongside work from other disciplines that the potential of comics studies has a chance to be fully realized.

The reception of *philosophical* work within comics studies has been peculiar. Those describing comics studies hasten to tout its interdisciplinary nature, but only rarely is philosophy among the list of disciplines cited as contributing. More often than not, the interdisciplinary connections named are fields that substantially overlap like literature, visual studies, media studies, and communication. Indeed, in Hatfield and Bart Beaty's recent edited volume *Comic Studies: A Guidebook* (2020), which aims to provide a snapshot of the state of the art of this interdisciplinary field, no philosophers are included and the work by Cook, Meskin, and almost every other philosopher of comics goes uncited and undiscussed.

Some of the tension between comics studies and the philosophy of comics likely flows from differences in method and background assumptions. We suspect, for example, that philosophers' focus on extracting and making explicit arguments, theories, and theses will strike some outside of philosophy as stifling. For our part, we take it to be the best way to promote fruitful and productive intellectual disagreement. In the spirit of interdisciplinarity, we are hopeful that those working in comics studies who take seriously the project of engaging with philosophy will find this book as useful as we've found preceding work in both the philosophy of comics and comics studies. And, as an introductory textbook, we'll try to make clear where we're especially hopeful for promising comics studies work across disciplines.

While academics have a seemingly inexhaustible capacity for debating where to draw disciplinary distinctions, there is a different and arguably more important distinction within comics studies: the distinction between academic and nonacademic scholarship. Given the lengthy period throughout which the academy ignored comics, the historical research and preservation of comics and comics culture was, for a very long time, entirely the work of fans, critics, collectors, and creators. Some of this work is among the most historically rich and artistically insightful writing on comics. (A semi-recent sampling can be found in *Best Comics Criticism* (2010), although this tradition is a long and rich one arguably inaugurated by Colton Waugh's 1947 book, *The Comics*.) Good-faith engagement with comics studies therefore requires careful study of nonacademic work including fan discourse and both amateur and professional comics criticism. But we also need to be careful to distinguish work that is undertaken without academic standards like peer review, proper citation, and engagement with relevant literature. In addition, we should keep in mind that not everything academics do is thereby academic research. The key distinction between "the academic" and "the nonacademic" therefore concerns *research*, not the researchers.

A related, more difficult challenge concerns the kind of mental discipline with which we approach comics. We ought to do our best to pull apart our ways of thinking about comics as fans and enthusiasts from our scholarly, dispassionate ways of thinking about them as researchers. Indeed, as Marc Singer plausibly argues in *Breaking the Frames* (2018), comics studies has been unduly swayed by the practices and discourse of fans that extol the virtues of comics while too often failing to face up to some of their critical defects.

The distinction between academic and nonacademic discourse isn't easy to navigate. There are many things it leaves out. Most notably, neither category easily subsumes the writing produced by cartoonists and comics creators. These include prefatory essays, short pieces for edited collections, and interviews. The breathless praise that cartoonists heap upon giants of the medium in interviews can, for example, be treated as nonacademic fan discourse, but in the very same interviews, one often finds careful discussion of technique, production, and themes that equal any academic journal article for their sophistication, insight, and even scholarship. There is no easy or mechanical recipe for sorting opinions into academic and nonacademic categories, and, even if we could, this would not settle how much credence or attention they deserve. We should, however, remain sensitive to the fact that within the ecosystem of comics creation and criticism, there are different roles like fan, critic, creator, and scholar, and that individuals can often move across them in ways that are not immediately obvious. To point to one important example, Scott McCloud's watershed contribution *Understanding Comics* (1993) is a lively and innovative comic, which often features his unabashed expression of fandom, both for the medium of comics and for specific works. Despite this, *Understanding Comics* warrants (and has received) substantial consideration as either a precursor of or an early contribution to the philosophy of comics. So, although he's not an academic and *Understanding Comics* is not academic research, we can and should—so long as it is properly contextualized—engage with this work as one voice among many in comics studies and in the philosophy of comics.

4. How This Book Works

This book isn't an effort to defend a specific "philosophy" of comics. And, while one of our aims is to offer an introduction to this still relatively new field, another aim is to pose some new or underexamined philosophical questions about comics. A different aim of this book is to make some progress in answering a bigger, more daunting question: What would it mean to have a philosophy of comics? Put differently: what questions would we need to answer in order to have a comprehensive philosophical theory about what comics are, what they're like, and why they matter?

To answer that question, it's useful to think about parallel questions elsewhere in philosophy. Take the philosophy of music. Like comics, music involves a diverse array of practices and is focused on generating certain kinds of activities or artifacts. While there are salient differences, a comprehensive philosophy of comics demands many of the things we might also want out of a comprehensive philosophy of music.

Just as the philosophy of music seeks to provide an account of what musical compositions, performances, and scores *really* are, the philosophy of comics should provide us with an account of what comics, characters, genres, and adaptations are. Just as the philosophy of music, in an effort to situate itself against the broader backdrop of the philosophy of art, should remain cognizant of parallel phenomena in nearby fields such as the philosophy of theater or the philosophy of film, so should the philosophy of comics. And, just as the philosophy of music ought to explain apparent features of music—for example, how the same songs can be repeatedly performed, how different versions of songs might differ in their artistic and aesthetic properties, how works can be sampled or covered—the philosophy of comics owes us an account of the apparent features of comics—for example, how comics can have different instances, vary in their artistic and aesthetic properties across versions, and be adapted into other mediums. Much as the philosophy of music aims to make sense of distinctions between categories like classical and rock and the practices that shape these distinctions, the philosophy of comics owes us accounts of how the medium relates to genres like horror and superhero comics and non-genre categories like the ever-controversial label of *literature*. Finally, the philosophy of music includes questions about the ethics of the various practices involving musical works and performance. Some of these are exceptionally nuanced. For example, when is it morally wrong for someone to sing or perform a song with offensive or otherwise sensitive lyrics? When is it inappropriate for someone to perform in a tradition originating outside their own culture? In parallel, ethical questions within the philosophy of comics are rather complex in nature: What is morally required when we reprint old comics? How are comics related to potentially morally loaded categories like pornography? What does respect for marginalized groups require or rule out when we create comics?

It should be clear that a philosophical account of any large-scale human activity like comics or music will have numerous moving and carefully interconnected pieces. But, in arranging the following chapters, we hope to introduce some of the key pieces of a bigger picture, one that might help us see what a comprehensive philosophy of comics would look like. We start with definitional, conceptual, and ontological issues regarding the medium of comics and then turn to related metaphysical and epistemological issues regarding characters, interpretation, and truth in comics. We then explore some important aspects of comics and comics practice related to genres like horror and superhero comics before moving on to some ethical and philosophical puzzles about diversity and representation in comics. After carefully examining some non-genre designations like *literature* and *pornography*, we conclude with the connection between comics and other mediums by reflecting on the nature of adaptation.

To give you a sense of where various issues are explored, the following subsections provide a brief chapter-by-chapter summary. And, while this book can be read in a variety of different ways, a familiarity with Chapter 2 is regularly presupposed throughout subsequent chapters. Additionally, Chapters 4 and 5 are closely connected by a focus on the ontology of characters and truth in fiction. If you decide to skip over Chapters 4 and 5, we recommend reading them before turning to Chapter 10.

Chapter 2: What Are Comics?

This chapter dives into the messy and contentious debate about how, if at all, we should define the medium of *comics*. We'll explore competing approaches, deepen our familiarity with comics (and comics-like artifacts), and ask what hangs on the success or failure of philosophers' efforts to define the medium.

Chapter 3: Comics as Artifacts—Ontology and Authenticity

Comics raise a host of philosophical puzzles once we start thinking systematically about *what* and *where* they are. This chapter focuses on several ontological issues: How can we make sense of the *multiplicity* of comics— roughly, the fact that a given comic can be located in different places at the same time? How should we understand claims about authenticity and identity within the comics medium? For instance, how does looking at a reprint of a comic differ from looking at the original? We also explore ethical issues that arise in the practice of reprinting and especially recoloring comics.

Chapter 4: Does Superman Exist?

Characters pervade comics. Indeed, few comics are without them. But what kind of thing is a comics character? Are they merely ideas in the minds of readers or perhaps abstract artifacts crafted by the activities of creators? How ought we make sense of our discourse surrounding characters, and what does it take to create one?

Chapter 5: Truth in Comics

Building on the discussion of fictional discourse in the previous chapter, we explore the challenge of providing a theory of *truth in comics* and its connection to the complex phenomenon of comics canon. What principles drive our ordinary judgments about which claims to accept or reject about what happens within comics stories? And what happens when these stories are told over years and years, across different comics, and by a sprawling number of writers and artists?

Chapter 6: Genre in Comics

Like other mediums, comics are often partitioned and appreciated with regard to genres like romance or western comics. This chapter investigates the nature of genre categories in general and the contours of two specific comics genres: superhero and horror comics. What makes something a horror comic? What qualifies as a superhero comic? We then explore how certain philosophical views about genre bear upon the task of understanding comics practice at the intersection of superhero and horror comics.

Chapter 7: Representing Social Categories in Comics

Historically, the comics medium—especially mainstream superhero comics—has had a rather significant representation problem, and recent debates have brought the ethics of representation to the forefront of comics criticism. This chapter considers some of the moral and aesthetic dimensions of representation and the challenge of making comics inclusive of marginalized groups.

Chapter 8: Are Comics Literature?

The category of *literature* is a familiar but controversial one. Given that some comics are often described as "graphic novels," and in light of their changing cultural status, the relationship of comics to literature is a contentious affair. This chapter takes up philosophical work on the concept and category of *literature* with an eye toward analyzing what it might mean for comics to be literature and why it might matter.

Chapter 9: Comics, Obscenity, and Pornography

This chapter explores the nature of pornographic and obscene comics and the potential conflict between art and pornography. What is the nature of pornography, and when does a comic qualify as pornographic? How should we approach moral issues surrounding ostensibly pornographic comics, and when should we censure—or even celebrate—those creators who make them?

Chapter 10: Page, Panel, Screen—Comics and Adaptation

Comic adaptations have run amok in film and television. But what does it mean when we say that a character like Batman has been adapted into film or that a comic like Alison Bechdel's *Fun Home* (2006) has been adapted into a musical? This chapter examines the philosophical puzzles that arise when we think about transporting a work across forms or mediums. What features of a comic must be preserved for a film to count as a genuine adaptation of its source work? Are there artistic mediums that resist adaptation to or from comics? And what are the potential costs or benefits of adapting from one medium to another?

5. Recommended Readings

At the end of each chapter, we'll include a list of some recommended resources that explore relevant issues and, in many cases, dive deeper into the cases and complexities than we're able to do here. These lists are by no means complete, but we hope that they prove helpful in guiding readers in directions they might hope to go. (Throughout the book, we generally supply publication dates for works, though, in certain cases where, for example, serialization proves unduly complicated, we omit them.)

Philosophy through Comics

Academic volumes on philosophy through comics include McLaughlin's *Comics as Philosophy* (2005) and its follow-up *Graphic Novels as Philosophy* (2017a). Chris Gavaler and Nathaniel Goldberg's *Superhero Thought Experiments* (2019) is the most sophisticated, extended contribution to philosophy through comics, which defends superhero comics as a substantial source of philosophically rich thought experiments. In addition, there are numerous books devoted to popular philosophy through comics with titles like *Watchmen and Philosophy* (2009), *Green Lantern and Philosophy* (2011) and Mark D. White's *Batman and Ethics* (2019.) Note, however, that these books are typically more interested in characters and stories as they occur *across* comics and other mediums like film and television.

Philosophy of Comics

Meskin's "Philosophy of Comics" (2011) and the introduction to Cook and Meskin's *The Art of Comics: A Philosophical Approach* (2012) are excellent starting points. For the locus classicus of proto-philosophy of comics, see McCloud's *Understanding Comics* (1993). And though they are largely outside of the particular methodology within which we are working here, classic works of French comics criticism such as Thierry Groensteen's *The System of Comics* (2007) and *Comics and Narration* (2011) certainly qualify as *philosophical* and warrant attention. Several chapters of Gavaler and Goldberg's (2019) also focus on issues of authorship and interpretation in comics.

Philosophy in Comics

In the last ten years a number of comics explicitly devoted to philosophers or the history of philosophy have appeared. These include *LogiComix* (2009) by Apostolos Doxiadis and Christos Papadimitriou, which chronicles the life of Bertrand Russell, as well as *Heretics!* (2017) by philosopher Steven Nadler and cartoonist Ben Nadler. Michael Patton and Kevin Cannon's *The Cartoon Introduction to Philosophy* (2015) is a comics-based engagement with philosophical thought and Sam Kieth and William Messner-Loebs's *Epicurus the Sage* (1989–91) is a noteworthy, comedic portrayal of classic Greek philosophy. The philosophy website *Daily Nous* also features a running archive of philosophy comics—many of which are by professional philosophers.

Comics Studies

Comics studies has expanded rapidly in the last ten years, and there are a large number of collections that would serve as good starting points depending upon readers' interests. *The Secret Origins of Comics Studies* (2017) is a wide-ranging collection that covers the history of the field, and Benjamin Woo's "What Kind of Studies Is Comics Studies?"(2020) is an insightful discussion of where the field presently stands. Hatfield and Beaty's *Comic Studies: A Guidebook* (2020) is a recent introduction to the field. Hilary Chute's *Why Comics? From Underground to Everywhere* (2019) is an accessible, wide-ranging discussion of a variety of influential comics and key themes in comics studies. Karin Kukkonen's *Studying Comics and Graphic Novels* (2013) is an engaging survey of comics studies methods and interesting case studies. Charles Hatfield's *Alternative Comics* (2005) and Roger Sabin's *Adult Comics* (1993) are early and influential comics studies texts. Bart Beaty and Benjamin Woo's *The Greatest Comic Book of All Time* (2016) is data-driven exploration of the dimensions of cultural capital and prestige within comics.

Engagement in comics studies from psychology, linguistics, and cognitive science is quickly growing, and Neil Cohn's work, drawn together in *The Visual Language of Comics* (2014), is a natural starting point. Frank Bramlett's edited volume *Linguistics and the Study of Comics* (2012) offers a range of linguistics-driven inquiries into comics. For an art historical perspective, Andrei Molotiu's "Abstract Form: Sequential Dynamism and Iconostasis in Abstract Comics and Steve Ditko's *Amazing Spider-Man*" (2011) is an exemplary place to start. Roy Cook, Frank Bramlett, and Aaron Meskin's *Routledge Companion to Comics* (2016) is an exceptionally helpful resource for introductory, topic-specific surveys, as is Frederick Luis Aldama's *Oxford Handbook of Comic Book Studies* (2020).

Colton Waugh's *The Comics* (1947) is a very early critical overview of the emergence of the comic strip and its reception. Douglas Wolk's *Reading Comics* (2008) and Paul Gravett's *Comics Art* (2014) are insightful and wide-ranging contributions to comics criticism. Donald Phelps's *Reading the Funnies* (2001) collects a wealth of critical engagement with comic strips. Comics critic Tom Spurgeon's website, *The Comics Reporter*, remains a repository for rich and deeply informed interviews and reviews despite his death in 2019.

Comics History

David Kunzle's *The Early Comic Strip* (1973) is a founding contribution to the history of comics, tracing the development of European printing and broadsheets up to the nineteenth century. Thierry Smolderen's *The Origins of Comics* (2014) maps the subsequent period in which comics emerge as a more or less distinctive medium. Jean-Paul Gabilliet (2013) is a wide-ranging cultural history of American comics that covers significant ground. Blackbeard and Williams's *The Smithsonian Collection of Newspaper Comics* (1977) is an accessible collection of strips with a historically informed survey. R. C. Harvey's *The Art of the Funnies* (1994) and *The Art of the Comic Book* (1996) are useful resources. Amy Kiste Nyberg's *Seal of Approval* (1998) is a careful historical inquiry into the emergence of the Comics Code Authority. Sean Howe's *Marvel Comics: The Untold Story* (2013) is a popular and illuminating history of one of the most influential comics publishers. Recently, a variety of different approaches to engaging comics history have emerged, including creator-focused books like Spiegelman and Kidd's *Jack Cole and Plastic Man* (2001) and Charles Hatfield's book on Jack Kirby, *Hand of Fire* (2011), illuminating historical prefaces by cartoonists like Chris Ware and scholars like Jeet Heer can be found in various reprints of Frank King's *Gasoline Alley* (1918–59) and George Herriman's *Krazy Kat* (1913–44*)*. Qiana Whitted's *EC Comics: Race, Shock, and Social Protest* (2019) is a thematic engagement with a specific and influential comics publisher. For a comic book history of comics, see Fred Van Lente and Ryan Dunlavey's *The Comic Book History of Comics* (2017).

Comics Practice

The craft and practice of comics-making is a prerequisite for the existence of comics and, in turn, the philosophy of comics. Understanding how comics are made and the nature and variety of comics creators' choices is a daunting but necessary task. Some useful texts for learning about the production of comics include (but are hardly limited to) Jessica Abel and Matt Madden's *Drawing Words & Writing Pictures* (2008) as well as *Mastering Comics: Drawing Words & Writing Pictures Continued* (2012), Lynda Barry's *Making Comics* (2019), Ivan Brunetti's *Cartooning: Philosophy and Practice* (2011), Will Eisner's *Comics and Sequential Art* (1985), Dave Gibbons and Tim Pilcher's *How Comics Work* (2017). Nick Sousanis's *Unflattening* (2015) is a meditation on both the making of comics and the nature of the medium. Scott McCloud's follow-ups to *Understanding Comics, Reinventing Comics* (2000) and *Making Comics* (2006), are influential and wide-ranging.

2

What Are Comics?

---

1. Why Ask What?

Across philosophy, it's a common practice—one that traces back at least as far as Plato—to pose and attempt to answer *What Questions*. What is freedom? What are desires? What is beauty? It's not surprising, then, that when it comes to the philosophy of comics, philosophers have been especially interested in its big What Question: What are comics? This chapter examines some potential answers to this question and tackles some of the puzzles that arise upon considering them. Throughout, we'll introduce key notions that are especially useful for understanding what comics are and what they can be. Before doing all that, though, it's worth thinking just a bit more about the value of the "what are comics?" question. Why even bother asking it?

In Plato's dialogue *Euthyphro*, we're presented with a fictional exchange between his teacher, Socrates, and a local know-it-all, Euthyphro. Socrates asks Euthyphro what piety—or holiness—is. Euthyphro claims to know the answer and then offers a series of potential definitions. Socrates considers each of these carefully, showing that none are satisfactory. After Socrates has shown that Euthyphro is incapable of defining piety, Socrates concludes that neither of them *really* know what piety *really* is. Despite this superficial failure, the dialogue serves as an illuminating and instructive inquiry into piety and related concepts. This sort of outcome is a common one in Plato's dialogues. As it turns out, while many people act and speak as if they know what things like justice, knowledge, and love are, Socrates repeatedly shows that they are unable to define these concepts. So, in at least *some* sense, they don't know what justice, knowledge, and love are insofar as they can't define their object of inquiry.

Perhaps matters will prove similar in the case of comics. Perhaps, despite seeming to know perfectly well what comics are, we won't be able to define the concept *comic*. Either way, Plato's *Euthyphro* illustrates an important point: even if we are left without a definition, our understanding of something can be improved by *seeking* that definition. So, although Plato's dialogue ends with no definition of piety, at its conclusion we have still learned much about piety—often by learning what distinguishes it from other, nearby concepts.

Some philosophers have argued that the search for a definition of comics—much like any general search for definitions—might be more trouble than it's worth. For example, philosopher Aaron Meskin memorably implores: "Let's get beyond the definitional project" (2007: 376). But we believe that the search for a definition of comics, when viewed properly, is a valuable thing regardless of whether we succeed. This is because it involves carefully thinking through what features comics always or typically share and considering the vast diversity among comics. So, by the end of an attempt to define comics, we're likely to find ourselves with a richer understanding of comics even if we don't agree upon a uniquely acceptable definition.

Suppose, however, that we do find the right answer to the "what are comics?" question. What would such an answer be good for? There is, quite obviously, a lot we can do without one. We can certainly read, discuss, and make comics without being able to define the medium. Some have suggested, however, that the project of defining comics is crucial for comics criticism. For instance, comics critic R. C. Harvey claims that the proper "description" of comics is uniquely valuable for engaging in comics criticism. Specifically, he holds that his own characterization of comics as "a visual-verbal blend" is of particular importance:

> It also suggests a critical criterion: in the best examples of the medium, the words give a meaning to the pictures that the pictures otherwise lack, and vice versa. The blend creates a new meaning that is not present in either of the two vital ingredients alone without the other. I must emphatically add, however, that visual-verbal blending is only one of numerous criteria by which the cartooning artistry of comics should be judged—only one, albeit the first one. (2005: 22)

Now, Harvey might be right that *his own* model of criticism requires a characterization of comics as a visual-verbal blend. But, as Meskin (2007: 375) points out, "the fact that warranted evaluation and interpretation of an artwork requires knowledge of the sort of thing it is does not imply that knowledge of essence is also required." Put differently: there's simply no evidence that *all* comics criticism requires an *analysis* of comics. Just as jazz records can be reviewed and films critically panned without knowing how to define jazz or cinema, comics criticism simply does not hang on the prospect of successfully defining comics.

Although a definition of comics is not a prerequisite for comics criticism, there are intellectual and artistic projects where a definition would be helpful and others where it does seem required. If we wanted to write a comprehensive history of comics or teach a course exclusively on comics, we would have to decide what to include or exclude from the scope of our enterprise. (Notice that this is true even if we elect to treat certain works as borderline cases and, at the same time, disregard other works as *non*-borderline cases.) Similarly, if we wanted to edit a collection like *Best American Comics* or give prizes like an Eisner Award or the Prix Révélation at Angoulême, we might have to answer tough questions about what counts as a comic. Finally, when organizing libraries or archives, in order to make consistent decisions about which artifacts to keep and where to keep them, we require a policy that distinguishes comics from other artifacts. Indeed, that's why the Library of Congress has a Collections Policy Statement that defines comics (though only after lumping them together with cartoons): "comics and cartoons are defined as entities consisting primarily of one or more distinct illustrations (panels), which tell a story or convey an (often humorous) situation, often with the aid of text captions and/or dialog balloons." We'll return to this definition later on, but, for now, keep in mind that under the right circumstances, we might actually need to answer the question of what comics are. And, even if our preferred answer proves imperfect, it will quickly become clear that some answers are better than others.

2. How to Define Things

Throughout Plato's dialogues, certain individuals who claim to know what something like justice or knowledge is make an obvious mistake: they confuse knowing what a standard example or a typical instance of something is with being able to define the concept in question. To be sure, we often point to examples in order to show that we grasp the relevant concept. If an alien or a small child asked you what comics are, you might, for example, begin by pointing to the dog-eared *Usagi Yojimbo* volume on your desk. But when philosophers pose What Questions, they want more than a handful of examples. They want an *analysis*, which will provide the necessary and sufficient conditions for being an instance of the concept in question.

A *necessary condition* for being a thing of kind K is a feature that something *must* have in order to be a K but that does not, on its own, entail that something is a K. For example, a necessary condition for being a square is having exactly four sides but not all figures that have exactly four sides are squares. A *sufficient condition* for being a K is a feature that not every K needs to have but that would guarantee or entail that something is a K. For example, a sufficient condition for being an animal is being a rat but not all animals are rats. To give an analysis of *comics*, then, is to give a set of necessary and jointly sufficient conditions for being a comic.

Taken separately, necessary and sufficient conditions provide us with interesting information about comics but not enough information to answer the "what are comics?" question. For instance, learning that a necessary condition for being a comic is the inclusion of images isn't enough to help us distinguish comics from portraits or films. Similarly, claiming that a sufficient condition for being a comic is having a regular nine-panel layout doesn't tell us what it is that all comics have in common. In contrast, if we were to complete the following sentence, we *would* know the necessary and jointly sufficient conditions for being a comic:

Something is a comic if and only if _____.

If completed, this sentence would specify the feature(s) shared by and unique to comics. The answer to the What Question is therefore whatever correctly fills that blank.

In trying to fill in the blank, there are certain constraints that ensure our analysis is a satisfactory one. For example, we can't say that something is a comic if and only if it's a comic. That's true—trivially so, in fact—but it's *vacuous*, offering us no insight whatsoever. It's also *circular*: if our aim is to analyze the concept of *comics*, then if we use the concept of comics in our analysis, we're simply back where started: in need of an analysis of the concept of comics. This points toward a moral about analyses in general: no satisfactory analysis (or way of "filling in the blank") can be given using the concept we seek to define.

Circularity is one reason to reject analyses like the following: something is a comic if and only if it is treated like a comic; or something is a comic if and only if most people would say it is a comic. But there's another reason to reject these sorts of answers: they would mistakenly render people infallible in their judgments about which things are comics. For, if something is a comic just because we treat it as one, then, if we, for whatever reason, treated portraits, phone books, or snowshoes as comics, views of this sort implausibly entail that portraits, phone books, and snowshoes are therefore comics.[1] Presented with such views, a good question to keep in mind is one often attributed to Abraham Lincoln: "How many legs would a cat have if we called a tail a leg?" It's even more important, however, to remember his (alleged) answer: "Four. Calling something a leg doesn't make it one."[2]

Here's another thing we can't do: we can't say that something is a comic if and only if it is a nexus of grapho-iconic manifestation. This answer and others like it are unsatisfactory for a different reason: they're *uninformative* given the opacity of the terms involved. Now, that's partly because we just made up the term "nexus of grapho-iconic manifestation." But like a lot of terms that academics make up, it might sound informative (smart even!), but it provides no improvement in our understanding. In fact, there are some ways in which this answer is worse than the ones earlier because it might initially *seem* informative. (Full disclosure: we think this is a vice of some of the proposed definitions of comics that we *won't* focus on in this chapter.) To be clear, technical vocabulary and discipline-specific terminology are perfectly acceptable in analyses and we'll rely on them in our discussion here. We also think that a certain measure of indeterminacy is to be expected given that, as with most human artifacts, the distinction between comics and non-comics is occasionally a vague one. But, unless we have a good and independent grip on a term or concept, we should avoid using them in potential analyses. Another moral, then: any satisfactory answer to the What Question must be clear and informative enough to *improve* our understanding of comics.

There are additional constraints on adequate analyses, but the most important one is *extensional adequacy*.[3] Concepts like *dog, mirror,* and *comic* all have extensions—namely, those things to which predicates like "is a dog," "is a mirror," and "is a comic" are correctly applied. And, in defining these concepts, the necessary and sufficient conditions we provide need to coincide with the extension of the concepts in question. So, in the case of comics, an extensionally adequate definition will count all and only those things that are comics as comics. This might seem obvious, but it's the rationale behind the standard method for evaluating proposed answers to What Questions: the *method of counterexample*, which proceeds by proposing a definition and then trying to find a counterexample. In our case, a counterexample would be a *non*-comic that our definition says is a comic or a comic that our definition says is a *non*-comic. When presented with a compelling counterexample, we're obliged to either revise our definition or attempt to develop an entirely different one. We'll put this method to use shortly, but before we do so, it will be useful to establish some common ground in our thinking about comics and tackle some potential misconceptions.

2.1. Are Comics Art?

When talking about comics, critics often draw upon Will Eisner's preferred term "sequential art" or, less frequently, refer to comics as "the ninth art." (This latter term is a play on the tradition of dividing the "fine arts" into seven categories, with the eighth being television, videogames, or something else, depending on who you ask.) These are serviceable terms to employ in suitable contexts. But neither term ought to be confused with an analysis of what comics are. The most obvious reason to avoid this is because each term, when recast as an analysis, mistakenly requires that each and every comic is a work of art.

As we noted in the previous chapter, there is a subdiscipline of philosophy concerned with the nature and limits of art. We won't attempt to summarize the vast range of views about how to define art (or whether a definition is even possible). And, as philosopher Patrick Maynard notes, there is also an exceptionally broad notion of "art" that is sometimes operative when, for example, we talk about a company's "art department" (2005: 6). (*That* exceptionally broad usage seems to include more or less anything visible created by humans.) Our concern here is with the familiar but considerably narrower (along one axis) and broader (along another) sense of "art"—the sense that's relevant when we talk about supporting *the arts* or learning to appreciate art. Like symphonies, sculptures, and poems, we take it to be undeniable that many comics are artworks in this sense. And, as Meskin (2013: 575) argues, "it is unlikely that any plausible theory of art—essentialist or nonessentialist—could be marshaled to exclude all comics from the category." But we think it is similarly uncontroversial that at least some comics are *not* artworks.

The range of nonart comics is, in some ways, less well understood than that of art comics, given the sustained philosophical attention and interest traditionally afforded to artworks. At a first pass, nonart comics include instructional comics like those we use to assemble desks, informational comics that demonstrate how certain systems function, and advertisement comics that promote products. When these sorts of comics are not artworks, it's often because they're created with no ambition of audience or critical engagement *as artworks*. Such artifacts naturally find themselves evaluated in purely functional terms. (There are, however, instructional or advertisement comics that do retain a fair claim to being artworks—for example, Will Eisner's instructional comics for *Army Motors* magazine, Dan Clowes's *OK Soda* designs, or Chris Ware's book jacket design for a translation of Voltaire's *Candide*.) This does not, of course, mean that we can't praise some of them for being competently crafted or well designed—even *artistically* so. But the point stands: some comics are not artworks and, for this reason, we should avoid defining comics in any way that requires them to be.

2.2. Are Comics Cartoons?

Etymology is a poor substitute for philosophy. This is as true in the philosophy of comics as it is elsewhere. Obviously, comics need not be "comic" in the sense of being comedic or humorous. This linguistic association between comedy and comics is, however, inherited from the description of British humor magazines like *Life, Judge,* and *Puck* as "comic weeklies." The same association is notably absent in other languages. Instead, formal features of comics often play a parallel etymological role. In Italian, comics are *fumetti* (roughly, "puffs of smoke") on account of speech balloons. In Portuguese, comics are *quadrinhos* (roughly, "little boxes") while in French, comics are *bandes dessinée* (roughly, "drawn strips").[4] Like "comics," each of these names potentially misleads when it comes time to define comics—for example, silent comics are "smokeless," photo-comics aren't really "drawn," and circular panels aren't "boxes."

Cartoons, a category prominently associated with comics, have a similarly rich and closely related etymological history. *Cartone* was an Italian word for preliminary drawn studies produced in the course of making larger artworks. But, when the British humor magazine *Punch* undertook a satirical design contest in the 1840s, the term "*Punch's* cartoons" came into use and was quickly transformed into the broader term "cartoons," which referred broadly to humorous drawings.[5] In contemporary contexts, "cartoon" is often used to refer to a category of works that cuts across comics, animation, and other mediums, characterized by simplification, abstraction, and exaggeration. As Andrei Molotiu (2020a: 153) characterizes cartooning, it is a technique or practice consisting in "the graphic simplification of figurative shapes for the purposes of communication, humor, and so on in comic strip and comic book rendering (as well as, of course, in gag cartoons, animation, and other visual media)." This definition captures an important fact about cartooning—that it is a technique closely and importantly connected to the comics medium. And, while many comics artists describe themselves as cartoonists, this terminological fact does not entail that all comics are cartoons. For, as Molotiu's definition also makes explicit, cartooning is practiced across different kinds of visual mediums.

As philosopher Henry Pratt (2011) argues in his paper "Relating Comics, Cartoons, and Animation," there are more than terminological affinities between cartooning and comics. For example, Pratt considers whether certain features of comics production—for example, the rapidity, seriality, and poor legibility of early comics publishing—might explain the pervasiveness of cartooning in comics. Whatever one's view on this question, there is simply no way to tell the history of comics without drawing deeply from the history of cartooning. After all, many of the greatest achievements in comics are cartoons—for instance, Ernie Bushmiller's *Nancy* (1938–82) and Carl Barks's *Uncle $crooge*. Additionally, many of the most politically charged and morally fraught moments in comics history flow from the use of cartooning in service of caricature as a mode of social commentary.[6]

Despite the time-worn association between comics and cartoons, comics artists make use of diverse styles and techniques, some of which approach a remarkable degree of realism that often yields comics that are not readily described as cartoons. The use of photography, collage, and, with increasing regularity, certain digital techniques suggests that not only are many comics not cartoons but in some cases comics aren't even *drawn*—at least not in any familiar sense.[7] This isn't to say that the use of digital tools precludes the possibility of drawing, but that the advent of novel technology raises subtle and far-reaching issues about how to understand and characterize the activity of drawing.[8] In his 2005 book *Drawing Distinctions,* Maynard works through a large number of these philosophical concerns. Here, we'll simply note that there is no good reason to believe that comics must be cartoons or drawn via traditional means as evidenced by the increasingly familiar practice of assembling comics from digital materials or photographs.[9]

2.3. Are Comics Printed?

In Gregory Hayman and Henry Pratt's "What Are Comics?," they note that one potential approach to defining comics is "medium-based." On such a view, "comics are classified in terms of the material components by which they are typically produced" (2005: 419). And, since comics have typically been produced with ink on newsprint, this approach would require an analysis according to which comics must be printed artifacts. Hayman and Pratt rightly note that such a view enjoys no serious plausibility. Comics can be physically realized in diverse ways including the short *comic strips* that we encounter in newspapers and, after their emergence in the 1930s, the magazine-style format of the *comic book*. Current comics production is, of course, even more wide-ranging. Comics have migrated to the web, appearing in any number of digital contexts and formats. The 48-plus page album format is commonplace in European comics. *Tankōbon* volumes of manga standardly comprise previously serialized installments. Trade paperbacks in North America are free-standing, long-form works or collections of individual "floppies." Comics also occasionally find themselves painted on museum walls or enfolded into the long tradition of artists books.[10] The complexity and range of comics "delivery" resists any simple or comprehensive summary, and this provides ample reason to reject any analysis of *comics* that involves their material components or requires that all comics be physically printed.

A more difficult question is whether comics need to be *reproduced,* regardless of whether this is done via physical printing or online distribution. It is indisputable that the history of comics is intertwined with the history of printing and that comics have historically and typically functioned as a mass art (or at least as a mass medium). In this respect, they are profoundly different from paintings and much closer to novels or films. Consider, however, a three-panel story a student draws in their notebook over the course of a dreary philosophy class. Suppose this multi-panel drawing is never intended for circulation, much less reproduction. Does it therefore fall short of being a comic *because* it is neither reproduced nor *intended* for reproduction? Hayman and Pratt reject any kind of reproducibility constraint on comics, noting that such a view would require denying comics status to works that, from all appearances, seem to be perfectly good examples of comics. And, while Meskin (2012: 34–7) demonstrates that the relationship between comics and their reproduction is a complex affair, he shares in Hayman and Pratt's general assessment. We'll return to this issue in the next chapter, but we similarly reject any requirement that comics must be reproduced even if most of them are.

Given this remarkable diversity among comics, a challenge arises for the way in which we (and many others) talk about them. We've helped ourselves to the terminological assumption that comics are a medium and we've therefore talked about the project of analyzing *the comics medium*. Whether there is any such thing as *the comics medium* is, however, a contestable assumption. In their book *The Power of Comics*, Matthew Smith and Randy Duncan claim that "there is no distinct medium known as comics" (2009: 3) since comic strips and comic books differ significantly in their production and consumption. Smith and Duncan are right to note that, too often, scholars paper over the distinctions between comic books, comic strips, and other material or digital species of comics. At the same time, if we prioritize the differences among comics, we seem similarly required to divide up webcomics, manga, European albums, and other comics-related traditions into mediums of their own. For certain theoretical purposes—especially historical ones—this is a sensible choice, but if our interest is in what *unifies* these kinds of artifacts into a common category and, in turn, explains the comics practices that treat them as importantly unified, we require *some* term to mark the category that includes them. Largely as a matter of convenience, we follow others in using the term "medium," but if you find yourself with especially stringent reservations, we invite you to replace our talk of "medium" with the perfectly generic "category." Such an approach isn't without merit. For, as we'll see in the coming chapters, there is no universally agreed-upon list of precisely which kinds of *categories* we require for understanding comics. While talk of medium, style, and genre are fairly familiar kinds of categories, many theoretically important categories cannot be assimilated to these three. What, for example, should we make of categories like "literature," "film adaptation," "single panel cartoon," or "pre-Code horror"?

We've noted several misconceptions that might arise in a discussion about what comics are. These are each understandable enough, since it is quite natural to say things like "comics are cartoons" or that "comics are printed" or even that "comics are art." When we discuss comics and literature in

Chapter 8, we'll offer some philosophical strategies for understanding what's going on when people utter these sorts of claims. But, crucially, we shouldn't mistake this sort of loose talk as requiring each and every comic to have these features. On the contrary, if we make that mistake, we are likely falling into the same trap as Euthyphro: mistaking what's *typical* about comics for what is *essential* or *definitional* about them. As we turn to proposed definitions of comics, this will be a useful moral to keep in mind.

3. Text and Image

Comics include the expressive and aesthetic resources found in both written or text-based mediums and pictorial or image-based mediums. This doesn't entail, of course, that simply by stapling a poem onto a portrait, we've thereby created a comic.[11] Nor does it mean that any time we see artworks or artifacts with both text and image that we should treat them as comics. But it does mean that in order to understand comics, we need to understand, at least to some extent, how text and image work—and in the case of comics, how they work together. As you might expect, there is a staggering amount to say about these topics. Unfortunately, the wealth of insight in comics studies and the philosophy of comics can't be quickly summarized. In the next few sections, we'll settle for drawing out some of the central issues that prove especially important for assessing proposed definitions of comics.

First, a terminological preliminary. In what follows, we'll use "text" to pick out strings of symbols like words and sentences that represent or refer in virtue of linguistic conventions. We'll also use "image" as a general term, and when the relevant images clearly serve a depictive function (i.e., to represent some object, whether real or fictional), we'll typically call them "pictures." Disagreements in these areas abound, and there's no uncontroversial terminological choices available. As we'll see, matters are further complicated by the possibility of creating pictures of text and the cryptic but apt observation by Will Eisner that in comics, "text reads as image" (1985: 10). It is important, however, to avoid confusing the inclusion of pictures within comics with the fact that comics are structured by typically non-depictive images—most notably, the arrangement or layout of comics panels. We'll return to these issues later and point toward some useful resources in the "Recommended Readings" section. But for now, on to something more fun.

Figure 2.1 "The Invisible Man," in *Superior Stories* #1 (1955), Pete Morisi. The Invisible Man attempts to break into a home as the police arrive.

Let's start by reading through this excerpt from *Superior Stories* #1 (1955) (Figure 2.1). This story, drawn by Pete Morisi, is an adaptation of H. G. Wells's *The Invisible Man* (1897). In keeping with the reading practices of European and North American comics, it's meant to be read from left to right and top to bottom. (In contrast, Japanese manga are read right to left, though still top to bottom.) As a reader, notice that your attention is carefully guided by the panel layout. In principle, there are many ways you could distribute your attention across the page—for example, by looking at all the gun drawings at once or by focusing your attention on the three tiers rather than the pairs of panels in them. Despite any number of things you *could have* done, your attention to the page almost certainly proceeded through a fairly clear sequence as you attended to or "read" the panels in turn. While your attention might drift forward, backward, or to other features of the page, it will, on pages like this one, typically unfold in an intentional fashion guided by the layout.

On this page of "The Invisible Man," each panel is closed and rectangular. This is common enough, but panels need not be rectangular, nor do all panels need to be enclosed by lines. (*Open panels* have no drawn borders, often featuring a figure with no background.) The distribution and number of panels on a page—often called a *layout*—varies tremendously across comics.[12] Some comics vary their layouts from page to page; others stick more or less to the same layout. In some sense, the simplest layout is a *splash page* on which a single panel takes up the entire page, but alternative layouts abound and some enjoy remarkable geometric, narrative, and self-referential complexity. (Compare, for example, the layout of our page from "The Invisible Man" with Richard McGuire's "Here" (1989), discussed in Chapter 10.) And, while panel layouts are not (usually) themselves pictures or text, they are nevertheless part of the visual presentation of a comic. Among their many functions, they critically shape how we interpret the contents of panels. More often than not, the temporal sequence of the depicted contents of the panels is conveyed by the parallel ordering of the panels in reading sequence on the page.

It is tempting—especially when looking at our example—to conclude that each panel is a separate picture—roughly, a drawing of an event within a story. We might, for example, describe this page of "The Invisible Man" as consisting of six separate pictures. And, while that might be true in this case, comics layouts regularly violate this assumption. There are panels that include several distinct pictures, and there are pages in which the panels jointly constitute an image distinct from each of them separately.

There is therefore no simple correspondence between images and panels. In addition, there are panels that are plausibly thought to include only text (or perhaps only pictures of text). For these reasons, there is also no simple way to define the concept of a *panel* in terms of its shape or its relationship to picture or text. The best we can do is think about the role of panels in how we are supposed to read comics. They are the things that we, as readers, are intended to pay primary sequential attention to. They shape our gaze and our cognition as we engage, in an orderly way, with a comic. As readers, we attend to features of the panel, then turn our attention to certain juxtaposed panels or proximate texts that might appear across, within, or outside panels. This has prompted some, like Abbott (1986: 156), to claim that "[t]he panel is the fundamental unit of comic art." (Compare, however, cartoonist Art Spiegelman's remark that "[i]n comics the page is the basic unit of thought" [2008: 19]. We suspect that without theories of what it is to be fundamental or basic in comics, these and similar claims are too vague to be especially informative.)

An important part of controlling readers' movement through panels is the lettering. The work of lettering is complex, but a significant portion involves inscribing text and deciding the shape and placement of *speech balloons*— typically, white ovals with text and "tails" indicating a speaker. For this reason, letterers—comics creators responsible for placing much of the text on pages— use balloons to pull readers' eyes around the page. But, when they undertake this work, they are notably constrained by the primary attention we pay to the sequence of panels. The importance of lettering often becomes especially clear when we encounter illegible or otherwise poor lettering. It is, for instance, a remarkable and jarring feature of Winsor McCay's comics like *Little Nemo in Slumberland* (1905–27) that his scrupulously delicate drawing style is paired with slipshod, barely legible narration and speech balloons.

The significance of text within comics and its relationship with images are reflected in some of the more prominent philosophical pronouncements about the medium. In *The Aesthetics of Comics,* philosopher David Carrier (2000: 74) argues that the presence of speech balloons is a necessary condition for being a comic. Similarly, Harvey (2005: 21) claims that Hal Foster's *Prince Valiant* (1937–71) and similar works are not properly counted as comics since they eschew speech balloons, placing text only on the bottom of panels. And, while Hayman and Pratt (2005) and Meskin (2007) are among those who rightly point out that this yields an implausibly narrow view of comics, speech balloons remain the most easily identifiable common feature of comics and have a fair claim to being their most interesting piece of "visual technology," given their peculiar synthesis of linguistic convention and pictorial function.

Although speech balloons abound in comics, they've received little direct philosophical examination. Cook (2015c: 12) suggests that, conventionally speaking, they aim to prompt readers "to imagine hearing (or telepathically sensing?) the relevant characters speaking the dialogue (or thinking the thoughts) textually represented." But however we characterize the conventions regarding speech balloons, a puzzle remains of how to understand their relationship to the broader categories of text and image. Almost all speech balloons (or thought bubbles, for that matter) include text. But, at the same time, non-textual features such as the direction of their tails or their color and edges convey information about who is speaking and how they're speaking. So are speech balloons text or pictures, or something else altogether?

Notice that in all but the strangest of metacomics, speakers can't see speech balloons.[13] So, if they're pictures, they surely do not represent bulbous patches of white space and text floating in front of speakers. Could they be *pictures of sounds* and therefore function as a kind of cross-modal symbol? Probably not, since they convey grammatical information that's far richer than merely the phonological information—for example, a speech balloon that includes "Hawkeye" depicts something different from one that includes a soundalike such as "Hawk Guy." The most plausible view seems to be that speech balloons are used to depict speech acts or utterances of characters.[14] Like other *emanata* including motion lines, they are ways of drawing us talking that are intelligible only through learned conventions.[15]

While text prominently occurs in speech balloons, it serves a range of additional functions within comics. Following Pratt (2009a: 108) and philosopher Thomas Wartenberg (2012), there seem to be four primary functions of text within comics:

(a) *Speech Balloons*: In our "The Invisible Man" excerpt, speech balloons convey or depict the utterances of characters—e.g., "Thank heaven you've come." In a related manner, text within thought bubbles conveys the mental states or "inner speech" of characters—in this case, the titular Invisible Man.[16]

(b) *Narrative Captions*: Text occurs in narrative captions—sometimes called "box narration." In our excerpt, these narrative captions describe the Invisible Man's activities like walking towards the house. In other comics, such captions narrate from a first-person perspective, serving as a kind of comics analogue of the cinematic voiceover. Because narrative captions can describe events in third-person or first-person (and, in rarer cases, second person), they can function as an alternative means for describing the speech or mental states of characters as well as the broader world of the story.[17]

(c) *Onomatopoeia*: Onomatopoetic "sound effects" like *BOOM* or *ARRRRGHHH* standardly function as way to communicate sonic events that are typically not instances of speech. The comics practice of lettering such text regularly exploits a variety of interesting cross-modal phenomena—e.g., the visual information regarding the size, shape, and color of text often conveys the intensity and trajectory of sounds within the narrative world.

(d) *Depicted Text*: Just as text is sprinkled throughout the actual world, it is often plentiful in the worlds depicted within comics, appearing on book jackets, t-shirts, and billboards. Depicted text therefore functions in comics as a "part" of pictures. For example, the "CLOSED" sign on a storefront, the numbers on a clockface, or the "A" on Captain America's helmet are readable by (literate) characters within comics.

Alongside the primary functions of text just noted, text slips into comics in numerous additional, often paratextual, ways. Along with *indicia*—roughly, publication information, legal notices, and credits that often appear on the first page of comic books—comic books regularly include editorial notices, fan letters, story titles, and page numbers. In one of the more interesting intersections of text and image, text can serve a dual function. Consider,

Figure 2.2 *The Spirit* (March 30, 1947), Will Eisner. An April Fool's Day prank unfolds with action interspersed with the title of the comic strip. WILL EISNER and THE SPIRIT are Registered Trademarks of Will Eisner Studios, Inc.

for instance, the separate but interconnected roles of text in this installment of Will Eisner's *The Spirit* (Figure 2.2). Text-image doubling of this sort is a vivid example of how easily text can be read as image. It is also a cautionary reminder that no simple and comprehensive account of the relationship between text and image is possible in the face of inventive cartooning. But, despite the plasticity of text in comics, it is plausible that text and image do play certain *typical* roles in comics—indeed, it is only in virtue of exploiting reader expectations about what's typical that the inventiveness and peculiarity of examples like Eisner's *The Spirit* can be explained or appreciated.

Let's look again at our page from "The Invisible Man." Each of the six panels from this page includes both text and image. Now, imagine reading this page for the first time without any of the text. Not only would one surmise that it's a tale about a haunted, floating gun and axe, we'd have no clear sense of where or when the events occur. Now, imagine encountering just the text on the page in the absence of any drawn elements. Notice that the text, by itself, would not indicate whether it is being thought or spoken or who is thinking or speaking. In fact, it is only in concert with the apparatus of speech balloons and narrative captions that the text is made coherent. There is, it seems, a kind of mutual "say" of text and image in typical comics storytelling. This relationship has prompted some philosophers to seek an analysis of comics in terms of the "equal priority" that text and image exhibit.[18] Specifically, Wartenberg asserts that "it is characteristic of comics to give equal priority to the text and the pictures" (2012: 87).

According to Wartenberg, this sense of "priority" enjoyed by text and image in comics concerns how we interpret them in constructing the narrative world of the comic. In an illustrated novel, text has absolute priority in settling what is true according to the story, while any included images are merely supplemental. They depict the events of the story but, typically, lack the authority to specify additional truths about what happens within the narrative world. As Wartenberg points out, when it comes to comics, text and image are equally authoritative in determining what happens in the story conveyed. In contrast with anatomical diagrams or maps, the text in a comic is not *merely* a caption or a label for the images: it is a kind of equal partner to the image in settling what happens in the story-world. According to Wartenberg, this equal standing of text and image is the key to distinguishing comics from merely illustrated texts, since comics "give images and text equal ontological priority in determining the story-world the comic creates" (2012: 101).

We'll explore the question of what makes something true within the story of a comic in Chapter 5, but for the time being, let's assume that this admittedly blurry notion of "ontological priority" can be understood as a matter of relative authority in constructing the world of a story. If we do so, we can transform Wartenberg's remarks into a potential analysis of comics. For convenience's sake, we'll call this analysis the Equal Priority View:

> **Equal Priority View**: x is a comic if and only if the text and images of x have equal ontological priority in determining what is true according to the story-world of x.

The Equal Priority View captures something important about many comics. If we were to ignore text or image while reading them, we would be unaware of much that takes place according to the comic. As we've seen in our previous example, it would be exceptionally hard to sensibly interpret the images in "The Invisible Man" excerpt without the text and vice versa. This isn't to deny that in *some* comics, one could follow the narrative while ignoring the text or, conversely, read the extensive narrative captions and more or less ignore the pictures. But even in such cases, there are still facts about the story-world and characters within it—perhaps the look of faces or the physical relationships among characters—that are determined by the image. Conversely, the text in comics, even when limited, still serves to determine certain truths within the story-world—such as narrative captions that specify time and location or speech balloons that indicate the names of characters. This means that although our readerly attention might be unevenly distributed between text and image, they are nevertheless equally capable of fixing what is true *according to the story of a comic*.[19]

According to the Equal Priority View, comics are to be defined in terms of *how text and image function within them*—namely, how they generate story-worlds or truths according to a comic. Later, we'll encounter other definitions of comics that focus on the *formal features* of comics—roughly, what comics look like—and others that crucially involve the *history of the medium*. But having set out this potential analysis of comics, we can now ask: Is the Equal Priority View correct? Here's the good news: the Equal Priority View is noncircular, informative, and while the notion of "ontological priority" requires further clarification, it seems tolerably clear. The bad news: the Equal Priority View faces several counterexamples and, for that reason, seems extensionally inadequate.

Let's begin with a concern that Wartenberg himself notes but eventually dismisses. If there are works that involve image and text that exhibit the same equal priority as comics but aren't themselves comics, then the Equal Priority View counts certain *non*-comics as comics. And there do seem to be such works: illustrated children's books. While there are now (thankfully) many (excellent) comics made for kiddos, there are also non-comics for children in which text and image do equal work.

Although Wartenberg claims that in a children's book like *Goodnight Moon* (1947) by Clement Hurd and Margaret Wise Brown, the images are posterior to and serve merely to illustrate the text, there is little reason to think that the category of "children's illustrated book" is uniform in this regard. (This is, in part, because "children's illustrated book" seems to be less a genre or medium and more a functional category with distinctive readerly aims.) Take the case of *I Want My Hat Back* (2011) by Jon Klassen. In this children's book, the central plot device is a bear's striking failure to notice that his hat has been stolen by a rabbit. The rabbit's theft of the hat and the bear's comedic failure to notice are settled by the pictures in the book and indeed runs contrary to the text (or at least until the bitter dénouement). So, although Wartenberg claims that in such books "texts provide constraints on the illustrations, but not the other way around" (2011: 87), it's not difficult to find non-comics that are apparent counterinstances to Wartenberg's conjecture, where image and text function just as they do in comics. In such cases, the story-worlds seem to be constructed with text and image enjoying equal priority. And, if certain illustrated children's books do exhibit equal priority, then equal priority cannot be a sufficient condition for being a comic.

Faced with this putative counterexample, we have two options: we can either concede that the Equal Priority View is false or conclude that *I Want My Hat Back* and works like it are comics. Although the number of children's illustrated books that are comics is significant and quickly growing, there's no evidence from comics practice that children's books that exhibit equal priority are comics. We take this latter option to look even less plausible in light of the two additional counterexamples we'll now consider.

Our second counterexample to the Equal Priority View hinges on the connection between comics and narrative. For, although comics often serve as a vehicle for fictional narratives, this is by no means an essential feature of the medium. Nonfiction narratives in comics are plentiful. Autobiographical comics like Raina Telgemeier's *Smile* (2010) and Thi Bui's *The Best We Could Do* (2017) are critically lauded contributions to the medium. Long-form comics that trace historical narratives like Chester Brown's *Louis Riel* (1999–2003) and Derf Backderf's *Kent State* (2020) are often carefully researched and extensively detailed. Additionally, comics journalism—perhaps most familiar in the form of Joe Sacco's comics like *Safe Area Goražde* (2000) and *Paying the Land* (2020)—is a steadily growing category of comics that is not only nonfiction but explicitly aimed at understanding (nonfictional) reality. So, comics need not be works of fiction. But could there be some more basic *narrative requirement* to comics? Must comics always serve as vehicles for *some* narrative regardless of whether or not the narrative is a fiction?

Let's help ourselves to the simplifying assumption that narratives are stories (albeit potentially very, very short ones).[20] Given this assumption, our question about the narrativity requirement for comics turns on whether comics must always generate some kind of story-world. It is difficult to deny that some comics, composed of only a few panels and marked by what McCloud (1993: 72) calls non sequitur transitions—roughly, panel-to-panel transitions that might seem entirely disconnected—still yield *some* kind of story-world even if it's one driven more by ambience than story arc. In contrast to those cases where the story-worlds are patchy, fragmented, or vaguely defined, are there genuinely *nonnarrative comics* that actually tell no story whatsoever?

We believe so. Consider the genre or category of *abstract comics* of which the comic "I Was Just" (2020) is an example (Figure 2.3). This comic by Samplerman (a pseudonym of Yvan Guillo) is, like many of his comics, a splicing together and "remixing" of elements of other comics. Within it, the

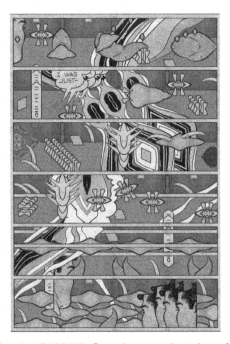

Figure 2.3 "I Was Just" (2020), Samplerman. A series of panels featuring nonnarrative shapes and forms.

absence of narrative precludes the generation of a bona fide story-world. When we attempt to read it as a more familiar narrative comic, the results are aesthetically interesting (if a bit disorienting) in part because, as Pratt (2009a: 107) notes, "the default phenomenology of comics reading entails looking for the stories that they tell." As a result, our gaze flits between panels and hits upon the text but comes up narratively empty. Ultimately, Samplerman's comic isn't intended to convey a story. It is instead a kind of aesthetic exercise of working within the comics medium to manipulate the technique of comics reading.

Of course, someone might insist that "I Was Just" just isn't a comic. They wouldn't be alone in this regard. In his groundbreaking history of early comics and European predecessors to comics, David Kunzle (1973: 2) proposed four conditions for being a comic strip:

> (1) There must be a sequence of separated images; (2) There must be a preponderance of image over text; (3) The medium in which the strip appears and for which it is originally intended must be reproductive, that is, in printed form, a mass medium; (4) The sequence must tell a story which is both moral and topical.

Kunzle advances these criteria in the course of delimiting the scope of his historical inquiry, so it is probably uncharitable to interpret him as attempting to provide a genuine analysis of comics strips (much less all kinds of comics). But, quite clearly, if such a view is true, it entails that abstract or nonnarrative comic strips are impossible. Despite this, when we look to critical practice, we find substantial evidence that abstract comics are, if not commonplace, readily available and standardly treated as comics. Along with the formal and stylistic similarities they bear to other comics, abstract comics appear in various comics collections. The artist behind "I Was Just" has been interviewed by venues like *The Comics Journal,* and his Samplerman work is included on various "Best of" comics lists. Additionally, there are collections of abstract comics—namely, Andrei Molotiu's seminal collection, *Abstract Comics* (2009)—published by comics publisher Fantagraphics—that have received considerable interest and attention from comics scholars. Additionally, the work of comics or *bande dessinée* collective, Oubapo, regularly produces nonnarrative comics subject to careful critical attention by comics scholars.[21] If "I Was Just" and works like it are comics, we must reject the narrative requirement on comics: some comics don't tell a story and so represent no story-world at all. And, if there is no story-world generated by a comic, then it looks like neither text nor image function in the way that the Equal Priority View claims to be essential to the medium.[22]

Here's a final concern with the Equal Priority View. Comics like Ricardo Delgado's *Age of Reptiles: The Hunt* (1997), Shaun Tan's *The Arrival* (2006), and Eric Drooker's *Blood Song: A Silent Ballad* (2002) are examples of what are often called "silent," "wordless," or "pantomime" comics: they include no text, so image alone is responsible for settling what holds true in their respective story-worlds.[23] But, if there is no text in a comic, in what sense do such comics exhibit equal priority of text and image?

The defender of the Equal Priority View might argue that their view concerns how text and image *could* be used, rather than how they are *actually* used. They might therefore claim that while *The Hunt* is over 100 pages without any text, *it could have incorporated text* and if it did, it would still be a comic. We grant that this is the most plausible way to apply the Equal Priority View to the case of silent comics but notice that it requires a controversial assumption: that after adding text into comics like *The Hunt* or *Blood Song*, we would still have the same comic we began with.

One of the most distinctive features of *The Hunt* and our other examples is precisely that they are silent comics. Their "silence" enormously impacts readers' experience, the look of the pages, and the comics' critical reception. For this reason, if we did insert text into these comics, it seems as though we would have thereby created new and importantly *different* comics. (In contrast, modest changes to the drawings or narration in most comics would not have this consequence.) But, if we're now talking about a comic numerically distinct from *Age of Reptiles: The Hunt*, it seems very strange to claim that *it* is a comic because we could have made a very *different* comic, *Age of (Chatty) Reptiles: The (Conversational) Hunt* which is similar but that includes text. We think this shows that the Equal Priority View cannot adequately account for the status of silent comics without making controversial assumptions—in particular, that we can transform comics in quite radical ways and still be left with the very same comic we started with.

3.1 Standard Features and Essential Pictures

Despite the problems we've noted, the Equal Priority View gets *something* right. In many comics—perhaps even in *most* comics—text and image do exhibit equal priority. We suspect this is reason to believe that while equal priority does not define comics, it is what Kendall Walton and others would describe as a *standard feature* of the medium. According to Walton (1970: 339), features of artworks admit of a useful threefold distinction into the *standard*, the *contra-standard*, and the *variable*:

> A feature of a work of art is *standard* with respect to a (perceptually distinguishable) category just in case it is among those in virtue of which works in that category belong to that category—that is, just in case the lack of that feature would disqualify, or tend to disqualify, a work from that category. A feature is *variable* with respect to a category just in case it has nothing to do with works' belonging to that category; the possession or lack of the feature is irrelevant to whether a work qualifies for the category. Finally, a *contra-standard* feature with respect to a category is the absence of a standard feature with respect to that category—that is, a feature whose presence tends to disqualify works as members of the category.

While we've already noted that not all comics are artworks, we think this threefold distinction nevertheless applies to artifacts like comics, too. In this spirit, Meskin (2007: 370, 372) suggests that features like conveying a narrative and including speech balloons are plausibly viewed as standard features of comics. Alongside them, we suspect that equal priority deserves a place. The misstep in the Equal Priority View arises from accepting an overly broad generalization that something is a comic just in case it exhibits equal priority.[24]

Within comics, we find a remarkable variety of interrelations between image and text governed by shifting and complex interpretive principles. The work of grasping and deploying these principles is surely one of the more interesting features of the medium, and it shapes the kinds of aesthetic engagement we have with specific comics. In Adrian Tomine's short piece "Translated, from the Japanese," (1995), first-person narrative captions relay a personal story paired with a sequence of apparently disconnected panels, whose relationship requires subtle inferences and careful imaginative extrapolation. Contrast that with the variable relationship between text and image in Richard Corben's adaptation of Edgar Allan Poe's *The Raven* in *Creepy* #76 (1974), which features the poem's text as narrative caption, spoken dialogue, and as direction for a complex series of visual reversals (most of which depend upon the reader's prior familiarity with the source text). Uncovering how text and image work across comics is an indispensable critical project, but the vast diversity of text and image relationships in comics is reason to suspect that the Equal Priority View imposes an implausible homogeneity on the medium.[25]

Before turning to another strategy for defining comics, there's an issue about text and image that warrants consideration. In evaluating the Equal Priority View, we saw that comics don't need to include text. But what about the parallel requirement that comics must include pictures? Could there be a comic without pictures, consisting entirely of text? In "Do Comics Require Pictures? Or Why *Batman #663* Is a Comic" (2011), Cook argues that under the right conditions, a *comic book* might indeed be entirely text-based. For Cook, thinking through this possibility is necessary in order to make sense of peculiar comic books like *Batman #663* ("The Clown Laughs at Midnight," 2007), which is an individual issue of the series, *Batman* (Vol. 1, 1940–2011). The issue—written by Grant Morrison and lettered by Todd Klein—includes only a very limited number of drawings by John Van Fleet and an overwhelming preponderance of text.

Cook contends that *Batman #663* is rightly viewed as a comic given what we know about the comics practice surrounding it—for example, that it is written, reviewed, and collected as part of a long-running comics series. But he also notes that we can readily conceive of a hypothetical issue much like *Batman #663* that's *entirely* void of pictures or substantial illustrations. This hypothetical comic would, according to Cook, be a counterexample to what he calls the *pictorial thesis*, which is the requirement that comics have pictures as parts. In assessing the pictorial thesis, Cook derives an important insight: the status of something as a comic often depends upon *extrinsic features* of that thing, most notably whether it is a part of a serial work published or printed in installments. A work like *Batman #663* can, in effect, *inherit* its status as a comic by virtue of being just one small part of a longer serialized comic—in this case, the *Batman* series. In contrast, a work consisting entirely or almost entirely of text that is not a serialized work would have no plausible claim to being a comic. This means that we need to be particularly careful to note whether or not artifacts are serialized when we assess their status as comics. It also highlights the significance of seriality for understanding comics more generally—partly for that reason, we'll return to the nature of seriality in Chapter 5.

4. Sequence

As we noted earlier, comics guide our attention from panel to panel. And, when comics convey narratives, it is typically through the intentional ordering of panels in some kind of sequence. This feature has led some to seek an analysis of comics in terms of their *sequential character*. This approach is implicit in Will Eisner's description of comics as a "sequential art." The most influential attempt to define comics, defended in McCloud's *Understanding Comics*, proceeds along just these lines. After considering a variety of definitions and subjecting them to the method of counterexample, McCloud offers the following proposal: comics are "juxtaposed pictorial and other images in deliberate sequence, intended to convey information and/or produce an aesthetic response in the viewer" (1993: 9).[26]

Before evaluating McCloud's definition, a few points of clarification are needed. First, for McCloud, linguistic items like words are included in his usage of "images," and what we've been calling pictures, he refers to as "pictorial images." Second, McCloud requires that sequences be deliberately produced and therefore the product of some (though perhaps quite limited) kind of creative intention. Consider, however, a remarkable circumstance in which three discarded pictures—say, a magazine cover featuring a dog, a discarded box with a pizza logo on it, and a child's drawing of a dog eating a pizza—are blown together by a gust of wind, giving rise to something that can be read as a short gag strip of a dog stealing a pizza. Since McCloud's definition requires the presence of creative intention in the generation of sequences, this windblown "pizza dog" sequence would not count as a comic. We'll return to this particular consequence of McCloud's view later in this chapter.

The concept of *juxtaposition* figures prominently in McCloud's definition and in his efforts to distinguish comics from other mediums like film and television. Although these mediums present pictorial images in deliberate sequence, they do so by presenting different pictorial images in a single place though at different times. McCloud argues that "each successive frame of a movie is projected on exactly the same space—the screen—while each frame of comics must occupy a different space. Space does for comics what time does for film!" (1993: 7).

Juxtaposition—understood as something like spatial adjacency—is, according to McCloud, an essential feature of comics. He further claims that juxtaposition underwrites a prominent *cognitive* feature of comics, a feature characteristic of what happens when we read comics: the phenomenon of *closure*. When presented with two juxtaposed images separated into distinct panels, we are disposed to incorporate them into a distinctively unified reading experience. In this way, the separation *between* pictorial images—the "gutter" that divides them—plays a key role in

McCloud's account of comics. As he says, "in the limbo of the gutter, human imagination takes two separate images and transforms them into a single idea" (1993: 66).

McCloud's proposed definition isn't the only attempt to define comics via their sequential nature.[27] Hayman and Pratt offer a related definition, partly inspired by McCloud's. According to Hayman and Pratt's analysis: "*x* is a comic if and only if *x* is a sequence of discrete, juxtaposed pictures that comprise a narrative, either in their own right or when combined with text" (2005: 423).[28] In this section, we'll focus on what we take to be the core of these and other sequence-based analyses of comics. In doing so, we'll omit the final clause of McCloud's account and continue our practice of taking "image" to refer to non-textual items. We then arrive at the following definition:

Deliberate Sequence View: *x* is a comic if and only if *x* is a deliberate sequence of juxtaposed images.

In assessing the Deliberate Sequence View, we can begin with an objection McCloud discusses in *Understanding Comics* (1993: 20–1). For something to be a juxtaposed sequence of images, it must consist of at least two images. But in "single panel comics," there seems to be only a single panel left unjuxtaposed. Artifacts of this sort therefore fail to satisfy the juxtaposition requirement and, according to the Deliberate Sequence View, fail to qualify as comics. While we might point to some single panel comics like the example in Figure 2.4 from R. F. Outcault and assert that they do include a plurality of images (e.g., the various figures considered in isolation), this is neither true of all single panel comics nor does it adequately capture McCloud's intended sense of juxtaposition, since there's no apparent use of a gutter or the kind of disunity in visual or narrative elements that would warrant positing distinct panels.

Given McCloud's general approach to understanding comics, the verdict that single panel artifacts are not comics might seem understandable—after all, they very rarely give rise to the kind of closure McCloud takes to be of special importance for comics. McCloud is also quick to note that single panel works like Jackie Ormes's *Patty-Jo 'n' Ginger* (1945–56) or Gary Larson's *The Far Side* (1979–present) are often rightly described as *cartoons*, which, given the prevalence of cartooning in the comics medium, might account for the temptation to assimilate them into the category of comics.

Unfortunately for the Deliberate Sequence View, once we scrutinize comics practice, we find little evidence that McCloud is tracking a distinction

Figure 2.4 "At the Circus in Hogan's Alley" (May 5, 1895), R. F. Outcault. Neighborhood children and animals put on a circus performance.

between comics and non-comics. Instances of *Patty-Jo 'n' Ginger* and *The Far Side* almost always consist of a single panel, and both Ormes and Larson are standardly treated as contributors to the same medium as cartoonists like Bill Waterson and Lynn Johnston, whose strips typically involve multiple panels. Collections of political and newspaper cartoons, regardless of the number of their panels, are frequently reprinted together. It is therefore *at least* a demerit of McCloud's definition that single panel works are held apart from comics when the critical, historical, and commercial aspects of comics recognize no similarly strict distinction. So, although McCloud is fairly clear that his definition gives a heterodox treatment of single panel works, there seems to be no way to both respect comics practice and resist the objection from single panel comics. This is bad news, then, for the Deliberate Sequence View.

The objection from single panel comics works by noting a discrepancy between the critical practice surrounding comics and the formal features identified in the Deliberate Sequence View. And, while this is the most influential objection to sequence-based views like McCloud's, it isn't the only potential challenge of this kind. The Deliberate Sequence View entails that the deliberate juxtaposition of images is sufficient for being a comic. But this raises a number of questions about what it takes for images to count as juxtaposed. Is there a maximum distance between them? Imagine, for example, a potential comic with panels placed miles apart. Is that an adequate sort of juxtaposition? Merely pointing out that defining *juxtaposition* is difficult falls short of providing a decisive objection, however. It is unreasonable to expect that each and every term in a definition will admit of its own simple analysis. Additionally, given paradigm instances and non-instances of juxtaposition, we do seem to have a fairly clear grasp of which cases of juxtaposition are genuine and which are borderline. Notice, however, that in panel layouts, juxtaposition comes in a staggering diversity of forms. Some page layouts feature only two panels, with one above the other. Others are peppered with all sorts of irregular panels. Things only get wilder from there. There is, it seems, no privileged horizontal or vertical notion of juxtaposition even if comics readers typically progress in a fairly stable order.

Look once again at our example involving "The Invisible Man" (Figure 2.1). This is only one page from a longer feature, but on its own, it clearly constitutes a deliberate sequence. In fact, these panels compose a surprising number of deliberate yet overlapping sequences: all of the panels apart from the first panel, all of the panels apart from the last panel, the two panels in the middle tier, and so on. Once we note that the panels above and below a given panel are products of deliberate juxtaposition, we can recognize that there are numerous sequences that satisfy the conditions set out by the Deliberate Sequence View.[29] The problem here is that the Deliberate Sequence View *over-generates* comics, since myriad arbitrary parts of comics and the entire comic equally satisfy the sufficient condition for being a comic. The Deliberate Sequence View therefore entails that things that we don't ordinarily treat or think of as comics—the juxtaposed *mere parts* of comics—are errantly deemed to be comics.

The structure of this problem isn't unique to comics. Here's a parallel one: notice that you (presumably) believe there to be exactly one person sitting in your chair: *you*. You also believe that if you lost your pinkie finger, you would continue to exist. It seems, then, that there is an object that is a part of you (namely, you minus your pinkie finger) that has everything it takes to be a person. But why doesn't that object—you minus your pinkie finger—count as a person *right now*? If we are forced to count it, along with all the other objects that are you *minus* this-or-that small cluster of cells, it now looks like we are forced to conclude that there are, in fact, a vast number of persons sitting in your chair after all.

The moral typically drawn from reflecting on the case of persons and their parts is that certain concepts like *person* or *boat* or *rock* are border-

sensitive in a distinctive way. They are *maximal* concepts. If, for example, something is a volcano, then there is no smaller part of that thing that is almost as big as it and also a volcano. As Ted Sider (2001: 357) observes: "Maximality is everywhere. Very large proper parts of houses, tables and chairs, rocks and mountains, persons and cats, are not themselves houses, tables, chairs, rocks, mountains, persons or cats."

We take it that the concept of *comic* is a maximal one. There are, of course, comics that might be parts of other comics—for example, the *Tales of the Black Freighter* might be seen as a comic that is part of *Watchmen* (1986). But not just any part of a comic that satisfies the conditions set out in the Deliberate Sequence View is a comic. And, without some way of capturing the maximality of comics within the Deliberate Sequence View, we end up with a view of comics analogous to a view on which there are myriad persons sitting in your chair with you. Since the Deliberate Sequence View is not equipped to avoid counting arbitrary *mere parts* of comics as comics, it delivers another incorrect verdict about the conditions for being a comic.

Is there some way to revise the Deliberate Sequence View to avoid this problem? Perhaps comics are just the *biggest* deliberate sequence of juxtaposed images on a page. Setting aside the fact that some comics aren't on pages, the Deliberate Sequence View can't be fixed in this way. Deferring to size alone would, for instance, deliver the mistaken result that all of the comics on a Sunday newspaper page are a single comic in virtue of being placed there by an editor. Perhaps, instead, we might revise the Deliberate Sequence View by saying that something is a comic if and only if it is a *complete* deliberate sequence of juxtaposed images? This is more promising, but, if we pursue this revision, we now require an account of what it means to be a "complete" deliberate sequence. Such an account might be possible, but it is an exceptionally difficult task. Consider, for example, the fact that serialized comics are intended to be parts of an ongoing comic and are therefore incomplete for years on end. So, if we interpret "complete" as something like "series within a final published installment" then it turns out that ongoing comic strips installments aren't even parts of comics much less comics themselves—at least not until the final installment is put to (web) page.[30]

Whether the Deliberate Sequence View can meet this worry regarding maximality, the single panel objection remains. Each of these challenges dims the hope of defining comics purely in terms of their sequential features. (This isn't to say the Deliberate Sequence View is entirely formalist; it does, after all, involve intentions.) But, it will now be useful to consider an objection that threatens to undermine the Deliberate Sequence View along with *any* formalist analysis of comics.

5. History

In presenting his definition of comics, McCloud claims that the history of comics is far more extensive and considerably more inclusive than is usually acknowledged. This is because, on McCloud's view, the medium of comics subsumes a huge and diverse range of artifacts ranging from the Bayeux Tapestry, which is a twelfth-century British tapestry, to Mixtec Codices, which are pre-Columbian deerskin screenfolds. Since these and other artifacts involve juxtaposed images in deliberate sequence, they satisfy McCloud's definition and are therefore counted as comics by the Deliberate Sequence View. While this result has the rhetorical effect of connecting comics to remarkable works of cultural and historical importance, it raises serious questions. For example, few critics would think to even consider the Bayeux Tapestry as the greatest comic of all time and in the myriad historical studies of the Bayeux Tapestry or works like it, the word "comic" almost never appears. Similarly, it is no apparent deficit of a comic collection in a library or archive to omit the kinds of historical materials like codices and tapestries that McCloud mentions. It therefore looks as though the Deliberate Sequence View misclassifies a vast range of historical artifacts as comics. As Meskin (2007: 376) develops this objection, the problem with the Deliberate Sequence View and others like it is that they fail to respect important historical facts about when and how the medium of comics emerged:

> Their biggest flaw is their failure to attend to the historical specificity of the medium of comics. . . . The art of comics, which began in the middle of the nineteenth century and developed largely out of eighteenth- and nineteenth-century British humor magazines such as *Punch*, can and should be understood on its own terms and by reference to its own history.

If Meskin is correct, there is reason to reject any formalist definition of comics, since the medium of comics is a *historically specific* one. To this end, Meskin claims that part of what it is to be a comic is to be connected to the history of comics that emerged in Western Europe in the eighteenth and nineteenth centuries. The details of this tradition have, following Kunzle, been subject to increasingly comprehensive and subtle inquiry, moving well beyond seminal figures like William Hogarth, George Cruikshank, and Rodolphe Töppfer. The project of understanding comics is, therefore, fundamentally connected with the project of charting the history of printing, cartooning, and publishing. It would therefore be impossible without the work of historians of comics and historians of printing.

To be sure, those of us interested in understanding comics ought to be concerned with the historical trajectory of the medium, but it's important to be clear about what Meskin's objection means for the project of analyzing comics. If comics are a historically specific medium, then even if something satisfies all relevant formal criteria, it would only be rightly categorized as a comic if it were appropriately connected to the history of comics as well—for example, by relying on techniques informed by the history of comics production, by aspiring to replicate features of prior comics works, and so on. Let's call this *the historical constraint* on comics.

The historical constraint has profound consequences for the epistemology of comics—roughly, how we know which artifacts are comics. The presence of panels, images, juxtaposition, and other formal features is, if not always, almost always perceptually detectable. And, on formalist views about comics, one can often, at least in principle, determine whether something is a comic on the basis of its perceptible features. In contrast, the historical constraint entails that certain imperceptible features are essential to comics. The property of being a comic would therefore be akin to features like being an uncle, having a Ph.D., or having visited Belgium. You can't see or hear that something has these properties. You can, at best, *infer* that something has them.

Importantly, the historical constraint isn't, by itself, an alternative analysis of comics. There are many things produced by comics creators that are appropriately connected to the history of comics but that are not comics. These include trade magazines about comics publishing, certain ads for comic books, sketches in the backs of artists' notebooks, and posters of superheroes. The historical constraint is, for this reason, most naturally treated as an additional clause that we might append to a proposed definition of comics like the Deliberate Sequence View. This would, for example, deliver the following revised analysis:

Historicist Deliberate Sequence View: x is a comic if and only if x is a deliberate sequence of juxtaposed images *and* the production of x is appropriately historically connected to the tradition that began in the middle of the nineteenth century and developed largely out of eighteenth- and nineteenth-century British humor magazines.

Alternatively, if Meskin is correct, the historical constraint is a fact about the nature of the comics medium that provides compelling evidence that comics simply cannot be defined. (This latter result would bear out Nietzsche's memorable quip that "nothing with a history can be defined.")

So, should we accept the historical constraint on comics? Well, let's consider a hypothetical scenario. Suppose that independent of the European printmaking tradition that Meskin cites, another printmaking tradition emerged in a manner that was totally separate. Suppose that out of this other tradition, works appeared with speech balloons, panels, and all the other standard features we associate with comics. Would we *really* insist that these works aren't comics solely because they aren't historically connected with Western European printmaking?

We think not. And, interestingly, there's arguably an example where something reminiscent of this happened: Japanese manga. The rich and long-standing printing tradition in Japan emerged separately from that of Western Europe. Subsequently, at several junctures, this tradition was impacted by the arrival of artifacts like British humor magazines and, much later, American comic books. Given the ongoing debate regarding the history of manga as well as the vagueness of the notion of an "appropriate historical connection," it is controversial whether manga actually constitutes a counterexample to the historical constraint. (We certainly don't believe so.) But, as Holbo (2012) argues, the history of manga is evidence that there *could have been* a historically distinct tradition of the right sort and, if there were, it would seem implausible to insist that the works produced within it are not comics.

If the historical constraint doesn't set the limits of which things are comics, what can it *really* do to help us understand the nature of comics? As Meskin (2007) argues, historical understanding of comics is critical for understanding its status as a hybrid medium. Following Jerrold Levinson (1984), Meskin argues that the question of whether comics are hybrids is best understood as a historical rather than formal one. So, while Roger Sabin (1993: 9) insists that comics are not "some hybrid form between 'literature' and 'art,'" Meskin (2007: 236) notes that "[o]n this historical conception of hybridity, the question of whether the art form of comics is a hybrid is not a question about a relationship between words and images in them (which, after all, can vary widely), but rather a question about genealogy." For this reason, understanding the hybrid nature of comics requires not just attending to their formal or structural features but looking backward to what techniques *within comics* emerged from printmaking techniques like engraving and lithography as well as practices like narrative fiction writing.

It is easy to mistake the rejection of the historical constraint in defining comics for a broader dismissal of history in philosophizing about comics. But, as Meskin's examination of the hybridity of comics makes clear, just because history doesn't constrain *which things are comics*, it doesn't mean that history doesn't importantly shape *how we understand comics*.

6. Picture-Reading

With the Equal Priority View and the Deliberate Sequence View proving to be unsatisfactory, we're forced to go back to the drawing board yet again. In this section, we'll explore one last approach to defining comics.

Let's start by thinking about certain historical relatives of comics. Not the storytelling ones, mind you, but other ephemeral, disposable, printed things like playbills, tickets, and product flyers. The idea of defining a ticket or an advertisement in formal or historical terms should sound odd to you. Such items aren't constrained by what they look like. Nor is it plausible to think that the notion of a ticket is historically specific like, say, ballet or pasta. Tickets and advertisements are distinguished by *what they do*: they are *functional* artifacts. Tickets are things that can be exchanged for specific goods and services. Advertisements are inanimate things that promote something, whether it is a business, product, person, or activity. Any analysis of these two notions that wasn't predominantly concerned with what tickets and advertisements *do* seems all but hopeless. What, then, should we think about a parallel *functional approach* to defining comics?

It's not hard to think of the name "comics" in this context. While one might be tempted to claim that the function of comics was to produce the responses we associate with comedy, comics have long expressed sentiments other than the straightforwardly comedic (e.g., the wistful or the ironic). And it's surely not true now. But this much is plausible: comics, like tickets and advertisements, do have a *characteristic use* as objects. They are things for individuals to attend to and to think about, and they are to be attended to and thought about in a distinctive fashion. Just as tickets are to be redeemed, comics are to be "read." If that's correct, then comics are ultimately a functional artifact rather than one that can be defined formally or historically.

As we usually put it, comics are for reading. Notice, however, that talk about "reading comics" involves yet another linguistic accident. While most comics involve text, we know that many do not. So whatever reading we do when we engage with comics, it is not the same activity as the reading we undertake when we engage with a novel. To see that the practice of reading comics is sufficiently different from the practice of reading novels or poems, notice that we regularly find people unfamiliar with comics expressing puzzlement or confusion about how to "read them properly." In fact, in Wertham's *Seduction of the Innocent*, we find the activity of reading comics singled out as a distinctive (and pernicious!) activity quite different from the reading of text:

> In the course of studying children with reading disorders who are at the same time great comic-book readers, I have found many who have developed a special kind of "reading." They have become what I call "picture-readers." Later I learned that not only children with reading difficulties, but also those with good reading ability, are seduced by comic books into "picture-reading." This is of course another point where comic books exert a pernicious influence on the general child population. (1954: 139)

Let's suppose, with Wertham, that there is a distinctive kind of activity for which comics are intended.[31] We can't think of a better name than Wertham's, so let's call it *picture-reading*. Describing the nature and nuance of picture-reading would require a comprehensive catalogue of "what it's like" to read comics or, as some philosophers might call it, the phenomenology of comics reading. And across comics studies, we find remarks, like the following from Jared Gardner (2015: 248), that attempt to get at its distinctive character:

> Part of the reason readers became so passionately attached to early comics was because of this investment of imaginative energy and narrative energies— the active filling in of all that cannot be represented in the panels on the page: sounds, detail, the action between the panels, etc. While such filling in is central to all meaning making in narrative across media, the fundamental *inefficiency* of comics as a narrative medium and its foregrounding in the formal space of the gutter between panels, the work required by the "gap" arguably entails from the outset a different level of investment than any other narrative form.

We won't develop a full theory of picture-reading here, but some central elements warrant comment. When picture-reading, we are open to incorporating one or more images into our unified attention. We're open to taking juxtaposed images as components of a narrative. We're open to finding closure among panels. We're open to taking text (or a solitary image) as determining what's true according to the narrative. Importantly, this *openness* isn't the same thing as expectation. We can picture-read in the absence of text and even in the absence of juxtaposed images. We can even engage in a kind of frustrated picture-reading in the case of nonnarrative abstract comics, where we seek to construct a narrative but are unable to do so. Importantly, the activity of picture-reading isn't defined by what it attends to but by what it is *open to attending to*. (Picture-reading also doesn't require a left-to-right ordering of attention, so there's no reason to think that it is distinctive to Western comics. It is just as much manifested in engagement with manga and other comics traditions.) The work of picture-reading is, importantly, a learned mode of engagement that involves sensitivity to sequential panel layout, closure, and various means of quasi-compositional interplay between text and image. [32]

It's easy to get a conceptual grasp of the activity of picture-reading, especially for those who have regularly undertaken it. But we also face a difficult question: What kind of activity is picture-reading? Is picture-reading a *psychological activity* in the sense that whether or not we are doing it is ultimately a cognitive or neuroscientific matter? Or is it a *sociocultural activity*, one that, of course, involves cognition but that is circumscribed by sociocultural conventions? If that distinction seems murky, compare the activity of being polite with the activity of remembering a past event. Each involves human cognition, but whether you're being polite is not something cognitive scientists are plausibly in a position to settle. In contrast, remembering a past event is an activity principally distinguished by cognitive science.

Different views about what kind of activity picture-reading is yield quite different results when it comes to defining comics. If we take picture-reading to be a special kind of psychological state, then our definition will depend upon empirical verdicts that issue from cognitive science. If, for example, there is no empirical support for the hypothesis that an individual reading a single panel comic and an individual looking at a painting like the *Mona Lisa* are in importantly *different* cognitive states, then this view would entail that single panel comics aren't comics after all. If, however, we take picture-reading to be not a narrowly psychological activity but a sociocultural one, our account of comics is not as clearly dependent upon what cognitive scientists discover about our psychological engagements with comics. To be sure, the work of psychologists and linguists is valuable for understanding picture-reading, but we take it that what does and does not count as picture-reading is, in important respects, a sociocultural matter—one more like being polite than remembering a past event. For this reason, it cannot be discerned solely through psychological means. Moreover, whether we are correct in describing individuals as picture-reading single panel comics, abstract comics, and other would-be comics depends to a large extent on the sociocultural practices that surround comics.

One consequence of this view is that there might well be importantly different cognitive activities involved with comics. As linguist Neil Cohn argues, thinking about certain comics through the lens of cognitive linguistics yields fruitful insights for understanding how we communicate through graphic expressions. At the same time, while many comics involve what Cohn calls a "visual language," we ought to be careful to note that the concept of a comic is not itself a linguistic or cognitive concept. As he puts it, "[w]hile 'visual language' is the biological and cognitive capacity that humans have for conveying concepts in the visual-graphic modality, 'comics' are a sociocultural context in which this visual language appears (frequently in conjunction with writing)" (2012: 113). For much the same reason, we take it that picture-reading ought not to be confused with a distinctive kind of psychological state any more than comics ought to be confused with what Cohn would claim to be the "visual language" on which comics rely.

Provided that we're careful about how we understand picture-reading, we can draw upon this notion in attempting to define comics. But considerable care needs to be taken. In doing so, we can turn back to the intentions that surround the creation of a comic. Drawing upon a suggestion that Meskin (2007: 375) briefly mentions, we might propose the following definition:

> **Intentional Picture-Reading View**: x is a comic if and only if x is aptly intended to be picture-read.

This view shares an affinity with certain approaches to the project of defining what it is to be an artwork. For example, Levinson (1979: 234) presents his account of artworks as follows: "a work of art is a thing intended for regard-as-a-work-of-art, regard in any of the ways works of art existing prior to it have been correctly regarded." The analogy between this proposal and the Intentional Picture-Reading View (hereafter, the IPR View) flows from the view's commitment that something is a comic just in case it is intended for regard in a certain way—namely, as a thing to be picture-read.

On the IPR View, comics are distinguished by whether or not their creator aptly intended them to be regarded with a certain kind of attention. This kind of attention need not be culturally specific. Comics creators need not have deep ties to the history of printmaking in Western Europe. They need only have undertaken (or somehow come to grasp the activity of) picture-reading themselves. So, although manga and European comics are read in different directions, they are each rightly described as being intended for picture-reading. Similarly, there is no barrier to picture-reading single panel or silent comics, since juxtaposed images and text aren't required for picture-reading. Only an *openness* to incorporating juxtaposed images into one's pattern of attention is required. Finally, abstract comics are intended to be picture-read precisely because of the aesthetic properties that emerge when we find our openness to narrative stifled by such cases.

Like most other artifacts whose nature depends on the intentions of their creators, not just any intention suffices. Hence the qualification that these intentions must meet minimal success conditions. Just as intentions alone cannot guarantee that something is a cheesecake or origami, intentions alone cannot magically transform clouds or pencil shavings into comics. Aptly intending something for picture-reading involves, among other things, the fact that competent audiences would be able to picture-read it and that competent audiences would recognize it as an attempt at producing something for picture-reading. In the case of the aspiring avant-garde comic artist who, in making a stack of pancakes, creates something that they intend for others to picture-read, we take it that although the resulting artifacts might be interesting, they nevertheless fall short of being comics.

Take another case. Suppose that a gallery owner, Aggie, hangs three paintings on the wall of the gallery and, moments before opening, realizes that there's a comics convention across the street. Aggie immediately decides to make a comic, so she looks over the drawings and thinks to herself: "Bamf! That's now a comic on that there wall!" Is that the right kind of deliberation? According to some, the answer is a tentative yes. As Picone (2013: 48) remarks:

> One could even reasonably assert, perhaps to the indignation of a few, that an art museum is an example of experimental comic art in everything but name only and that, conversely, a work of comic art is a sort of paper museum (or web-based museum, in a growing number of cases) where the spatio-temporal gaps between panels are simply greatly reduced compared to the those of the museum exhibit.

Would a competent comics reader recognize Aggie's artifact as a comic? Perhaps under some conditions (e.g., if the paintings were suitably reminiscent of a comic) but surely not under other conditions. This, we suspect, is where we ought to expect and therefore accept vagueness in a proposed definition of comics. More generally, the notion of an "apt intention" is liable to seem shot through with vagueness, but it's the kind of vagueness that attends the definition of almost all human artifacts insofar as mere intentions rarely suffice to settle what kind of artifact something is. It is, moreover, an inherently normative vagueness in the sense that intending can go better or worse. And, again, this seems the right verdict: comics practices are human practices, so the definition of comics is going to be bound up with how we act and evaluate things.

So far, so good. But when we look backward to our diet of examples, we can see where potential problems do arise for the IPR View. Earlier, we noted that views like the Deliberate Sequence View over-generate by counting remote historical artifacts like the Bayeux Tapestry as comics. What should the defender of the IPR View say to such a challenge? With regard to the Bayeux Tapestry, the defender of the IPR View should grant that while we can presently use our techniques of picture-reading to engage with diverse historical artifacts, the sociocultural activity of picture-reading in its current form had not yet arisen when it was created. While the creators of the Bayeux Tapestry intended for it to be looked at and read *in some sense*, the proponent of the IPR View will claim that picture-reading has a distinctive history and that while it can emerge in different historical contexts, it simply was not operative in the context in which the Bayeux Tapestry was created. In this way, history matters in what counts as a comic insofar as what intentions are available to creators depend upon historical and sociocultural contexts. Put a bit differently, for the IPR View to deny that the Bayeux Tapestry and other artifacts are comics, a distinction is needed between picture-reading as a historically specific activity and a more general, arguably universal, activity of pictorial storytelling.

Intentions play a key role in explaining the response of the IPR View to a puzzle we noted all the way back in Section 4: What should we make of a windblown series of images that come together in a manner that makes them perfectly suitable for being read as a comic? Given the requirements of the IPR View, there's no way to count such things as comics. And, while such things are surely exceptionally rare, they do raise the kind of problems with the epistemology of comics we noted in connection with the historical constraint. If it turns out that what you thought was your favorite comic is, in fact, a fantastic accident of juxtaposed images, then—somewhat shockingly—you would be mistaken in your belief that it was a comic in the first place. Since "accidental comics" of this sort occupy no meaningful place in the critical practice around comics and since philosophers disagree wildly about how and when to worry about these sorts of skeptical scenarios, we take this to be an open question rather than a damning objection—one that any defender of the IPR View owes a nuanced treatment of.

Alongside these challenges regarding absent or bizarre picture-reading intentions, the defender of the IPR View encounters another problem that stems from the sheer complexity of intentions relevant to comics production. When a comic has a single creator, it is somewhat straightforward to talk about what that artifact is intended for. But, in collaborative contexts—some of which run for years upon end—an account of comics that relies upon intentions will require a plausible account of who forms the relevant intention and why the intentions of *that* individual (or group of individuals) prove uniquely relevant. Those wary of relying upon intentions in defining anything are sure to find this an especially forbidding project, but understanding the attitudes and aims of collaborative comics creation is not a kind of complexity we can simply ignore; it is an integral part of grappling with comics history. And, if it is work that needs to be done in making sense of comics, we should, in principle, be open to incorporating it into our definition of what comics are.[33]

7. The Why Question

We've explored a large number of ways we might try and define comics. None avoid challenges, but some fare better than others. And, in some cases, there are options for proposing revised accounts or for developing a broader philosophy of comics in which certain consequences might prove more palatable. For example, while the Deliberate Sequence View seemed to be sunk by the single panel objection, perhaps if one developed a broader view—echoed in the Library of Congress policy—that gives precedence to the unified category of comics *and* cartoons rather than comics alone, the force of this objection can be mitigated. And, as we've also seen, there are various ways to refine approaches like those premised upon picture-reading into specific definitions of comics. For now, we'll conclude this chapter by noting an issue that is often ignored in discussions about defining comics.

We started this chapter by talking about Plato's *Euthyphro*, so let's bring things full circle. In that dialogue, Plato raises a dilemma for Euthyphro's claim that something is pious if and only if it is loved by the gods. This dilemma arises because even if this claim is true, we are left with a crucial yet unanswered *explanatory* question: Are things pious *because* they are loved by the gods? Or are things loved by the gods *because* they are pious? Depending on one's answer, facts about piety might explain what the gods love. Or, alternatively, the arrow of explanation might point in the opposite direction: facts about what the gods love explain facts about what is pious. These are importantly different views: one on which facts about piety are explanatorily *prior* to facts about the gods and another on which facts about what the gods love are explanatorily *prior* to facts about piety.

The Euthyphro dilemma is an illustration that even if certain concepts coincide, there remain open and important questions about the direction of explanation. This is true in the case of defining comics, too. Suppose, just for a moment, that McCloud's definition of comics is extensionally adequate. On such a view, something would be a comic just in case it is a deliberate sequence of juxtaposed images. And, since McCloud claims that deliberate sequences of juxtaposed images generate closure (of the relevant sort), something would also be a comic just in case it generates the right kind of closure. If so, an important *Why Question* is still left open: Why are things comics?

Suppose we were talking about our old volume of *Usagi Yojimbo* stories. We might give two different answers, each of which is consistent with McCloud's definition. The first claims that the volume is a comic because it generates closure. The second claims that it is a comic because it consists of juxtaposed images in deliberate sequence. We take it that first would be a far better answer than second. (To be clear, we don't think either is correct. We're just using them as examples.) That's because when it comes to the job of explaining *why* something is a comic, its function, effects, or sociocultural role seem to provide a better explanation of its status than highly specific formal features. (In this regard, comics and categories like *haiku* seem very different.) Perhaps that's correct, but even if it isn't, the fact stands: even if definitions are extensionally equivalent, they can fare better or worse when it comes to explaining what unifies comics together. This is, in part, why providing a definition of comics that just lists each and every comic ever can't be made satisfactory: the fact that a comic is on such a list is a shoddy explanation of why that thing is a comic in the first place.

The final takeaway here is that in assessing potential definitions of comics, our interest shouldn't be exclusively on making sure that our answer to the "what are comics?" question is extensionally adequate, though that's undeniably important. A good definition of comics should, at the same time, furnish us with a plausible answer to the question of why this-or-that comic is a comic. So, if you find yourself seeking to carve out a definition that includes a carefully delineated class of artifacts you deem to be all and only comics, keep in mind that whatever proposal you arrive at ought to yield an answer to the Why Question along with the What Question. Perhaps that answer will turn on the psychological effects common to all comics, the way in which text and image interact in all comics, or, as we've suggested, their intended role as material for picture-reading.

8. Recommended Readings

This chapter has covered a lot of varied ground, ranging from the definition of art to cartooning to the metaphysics of artifacts. Throughout, we've included various pointers to important contributions to these various areas of research. When it comes to the philosophical project of defining comics, a natural starting point is, of course, McCloud's *Understanding Comics*. Cartoonist Dylan Horrocks offers an extended response in "Inventing Comics: Scott McCloud Defines the Form in Understanding Comics" (2003). Meskin's "Defining Comics?" (2007) is a starting point for understanding the historicist challenge to McCloud's and other broadly formalist views. Meskin's follow-up piece, "Defining Comics" (2016)," usefully expands on these issues.

Along with the resources noted in the previous chapter and throughout this one, Pascal Lefevre and Charles Dierick's *Forging a New Medium* (1998) is a valuable historical collection. Within comics studies, the work of Thierry Groensteen on the specificity or definition of comics exerts continued influence especially in light of the translation of his *The System of Comics* (2007) and *Comics and Narration* (2011) into English. For those interested in semiotic approaches, see Sylvain Bouyer's "There Is No Specificity at the Number You Dialed" and its sequel in Miller and Beaty's *The French Comics Theory Reader* (2014). For a perspective on the trajectory of attempts to answer the What Question alongside detailed rhetorical analysis and an approach that meshes philosophy *of* comics with philosophy *through* comics, see Jason Helms, "Is This Article a Comic?" (2015) and *Rhizcomics* (2017).

3

Comics as Artifacts—
Ontology and Authenticity

1. Where Are Comics?

Comics are social artifacts. Unlike anthills and snow drifts, they're produced by humans and their production occurs against a complex backdrop of history, technology, and culture. Their reception by fans, scholars, and society at large is no less complex. It's a sprawling, messy affair involving any number of interconnected activities like reading, creating, and collecting. Any plausible *ontology* of comics—roughly, a philosophical theory about the nature of comics as artifacts—will be a complicated affair, since it ought to reflect the social complexity of comics practice.

This chapter is intended as an introduction to the ontology of comics, touching upon some of the conceptual challenges that arise in trying to develop a plausible and logically consistent theory of what kinds of things comics are. Importantly, this isn't the same project as defining *comics*. Instead, it aims to account for the most general features of comics by placing them within a broader theory of human artifacts. In this way, it's compatible with a host of different views about the proper definition of comics. And, as we'll see, a satisfactory ontology of comics requires that we distinguish between different and often conflicting norms that shape how we think and speak about comics.

It might seem a bit surprising that comics can be a source of thorny metaphysical troubles. After all, we do appear to know quite a lot about them. We know, to varying degrees, how to read, make, collect, and critique them. In fact, if you've spent much time around comics, you've likely internalized an implicit sort of theory about how comics work—for instance, about how series, issues, panels, stories, and other elements of comics relate to one another. For most purposes, this implicit theory is perfectly serviceable and leads to few paradoxical results. But, once we start asking apparently straightforward questions about comics, this implicit theory likely reveals itself to be unfortunately limited in scope. Consider, for example, a question about comics on which this implicit theory offers very little guidance: *Where are comics?* For example, where *exactly* is Daniel Clowes's comic, *Eightball* #18?

A plausible ontology of comics should be able to provide a principled answer to this question. Of course, this answer might prove surprising or contentious, but the lack of an immediately plausible answer is some evidence that our implicit theory of comics only goes so far. It's at such a point that the philosophical work of ontology often begins. That isn't to say, however, that we don't have *some* intuitive guidance regarding what plausible answers look like. It seems, for example, obviously false to say that *Eightball* #18 is on Venus. At the same time, it doesn't seem *obviously* true to say that *Eightball* #18 is in Seattle, even if someone is there, reading a copy of it right now.

Perhaps we can make headway in answering the question of where *Eightball* #18 is by drawing on some largely uncontroversial claims. We know that the series was published by Fantagraphics beginning in 1989 and that this particular issue hit stores in February of 1997. We also know that it had a substantial print run of at least 20,000 copies and that these copies are now strewn across the world. One is in a basement in Ohio. Another is in a comic store in New York City. Others have sadly but surely found their way into landfills. Even though we know all these facts, there still seems to be no simple or straightforward way to complete the following sentence: "*Eightball* #18 is located _____."

A tempting strategy is to determine where a particular instance of *Eightball* #18 can be found and answer by offering *that* specific location—for example, by saying that *Eightball* #18 is in a basement in Ohio. While that might be true, such an answer mistakenly implies that *Eightball* #18 is located *only* in a basement in Ohio. After all, if *Eightball* #18 is *only* in Ohio, then it can't *also* be in NYC—but it's surely in Ohio no more and no less than in NYC.

Here's a second potential answer: comics are nowhere at all. The quick argument in favor of such a surprising verdict is that *Eightball* #18 is an abstract entity, like the number seven or the property of *fragility*. It's just not the same kind of thing as its particular instances. For, while each instance of *Eightball* #18 has a location, *Eightball* #18 itself is a fundamentally different kind of thing—something that exists outside of physical space. As we'll argue in the next chapter, that might be the right thing to say about comics *characters* but it's far less plausible as a claim about comics themselves. It is, for example, exceptionally hard to reconcile the view that *Eightball* #18 is an abstract entity lacking any spatial location with the commitments of comics practice—in particular, that comics are created material artifacts, much like top hats and writing desks. Although there's little reason to expect a simple answer to the question of where a comic like *Eightball* #18 is located, announcing that comics are abstract or immaterial entities is, to our minds, a philosophical last resort.

A more promising answer to our location question claims that *Eightball* #18 is *entirely* located where each of its instances is located. According to this "multiple location" answer, *all* of *Eightball* #18 is located in a basement in Ohio and, at the very same time, *all* of *Eightball* #18 is located in an office in Seattle, and in a store in NYC, and so on. The good news: this answer avoids privileging one location over all others. The bad news: we're now neck deep in weird metaphysics. That's because if a comic can be entirely located in different places at the same time, then it's quite unlike familiar material objects like the Eiffel Tower, Abraham Lincoln, and your favorite mug. When we inquire into the location of material objects like the Eiffel Tower, a satisfactory answer will specify its *unique* location—for example, that all of the Eiffel Tower is located in a park in Paris. More generally, material objects seem to have a single location in space that's determined by the location of their respective parts. They are not—and cannot be—entirely located in distinct places at the same time. So, if we claim that comics like *Eightball* #18 are entirely located in many different places, we're committed to the striking claim that comics are, in at least this important respect, quite different from ordinary material objects.

Perhaps you're wary of the seemingly spooky claim that *Eightball* #18 and other comics can be *entirely* in one place while, at the same time, being in an *entirely* different place. You might propose instead that *Eightball* #18 is a scattered material object, like an asteroid belt or an archipelago. For example, as a scattered material object, the landmass of Michigan is partly located in the Upper Peninsula because it has that peninsula as one of its parts. It's also partly located in the Lower Peninsula—again, because it has *that* peninsula as a part. While the landmass of Michigan is *partly* located in these places, there is only one place at which it is *entirely* located: the total spatial sum of the two peninsulas (as well, of course, as the various islands). Can we say the same thing about the location of comics? On the resulting view, *Eightball* #18 is partly in a basement in Ohio, partly in an office in Seattle, and so on, but it is *entirely* located only at the sum of all of these various scattered regions.

This answer offers a way to make sense of the location of comics by positing that comics are ultimately scattered material objects. Unfortunately, upholding this claim requires that we accept some pretty implausible conclusions about comics. For example, if *Eightball* #18 is *really* just a material object scattered across the globe, then *Eightball* #18 is also a thing that weighs over 500 lbs. For, if we put all of this object in one place, it would tilt the scale at least that much. But no one believes *Eightball* #18 is anywhere near that heavy. Similarly, this scattered object also has tens of thousands of pages. But according to just about everyone, *Eightball* #18 has only forty-four pages. What gives?

The problem here is that *Eightball* #18 isn't just a scattered material object: it's a *multiple object*—a thing with multiple *instances*, each of which share common features in virtue of which they are instances of *Eightball* #18. Not all parts of the scattered material object made of the thousands of copies of *Eightball* #18 are instances. In fact, very few are. For example, a scattered object consisting of the first page of every issue of *Eightball* #18 is not an instance of *Eightball* #18. Why not? Well, no matter how many times you might try to read *that* object, it can't provide you with the right kind of access to *Eightball* #18. It's only by reading something with the *right* forty-four pages that you can actually read *Eightball* #18. And when Fantagraphics printed *Eightball* #18, they set out to produce and sell genuine instances of the comic, not just arbitrary portions of some massive thing made out of paper and ink.

We think that posing questions about the location of comics is a useful way to illustrate how puzzling the ontology of comics can be. And, while questions about *location* are not among the most important ones regarding comics, they draw out what is arguably the most significant ontological feature of comics: their multiplicity. Since our project is to make sense of our common thought and talk about the features of comics, exploring what it means to say that comics are (or are at least typically) multiples will be our first order of business.

2. Multiplicity

The natures of artworks differ to a remarkable extent. Compare, for example, a carefully accompanied ballet recital, an improvised jazz standard, and a towering piece of modernist sculpture. As we consider the sprawling variety of artworks, a key difference often emerges which separates *singular artworks* from *multiple* ones. Examples of the former kind—artworks that are ontologically unique—include paintings like Picasso's *Guernica* (1937), carved sculptures like the Hellenistic masterpiece *The Winged Victory of Samothrace* (*c.* 190 BCE), and numerous other forms like murals, totem poles, and site-specific works. Intuitively, singular artworks are one of a kind. Reproductions of them might share some of their features—indeed, they might look remarkably similar. But, despite their similarity, reproductions of singular artworks are aesthetically, commercially, and, in many other ways, secondary or inferior to the original work.

Unlike singular artworks, multiple artworks admit of many instances. Films, musical recordings, ballets, poems, novels, cast statues, and photographic prints produced from negatives are all *multiple artworks*. They can have *instances* in different places at the same time, each of which are equally legitimate objects of appreciation and engagement.[1] Given their multiplicity, artworks like novels can be readily purchased and admit of not only multiple instances but indefinitely many instances. It is, for example, a simple matter to acquire and read John le Carré's *The Secret Pilgrim* (1990), since prose novels are a multiple medium par excellence.

Multiples like prose novels have a perfectly familiar but ontologically distinctive capacity. By virtue of someone reading a specific material object—namely, their copy of *The Secret Pilgrim*—and you reading a different material object—your copy, perhaps with a different cover or in a different typeface—we are each capable of having read *the very same thing*. Each instance of a multiple artwork is a way to "access" the artwork that is somehow realized or manifested through its instances. In contrast, while you might be able to gather what *Guernica* looks like from photographic reproductions in books or on postcards, there is a clear sense in which you haven't actually *seen* it—

at least not by relevant aesthetic standards—without going and looking at *Guernica* itself.

Unlike singular artworks, multiple artworks are accessible through any of their instances, which, in the case of novels, films, and recordings, are typically reproduced through mechanical techniques like printing. So, while it would be lovely to thumb through le Carré's original manuscript of *The Secret Pilgrim*, you can genuinely read *The Secret Pilgrim*—or any other novel—without ever observing its original manuscript. In this way, when it comes to multiple mediums—mediums made up of artworks that exhibit multiplicity—any old instance will do.

Comics are a multiple medium. The kinds of artifacts that comics readers read, comics creators create, and comics collectors collect are typically (though not exclusively) instances of multiples. Whether our interest is in newspaper strips, minicomics, floppies, trade paperbacks, *tankōbon*, or webcomics, in reading a specific instance of a comic, we are able to read the comic itself. As with novels, there seems to be no better way to access or appreciate a (non-web) comic than by reading a printed instance of it. And, while original art created in the production of a comic is often a sought-after and interesting artifact, that original art is an inferior or at least nonstandard way of attempting to access and appreciate the comic produced from it. (That's not to say that original comics art isn't fascinating or valuable or that it might not be a superior way to appreciate artistic technique or a specific stage of the comics' production.)[2]

Does the fact that comics are a multiple medium mean that *all* comics are multiples? No. As we argued in Chapter 2, a doodle on your napkin could, under the right conditions, be rightly categorized as a comic and that might be true even if it were neither printed nor intended for printing. As a category of human artifacts, *comics* are impressively diverse. That said, it's plausible that *most* comics are multiples and it's evident that comics practice is overwhelmingly focused on comics that are multiples. It's in this *typical* sense that comics are a multiple medium. And it's for this reason that a key ontological question about comics concerns how we ought to understand their multiplicity. If, for example, we hope to answer questions about where comics are and what they're like, non-multiple comics like the doodle on your napkin prove far easier to make sense of than multiples like *Eightball* #18. And, when it comes to the latter case, we need a theory about the multiplicity of comics before we can make sense of how comics can be in two, three, seven thousand, or indefinitely many places at once.

Like television and certain kinds of film, music, or visual art, comics are not only a multiple medium but also a *mass* medium. Instances of comics like Raina Telgemeier's *Smile* (2010), *Shonen Jump* (1968–present), Hergé's *The Adventures of TinTin* (1929–86), and various *X-Men* and *Batman* titles are incredibly numerous, selling into the millions. Within certain aesthetic and philosophical traditions, mass art of this kind is often relegated to a secondary aesthetic status. In contrast, art that is not massively reproduced is often claimed to enjoy greater expressive or individualistic virtues.

Philosophical debate over the status of mass art is carefully examined in Noël Carroll's *A Philosophy of Mass Art* (1998), but it's worth noting that the assertion that comics is a mass art should not be interpreted as the claim that each and every comic is subject to mass reproduction. Some comics are printed in exceptionally small numbers (or not at all). Although the philosophical issues raised by mass art are important for critical purposes, the distinction between mass multiples and non-mass multiples is of limited *ontological* significance. It is important to keep in mind, however, that the methods for producing and distributing comics vary enormously. There are, for instance, plenty of avant-garde comics projects that range from exotic printing techniques to hybridized multimedia comics to site-specific comics splashed across the walls of fine art galleries. Despite this variation, our focus will be on making sense of the multiplicity of "typical" comics if only because *avant-garde* projects frequently set out to self-consciously interrogate precisely the typical norms of comics production and reception.

Our discussion will draw heavily on the investigation of multiplicity in Meskin's "The Ontology of Comics" (2012). Meskin, in turn, draws upon a threefold distinction from Stephen Davies (2003) regarding the ways in which artworks or artifacts can be multiples: *performative* multiplicity, *exemplary* multiplicity, and *encoded* multiplicity. In the rest of this section, we will ask *in what way* comics are multiples and, in doing so, explore why comics—unlike, say, objects like *Guernica,* Abraham Lincoln, or the Eiffel Tower—are able to be in many places at once.

2.1. Are Comics Performed?

While plays are often read, their scripts are produced for the purposes of facilitating performance. Similarly, scores of musical compositions are read by musicians and composers but are ultimately intended as guides for musical performance. On account of their parallel structure, scripted plays, scored musical compositions, and other artworks like choreographed dance pieces are all *performative multiples*. They have instances in virtue of individuals acting in compliance with something like guidelines or instructions. As S. Davies (2003: 161) puts it, an artwork that is a performative multiple generates instances "through writing and issuing a set of instructions for the production of its instances addressed to their performers or executants."

Are comics performative multiples? Well, instructions often play an important role in their production. Some writers produce lavish scripts that are treated as a guide to how artists ought to visually realize a story. And, when comics are printed, color guides have historically been an instructional tool for ensuring that the printed comics reflect the intentional choices of the colorist. But the fact that comics production often involves instructions falls well short of showing that comics are performative multiples.[3]

It's also important to note that holding comics to be performative multiples does not require us to believe that comics are themselves performances—presumably of printing technique. Given the dubious quality of much comics printing, this would be an extremely surprising discovery. Among other things, it would fail to explain the widespread disinterest in the ins and outs of comics printing practices. After all, if comics were themselves performances, one would expect World Color Press in Sparta, Illinois—where the overwhelming majority of American comic books in the 1980s were printed—to have been considerably more famous! On the more plausible interpretation of the view that comics are performative multiples, comics are artifacts intended for use in some kind of performances in the manner of scores or scripts.[4]

If you hope to defend the view that comics are performative multiples, your best bet might be to adapt the distinctive view about literary works defended by Peter Kivy in *The Performance of Reading* (2006). According to Kivy, literary novels are performed, typically silently and privately, by their readers. Roughly speaking, each reading of a novel constitutes a kind of solo performance, which takes its instructions from the author in the form of the text. Kivy's defense of this view is layered and complex, but a crucial component of it is premised upon facts about the historical practice of reading, which, as Kivy argues, was predominantly a performative practice in the West until *scriptura continua*—roughly, text without space inserted between words—was abandoned and the inclusion of spaces between words facilitated the development of silent, solitary reading. On Kivy's view, the reading aloud of a literary work was, prior to the advent of this new writing technology, a performance. Furthermore, according to Kivy, our present readerly practices are close enough in kind to still be rightly viewed as performances.

If comics are performative multiples, this might be on account of the fact that they suitably resemble literary novels *and* because Kivy's argument regarding the performance of literary novels is sound. But, leaving aside whether Kivy is correct about literary works, the divide between the literary works he has in mind and artifacts within the comics medium is large—large enough, it seems, that we should deny that comics are instructions for silent, solitary performance.

Notice, for example, that we often find authors of literary novels offering public performances of their works, which standardly consist in an author simply reading the text of a novel aloud. On Kivy's view, this is merely to make public a performance that is (at least in present day) typically done silently and solitarily. In contrast, there is no remotely straightforward way to transform the activity of reading a comic into a public performance of that very comic. Not only is it impossible to read aloud wordless or "silent" comics, the complex interaction of diegetic text, panels, speech balloons, thought bubbles, and other formal elements means that any simple strategy for performing comics will typically lead to something incomprehensible to the audience. This is because the interaction of text and image in comics precludes us from following any straightforward norm such as "read the text aloud in its order of appearance." And, while comics can be described in sequential order or woven into multimedia presentations or even audiobooks, such things are more plausibly viewed as adaptations or commentaries on comics than as genuine performances of the comics in question. (We'll examine the nature of comics adaptations in Chapter 10.)

The fact that there are no remotely familiar norms for publicly performing the reading of comics as one might publicly perform the reading of novels is good evidence that our silent solitary readings of comics are not performances. Importantly, this isn't to deny the cognitive complexity and internal vivacity of reading comics; it's just that the tradition of comics reading isn't a performance tradition and so comics are neither performances nor instructions in the manner of scripts or scores. Although the complexity and potency of what happens within the minds of comics readers is surely as rich as the performing of scripts or scores, there is no compelling reason to believe that this complexity entails that comics readings are *performances*. We must therefore look to our other options in our effort to make sense of the multiplicity of comics.

2.2. Are Comics Exemplars?

One way to frame our question about the multiplicity of comics is to ask: What would it take to create an instance of a specific comic like *Eightball* #18? When tackling a parallel question about novels, a straightforward answer is available: in order to create an instance of le Carré's *The Secret Pilgrim*, all we have to do is fashion an artifact that appropriately resembles the author's original (or perhaps corrected) manuscript. Importantly, our new instances of *The Secret Pilgrim* need not resemble le Carré's manuscript in every respect. The original manuscript might be unbound, on A4 paper, inscribed in longhand, and located in a desk drawer in England, but new instances don't need to have any of these features. By and large, the only required resemblance between instances of *The Secret Pilgrim* and the original manuscript is that they are alike with respect to the inclusion of the same words in the very same legible sequence.[5]

Exemplary multiples like novels have their instances solely in virtue of those instances resembling a designated *exemplar*—usually, a manuscript or a canonical performance—in respects that are relevant to the category of artwork or artifact. As S. Davies (2003: 159) says, "a novelist produces a manuscript that is both an instance of her novel and a model with the normative function of setting the standard that other instances of her novel must emulate." For this reason, mediums like the novel that exhibit exemplary multiplicity are also mediums in which the initial product of creative activity (e.g., the manuscript) is an instance of the work and therefore a perfectly good way to access and appreciate it. In this respect, exemplary multiplicity differs from performative multiplicity, since access to instructions like scores and scripts is a derivative or secondary way of engaging or appreciating an artwork. Consider, for example, that reading a musical score rather than hearing it performed hinders the proper evaluation of the musical piece, since the score is principally a means for generating performances.

The fact that artworks like novels are exemplary multiples has wide-ranging consequences. Here's one of particular interest: if all that's required to create an instance of an artwork is the production of something that suitably resembles an exemplar, then this suggests that it is impossible to forge instances of that artwork. This is because if suitable resemblance guarantees that something is an instance of an artwork like a novel, then any competent attempt at copying it will thereby succeed in generating a genuine instance. (Of course, someone might produce unlicensed or illegal instances of a novel, but the legal issues raised by such instances are no barrier to being instances of the novel, ontologically speaking.) For this reason, exemplary multiples are typically viewed by philosophers as *allographic* rather than *autographic* artworks or mediums, where only autographic artworks or mediums are those susceptible to forgery.[6] Contrast, for example, a perfect look-alike reproduction of any instance of *The Secret Pilgrim* with a perfect look-alike reproduction of an Albrecht Dürer woodcut like *Four Horsemen of the Apocalypse* (1498). As an allographic medium, being a look-alike of an instance of *The Secret Pilgrim* guarantees that a novel is therefore a genuine instance of *The Secret Pilgrim*. In contrast, although Dürer's woodcut is a multiple artwork, a mere facsimile of it will, if it lacks the proper production history, fail to be a genuine instance. Rather than being an instance, it will be a mere copy or, if used nefariously, a forgery.[7]

Meskin (2012: 42) argues that comics are typically autographic rather than allographic. So, unlike novels but much like paintings or fine art prints, comics admit of potential forgery:

> The production of an authentic instance of a traditional comic requires mechanical reproduction from a template. In the case of most traditionally produced comics the particular template is the collection of printing plates that are used to print the token comic. No token comic is an authentic instance of a relevant comic type unless it was produced mechanically by means of those printing plates or, *perhaps*, by mechanically copying another genuine instance (or another set of plates made from the original art) which may serve as a surrogate template. It is because of this that the distinction between original and . . . forgery in the case of comics is significant.

If Meskin is correct, then looking exactly like *Eightball* #18 isn't enough for something to count as a genuine instance of *Eightball* #18. A perfectly faithful, hand-drawn reproduction of a comic will, for example, fall short of being a genuine instance. This is because in order to count as an authentic instance of *Eightball* #18, a certain kind of production history is required—for instance, that it be printed with specific printing plates or digital file originally used.

On this autographic view, the history of a comic—not merely how it looks—matters for determining whether it might count as an authentic instance. In the same way that a certain historical process renders the autograph of a celebrity significant—namely, that *their very hand* signed the page—a certain historical process is part of what settles whether a comic is an authentic instance. And, if comics are autographic rather than allographic, they cannot be exemplary multiples—their multiplicity must be a matter of something more than their similarities with an exemplar.

2.3. Are Comics Encoded Multiples?

S. Davies (2003) describes a third kind of multiplicity, one shared by some forms of photography, printmaking, sculpture, film, and music recording. *Encoded multiplicity* involves the production of an "encoding" such as a master tape, a cast for a statue, a photographic negative, or a digital file. To create an instance of an encoded multiple artwork, the encoding or *matrix* is "decoded" through some specific (typically mechanical) process. Molten metal is poured into a cast. Chemicals and light are applied to photographic negatives and paper. A cassette is run through a VCR or a tape deck. According to S. Davies, the matrix produced in order to decode and create instances is not identical with the artwork of primary interest. A statue isn't the cast: it's the "decoded" statue. A photographic work isn't the negative: it's the "decoded" print. A film or album isn't the cassette: it's the playing of the recording. Encoded multiplicity therefore involves a two-stage process: the encoding or creation of a matrix and its subsequent decoding, which when properly undertaken creates instances of the multiple artwork.[8]

A historical reason to believe that comics are encoded multiples is that prints like woodcuts, lithographs, or *gyotaku* are encoded multiples, and the traditions of printmaking and comics production are distinct but intimately connected. The development of woodblock printing, movable type, and lithography are watershed moments in the history of printmaking, but they are equally important for the emergence of the comics medium. Works that straddle the divide between comics and printmaking—often called "proto-comics"—like Lynd Ward's wood engravings, William Hogarth's engraved version of *The Rake's Progress* (1732–4), or Max Ernst's *Une Semaine de Bonté* (1934) are further evidence for the inseparability of the history of comics from the history of printmaking. It seems natural, then, to view comics as encoded multiples for much the same reason that we standardly take printmaking to be an encoded multiple medium—though, as Cook and Meskin (2015) point out, there are salient differences, for example, with regard to status of editions and instances as distinctive works.

Taking comics to be encoded multiples also provides us with a general framework for understanding the often complex and variable character of comics production. Just as the process of "encoding" a matrix is usually a large undertaking in filmmaking, comics production regularly comprises a host of activities including script writing, penciling, inking, lettering, revisions, the production of color guides, paste-ups, and many additional tasks or variations thereof. But all this work aims at the production of a matrix to be used in order to "decode" instances (whether mechanically or digitally), and those instances are the artworks and objects of intended aesthetic engagement. In this spirit, we do find comics creators suggesting that authentic instances are only produced via the printing of comics and not before. Rather famously, Art Spiegelman remarks that "comics just aren't complete 'til they're printed." (2008: 3) And that's true even if—as we believe—the original art produced in standard creative processes are also rightly categorized as comics. (It's just that the printed works rather than material generated in their production process are the comics of primary appreciative interest.) This sentiment is echoed by cartoonists Jessica Abel and Matt Madden (2011: vii):

> Comics is a printed medium. And now it's also a digital medium. What it isn't is a *direct* medium, like drawing or painting: there is no "original" comic to read. The pages that have the ink on them may be beautiful to look at and they may offer loads of information for fans and researchers, but most people will agree that it's not really a comic until it has been reproduced.[9]

No account of the ontology of comics that ignores digitally produced and distributed comics has any hope of being comprehensive. The good news, then, is that a view of comics as encoded multiples can also account for the multiplicity of digital comics, broadly construed. Meskin (2012: 38) says:

> Instances of traditional comics are produced mechanically by various means of printing (the transfer of ink from engraved plate to paper). The engraved plates from which comics are printed are, then, encodings and the production of prints is their decoding. Webcomics are literally digitally encoded and decoded by software on your home computer. Moreover, neither the original art (Bristol Board, proofs, etc.) nor the plates made from that art that are used in reproduction of a standard comic are typically counted as instances of that comic. The drawings from which *Action Comics* #1 was made do not constitute an instance of that the comic.

With this account in view, let's turn now to an argument against the *encoded view*—that is, the view that comics are encoded multiples—that needs to be addressed. This objection concerns the epistemic access creators have to their own comics.

Comics creators—including pencilers, inkers, letterers, and colorists—are standardly taken to have an expert understanding of and distinctive access to the comics that they make. If comics are encoded multiples, there's something prima facie puzzling about this practice, since comics creators might spend little or no time at all inspecting authentic instances of their comics. After all, we can easily imagine circumstances under which a comics creator never actually reads the comic itself and inspects or examines only the original art used for the creation of the matrix. But, if comics are encoded multiples, the matrix that is decoded in the production of a comic (e.g., a digital file, printing plate, or, by extension, original art) is not actually an instance of that comic. There is, then, a notable sense in which the encoded view holds that comics creators can find themselves at arm's length from their own comics. It is therefore unclear how to make sense of their de facto authoritative knowledge regarding their creations when, according to the encoded view, they might have never even seen the comics they wrote, penciled, inked, and so on.

This objection continues: the only way to explain the knowledge that comics creators possess regarding their creations is to hold that, contrary to the encoded view, original art, certain digital files, production photographs of original art, and perhaps even printing plates do count as instances of the comics they are used to create.[10] Such a view would hold, in effect, that original art produced for comics is much like the manuscript of a novel: its role in the creative process is different, but it is no less of an authentic instance than the decoded artifact.

This objection puts some pressure on us to grant that matrices are authentic instances of comics. But the defender of the encoded view has a way to counter this objection and to explain the epistemic authority of creators with regard to their creations without holding matrices to be authentic instances. That's because as expert craftspeople, comics creators are typically in a position to know with considerable accuracy how a comic will turn out after observing it at certain unfinished stages. And, quite often, the matters on which comics creators are authorities concern why a comic looks the way it does, how it aims to tell a certain story, or what the process of producing it involved. Knowledge of this kind need not require careful inspection of authentic instances. We are therefore under no serious pressure to insist that matrices are authentic instances when it comes time to explain creators' knowledge of their own comics: quite often, everything they need to know concerns themselves, the matrix they've produced, or the standard practices involved in decoding it.

If we accept S. Davies's taxonomy of performative, exemplary, and encoded multiples as exhaustive, Meskin's assessment that comics are encoded multiples seems highly plausible. It's important, however, to remember that in claiming that comics is a multiple medium, we claim only that comics are *typically* multiples. As we argued in Chapter 2, comics are artifacts aptly intended for picture-reading and the variety of such artifacts is potentially enormous. Some are reproduced; some aren't. Some are encoded multiples—in fact, the vast majority of comics on which comics practice is focused are encoded multiples. But could there be comics that aren't encoded multiples? We think so. The doodle on your napkin is created through a one-stage rather than a two-stage process of encoding and decoding. And, if we imagine an avant-garde comic circulated as a stencil to be painted on walls, we suspect that it could in principle be an allographic rather than autographic comic.

You might be tempted to object that these various exceptions undercut the significance of Meskin's case for viewing comics as autographic, encoded multiples. To the contrary, we think it actually reinforces the importance of that conclusion. Comics admit of enormous potential diversity, so the fact that they are typically *anything*—not to mention typically encoded multiples—is a fact that can shed crucial light on the link between what kinds of things comics are and how comics are created. As we'll argue in the next section, the view that comics are typically encoded multiples provides us with some foundational insights into how questions of identity and authenticity function within comics practice.

3. Authenticity

According to the ontology of comics that Meskin defends, comics are encoded multiples, typically produced through a (broadly) two-stage process of encoding and then decoding. They are also typically autographic and so are, in principle, subject to forgery. If that's correct, what does it mean for the practices of preserving and especially reprinting comics?

Suppose we find ourselves with an old comic strip that we've only just discovered and that we are desperate to share with others. After some research, we determine that it's absolutely anonymous, with no chance that the creator or publisher might still be alive. We also determine that the original art and printing plates have been destroyed. Is there any way we can create another authentic instance of the strip for distribution? Suppose we actually go ahead and mechanically copy and reprint the strip. Have we made an inauthentic instance? Or, weirder still: Have we created a new, distinct comic strip that just looks exceptionally similar to the one with which we began?

In broaching this issue, it will be useful to again focus on Meskin's remarks as our starting point: "No token comic is an authentic instance of a relevant comic type unless it was produced mechanically by means of those printing plates or, *perhaps*, by mechanically copying another genuine instance (or another set of plates made from the original art) which may serve as a surrogate template" (2012: 42; italics from original). A lot hangs on Meskin's italicized '*perhaps*' and depending on which way we go, we end up with two importantly different views about authenticity in comics.

If we *can* use surrogate templates to create genuine instances, then reprints are potentially a way to make new authentic instances. On what we will call the *Loose View* of authenticity, under the right conditions and with the appropriate means, we can generate authentic instances without the original matrix. And, while fine-grained details are crucial in developing the Loose View, let's suppose, for the moment, that at least one way to create authentic instances is by mechanically copying an authentic instance to produce a "surrogate template" from which we can then print new genuine instances. If so, the Loose View holds that it is still possible, even without original printing plates, for us to make authentic instances of our newly recovered comic.

If we treat Meskin's '*perhaps*' the other way, we end up with what we'll call the *Strict View* of authenticity. On this account, we *can't* use surrogate templates to create novel authentic instances since authenticity requires that a comic be produced via the original matrix.[11] So, if the Strict View is true, it's simply no longer possible for us to make new authentic instances. With the destruction of the original matrix, the number of authentic instances of a comic can only dwindle and can never grow as time passes.

How we should evaluate these two accounts of authenticity? What can be said in favor of the Strict View over the Loose View? Quite obviously, the Strict View draws a sharp dividing line between authentic instances and mere reprints. And, for certain philosophical purposes, this sharp divide might be used to explain the fact that original comics and their reprints are often treated in very different ways. This is, in part, because reprints have significant aesthetic properties that originals do not. Perhaps most importantly, reprints are standardly evaluated for their fidelity to original comics, but it makes no sense to ask how faithful an original comic is to itself. As we'll discuss in the next section, it can be a serious technical challenge to capture the color palette and overall look of comic strips when reprinting old newspaper comics on high-quality paper with digital printing technology. But original comics simply are not subject to judgments of fidelity.[12] (It's important to note, too, that for some comics, it is reprints rather than originals that become objects of central critical or appreciative focus—for example, the colored and, in some cases, recolored and collected reprints of portions of Chris Ware's *Acme Novelty Library* (1993–present) such as *Jimmy Corrigan, The Smartest Kid on Earth* (2000) eclipse the attention paid to the original instances.)

Only reprints are able to succeed or fail with regard to their fidelity to authentic instances. And the Strict View easily captures this fact by unambiguously distinguishing original comics from their reprints. For, if the original matrix hasn't been used, reprints simply aren't instances of the original comic. They're either inauthentic instances of the comic or, in certain circumstances, a numerically distinct comic altogether. Depending upon what they purport to be, they're to be assessed in different ways—namely, by their capacity to approximate the appearance of the original comic. In contrast, the Loose View seems forced to admit the possibility of reprints that are also authentic instances and so are, at the same time, properly assessed for their fidelity to other authentic instances. But applying these conflicting aesthetic standards to comics is incoherent: everything is perfectly faithful to itself, after all. This suggests that the Loose View can't give a straightforward account of fidelity or, by default, entails that authentic reprints essentially exhibit perfect fidelity. And that suggests that the Loose View is poorly positioned to explain how comics practice actually treats reprints.

Here's a second argument for the Strict View. The variety of comics reprinting practices varies wildly and gives rise to reprints that differ in myriad ways from earlier comics. Black-and-white reprints of previously colored comics are commonplace, as are newly colored reprints. Comics that originally appeared as a single daily strip are often reprinted in immediate sequence alongside years' worth of installments. Changes in size abound with newspaper strips enlarged and, in some cases, comic books are resized upwards or downwards (often in conformity with the size of Bristol boards or popular formats). Comic books that first appeared with a variety of different advertisements are standardly reprinted and collected in formats without advertisements or even without their original cover art. These various changes yield markedly different aesthetic results. For instance, a previously surprising "reveal" that was discovered upon flipping a page might be rendered far less shocking because different pages of the reprint now face one another.

A virtue of the Strict View is that it avoids what seems like an impossible task: specifying exactly what would be required in order to generate an authentic reprint. If reprints can be authentic even in the absence of the original matrix as the Loose View claims, we would seem to be owed principled answers to questions like the following: Can authentic reprints alter the colors of the original? How about the size? Or the order of serialization? In what ways can the line art, lettering, and paper quality permissibly differ? Put simply, it seems impossible to give a principled account of what's required for an *authentic* reprint. It would be preferable, then, to avoid the Loose View which saddles us with an apparently unanswerable question. So, while the Strict View does owe us a general account of what features increase or decrease the fidelity of a reprint, it does not require us to specify the precise boundary point between authentic and inauthentic reprints.

The Strict View is the most demanding sort of view of authenticity in comics. In virtue of that status, it enjoys certain theoretical advantages like the ones just noted. At the same time, it also incurs objections that will push us to think carefully about the different practices that surround comics. The most pressing of these objections begins by asking what it means to have read a specific comic.

3.1 Reading and Owning Comics, Authentically

When we engage in discussions about comics, we regularly find comics readers talking about comics that they have and haven't read. And, when they do so, there's a clearly recognized sense in which someone can truly claim to have read Kazuo Koike and Goseki Kojima's *Lone Wolf and Cub* (1970–6) without having read the original manga in Japanese. Similarly, fans will discuss whether they've read the first issue of Stan Lee and Jack Kirby's *Fantastic Four* (1961) even if they've never even seen an authentic instance and have had access solely to reprints. Readers are exceptionally likely to claim, after reading, say, the *Showcase Presents* edition of Robert Kanigher and Ross Andru's *The War that Time Forgot* (1960–8), that they have successfully read the stories it reprints. And this is true despite the fact that the *Showcase Presents* reprinting was made by (roughly) scanning photographs of film preservations of original issues and publishing them in black and white on newsprint. These readers might remark that they don't own or perhaps haven't seen the original comic books, but a cursory look at the norms of reading within comics practice makes clear that suitably produced reprints are perfectly acceptable ways of reading original comics.

The problem for the Strict View is that if we hope to make sense of how reading works in comics practice, we seem forced to count reprints as authentic instances. But, since the Strict View entails that reprints are not authentic instances of the comics that they reprint, it seems to do a poor job of making sense of our talk about reading comics and, in particular, our judgments about which comics different individuals have read. In pressing this objection, one might argue that the Strict View entails that, quite unwittingly, scholars studying or readers enjoying reprints are up to something quite strange. They're actually reading look-alikes that falsely purport to be instances of original comics or, perhaps more charitably, prosthetically reading authentic instances *through* their reading of inauthentic instances.

We think the Strict View can meet this objection but doing so requires that we distinguish between some of the practices that surround comics and the way in which these practices are driven by importantly different norms. For present purposes, it will be useful to make a rough distinction between two general kinds of activities: *readerly practices* and *collecting practices*. This is not to say by any means that these are the only kinds of comics-related activities; obviously, without *creative practices*, neither readerly practices nor collecting practices would be possible. They are, however, the two primary practices most relevant to our concerns here.

Readerly practices are, by leaps and bounds, the most familiar comics-related activities. They're undertaken by anyone who competently engages with the content or form of any given comic. These practices range from the casual, leisurely reading of a comic strip in a newspaper to perhaps the most rarified readerly practice: the careful, deliberative study of the content of a comic. Importantly, comics reading—or, as we called it in Chapter 2, picture-reading—isn't merely the activity of looking at comics. An artist might study every page of a comic, perhaps out of sequence, observing the inking, but given the nature of their attention, do something other than actually read it. While it remains an under-discussed philosophical issue of how to define picture-reading, it is an activity largely insensitive to fine-grained distinctions regarding authenticity. We take the activity of picture-reading to be essentially *recognitional* in nature: if someone has read a comic, they can generally recognize it—roughly put, they know what it looks like, can more or less reliably identify it, and recall the appearance of its constituent parts, and so on. Since readerly practices are driven by recognitional norms, a reprint of sufficient quality is, for the purposes of reading, no more or less an instance of a comic than an original printing.[13] Each affords the same possibilities for readerly practice and when engaging with comics principally as readers, standards for identity and authenticity are more or less irrelevant.[14]

Collecting practices are arguably more diverse than readerly practices but also less widespread. They range from the sale and purchase of comics as collectibles to the archival and historical preservation of comics, whether in the form of original art, printed strips, or digital records. These practices are informed not merely by recognitional norms but crucially by norms concerned with historical authenticity and material rarity. As Cook and Meskin (2015: 62) describe them, "these practices (like the practices surrounding many collectibles) focus on scarcity and other aesthetically irrelevant properties of particular instances." For almost anyone interested in comics collecting, authentic original printings of comics are treated in fundamentally different ways than reprints (e.g., in monetary value) and for those interested in preservation of the historical record, replicas and reprints are, at best, proxies for the objects of central interest: authentic, historical instances. Just as a replica of Abraham Lincoln's pen is of vastly less interest than Lincoln's actual pen, when we're engaged in collecting practices, originally printed strips receive importantly different treatment than look-alike reprints. Because of this sensitivity to historical properties of artifacts, judgments of authenticity are of central relevance when we're engaged in collecting practices. A contrast between these practices is therefore clear: when our interest is in readerly practices, authenticity matters only quite rarely, but it is a foundational concern of collecting practices.

To get a sense of how these different practices shape our judgments of authenticity, consider the following pair of more or less hypothetical questions—one about what it takes to *read* a comic and one about what it takes to *own* a comic:

Reading Question: Agatha just purchased a copy of Sloane Leong's *Prism Stalker* #2 (2018). Edie can't find a copy at her local comic book shop, but is able to briefly borrow Agatha's. Without looking at Agatha's copy, Edie runs down to the office supplies store, digitally copies each page, and then staples the copied pages together. She then returns Agatha's comic. Later that day, Edie flips slowly through her copied material, looking and reading carefully. Excited, she calls Agatha to talk about how *Prism Stalker* #2 is great and even better than the first issue. But has Edie actually *read Prism Stalker* #2?

Ownership Question: Glynis is a tremendous fan of the work of artist Sanho Kim and an avid collector of original comic art. Over the years, she's purchased numerous pages of Kim's work. She's especially excited to learn that, with her purchase of the original cover art to *Ghost Manor* #5 (1969), she now owns all of the original art used for that issue. As Glynis casually looks through her comic collection, she realizes that, while she owns all of the original art used to produce the issue, a printed version of *Ghost Manor* #5 is not in her collection. So, does Glynis actually *own Ghost Manor* #5?

These are undeniably weird questions. And, as we think through them, things only get weirder. There is, for example, very little temptation to claim that Agatha owns a copy of *Prism Stalker* #2. But, if she doesn't actually own a copy, how could she have gone about reading one? We think this points toward the peculiar and important ways in which the norms of readerly and collecting practices conflict and intersect with one another.

It seems—to our mind, anyways—that Agatha has read *Prism Stalker* #2 provided, of course, that she did a suitably competent job copying from Edie's authentic instance. In much the same way that reprints can provide *readerly* access to older comics, Agatha managed to acquire readerly access (albeit unlawfully and arguably unethically). But, as we consider questions of *ownership*, it also seems true that Agatha doesn't own a copy of *Prism Stalker* #2. When we have collecting practices in mind, it is natural to say that Glynis doesn't actually own a copy of *Ghost Manor* #5 even if she does own an artifact remarkably important for its production.

What matters most for our purposes is that as we move from questions about reading to questions about collecting and ownership, our standards for what counts as an instance seem to change. When our focus is on reading and questions of content, the norms of readerly practice determine which artifacts we can treat as instances of a comic. These standards are quite generous, including almost any competent reprint (provided that it meets the standards of ordinary reading practices). But when we talk about ownership and collecting, our attention to the norms of the latter practice becomes more salient and, in turn, production history and material rarity shape our judgments of what counts as an instance of *Prism Stalker* #2 or *Ghost Manor* #5.

In some contexts—namely, those where we're interested in readerly practices—Edie has *Prism Stalker* #2 and can perfectly well read it. In other contexts, where we're focused on collecting and authenticity, she doesn't seem to have *Prism Stalker* #2. In that second context, it seems odd to say that she has read it. But, notice, that merely by talking about whether or not she has read it, we thereby change the linguistic context, inching back to the previous context and its looser standards. If we're right, what counts as an instance of a given comic varies significantly depending on whether we're speaking in a context primarily concerned with readerly or collecting practices. (Yet another shift in standards occurs when we are primarily concerned with creative practices—for example, we think that, in such contexts, speakers are far more likely to talk as though original artwork is an instance of a comic.) We take contextual variation in what counts as an instance to be highly plastic, but we also think that it's crucial to avoid an "anything goes" relativism about instances, since views of that sort are unable to explain the systematic behavior of judgments of fidelity and value in comics practice. For example, no amount of wishing or linguistic sleight of hand can turn your reprint of *Suspenstories* #22 (1954) into an authentic instance.

Here's our rough proposal, which admittedly requires more elaboration than we can give it here: the Strict View accurately reflects the judgments of authenticity that are part and parcel of collecting practice. To the extent that authenticity matters within comics practice, it's almost always when we're engaged in collecting practices rather than readerly ones. By contrast, the readerly practices that surround comics—which are more familiar to most people—are largely insensitive to the distinction between authentic and inauthentic instances. For most readerly purposes, a look-alike comic is just as viable a means for reading a comic as the original. It would, for example, be highly misleading to say that you own *Fantastic Four* #1 without adding that what you own is a reprint of the issue in a larger reprint volume. In contrast, it seems far less misleading to say that you've read *Fantastic Four* #1, since whether your access was to an authentic instance or a reprint is of little significance for readerly practice.

Let's step back and face up to the objection against the Strict View on the grounds that it can't make sense of readerly practices. On the contextualist version of the Strict View we've sketched, we take it that authenticity plays a minimal role in comics reading, and when our focus is on comics reading, what counts as an instance is much broader than what the Strict View would count as an authentic instance. But when we turn our attention to collecting practices—as we do when we ask whether Glynis owns *Ghost Manor* #5— our standards change and we become increasingly sensitive to questions of authenticity. It's in those latter contexts that we are inclined to deny that Glynis owns *Ghost Manor* #5. If we apply the demanding standards of collecting practice, it can therefore seem puzzling that Edie might have read *Prism Stalker* #2 given that those standards invite us to believe that she is without an authentic instance. But, we should simply reject the interpretation of this question that tries to apply the standards for being a genuine instance in collecting practices to matters that are fundamentally concerned with readerly practices. We often need to be careful when moving from context to context to avoid finding paradoxes where there are none. In the same spirit, it's not a genuine paradox that Gomer is tall and short so along as we're clear that we mean he's tall *for an NBA player* and short *for a redwood tree.* And in a similar spirit, *for collecting purposes,* Edie doesn't have a copy of *Prism Stalker* #2 even though *for readerly purposes,* she's holding one right now.

4. Putting Comics in Their Place

We started this chapter by posing the question of where comics are located. It would seem unfair if we didn't offer up our best attempt at an answer.

We think the most promising way to reply to questions about the location of comics is to help ourselves to what we learned earlier: that comics are typically encoded multiples and that authentic instances stand in very specific causal and historical relationships to the matrices that produced original instances. Of course, in some contexts—those driven by readerly practices—authenticity matters little and, for that reason, what counts as an instance of a comic is a fairly loose affair—reprints will therefore be appropriately included. We also know that even if something has the right history, it might fall short of being a well-formed instance if, say, it's ripped to shreds by the cat.[15] To develop a plausible answer to our question regarding location, our first step is to begin by posing the following question about comics like *Eightball* #18: What properties do all *well-formed* instances of a comic share?

How can this answer help with locating comics? When we ask how many pages *Eightball* #18 has, what the art on the cover looks like, or what story it tells, we take the standards for our answer to be given by what's true of all well-formed instances. (When we pose this question in collecting contexts, the class of instances is narrowed further to *authentic* ones.) For example, it is true that *Eightball* #18 has forty-four pages *just in case* each well-formed instance has forty-four pages. Similarly, it is false that *Eightball* #18 is triangular *just in case* no well-formed instance is triangular. Put roughly, this way of interpreting talk of *Eightball* #18 is a way of *simulating* reference to a paradigm *Eightball* #18 (or any other comic, for that matter) because claims are true about *Eightball* #18 *just in case* they are true of *all* well-formed instances.

Roughly speaking, this account tries to make our intuitive but implicit conventions for talking about comics explicit and systematic. It does so in a way that holds us to be talking about nothing more and nothing less than all of the well-formed individual instances of comics. There are a variety of different philosophical tools for refining this sort of proposal—most notably, the semantic technique of supervaluation.[16] We won't dive in here, but we'll instead point to how this might give us an answer to the question of where comics are located.

Is it true that *Eightball* #18 is in a basement in Ohio? While that's true of at least one instance, it's certainly not true of all well-formed instances. So, no, it's not true that *Eightball* #18 is in a basement in Ohio. Importantly, it's also not false that *Eightball* #18 is in a basement in Ohio, since it's not true that all well-formed instances are outside of Ohio. That means the claim *Eightball* #18 is in a basement in Ohio is indeterminate: neither nor true false. (Importantly, that's perfectly consistent with it being true that an *instance* of *Eightball* #18 is in Ohio.) What about an example we started with: Is *Eightball* #18 on Venus? As it turns out, there are absolutely no well-formed instances of *Eightball* #18 on Venus, so it's not true that *Eightball* #18 is on Venus. In fact, it is true that *Eightball* #18 is on this very planet.

Generalizing from these cases, what's true about the location and composition of *Eightball* #18 is just what's true about all of its well-formed instances. It's smaller than a house. It's made of paper. And so on. Interestingly, if we collected absolutely all well-formed instances and put them in a warehouse in Seattle, it *would* be true that *Eightball* #18 is in a warehouse in Seattle. But, typically, claims about the location of *Eightball* #18 will be indeterminate even while claims about the location of specific instances are determinate. But, since each well-formed instance of *Eightball* #18 is a material object, it is also true that *Eightball* #18 is a material object.

This approach to the ontology of comics leaves us with a general recipe for making sense of claims about comics and, in some cases, for determining what's true about them. It also acknowledges that depending upon our activities, the significance of authenticity can vary and, in turn, shape which claims we might accept in different contexts. In the last section of this chapter, we'll explore the significance of authenticity in reprints for not just the ontology of comics but the ethics of comics as well.

5. Recoloring

As we've noted, the practice of reprinting comics is a common one. And, when it comes to accessing comics from the past, it's quite often the best we can do. Although we've argued that reprints are not authentic instances of original comics, they are nevertheless a viable means for reading the comic they reprint as long as reasonable standards of fidelity are met. For this reason, when we evaluate reprints, the standard question to ask is how faithful they are to the original comics. Generally speaking, the most faithful reprints are those that best approximate the look and visual experience of reading authentic instances. But this virtue of fidelity isn't the only aesthetic virtue and, in many cases, the pursuit of fidelity is in tension with other aesthetic concerns.

Suppose, for example, that we were interested in reprinting the first year of *Secret Agent X-9* (1934) by Dashiell Hammett and Alex Raymond. We might reprint a volume of this daily strip by placing a single installment on each page. Very roughly, this seems to approximate readers' historical engagement with the series, placing each installment in relative isolation from preceding and subsequent ones. Alternatively, we might decide to place several installments on each page of the reprint volume in order to facilitate continuous reading. The former option is perhaps a more faithful reading experience of the original comic. It might also leave us more inclined to study Raymond's "opaque, monotonous elegance" (Phelps 2001: 9) and appreciate the isolated panel designs of the strip. In contrast, the latter option will bring the various strips together in a way that fosters a more cohesive reading experience. It might therefore amplify the continuity of the storytelling, rendering Raymond's plotting more coherent, even if it minimizes the dramatic sense that each installment is a vital cliffhanger.

The creative practice of reprinting is rife with these sorts of choices, since any reprint effort is forced into a variety of aesthetic trade-offs. In reprinting comics, it's all but impossible to avoid decisions about the size and design of the reprinted page, the size and quality of the reprinted image, the quality of the paper and binding, the inclusion of supplementary material like original advertising, as well as numerous additional decisions. Historically, major publishers have been minimally interested in these concerns, focusing squarely on profit at the expense of aesthetic virtues. But, with the emergence of critical, scholarly, and historical interest in older comics and cartoonists, reprint projects that involve careful aesthetic consideration are increasingly commonplace and often take seriously the challenge of how to reconcile the pursuit of fidelity with, say, readers' curiosity about artistic techniques.

As reprints receive greater care and attention, a familiar complaint within critical practice concerns the preservation of color design. Reprinting comics that were originally cheaply printed on low-quality newsprint raises a litany of challenges. Not only has the typical method for color production changed significantly (e.g., the emergence of digital coloring tools rather than old school color separation), but, even when publishers are able to use the original color guides, advances in printing technology and the desire for "deluxe" reprints leave reprint projects with the challenge of how to use modern, high quality resources to deliver something that looks like the product of an older, often low-quality process. For example, what a color guide looks like when followed on fifties newsprint differs markedly from what it looks like when executed with contemporary printing technology. It's therefore quite common to find reprints that, intentionally or not, look quite different from authentic instances.

An increasingly standard practice in reprinting—partly motivated by this practical challenge—is to digitally recolor copies of original art or copies of authentic instances. As we'll see in a moment, this practice has been advertised as a means for improving or "remastering" comics. Importantly, there's no sharp or uncontroversial divide between *un*recolored and recolored reprintings insofar as any reproduction process will involve tools, digital or mechanical, that involve some unavoidable alteration. At the same time, reprinting practices vary greatly in the intended extent of recoloring, ranging from those that pursue all possible fidelity to those that actively attempt to transform the appearance of the comic. In the latter category, numerous reprint projects have sought to wholly recolor reprints and, in effect, replace the contribution of the original colorist. It's this sort of case which will be our focus here, since these kinds of projects raise an obvious question: When should we recolor comics? And when should we strive for the best approximation of original comics? (In what follows, we'll take talk of "recoloring" to concern the sort of comprehensive recoloring just described.)

In posing these questions, we ought to distinguish—to whatever extent we can—between two kinds of considerations. The first sorts of considerations are aesthetic. A comic marred by dreary color design or limitations in its original printing could, at least in principle, admit of improvement with more lively or vibrant color design. That said, the use of digital coloring tools might sap the bold feel that comes through with original palettes and printing techniques. Quite obviously, disagreement is all but guaranteed when it comes to these aesthetic matters.[17] Most readers, we suspect, will likely find some recoloring projects aesthetically successful and other efforts to be aesthetically disastrous. Importantly, however, these kinds of considerations are concerned exclusively with the *aesthetic* features of comics.

A second species of consideration—ethical ones—are rarely brought to bear in the evaluation of recoloring comics. After all, how could *ethics* really impact the project of recoloring a reprinted comic? It's not hard, however, to see how ethics could, at least in principle, rule out certain kinds of recoloring. Suppose, for example, after the death of a cartoonist who colored their own autobiographical work, a callous publisher decided to produce a recolored reprint in which the skin tones of the main characters were radically altered in order to imply different racial identities. Recoloring a comic in this way surely raises ethical concerns, not only because of potential misrepresentation but also out of a duty to respect the deceased cartoonist's storytelling intentions. In at least some cases, there is therefore an obvious ethical dimension to the project of reprinting. Moreover, since colors rather than linework or dialogue are far more likely to be altered in reprints, color design is, by default, the facet of reprinting in which aesthetic or ethical considerations are most likely to arise.

While aesthetic and ethical considerations should, when possible, be distinguished, the actual relationship between aesthetic and moral value is famously contentious. Our ethical reservations about reprinting a comic that depicts a morally heinous act or horrific political sentiments might be amplified by the fact that the comic is engrossing and beautiful. Additionally, there can (or so it seems to many philosophers) be moral obligations regarding the production of aesthetic value, such as a duty not to glamorize despicable actions.[18] We won't try to catalogue the interplay between moral considerations and aesthetic properties here. Nor will we take up the broader menu of ethical questions that some like Pratt (2009b) and Robison (2016) have considered about the entire medium of comics. Instead, we're interested in what, if any, distinctively and separably ethical considerations might caution against recoloring.

A phenomenon that can shed some useful light on the recoloring of comics is the practice of colorizing originally black-and-white films that became increasingly common in the late twentieth century. Since film, like comics, is typically an encoded multiple medium, some of the arguments for the immorality of colorizing films can be extrapolated to the case of comics. For instance, a largely unconvincing argument for the immorality of colorizing films and, in turn, recoloring comics is that it violates a duty we have to preserve the works as best we can. Although we might have a duty to preserve some authentic instances of a comic in much the same way that we have a duty to preserve paintings or sculptures, comics is a multiple medium and reprints are not authentic instances of an original work. As James Young (1988) argues regarding film, provided that the creation of reprints does not require the destruction of, say, rare original comics, there is no clear sense in which producing reprints degrades the original artifacts that we might have a duty to preserve.[19]

A different line of argument contends that colorizing films is unethical insofar as it fails to adequately respect the creative intentions of the filmmakers who produced the film in the original black and white.[20] In response, some defenders of colorization hold that filmmakers might have been perfectly content or especially pleased for their work to have been in color, since technological or fiscal limitations were a familiar reason that some films originally appeared in black and white. In addition, defenders of colorization have noted that black-and-white versions are still available and that if provided with notice of the post hoc colorization of the film, there's a clear sense in which filmmakers' wishes are respected. After all, films are also regularly presented in many ways that run contrary to filmmakers' wishes— for example, with commercials inserted, on television sets, in varying aspect ratios, with subtitles, and so on.

In the case of comics, evaluating a parallel line of argument is no easy matter, given the complexity of comics production. Historically, it has been fairly common for writers and artists to have only limited contact with colorists responsible for their comics. It would also be exceptionally rare for them to interact with those directly responsible for the production of the color separations or printing plates used in the printing process.[21] Perhaps for this reason, a prevalent view—one that we don't find particularly plausible—is that the primary creative effort of a comic consists in its writing and drawing. The work of coloring a comic is therefore deemed a secondary element of production, so the artistic intentions of the writer and penciler (or inker) are the only ones that require upholding. And, since there are numerous ways that a comic might be colored that are consistent with these intentions (e.g., pencilers often do not produce color guides for printing), there is no important sense in which recolored reprints are likely to violate creative intentions worth preserving. So long as there are no radical changes—such as rendering Batman's cape in plaid—a significantly broad range of color designs will be acceptable.

As we'll suggest shortly, this defense of recoloring comics involves an implausible view of the role of colorists. But it's also important to note that black-and-white reprints of comics originally in color are commonplace and obviously fall short of what their original creators envisioned for the final product. Importantly, however, such reprints hardly seem to be unethical for failing to respect creative intentions. By way of analogy, they seem to be the comics equivalent of showing films on televisions with commercial interruptions. They are evidently inferior ways of accessing the original comics from which they are ultimately derived, but those who access the work in this way are standardly aware of this fact. Such reprints are, it seems, a kind of aesthetic compromise that all hands are willing to accept. Respect for intentions is therefore a shaky foundation on which to erect an argument against recoloring comics.

For those who would pursue this line of argument, some account of how to ascribe credit for the creation of comics is required. Philosophical efforts that seek to shed light on this issue have focused on the question of authorship, seeking to determine the structure and nature of comics authorship. Mag Uidhir (2012), for example, develops an account of authorship specifically with comics in mind. Mitchell (2016) explores a range of potential accounts of comics authorship. Gavaler and Goldberg (2019) take the variable and typically collaborative structure of comics production to warrant positing what they call a *pluralistic author*—namely, an irreducibly plural entity that has genuine intentional states of its own that are not analyzable in terms of the individual intentions of contributors. For those who aim to defend the view that comics have authors, there is a range of intriguing views on the table. As it turns out, we (namely, the authors of *this* book) are of two minds on the question. One of us would deny comics have authors at all and hold, instead, that there is no theory of authorship that we can or should impose on the comics medium beyond its own structures of creative contribution. And one of us finds elements of Mag Uidhir's and Gavaler and Goldberg's views tempting at least insofar as it might seem to run contrary to comics practice to deny that comics have authors. This issue will remain, however, one of the topics in the philosophy of comics we'll leave more or less unexplored.

A different argument against colorizing films and, by analogy, recoloring comics is that such efforts distort a historical record of the medium that we ought to preserve. As critics of this argument have noted, this kind of distortion seems to be of an exceptionally limited kind. Those watching a colorized version of *Gone with the Wind* (1939) may perhaps form the mistaken belief that color film technology was available when the film was created. But, again, this can easily be addressed by noting for audiences that the work has been colorized. (Against this assessment, see Levinson (1990).) Moreover, this potential historical distortion regarding film technology is an exceptionally narrow historical distortion in comparison to, say, the large-scale errors about history that might arise from viewing *Gone with the Wind* and many other colorized films. This argument against recoloring therefore threatens to commit us to a sweeping (and pretty implausible) case against the ethical permissibility of historical fiction.

When it comes to the parallel issue in comics, the historical distortions are even more limited in nature. While digital color manipulation is a relatively novel development, color printing has long been available. More generally, reprints typically differ from authentic instances in a host of different ways including size, layout, paper quality, and surrounding material. There's little reason to believe recoloring raises ethical issues that these other discrepancies do not. And, since these discrepancies give us no serious moral pause, this argument against recoloring also seems to fail.

There is, to our minds, no compelling and perfectly general ethical case against recoloring reprints. Instead, we take it that the most important ethical consideration in recoloring reprints is historical but highly specific in nature: it emerges only from careful consideration of equity and diversity within mainstream comic book production. To draw out what we take to be the main moral hazard in recoloring reprints, it will be useful to turn to a recent case study.

In 2020, DC Comics published *Absolute Swamp Thing* by Alan Moore, Vol. 1, which reprints a substantial portion of Moore's run on *The Saga of the Swamp Thing* (issues #20–34, plus an annual), with original pencils by Steve Bissette and inks by John Totleben. Few horror comics have enjoyed the critical esteem of Moore's run on *The Saga of the Swamp Thing*, which has been critically lauded as a watershed moment in contemporary horror comics. This reprint edition was billed on Amazon.com as debuting "completely new coloring for every page, crafted exclusively for this definitive collector's edition by legendary color artist Steve Oliff." On the basis of this sales pitch, one could justifiably be excused for not knowing that most of the original run was colored by Tatjana Wood, whose inventive and frequently psychedelic strategies for complementing the loamy greens of the titular character evoke an eerie, volatile atmosphere in the comic.

As we've argued, in keeping with the Strict View, *Absolute Swamp Thing* is not an authentic instance of the original comic (or, more accurately, does not contain instances of the original comics). It is, instead, a reprint that inherits many features of the original(s). It departs from other reprints of *The Saga of the Swamp Thing* insofar as the coloring, undertaken by Tatjana Wood using the pre-digital color printing methods of the 1980s, is replaced by Oliff's digitally produced and digitally printed work. What, you ask, could be morally concerning about that?

Taken in absolute isolation from sociological and historical facts regarding the comics industry: nothing. But the decision to solicit, print, and sell a reprint of *The Saga of the Swamp Thing* and present it as a "definitive collector's edition" happens against the backdrop of a comics industry in which women have been vastly underrepresented. (This is to say nothing of the underrepresentation of those with nonbinary gender identities.) At most, a handful of women were able to work as writers and pencilers or inkers in mainstream comics of the 1980s. A far more likely role in which to find women working in comics was as colorists or as letterers. Some leading women colorists of the 1980s include Glynis Wein, Adrienne Roy, Richmond Lewis, Lynn Varley, Elizabeth Berube, Christie Schiele, and Tatjana Wood. This range of women artists working as colorists—but who were afforded little or no opportunity to write, pencil, or ink comics at DC or Marvel— lends credence to the fact that systemic sexism was a factor within the industry. And, as noted previously, the work of colorists is too often treated as creatively secondary to the writing, penciling, and inking within comics and derogated to what would be deemed the "the production side" of comics publishing.

Again, while *Absolute Swamp Thing* is a reprint and therefore not an authentic instance of the comics it reprints, it is nevertheless a viable way to *read* those comics. And, as it's presented by DC, it's something close to *the best* way to read *The Saga of the Swamp Thing*. By recoloring a reprint and actively excising Wood's contribution, DC directly contributes to the pattern of not only marginalizing women's contributions to comics but effectively erasing Wood's contribution to and historical significance for a critically esteemed and massively successful comic. The ethical problem that arises is therefore a product of the wrongful marginalization of women creators in mainstream comics, which regularly limited their opportunities, confining their contributions to those aspects of comics which were errantly treated as inessential and replaceable.

Since readers who are unaware of Wood's original color work will, in keeping with readerly norms, take themselves to have read *The Saga of the Swamp Thing*, this recoloring not only subtracts Wood's contribution but renders the absence of her contribution exceptionally difficult for audiences to detect or appreciate. (Wood receives a small credit line with "Original Series Coloring by.") Not only is Wood's contribution erased from reader experiences, its absence, in virtue of the norms of readerly practice, ends up hidden from critical view. Interestingly, when it comes to black-and-white reprints, the moral hazard of erasing contributions seems significantly less serious. For, when comics like *Tales from the Crypt*, initially colored by Marie Severin, are reprinted in black and white, they are quite evidently lacking in original fidelity. And, unlike the case of *Absolute Swamp Thing*, even if Severin's contribution is not preserved, they're not being actively obscured by recoloring, either. Readers are, for instance, standardly aware that they're engaged with something deficient with respect to the original comics.

Our claim here isn't that recoloring is always morally wrong or even that it's typically morally wrong. Quite often, it seems perfectly unobjectionable. Our claim, instead, is that when the practice of recoloring obscures the historical contribution of individuals who belong to groups historically marginalized within comics production (or historically marginalized, full stop), recoloring is unethical absent substantial measures taken to clarify the contributions of the colorists involved. The best practices for recoloring reprints in a way that makes clear the historical creative contributions are, we take it, the kind used in collections like Greg Sadowski's *B. Krigstein Vol. 1, 1919-1955* (2002). That reprint project recolors Bernard Krigstein comics while including samples of the original color work of Marie Severin, comparisons of the recolored and original versions, and explicit credits and discussion of Severin and other colorists' contributions. As Sadowski's and other volumes show, it's entirely possible to actively honor and preserve the historical contributions to comics while attending to aesthetic virtues other than fidelity. And, especially when it comes to historically marginalized groups, this is precisely what the ethics of recoloring and reprinting requires.

6. Recommended Readings

As should be evident from this chapter, Meskin (2012) is a key contribution to this part of the philosophy of comics and Cook and Meskin (2015) carefully explore the relationship between the norms of printmaking and comics. With comics studies, discussion of the materiality and production of comics is wide-ranging. Brian Evenson's *Ed vs. Yummy Fur, or What Happens When a*

Serial Comic Becomes a Graphic Novel (2014) is a careful study of a reprinting and collecting project. The status of original art and its role in production features in Andrei Molotiu's (2020b). The status of comics as mass art and its critical and aesthetic implications are ready topics of discussion within comics studies. See, for example, Gardner (2012), which maps the trajectory of comics alongside other storytelling mediums. A recent examination of materiality in comics especially as it relates to webcomics is Kashtan (2018). See also Tinker (2007) on material form and alternative comics. Van Camp (1995) is an excellent overview of the trajectory of the colorization debate regarding films.

4

Does Superman Exist?

1. "The House Where Superman Was Born"

A silvery, triangular sign posted in front of 10622 Kimberely Avenue in Cleveland, Ohio, reads: "This is the house where Superman was born." The house is famous for being the childhood home of Superman cocreator Jerry Siegel and the frequent site of collaboration between Siegel and Joe Shuster, Superman's other cocreator. In fact, there's a fair chance that the first Superman comics were written and drawn in this house. But is it really the house where Superman was *born*?

If you ask most people where Superman was born, they'll almost certainly answer: "Krypton." But those same people—after a moment's reflection— will soon recall that Superman is a fictional character like Sherlock Holmes or Scooby Doo. Unlike flesh-and-blood creatures, fictional characters aren't the kind of thing that can be *born* in any literal sense. So, after some chin scratching, you'll likely receive a revised and very different answer: "actually, nowhere, I guess."

The fact that we can interpret this question in two very different ways and arrive at two very different answers is evidence of a crucial distinction in the thought and talk surrounding fictional entities like characters, stories, settings, and so on. (For short, we'll call this *fictional discourse*.) This distinction arises because there seem to be two importantly different ways of thinking or speaking about fiction. On the one hand, we often find ourselves concerned with "internal" claims, the truth or falsity of which depend upon what happens "within" a fiction. For example, when we note that Superman's home planet was destroyed or describe how he manifests superstrength, we're making internal claims. On the other hand, we also find ourselves thinking or uttering "external" claims" that are, in some sense, speaking "outside" the fiction in question. We're making external claims, when, for example, we report which character is more famous in popular culture or is owned by a particular company. When uttering external claims, our interest is typically in whether or not our claim is true *simpliciter*.[1] But, when we utter internal claims, we are typically interested only in whether our claims are true *according to the fiction*.

The Superman sign in Cleveland is a useful example of how this internal-external distinction helps us make sense of fictional discourse. There are, for instance, two natural interpretations of the claim that 10622 Kimberely Avenue is the house where Superman was born. The first interpretation is an external claim, made *outside* the Superman fiction, which conveys that the character was created in Cleveland. The second interpretation treats the sign as making an internal claim about the Superman fictions that appear in *Action Comics, Superman,* and other DC Comics. It entails that within these fictions, Superman was born in Cleveland. To make explicit that this claim is internal rather than external (and that it concerns the Superman fictions), we can append a prefatory clause like "According to the Superman fictions . . ." or "In the Superman fictions . . ." to generate the following:

(1) *According to the Superman fictions,* Superman was born in Cleveland, Ohio.

(1) is, of course, false. On the contrary, a different internal claim is true:

(2) *According to the Superman fictions,* Superman was born on Krypton.

Note, however, that the truth of (2) and the following *external* claim are logically independent of one another:

(3) Superman was born on Krypton.

And, while (3) is *actually* false, (2) is still true. Since there is no planet Krypton, nothing—not even Superman—was born there. Despite this, speakers will often utter claims like (3) and omit the preface "According to such-and-such fictions . . ." in their efforts to express claims like (2). (If you're curious why this happens, consider how tedious it would be to recap a comic to a friend while constantly including the preface "According to the *Whatever Happened to the Man of Tomorrow* fiction . . .".) This is one of many practical challenges that arise when it comes to interpreting fictional discourse, but throughout this chapter, we'll seek to be as clear as possible and therefore include the "according to" prefix whenever appropriate. Notice, however, that once we draw this distinction between internal and external claims, the peculiar response we received to our earlier question about Superman's birthplace makes perfect sense: there are two ways to take the question and, depending on how we interpret it, we arrive at two very different answers.

The internal-external distinction is the centerpiece of many philosophical attempts to make sense of fictional discourse. And, since discourse about comics is among the most complex species of fictional discourse, providing a philosophical account of it and its role in comics practice is an important part of any broader philosophy of comics. In this chapter and the next one, we'll examine issues that arise when we consider the claims that make up fictional discourse. For now, our focus will be on philosophical issues concerning fictional characters, which are, of course, exceptionally frequent subjects of these claims. In doing so, we'll examine several approaches to the ontology of fictional characters and explore how they connect up with the critical—and especially the *creative*—practices surrounding comics.

2. Why Believe in Superman?

No satisfactory philosophy of comics can deny the existence of comics. After all, if there's anything that deserves to be called a nonnegotiable commitment of the comics practice surrounding comics, it's that *there are comics*. But what about comics *characters* like Sluggo, Tintin, and Fin Fang Foom? Are we required to affirm their existence as well? And, if we do, does this deliver a philosophy of comics that's inconsistent with what we would otherwise believe about the world (e.g., that there aren't superheroes or giant flying dragons or talking cats and dogs)? We'll begin by arguing that comics practice strongly supports a view called *fictional realism*—roughly, the view that fictional characters do indeed exist.

Let's start by considering the following excerpt from *The Comics Journal, #95* (1984):

> The 30-year old British character, Marvelman, which is owned by London's Quality Communications, has become an object of contention. Marvel's British arm, Marvel Comics Limited, is asking Quality to cease publication of Marvelman on the grounds of copyright infringement. Ironically, the Marvelman character has been in existence longer than the United States' Marvel Comics Group, having been created and copyrighted in 1954.

This excerpt is typical of fictional discourse regarding comics characters, especially when issues about creator credits, creator rights, and copyright are involved. The author of this article, Tom Heintjes, indicates when Marvelman was created (as well as copyrighted), notes that Marvelman is owned by Quality Communications, and describes the character as British. These claims are external ones, largely unconcerned with what is true according to the Marvelman fictions. It is not, for example, true according to the Marvelman fictions that he was copyrighted in 1954. That said, some claims can be true both internally and externally—for example, Marvelman is British in the Marvelman fictions and British insofar as the character was created in Britain by British comics creators. (In 1985, Marvelman was rechristened as "Miracleman" to avoid legal complications with a noted comics publisher.)

The case for fictional realism flows from an effort to make sense of this discourse. If it is true that Marvelman is owned by Quality Communications, that Marvelman was created in 1954, and that Marvelman has existed longer than the Marvel Comics Group, then Marvelman must exist. For, if Marvelman didn't, none of these claims could be true. And, if we reject the truth of all external claims of this kind—namely, those that feature comic book characters—there is no way to make sense of the fictional discourse surrounding comics. We would, for instance, seem required to deny that Superman is an oft-imitated character, that Scrooge McDuck is more popular than Krazy Kat, and that Simple J. Malarkey—a character from *Pogo* (1948–75)—was one of several satirizations of Joseph McCarthy.

In another context, Maria Elisabeth Reicher (2016: 62) offers remarks which can be helpful in summarizing one plank of this general argument for fictional realism—especially as it concerns the legal practices that connect up with comics practices:

Copyright law and jurisdiction provide a considerable amount of data that should be taken into account by an ontology of works. If such an ontology were in conflict with relevant and widely accepted parts of copyright law and/or approved jurisdiction, this would be a prima facie reason against it.

The implication is that since we ought to account for the intelligibility of copyright law and other legal claims, we have reason to believe that characters do exist—or, as philosophers often put it, to accept characters into our ontology.

Admittedly, it might seem surprising to say that Superman exists. But it's important to show why fictional realism—the view that fictional characters exist—doesn't require us to believe anything *wildly* implausible. For instance, fictional realists hold that it is true, both inside and outside of Superman fictions, that Krypton exists. But they also hold that, external to the fictions, Krypton is a *fictional* planet. It is not *really* a planet any more than a rubber duck is a duck. In this regard, fictional realists rely upon a critical distinction between the properties that fictional entities *instantiate* and the properties that they are *ascribed*.[2] And, while Krypton is ascribed the property of *being a planet*, it does not instantiate this property or such properties as *having such-and-such mass* or *having been destroyed in a planetary apocalypse*. Instead, it instantiates properties like *appearing in Superman fictions* and *being copyrighted by DC Comics*.

To get a firmer grip on the fictional realist framework, let's return to the case we started with. According to the fictional realist, Superman *instantiates* properties such as *being created by Jerry Siegel and Joe Shuster, appearing in over a thousand DC Comics*, and *inspiring the creation of hundreds of derivative characters*. In contrast, Superman does not instantiate, and is merely *ascribed*, properties like *being from Krypton, having saved the world countless times*, and *having dark hair*. Generally speaking, the properties that a fictional character is ascribed are determined by what is true according to the fictions in which they appear. In contrast, the properties fictional characters instantiate depend upon how our—the actual, nonfictional world—*really* is—for example, Superman *really* is a fictional character, not a sentient Kryptonian, and Superman *really* was created by Siegel and Shuster, not by Jor-El and Lara. To see that these are two importantly different though independently coherent ways of thinking and speaking about characters, notice that Superman instantiates the property of *being over eighty years old in 2020*, even though he is not ascribed this property within the comics.[3] Since nothing can be eighty years old and, at the same time, not eighty years old, the fictional realist uses the distinction between instantiated and ascribed properties to make sense of what would otherwise be incoherent claims.

If you're still skeptical about admitting the existence of Superman, let's consider an analogy. Suppose that, after philosophical reflection upon the peculiar nature of mathematical entities like numbers (e.g., their imperceptibility and lack of spatial location), you were inclined to deny their existence. Having done so, you would have no straightforward way to make sense of mathematical practice, given that mathematicians debate, prove, and reject claims like "seven is a prime" and "there is no universal set." For just this reason, many philosophers of mathematics accept *mathematical realism*—roughly, the view that mathematical entities like numbers exist.

Now, you might be tempted to point out an important disanalogy between Superman and the number seven: fiction seems to be quite different from mathematics, since what distinguishes fiction from "reality" is that there are no fictional entities. They simply do not exist. This is a core commitment of *fictional anti-realists*: those who deny that there are any fictional entities. Importantly, fictional anti-realists seek to account for *some* of our fictional discourse by treating internal claims about fiction as akin to the (often false) testimony of individuals. So, for example,

(5) According to the Superman fictions, Superman has heat-vision.

is treated much like:

(6) According to Billy, Billy's dad has heat-vision.

While the embedded claims are true *according to* the relevant fictions, when they are unembedded, they are obviously false: Superman doesn't have heat-vision and neither does Billy's dad.

The problem for fictional anti-realism arises not when it comes to internal claims but when we try to make sense of external claims like the ones in the reportage about Marvelman. Such claims don't seem to be put forward as fiction or as idle storytelling but are instead reports of historical fact. And, since there is no Marvelman fiction according to which Marvelman was copyrighted in 1954, the fictional anti-realist has to deem the claims that make up the Marvelman report as a series of falsehoods (or, worse still, as claims that are so confused that they don't rise even to the level of being false). And, while there are sophisticated and powerful forms of fictional anti-realism available, none are motivated by considerations internal to comics practice and none seem to fare better than fictional realism in making sense of this practice. So, rather than diverting our attention to the broader metaphysical issues that *might* favor fictional anti-realism, we will, in what follows, proceed as fictional realists. Among other benefits, this permits a straightforward construal of the claims about characters that pervade comics practice: claims like "the Katzenjammer kids were heavily inspired by Max and Moritz," "no Marvel characters created after the sixties have matched Spider-Man in popularity," and "X-23 is a gender-swapped Wolverine."

Equipped with the framework of fictional realism, we might be able to explain away the intuition that motivates many fictional anti-realists— namely, that fictional characters aren't *real*. That's because we are often inattentive to whether or not we are speaking "within" a fiction. This leads us to sometimes conflate the external claim that Krypton exists, which affirms the existence of an abstract fictional character, with the claim that Krypton instantiates properties like *being a planet*. For, even if the former claim is true, the latter claim is obviously false. For the fictional realist, once we appreciate that fictional entities are radically different from ordinary entities like humans and tables—for example, the latter but not the former have masses and shapes—we can explain away the intuition that fictional characters do not exist as actually supporting a different judgment perfectly compatible with fictional realism: that fictional characters are not *really* planets, people, or in immediate peril. They're just fictional characters.

Now, if we grant that comic book characters really do exist, fictional realists are saddled with some increasingly difficult questions. Chief among them: What properties do comic book characters actually instantiate? Are they in our heads? Are they outside of space and time? With these questions in mind, we'll now explore a few leading views about the nature of characters.

3. What's Superman *Really* Like?

The history of superhero comics is marred, not only by disputes over the ownership of characters but also by disputes over credit regarding the creation of characters. In the middle of one such dispute, comics creator Neal Adams offers an explicit claim for legal purposes, saying, "I alone created the character of 'Ms. Mystic.' All of the artwork that I have published has been derivative of my own original 'Ms. Mystic' creation" (*The Comics Journal* #162 (1983)).

A somewhat notorious dispute—concerning the creation of Spider-Man—is instructively thorny in its complexity. While different histories have been offered, Steve Ditko—vexed by public discussion of his contribution and those of Stan Lee and Jack Kirby—poses a question in his essay, "An Insider's Part of Comics History: Jack Kirby's Spider-Man":

> That which is relevant can be seen by examining the first Spider-man story and comparing it with what is known of Jack's Spider-man. Surely they are not identical "creations." Are there no important differences? Only minor, unimportant ones? Are the similarities major or minor? Which essential elements, in both, would make them belong to one "idea," one "creator"? (2002: 59)

Our interest here isn't in adjudicating the historical details of Spider-Man's creation but in considering more carefully the view about characters implied in Ditko's discussion: that fictional characters are ideas. Is this a plausible view of what characters *really* are?

There is a wealth of historically influential but importantly different senses of "idea." On a particularly prominent and intuitive one, ideas are *mental particulars*. The "mental" part is evident enough, but the "particular" part requires a bit of explaining. Rather than taking ideas to be shareable or "universal" entities such that you and I share *the very same idea* of Spider-Man, the view that ideas are *particulars* (in this sense) entails that you have an idea of Spider-Man and I have a distinct idea. Similarly, Siegel and Shuster each possess different ideas of Superman. Of course, their respective ideas are likely quite similar (though they could be markedly different), but, in general, this view takes ideas to be something like individuals' unique mental representations of things like Spider-Man or the Eiffel Tower.

Is it plausible that characters like Spider-Man or our flagship example of Superman are ideas in the sense of being this kind of mental particular? Not really. Superman cannot be numerically identical to *all of our ideas* of Superman. After all, there are individuals out there with mistaken beliefs about Superman—for example, that his real name is Steve Rogers or that he's from the planet Thanagar. Faced with these inconsistencies, we might be tempted to say that Superman is identical with all the "correct" Superman ideas, but this raises the question of what the "correct" ideas could be checked against given that Superman would just *be* those ideas. Notice, also, that Superman could exist even if most of these ideas didn't. For instance, you might never have encountered Superman and so *your* Superman idea might not exist. But if Superman just is *your* idea (or someone else's), we would be unable to make sense of the obvious fact that Superman could have existed even if you had never acquired a Superman idea.

Ditko's remarks make clear that he thinks creators' initial possession of an idea is especially important. Perhaps, then, we could identify a character with the specific mental representations possessed by their creator. Such a view would entail that Superman is identical to the Superman ideas possessed by cocreators Siegel and Shuster. But, while Siegel and Shuster's ideas of Superman were surely very similar, there is no guarantee that they were exactly the same in what they took to be true of Superman. Is Superman therefore Siegel's idea? Or Shuster's? Neither answer seems plausible, and picking one over the other seems arbitrary. Moreover, Superman cannot be identical to the sum or collection of each of their Superman ideas. Since Siegel and Shuster are now deceased, there are, quite sadly, no Superman ideas lingering in their minds. And, since Superman still exists, this is yet another reason to believe that Superman cannot be a specific mental particular of this sort. We'll return to another, more sophisticated account of ideas and the roles they might play when we discuss stories and adaptation in Chapter 10, but for now, it's best to put the view that characters are ideas aside.

Moving on: similar lines of argument caution against views that would identify fictional characters like Superman with certain material objects rather than mental particulars. While preliminary sketches and the original art of *Action Comics* #1 (1938), not to mention the comic itself, are intimately connected with Superman's creation (as are some earlier, unpublished works), Superman is not identical with any one of those sketches, original artworks, or even the totality of *Action Comics* #1. Each of these material artifacts could be destroyed and, despite this loss, their destruction wouldn't ensure the destruction of Superman. Even in the tragic event that all the material traces of Superman comics up to this very day were destroyed, it seems possible that, tomorrow, DC Comics might set out to produce a new Superman comic to replace all the old ones. There is, it seems, no material artifact with which we can identify Superman.

For most fictional realists, the implausibility of identifying characters with mental particulars or material artifacts motivates a *platonist view* of fictional characters, which entails that Superman has more in common with mathematical entities like numbers than with drawings or ideas. According to platonism about fictional characters, Superman and Krypton are *abstract entities*. Importantly, this sense of "abstract" is orthogonal to the sense of "abstract" in talk of non-representational "abstract" art or comics like the kind discussed in Chapter 2. Instead, it is a term drawn from a family of philosophical theories that descend from Plato's metaphysical views and which hold that reality divides into two categories of entities: *concrete* entities like electrons, hacksaws, and planets and *abstract* entities like mathematical entities, universals, and meanings. Debate abounds about where to draw the line between the abstract and the concrete and how to properly characterize each side of the divide. Roughly speaking, concrete entities are the kinds of things that one could, in principle, bump into, destroy, or investigate empirically. In contrast, abstract entities seem to lack spatial locations and have no ordinary physical properties. For instance, according to platonists about numbers, the number seven exists, but it would be a category mistake to say that it exists anywhere in particular (a bunker in Omaha?), that it could be destroyed (via a surface-to-number missile?), or that we can directly perceive it. (Platonists are careful to distinguish between a written numeral like "7" and the thing that numeral refers to.) And, while platonism is a common view in the philosophy of mathematics, philosophers have also argued that a broad range of entities like meanings, universals, and possibilities are abstract rather than concrete.

The platonist view of fictional characters can be defended in a few different ways. First, if platonists are correct that reality divides into the abstract and the concrete, and there are no concrete things like mental particulars or material artifacts with which Superman can be identified, then, by process of elimination, Superman must be an abstract entity. This is, however, far from a conclusive argument, given that some philosophers deny that reality perfectly divides into abstract or concrete entities as platonists often claim. Second, platonists can point to the analogies between Superman and the number seven and, in doing so, provide positive evidence that fictional characters like Superman can't be concrete entities. This strategy is more promising. After all, much like the number seven, there seems to be no particular place in which Superman is located. And, just as it sounds bizarre to insist that the number seven is on Earth, it sounds similarly bizarre to insist that Superman is in New York. Additionally, while we are able to see groups of seven things or to reason using numerals that refer to the number seven, platonists deny that we can ever see the number seven itself. One might similarly claim that while we can see drawings of Superman or read stories that name him or describe the circumstances of his creation, there is no clear way to make sense of someone's desire to see the "real" Superman. According to the platonist about fictional characters, this is because like the number seven, Superman is an abstract entity: it has no shape, color, or mass despite the fact that according to Superman fictions, Superman has a shape, color, and mass.

Platonists about fictional characters can exploit similarities between Superman and the number seven to motivate their view. But what about dissimilarities between fictional characters and numbers? Two are of particular importance. First, it seems quite plausible that Superman came into existence in the 1930s, so he did not exist before that time but has existed ever since. In contrast, the number seven bears no similar relation to specific times, since most platonists hold that mathematical truths are necessary and eternal. (Words like "seven" or "sept" did come into use at specific times, but, again, we ought not confuse things with their names.) So, although Superman and the number seven are without spatial location, it does seem that fictional characters like Superman have locations in time.

Second, abstract entities are often characterized as causally inert entities that exist outside of the "causal order" of the concrete world. The number seven was not created with the Big Bang. Nor could be it destroyed through any physical process. It simply isn't *that* kind of thing. But, as we noted at the outset of this chapter, Siegel and Shuster created Superman. Moreover, comics practice regularly involves claims about creation, influence, and inspiration that concern fictional characters, which seems to entail that characters do stand in some kinds of causal and temporal relationships.[4]

In the face of these disanalogies, platonists typically pursue one of two options and as a result, two kinds of theories about fictional characters emerge. According to the *plenitudinist platonist* about fictional characters, our talk about the creation of Superman and other characters should not be taken at face value. Such entities are *not* created and do not, in fact, come into existence at specific times. The plenitudinist rejects the alleged disanalogies between Superman and the number seven and holds, instead, that they are alike with regard to causation and creation because neither kind of abstract entity is created or able to enter into causal relations. So, while the plenitudinist offers a unified view of abstract entities, this is a philosophical virtue gained only at the expense of doing violence to comics practice—for example, by denying claims like "Superman was created before Wolverine." Additionally, the plenitudinist also owes us an explanation of why it *seems* like Siegel and Shuster created Superman. To this end, plenitudinists posit a limitless *plenitude* (hence the name) of fictional characters, all of which populate a vast abstract realm. These characters are not created through human activities but during what we would ordinarily describe as "creation," they are instead "picked out" by our fictional practices and ascribed properties by the authors of fictions. For plenitudinists, the activity we usually call "creating characters" therefore involves somehow *singling out* abstract entities and producing fictions according to which those abstract entities have certain properties.

Unfortunately, the plenitudinist view faces significant problems in making sense of how to distinguish among the vast plurality of potential characters. There are, for example, infinitely many candidate entities that Siegel and Shuster could have indicated rather than the one we now refer to with the name "Superman." Recall that since fictional characters do not instantiate properties like *being a planet* but are only ascribed such properties, it is unclear how any properties they instantiate could distinguish them from one another prior to being picked out by an author. What, if anything, explains how or why they indicated the exact one they did? As Amie Thomasson puts this point in her case against plenitudinism regarding literary characters:

> For the descriptions provided in literary works fail to completely specify what the characters described in them are like, leaving indeterminate a wide range of properties such as, typically, a character's blood-type, weight, diet, and mundane daily activities. Thus we run into trouble immediately. . . . Selecting any one as identical with a particular character seems hopelessly arbitrary. (1999: 17–18)[5]

Plenitudinism scratches a metaphysical itch: the desire to sustain the analogy between fictional characters and numbers. But it generates philosophical complexity in ways that offer us no help in understanding comics practice.

In contrast, plenitudinism's primary platonist competitor, *artifactualist platonism*, takes critical practice largely at face value. To get a sense of the artifactualist view, consider a brief summary by one of its defenders, Saul Kripke:

> It is important to see that fictional characters so called are not shadowy possible people. The question of their existence is a question about the actual world. It depends on whether certain works have actually been written, certain stories in fiction have actually been told. The fictional character can be regarded as an abstract entity which exists in virtue of the activities of human beings, in the same way that nations are abstract entities which exist in virtue of the activities of human beings and their interrelations. . . . [A] fictional character exists if human beings have done certain things, namely, created certain works of fictions and the characters in them. (2011: 63)

According to artifactualism, fictional characters are abstract entities. But, unlike plenitudinism, artifactualism holds that fictional characters are *artifacts*. In this respect, they are akin to more familiar artifacts like sundials, arrowheads, and armchairs, insofar as they were brought into existence by intentional processes. Of course, *unlike* those things, fictional characters are *abstract* artifacts: they lack locations in space and are without shapes, masses, or colors. Importantly, not every human creation is an artifact. Some human creations like traffic jams or footprints are brought into existence (typically) without any intentions for use or creation. Fictional characters are, in contrast, entities intended for use in the generation of fictions or as targets for depiction in drawings. In the case of comics, they serve as subjects of stories aptly intended to be picture-read.

According to artifactualism, fictional characters are analogues of other abstract artifacts like stories, jokes, and recipes. They typically, though perhaps not invariably, have creators. Their creation usually presupposes a complex array of norms, practices, and behaviors that serve as the backdrop against which human intentions are sufficient for creating something. In turn, these practices allow these creations to be used in various ways. Just as nothing would be an ashtray if no one had ever smoked and nothing would be an armchair if no one ever had arms, nothing would be a fictional character if there were no norms of fiction and storytelling. But, since there are such practices, individuals are, under the right conditions, able to create these artifacts.

To return to our example from the start of this chapter, individuals like Siegel and Shuster can set out and succeed in creating an abstract artifact like Superman, which instantiates properties like *being abstract* and *being created in the 1930s* as well as being ascribed properties like *being from Krypton*. So, if artifactualism is true, it might well be true that Superman was created at 10622 Kimberely Avenue in Cleveland, Ohio. ("Born" is, however, a bit of stretch and, at best, a metaphor for Superman's creation.) In this way, artifactualism proves to be a useful tool for making sense of comics practice. And while difficulties and objections inevitably arise, the view is meritorious enough to remain within our focus for now. With this artifactualist theory in hand, then, we are in a position to take up the question that troubles Ditko in his discussion about Spider-Man's origin: What's involved in the *creation* of a character?

4. Collaboration and Creation

The artifactualist view of fictional characters did not initially emerge from reflection on comics and comics characters. Instead, its proponents developed and defended artifactualism largely with a focus on novels, plays, and short stories. We've argued that such a view ought to be extended to the case of comics, but, if we're going to be artifactualists about comics characters, some work is required to reconcile artifactualism with common features of comics that distinguish them from what we'll call *the standard case*—that is, single-authored, non-serialized, unillustrated text-based stories. As we'll see, extending the artifactualist framework beyond the standard case raises a variety of distinctive challenges. At the same time, it also provides a chance to shed light on philosophical puzzles regarding how characters are created and deployed within comics. Let's start, then, by considering how comics might differ from the standard case with regard to their actual production.

As noted in the previous chapter, there is enormous diversity in the ways in which comics are made. Partly for that reason, cataloguing the tools, techniques, and methods that comics creators deploy is a substantial aspect of comics practice. Given both the diversity of comics-making and the complexity which creative processes can involve, we'll make no attempt to answer the question "how are comics made?" Instead, we'll settle for describing a fairly typical model of collaboration within comics production and explore how it bears upon the creation of fictional comics characters. To that end, we'll start, first, by describing what comics production *sometimes* looks like in the case of what we might call *auteur comics*—that is, comics produced entirely by one person—though, again, we're mindful that this represents just one among countless ways to produce a comic.

Let's suppose that the production of our hypothetical auteur comic begins with a purely text-based script that describes the intended content of the comic's pages. Next, our auteur creator produces some "thumbnail" layouts of pages as well as rough sketches. Relying upon these, they produce some pages drawn in pencil. These pages are then inked with an eye toward contrast and clarity or perhaps simply to facilitate the printing process. Later, they're lettered and subsequently undergo one of many potential coloring processes. Importantly, our auteur creator might swap the order of these tasks on an individual page or even within a single panel. Other additional tasks might also be incorporated into the production—such as including paste-ups of preexisting lettering, using photo collage or screentone, or applying solution to craft-tint boards, ad infinitum. Finally, toward the end of the production process, our auteur undertakes some revisions and after printing some initial proofs, they elect to tinker with various features of the comic before undertaking a final print run.

Outside of auteur comics, however, this process can look much different and typically involves the work of multiple contributors. Historically, the prevailing division of comics labor in North American comics was largely prompted by economic considerations—specialized focus on domain-specific tasks like penciling, inking, and lettering increased the speed with which comics outfits like the Iger and Eisner studio or Chesler shop were able to produce comics.[6] There are, of course, numerous other ways to structure collaborative comics production. It is, for instance, common practice for manga artists to have assistants who aid them with drawing backgrounds. (That's not to say assistance in drawing backgrounds or finishing figures isn't part of North American or European comics practice; it's just that this aspect of North American comics practice receives little attention.)

The institutionalized collaboration common in mainstream American comics typically divides the work of writing from the work of penciling and in turn inking, lettering, and coloring. As it turns out, the following example proves to be a fairly typical one. In the first issue of the 1986 series *Power Pack*, Louise Simonson and June Brigman are credited as creators, with Simonson credited with the script and Brigman as penciler. Bob Wiacek is credited as inker, Joe Rosen as letterer, and Glynis Wein as the colorist. Two editors are mentioned: Carl Potts, who edited the series (which typically involves managing the creative team and providing critical feedback), and an "editor-in-chief"—in this case, Jim Shooter, who oversaw Marvel's various comics lines. In addition to those listed, individuals responsible for any other production are uncredited—for example, those involved in the color production and printing process. (As one moves backwards through comics history, credits or even "signed" work grow increasingly rare.)

By attending to these features of comics production, we can gain some insight into the creation of comics characters, since a cluster of new ones appeared in *Power Pack* #1, including the titular "pack" of Power children. In an interview thirty-five years after the series first appeared, Simonson and Brigman describe their collaboration, which gave rise to the creation of the *Power Pack* characters:

Who contributed what as far as the original concept for Power Pack?

Simonson: I wrote. June designed the look of the book—including the costumes—and drew the story beautifully. Together we told the story. June's work was so reality based; the kids' expressions, gestures and interactions felt so right; scripting was easy. Our editor, Carl Potts, was great. He helped with important things like thinking [of] a proper title for *Power Pack* and in helping June design [the team's spaceship] Friday.

How did Power Pack change as it went from planning stage to reality?

Simonson: It didn't, really, at least from the writer's perspective. The first plot I showed Shooter was the story you see as the first issue. Of course, I then had to flesh out the next three issues. June, of course, had to design everything and everyone. Aside from the Pack and their parents, she had to design two races of aliens: Kymellians and Snarks. And Friday. And the dad's invention. And the villainous Carmody.[7]

In cases like this one, where key features of characters are determined by a plot written in advance and other key features of characters are determined by drawn designs, we have what might seem like a tolerably clear model for the creation of comics characters. The creators are just whomever produces the script that introduces the character as well as whomever draws the character in their first appearance. (In those cases where someone is both writer and penciler, there is a unique creator.) In the case of *Power Pack*, this seems to be precisely why Simonson and Brigman are explicitly credited as "creators" of the Power Pack. This also seems to be the model of collaboration within which Siegel and Shuster created Superman. But, given the massive variation in approaches to comics production, this is just one of a multitude of ways in which comic book characters are created.

How, for instance, should we assign creator credits when a writer generates lavish, massively detailed scripts accompanied with fully developed character sketches but doesn't actually pencil the issue in which a character first appears?[8] And what about cases like Spider-Man, in which a highly schematic story is provided for a cartoonist who generates the visual design for a character and also crafts the majority of the initial story in which the character first appears? Deviations on these cases abound and once we factor in revisions to pencils and story, the creation of characters often proves to be an exceptionally convoluted process.

In stark contrast to the standard cases like stand-alone novels that artifactualists focus on, the remarkably collaborative nature of comics production brings a thorny question in the philosophy of fiction to the forefront. This question concerns not *what* was created but *who* is correctly described as a creator of comic book characters. Let's call this the Creator Question:

Creator Question: Under what conditions is an individual the creator of a comic book character?

The murkiness and controversy surrounding creator credit are all too evident in comics practice—in part, of course, because of the fiscal stakes that come with ownership and copyright. Among other disputes, we regularly find disagreements over who was the sole creator of a character, who should be counted as a cocreator, and, in perhaps the most intractable debates, disagreement about whether a character was "cocreated" or merely "created with," as in the case of Bob Kane and Bill Finger's Batman. Can philosophy intervene with a conclusive answer that settles these debates and correctly specify how to apportion responsibility for a character's creation?

Probably not. Recall that—according to the view currently on the table— fictional characters are not just abstract entities but also artifacts. Like other artifacts, their creation is embedded in a (typically) preexisting range of practices, attitudes, and norms. Consider the case of another collaboratively produced artifact: houses. We could engage in an intensive effort to develop a philosophy of houses in hopes of answering the question: Who *really* created the house? But, in doing so, we suspect that this would not uncover any implicit albeit conclusive principles which settle, once and for all, who gets the credit. More likely, we would subtly mischaracterize the norms, attitudes, or practices surrounding the creation of houses and, in turn, impose some verdict about house creators that isn't a genuine consequence of the norms, attitudes, or practices surrounding houses. That's because these norms, attitudes, and practices are simply indeterminate in key respects.

Much as vagueness occurs in natural languages because maximum clarity and absolute determinacy are rarely an aim of communication, it isn't an aim of comics creative practices to yield fully determinate rules about how to settle, with absolute precision, standards for deciding who created a character. Instead, these creative practices aim primarily at things like creating *good* characters, ensuring that comics are created in a timely fashion, and making comics accessible to certain kinds of readers. Any robust agreement about how to answer the Creator Question is, for this reason, a kind of by-product of the aims of creators, like receiving critical praise and financial compensation for their work. It's no mystery, then, why there's widespread controversy about who created which characters: there is, at present, no correct way to fully answer the Creator Question.

Now, while there's *presently* no correct answer to the Creator Question, it doesn't mean that there's no room for philosophical inquiry here. There is, for example, ample disagreement about certain potential necessary conditions for being the creator of a character—for example, whether character creation must be accompanied by the explicit intention to create a character rather than, say, merely engaging in idle doodling. But, at best, these potential necessary conditions would place constraints on possible answers to the Creator Question. The more interesting prospect comes when we note that creative practices change, deepen, and evolve, and, in this regard, it's clear that the comics practices surrounding character creation reflect an increasing sensitivity and search for specificity. This, in turn, shapes the relevant practices to the point where we now regularly find creators explicitly discussing and deciding upon how to assign creative credit and, in some cases, opting for distinctive ways to do so (e.g., the language of being a "creator with" rather than a "cocreator"). Could these practices change in such a way that we might someday arrive at sufficient clarity to generate an answer to the Creator Question? Put differently: if it became an aim of comics creative practices to get absolutely clear about who does and doesn't count as a creator of a given character, would we therefore have an answer to the Creator Question?

Sociologically, this seems exceptionally unlikely, but philosophically, it raises a different worry. Wouldn't this mean that by changing comics practices, we change the "metaphysical ground rules" that govern abstract entities and their creation? Not really. We shouldn't think that as comics practice changes, reality itself is transformed in some mysterious way. The natural model here is that expressions like "created" are exceptionally vague and admit of a wide range of potential sharpenings or disambiguations. Comics practice leaves matters highly unsettled about what we mean when we call someone "the creator" of a character, but, if greater determinacy were sought out, all we'd be doing is getting clearer about what we mean. Put differently, we'd simply be narrowing the range of candidate meanings for a claim like "Simonson and Brigman created Power Pack." It's worth noting, however, that this potential indeterminacy in meaning is one reason why proper attribution of credit is so crucially important to the preservation of comics history. If we allow larger and more powerful figures in comics history—like specific companies—to determine what and who counts as a creator, it's less and less likely that the contributions of individual writers, artists, editors, and others will be rightly acknowledged as creators. Instead, we're likely to see companies rather than individuals more commonly claimed to be the *real* creators of characters.

Given the indeterminacy of the norms of comics practice, determinately answering the Creator Question isn't in the cards. Perhaps, then, we can make headway in understanding another, different aspect of character creation and answer a different question: What does it take for comics characters to be created? What, for instance, was needed to bring Spider-Man into existence? Was it the first printing of *Amazing Fantasy* #15 or was it the act of Ditko delivering his finished pencils to Flo Steinberg at the Marvel office? Perhaps (though less plausibly), it was the moment Stan Lee decided that since "Hawkman" was taken, Marvel needed a character called "Spider-Man"? Suitably generalized, these would all deliver potential answers to what we'll call the Creation Question:

Creation Question: Under what conditions is a comics character created?

It might be natural, at least initially, to think that when characters are created, there must be a unique "magic moment" at which they "pop" into existence. But this would make them quite unlike most other artifacts, which are typically fashioned gradually, in stages, and come into existence over extended periods of time. And, if the creation of characters happens through thinking, writing, and drawing, it would be puzzling for the creation of characters to be instantaneous when these human activities are temporally extended. It's also tempting to think that a character would need to be somehow "finished" before they might be said to exist, but, as we'll note in a moment, the serial nature of many comics suggests that in a bulk of cases, there's no clear sense in which it's apt to describe a character as "finished." And, given that characters' names, costumes, and appearances can and often do change even after their first appearance, it would be strange to think that any distinctive aspect of a character would, on its own, suffice for a character's creation.

Perhaps we could claim that a character is created once there's a visual design *and* some measure of narrative detail. Notice, however, that some comics characters might not be depicted (or might not even be *depictable*) but nevertheless be created via text. In *Green Lantern* Vol. 2, #188 (1985), through a throwaway remark from a preexisting character, Alan Moore seems to have created a member of the Green Lantern Corps, Drktzy RRR, who is an "abstract mathematical progression." Similarly, in Moore's *1963* (1993), a Galactus-spoof named "Cosmax" features in a metafictional letters page where his exploits in a fictional prior issue are discussed. Pictures play no role in the specific creation of Drktzy RRR or Cosmax, so building a visual design requirement into any potential answer to the Creation Question seems to implausibly limit which characters can be created.

One way to make progress in answering the Creation Question is to provide plausible necessary conditions for the creation of comics characters. And, on that front, it is tempting to insist that a comics character is created only with the actual production of a comic featuring that character. And, while that might be a plausible view about what makes a character a *comics* character, it is, perhaps surprisingly, contrary to the creative practices surrounding comics. This is because upon closer inspection, comics practice suggests that characters can exist prior to the production, much less the printing of certain comics. For example, Dave Cockrum recounts the history of Nightcrawler—a character that appeared in *Giant Size X-Men #1* (1975)— as extending back to his time working on *Superboy and Legion of Super-Heroes* (1973–4): "When I became a pro and I was doing *Legion of Super-Heroes*, I proposed four new Legionnaires and Nightcrawler was one of them. But Murray Boltinoff's response was that he was too weird looking."[9] Cockrum similarly recounts creating other characters—for example, a monstrous character called Vampyre—that never even appeared in *X-Men* due to editorial concerns.

In a similar vein, throughout the 1990s characters frequently appeared in trade magazines, like *Wizard*, prior to their "first appearances" in comics. And, rather memorably, Joe Simon (1990: 184) recounts a hunt for comics characters not yet in print: "[Martin] Goodman could see that the monster fad was fast fading. He instructed Lee to start putting superheroes into his old monster titles. One title on the soon-to-be canceled list was *Amazing Fantasy*. Lee called Kirby in and asked him if he had any comic characters lying around that hadn't been used."

Respecting the critical practice of creators requires permitting that in some cases, characters are created prior to the production of the comics in which they appear (or, like Vampyre, even in the absence of any appearance). In this way, characters are essentially tied not to the material activity of producing comics but to the cognitive activities of the writers and artists who produce them. While we don't think that characters are ideas—at least not in the sense of being mental particulars of the sort discussed earlier—we take it that ideas do figure into the conditions necessary for character creation.[10] As best we can tell, the question of whether a comic character exists isn't a matter of whether or not that character appears in a comic but whether there is a representation of the character—linguistic or pictorial, in the form of a document or an idea—that is aptly intended for use in comics storytelling. So understood, characters are akin to tools for storytelling and their creation is bound up with irreducibly normative matters—namely, whether they might be aptly used. Mere names aren't aptly intended for use; mere drawings—in the total absence of narrative background—aren't aptly intended for use either.[11]

Our best bet, then, is that the right answer to the Creation Question is that a comics character x is created just in case there is a representation of x that is aptly intended for comics storytelling. This delivers the following view:

> **(Comics) Apt Representation Answer**: A comics character x is created if and only if someone creates a representation of x that is aptly intended for comics storytelling.

This can, we think, be generalized and therefore provides a plausible way of thinking about the creation of not just comics characters but characters in general:

> **Apt Representation Answer**: A character x is created if and only if someone creates a representation of x that is aptly intended for some variety of storytelling.

This is especially important for those who think that comics characters are not so much a *kind* of character as they are characters that happen to be most typically associated with the comics medium. Batman, for example, is a "comics" character insofar as he originated in the comics medium, but he is also a prominent character in mediums like film, television, and videogames. He is, it seems, not *just* a comics character but a character, full stop. The Apt Representation Answer helps us make sense of this, along with both characters seemingly more constrained to comics and characters typically associated with other mediums.

Admittedly, such a view makes it remarkably easy to generate characters. But that's a result that squares with how we typically think and talk about character creation. When in the 1960s, *Dial H for Hero* implored readers to send in their characters—many of which would appear in the comic—it was clear enough that comics characters are a dime a dozen.

Here's a diagnostic for applying the Apt Representation View and, in turn, determining whether a character has been created. Suppose that we have on hand a highly competent comics creator. If a representation of a character is aptly intended for some variety of storytelling—in this case, comics storytelling—then, were that creator supplied with the information encoded in that representation—whether pictorial, narrative, or idea-based—and be able to generate a more or less unexceptional comic strip or comic book, then it's likely that a character has been created. After all, this would be good evidence that the representation is aptly intended for comics storytelling.

The Apt Representation View deems that doodles on napkins, when paired with sufficient detail and an intention to be usable for some variety of storytelling, do suffice to create characters. (Not necessarily good ones, mind you.) We suspect that some competing views, which impose more stringent requirements on the creation of characters, are unable to make sense of much of the talk surrounding the creation of characters and will, for instance, be forced to deny that Cockrum created Nightcrawler prior to his appearance in *Giant Size X-Men* #1. Admittedly, such views enjoy a certain intuitive appeal, since the Apt Representation View does posit a vast multitude of comics characters that are wholly forgotten or have remained entirely unknown except to their creator. For our part, the right way to contextualize this verdict is by analogy with the historical sciences: Spider-Man and Superman are like *Tyrannosaurus Rex* or the wooly mammoth, but the history of comics characters is not made up solely of famous and successful characters any more than the history of life is made up solely of species that have been preserved in the fossil record. There are vast swathes of characters of which little or even no trace remains, but they are (forgotten) parts of comics history even so.

A final alternative to the Apt Representation View is to simply insist that no satisfactory answer can be given to the Creation Question, partly because of the complexity of comics-making and partly because of the inherent vagaries of human activity. According to what some philosophers have labeled "the brutal view," there are no necessary and sufficient conditions for the creation of characters.[12] Unfortunately, such a view comes with an obvious downside. If true, we seem to be without any way of understanding difficult cases for which we might hope such an account would provide guidance—for example, we cannot use the brutal view to help us understand the creation of Spider-Man. In fact, even if we had complete historical knowledge of Spider-Man's creation—including telepathic access to the inner mental lives of Ditko, Lee, and Kirby—the brutal view threatens to leave us without any means for adjudicating matters of character creation. Better, we think, to be proven wrong about how to answer the Creation Question than to prematurely abandon hope of answering the question of when characters like Spider-Man or Superman came into being.

5. Getting Serious about Seriality

There's a puzzle about the creation of comic book characters that marks a serious threat to the plausibility of artifactualism. This puzzle stems, in large part, from another feature of comics that differs from the artifactualist's standard case like the stand-alone novel: comics are regularly *serial* in nature. At first glance, non-serial fictions are written and published in a single installment, while serial fictions are published in a series of installments. Matters are further complicated, however, once we note that there are serial *publications* that are not themselves serial fictions—for example, comics anthologies like *Tales from the Crypt*, which consist of self-contained stories. Additionally, certain fictions might end up serialized in their publication, but, if they were produced with an eye toward being published in a single installment, they seem to be serial in a somewhat secondary or accidental sense. Now, while seriality is common across mediums—the Sherlock Holmes stories and Charles Dickens's works were frequently serialized—it seems that seriality is the norm in comics. Mainstream superhero comics are typically serial works that run for years upon years (provided they avoid cancellation) and some comics that are often treated as stand-alone, non-serialized comics, like Art Spiegelman's *Maus* or Chris Ware's *Jimmy Corrigan*, were first produced and published in serial form.

Efforts to make sense of the difference between serial and non-serial fictions are only recently underway in the philosophy of fiction in works like Caplan (2014) and Tillman (2016). (Within the philosophy of comics, the leading contributions are Cook (2013), Pratt (2013), and Mag Uidhir (2016).) It's worth noting, however, that as a reader, we shouldn't assume our engagement with non-serial fiction differs from serial fiction by being essentially uninterrupted. Practical facts about how we read (e.g., simple facts about human endurance) guarantee that novels are only rarely read in a single uninterrupted sitting. (Hence the importance of dividing novels into chapters!) And, while seriality requires that *some* readers' engagement with serial works will be interrupted, this isn't necessarily the case. For example, if you're reading an originally serialized work like *Maus* many years after its serial publication was completed, you can avoid the lengthy breaks in reading that were foisted upon those who read it as it was initially published. For these reasons, care needs to be taken in describing what, if anything, necessarily distinguishes our engagement with serial as opposed to non-serial works. For our purposes, however, the central point of interest—and the source of our puzzle for artifactualism—stems from what happens when we create characters in serial fictions.

As Roy Cook (2013: 272) notes, many superhero comics constitute "massive serialized collaborative fictions" (MSCFs), which he describes as follows:

> [M]assive serialized collaborative fictions are fictions that (i) have proper parts that are ordered by nonarbitrary sequences, both in terms of production and reception, and in terms of the diegetic ordering of the events portrayed within these fictions; (ii) are too large to be "absorbed" as a unified whole; and (iii) are authored by more than one individual.

As we'll discuss in the next chapter, the nature of *canoncity*—in effect, what "really happened" according to MSCFs—is a central concern for thinking through these sorts of fictions. But there's another concern regarding the cross-time collaboration that's involved in MSCFs, which stems from different creators being authorized to produce stories about characters that were initially created by different creative teams. (For this reason, it's common to talk about different creative teams' or creators' "runs" on a serial comic book—for example, Lee and Kirby's on *Fantastic Four* (1961–70) or Chris Claremont's lengthy run on *Uncanny X-Men* (1975–91).) As it turns out, this feature of seriality in MSCFs leads to a puzzle for artifactualism: it seems to entail the paradoxical verdict that the very same character can be created more than once.

Let's work through an example to see how this puzzle arises. Inspired by the vast success of *Crisis on Infinite Earths* in 1985, DC Comics subsequently pursued a series of company-wide crossovers in the 1990s including *Armageddon 2001* (1991) and *Zero Hour: Crisis in Time* (1994). A central figure in these stories is the villain, Monarch. Created by writers Archie Goodwin and Denny O'Neil and artist Dan Jurgens, Monarch's storyline involves a considerable degree of mystery about his real identity. (In fact, it was leaked prematurely to the comics trade magazines that he was Captain Atom, which led to a last-minute revision in the story.) This storyline culminates in the revelation that Monarch is Hank Hall, more widely known as Hawk from the late 1960s series, *The Hawk and the Dove*. That series and the characters in it were created by Steve Ditko and Steve Skeates, neither of whom were involved in the Monarch stories.

Even so, the serialized and collaborative nature of superhero comics, when understood in artifactualist terms, saddles us with a puzzle that stems from the following series of claims:

    i. Monarch is Hawk.

   ii. Ditko and Skeates created Hawk but not Monarch.

  iii. Goodwin, O'Neil, and Jurgens created Monarch but not Hawk.

Taken together, artifactualism's commitment to (i)–(iii) seems to entail a contradiction: it's both true and false that Ditko and Skeates created Monarch. Opponents of artifactualism therefore conclude that artifactualism yields incoherent results when we deal with MSCFs. And, since comics are often MSCFs, it looks like artifactualism can't help us make sense of comics characters.

As it turns out, this is an overly hasty conclusion. While the Hawk-Monarch case is a genuine puzzle, artifactualism is a rich theory, and it's able make sense of these claims so long as we carefully distinguish between the internal and external ones. In particular, when it comes to characters, it's especially crucial to distinguish between the properties they instantiate and those they are merely ascribed. While Hawk instantiates the property *being created by Skeates and Ditko* and Monarch does not instantiate this property, the character is merely ascribed the property *being identical to Monarch* just as Monarch is merely ascribed the property *being identical to Hawk*. Naturally, this wasn't true in the original *The Hawk & The Dove* series, but, as a serialized story, what is true according to the central continuity of DC Comics has changed over time. So, while the internal claim "According to the DC Comics fiction, Hawk is Monarch" is true, the external claim "Hawk is Monarch" is nevertheless false.

There are, in the present case, two distinct characters that, according to DC Comics continuity, are one and the same. This means that for artifactualists, facts about how many characters there are *according to the fiction* need not settle how many characters exist as abstract artifacts. There might, for example, be a single character that is, according to a fiction, multiple characters—as in those cases in which they're "duplicated" by some fantastic scientific device. The moral for artifactualists is that we need to be careful to distinguish what internal claims and external claims require. This means, of course, that we require a theory of what makes internal claims true or false in comics. This project, which is closely tied to the question of truth in fiction, will be our focus in the next chapter.

6. Recommended Readings

Philosophical literature on "creatures of fiction" like fictional characters is substantial, but some watershed contributions include van Inwagen (1977), Thomasson (1999), and Kripke (2011). Discussion of the internal-external distinction occurs across the literature, but see von Solodkoff and

Woodward (2017) and Friend (2007) for recent, accessible overviews. On the creatability of fictional characters, see Everett (2005), Friedell (2016), and Cray (2017), as well as Yagisawa (2001). On fictional objects in general, see Stuart Brock and Anthony Everett's collection, *Fictional Objects* (2015). For a nuanced discussion of characters and intellectual property laws, see James O. Young's *Radically Rethinking Copyright in the Arts* (2020). On abstract entities in general, see Cowling's *Abstract Entities* (2017).

Book-length comics studies engagement with specific characters—apart from Batman and Superman, of course—is quite limited when compared with research on creators, series, and genres. That said, recent character-focused anthologies include Peaslee and Weiner's *The Joker: A Serious Study of the Clown Prince of Crime* (2015) and Baldanzi and Rashid's *Ms. Marvel's America: No Normal* (2020).

Philosophy of comics focused on serial works is tackled directly in Cook (2013), Pratt (2013), and Mag Uidhir (2016). Broader philosophical work on serial fiction includes McGonigal (2013), Caplan (2014), Tillman (2016), and Kivy (2011: 76–97). A source of growing philosophical interest and productive comics-related attention is the status of reboots and retcons, which, as we note in the next chapter, is tackled in Gavaler and Goldberg (2019) and at length in Goldberg and Gavaler (2021).

5

Truth in Comics

1. Truth in Fiction

Grant Morrison and Richard Case's run on *Doom Patrol* (Vol. 2, 1987–93) is a mind-bending and genre-bending stretch of superhero comics. And, in *Doom Patrol* #22, Morrison places a logic puzzle at the center of its metafictional narrative.[1] After a group of philosophers write a fictional encyclopedia, the imaginary world it describes—Orqwith—begins to wreak havoc, destroying and reconstituting various chunks of reality. The baffling threat of a fiction that might gobble up the world spurs the Doom Patrol into action and when they storm into the center of Orqwith, they find two mysterious beings at its heart: a liar who speaks only falsehoods and a truth-teller who speaks only truths. The liar begins: "I am a liar and I do not know why there is something instead of nothing." The truth-teller follows: "I am an honest man and I do not know why there is something instead of nothing." Rebis—a member of the Doom Patrol—thinks hard and then asks the liar "Why is there something instead of nothing?" The liar responds: "There is something instead of nothing." And the fictional world of Orqwith promptly implodes. Later, another member of the Doom Patrol tries her best to summarize the puzzling events: "He said 'There is something instead of nothing.' Since that was a lie, then what he was really saying is that there wasn't something instead of nothing. That's when Orqwith collapsed." She hastens to add: "I think that's how it happened, anyway."

Even in an exceptionally weird comic like *Doom Patrol*, this plot point stands out for exploiting the most general structure of reality—logical structure—as a tool for combatting evil. It also makes evident something quite familiar about fiction: that unlike the real world, paradox and contradiction can roam free in fictional worlds where things can be, at the same time, true *and* false. Indeed, Morrison's implication seems to be that in acknowledging its own logical inconsistency, Orqwith—a fictional world aspiring to be part of the real one—confronts the fact that it simply can't be real, given the logical principles that govern truth and falsity. (Though, in this case, the fictional world happens to be nested within another fictional world rather than the real world.) Before turning to the question of truth in comics, it will be useful to consider these principles and their relation to fiction a bit more closely.

For our purposes, *truth* and *falsity* are properties of declarative sentences. Such sentences have these properties when they either succeed or fail, respectively, in accurately representing the world. *This* world—the very one we all live in—is a nonfictional place. It is also, according to many philosophers, a *complete* and *consistent* place: any apparent gaps in our knowledge or contradictions in our conceptions are really just that—gaps in *our* knowledge or contradictions in *our* conceptions—rather than anything like gaps or contradictions in the world itself.

On this sort of view, truth and falsity follow certain rules. Here's one: for any claim, either that claim or its negation (expressed using the symbol "~") is true. Or, more formally:

Law of Excluded Middle: For all p, either p or $\sim p$.

Either seven is a prime number or it is not the case that seven is a prime number. Either all humans are mortal or not all humans are mortal. Feel free to generate your own further examples, since this principle is supposed to apply to literally any declarative sentence. The Law of Excluded Middle requires that, logically speaking, the world is *complete*: it doesn't have *truth-value gaps*. So, for any claim we make about the world, either that claim is true or that claim is false. If it seems to be neither, that's good reason to think either that we've misunderstood or that our "claim" was really something else in disguise.

Here's another rule: it is never the case that for any claim, both that claim and its negation are true. Or, again, more formally:

Law of Non-Contradiction: For all p, $\sim(p\ \&\ \sim p)$.

It's false that all humans are mortal *and* that not all humans are mortal. And it's false that seven is prime *and* that seven is not prime. The same goes for any declarative sentence. The Law of Non-Contradiction entails that, logically speaking, the world is *consistent*: it doesn't have any *truth-value gluts*. That is, for any truth we can ascertain about the world, we can be sure that the negation of that truth is false. If it seems to be both, that's again good reason to think that we were confused about the claim we were starting with.

These two principles aren't merely constraints on the structure of reality itself. They're tools that we constantly put to use in our reasoning about the world. Given the Law of Excluded Middle, if we can show that p is false, then we can validly infer that $\sim p$ is true. And if we can establish that some p lands us in a contradiction, we know that $\sim p$ is true, since by the Law of Non-Contradiction, there are no contradictions. Appeal to these patterns of reasoning is at the core of all kinds of inquiry, philosophy especially.

Unlike the nonfictional world that we all live in, fictional worlds like the DC Universe need not be complete or consistent. In fact, they are rarely complete, if ever, and they are quite often inconsistent. But this should be no surprise: the conviction that the world is complete and consistent is rooted in the idea that our world is a thing to be discovered. Fictional worlds, on the other hand, are things that we create, and it would be a true labor of love and care to create a fictional world that is both complete *and* consistent. The norm, however, is that fictional worlds only collide with inconsistency either for storytelling purposes as in metafictional works like *Doom Patrol* #22 or as the result of inattention or other error. In a somewhat infamous example, Gwen Stacy meets her end in *Amazing Spider-Man* #121 (1973) at what is clearly depicted as the Brooklyn Bridge but which Spider-Man identifies as the George Washington Bridge. And, while we might contort our interpretation into holding Spider-Man to have simply misspoke, Stan Lee's subsequent remarks suggest that this inconsistency was, indeed, on account of error.

While inconsistent fictions raise fascinating problems, let's focus, for the moment, on gappy ones, which are incomplete with respect to the truth or falsity of certain claims. Take the familiar case of the Sherlock Holmes stories by Arthur Conan Doyle. How many hairs does Sherlock Holmes have according to these stories? Notice that it does not seem to be true according to the relevant fictions that he has exactly 50,000 hairs. At the same time, it would also be a mistake to hold that it's false that he has exactly 50,000 hairs. The fiction is simply silent on that matter. That's because the Holmes story and the characters in it are not a portion of a world that hasn't yet been discovered. They are instead a portion of an artificial world that hasn't been made and might never be. This isn't a problem unique to Sherlock Holmes's hair but a pervasive feature of fiction: fictions are *indeterminate* in all sorts of respects. In trying to understand how truth works in fiction, this feature of fictions needs to be accommodated.

The fact that the Sherlock Holmes fictions are indeterminate with respect to the number of hairs on Holmes's head isn't because Doyle never made that number explicit, even though doing so would perhaps have been the easiest way to settle the matter. There are many, many things that are true according to the Holmes stories but that remain implicit and go entirely unmentioned. Here are a few examples:

Sherlock Holmes has two nostrils.
Sherlock Holmes is smaller than Buckingham Palace.
Sherlock Holmes can't turn invisible at will.
Sherlock Holmes drank liquids when he was four years old.

Even though none of these claims are made explicit in the Holmes fiction (to our knowledge, at least), they are nevertheless true according to those stories. To be sure, they are of either limited or peculiar relevance to the stories, but, unlike the number of hairs on Holmes's head, viewing them as indeterminate—as neither true nor false—according to the stories would be exceptionally puzzling. Given what we know about the world of the Holmes fictions, the truth of these claims is required to make sense of what's going on. For instance, Holmes is taken to be more or less "normal" looking, so given that it's true that humans (typically) have two nostrils, it is an implicit truth that Holmes has two nostrils. England is also taken to be more or less as it was in the late nineteenth century, and since Holmes isn't a giant, it would be similarly baffling if Holmes weren't smaller than Buckingham Palace. Additionally, the laws of physics and biology are, according to the Holmes stories, just as they are in our actual world. So, since no humans can turn invisible at will, neither can Holmes. And, since humans cannot live without drinking liquids for a year, it is a dreary and not especially interesting truth that he must have drank liquids at some point when he was four. Cases like these make clear that truths in fiction far outnumber those truths made explicit.

In the last chapter, we sought to make sense of the external claims found in fictional discourse surrounding comics, like "Superman was created by Siegel and Shuster." As should be clear, however, we face an equally important task in understanding internal claims like "Superman was born on Krypton," which concern what is true according to Superman fictions. For philosophers, this project has typically focused on how to determine which claims are true in fiction and, more generally, what it means to say that a claim is true "according to such-and-such a fiction." In that spirit, our central question will be the following:

> **Truth-in-Fiction Question**: Under what conditions is a claim true according to a fiction?

Viewed one way, theories about truth in fiction aim to explain why readers arrive at often strikingly uniform verdicts about what does and does not happen within stories told to them. This is part of the reason why disagreements over interpretation often prove so hotly contested: because we find ourselves agreeing over so much when we engage with fictions, when our judgments do diverge, it becomes fascinating and controversial why this is so. This project of understanding truth in fiction has obvious implications for the philosophy of comics, since any adequate account ought to extend to the case of comics, which are a familiar medium for conveying fictions.

In this chapter, we'll start by focusing on what philosophers have said about truth in fiction in general and then narrow our focus to see what can be said about truth in comics in particular. Importantly, our discussion will be limited to the case of comics that tell fictions and will more or less set aside nonfiction comics. As we'll see, though, certain insights extend to both categories.

Before surveying some theories of truth in fiction, it's crucial to get clear about what these *aren't* theories of. Theories about truth in fiction are not general theories of literary interpretation. They are silent on how to discern the deeper meaning, significance, or aesthetic merits of fictions. They have nothing to say about the implicit messages of fictions, satirical or critical functions, or the values and knowledge they represent or impart to readers. Perhaps it is true that Holmes is a metaphor for human intellectual ambition, but, since it is not true *according to the Holmes stories* that Holmes is a metaphor, that claim and others like it aren't within the purview of theories of truth in fiction. Similarly, although Jonathan Swift's *Gulliver's Travels*

(1726) satirizes English high society, it isn't true according to *Gulliver's Travels* that the Lilliputians satirize English high society. Theories of truth in fiction therefore leave many, many questions about the interpretation of fictions in the hands of literary theorists.

Some literary theorists might object, however, that there's no difference between the tasks we've described, holding that it's as much a matter of interpretation whether Batman's cape is blue as it is whether Batman is a metaphor for neoliberal class politics. Notice, however, that if absolutely everything about a text is a contested matter of interpretation, we seem without any explanation of the remarkable unanimity regarding what's true according to certain fictions. And failing to account for this phenomenon is an easy way to render fiction wholly mysterious. For philosophers, then, the challenge that underlies the issue of truth in fiction is how to best explain this common uniformity in ordinary audiences' judgments about what is true, false, or indeterminate in the fictions they encounter. An account of truth in fiction aims to uncover the convention or principle that drives these judgments.

In trying to develop such an account, we might initially be tempted to claim that what's true according to a fiction is just what an author intended in producing that fiction. But, quite clearly, authors have intentions that outstrip what is true in their fictions—for example, their satirical or literary aims—and, in some cases, there is no reason to think that authorial intention is sufficient to fix what is true according to a fiction. Even if Doyle always intended for Holmes to have a mole under his left eye, if that sort of claim was never made explicit, then there seems to be no sense in which it is true according to the fiction itself. Suppose, for example, that Doyle had planned to mention it but forgot to do so. Upon having this pointed out to him, there are several interesting things he could say. He could note that he always imagined Holmes as having the mole or that he intended to make it true according to the fiction that had the mole. But, despite this, the fiction as he actually told it is not one according to which he has a mole under his left eye.

What do theories about truth in fiction look like? The locus of recent philosophical work on the topic is David Lewis's 1978 paper, "Truth in Fiction." There, Lewis endorses a general account of storytelling as a practice grounded in make-believe or pretense. Roughly put, make-believe or pretense involves a certain kind of imaginative activity akin to when we imagine how the day would have gone had we stayed in bed or what it would be like if we lived on Mars.[2] Lewis (1978: 40) sketches his view of the nature of fiction as follows:

Storytelling is pretence. The storyteller purports to be telling the truth about matters whereof he has knowledge. He purports to be talking about characters who are known to him, and whom he refers to, typically, by means of their ordinary proper names. But if his story is fiction, he is not really doing these things. Usually his pretence has not the slightest tendency to deceive anyone, nor has he the slightest intent to deceive. Nevertheless he plays a false part, goes through a form of telling known fact when he is not doing so.

With this view of fiction in hand, Lewis proposes his answer to the Truth-in-Fiction Question as a way of analyzing or understanding the prefix "According to fiction f . . ." which we deploy when making internal claims. And, while Lewis actually proposes two different analyses, we'll focus on just one of them here:

> **Known Fact View**: p is true according to a fiction f if and only if p would have been true had f been told as known fact.

Let's see what happens as we apply this. Suppose we're interested in figuring out what's true according to Doyle's Holmes stories. We start by entertaining a situation in which these stories are being told to us, not as fiction but as an accurate report of what has happened. This, of course, requires that we think about what things are like, not at our *actual* world but at possible worlds where the stories are accurate reports of what happened. There are, however, infinitely many such worlds. There is, for example, a world where someone accurately tells the Holmes stories but there are all manner of unmentioned, remarkable divergences from the actual world—for instance, everyone in Canada is a werewolf, grass is red in Uganda, and people usually have twelve toes. On the Known Fact View, we ought to disregard all the radically divergent worlds and focus solely on those worlds that are, on balance, most similar to the actual world in relevant respects. Something is true according to a fiction just in case it is true at *all of those* worlds.

   In all of the worlds that are on balance most similar to the actual world but where the Holmes fictions are told as known fact, Holmes has two nostrils, is smaller than Buckingham Palace, can't turn invisible at will, and drank water when he was four. Therefore, the Known Fact View delivers the verdict that all of these claims are true according to the Holmes fictions. And, since there will be some worlds where Holmes has exactly 50,000 hairs and other worlds where he instead has 40,000 or 60,000, it isn't true that he has 50,000 hairs. Nor is it false. The Known Fact View thereby entails that it is indeterminate and—given our previous discussion—this seems to be the correct verdict.

There's a problem with the Known Fact View, however. As we noted earlier, truth in fiction doesn't behave like truth in reality. It is common to find inconsistency and contradiction in fiction whether by accident (e.g., in the case of sloppy storytelling) or by design (e.g., in the case of fantastic and outlandish stories). So, while the view does well in capturing incomplete fictions, it is unable to accommodate inconsistent or contradictory ones. That's because there is no way to tell stories as known fact if they include contradictions, explicit or otherwise: if they're contradictions, they can't be known and they can't be facts.

The inability of the Known Fact View to address inconsistent fictions has prompted a number of alternatives which seek to remedy this problem. Gregory Currie, in his book *The Nature of Fiction* (1990), offers the following account:

> **Fictional Belief View**: p is true according to a fiction f if and only if it is reasonable for the informed reader to infer the fictional author of f believes that p.

Central to the Fictional Belief View is the notion of a *fictional author*—distinct from the actual author of the story. Currie describes the fictional author as "a fictional construction" who "speaks to an audience of his own time and, most likely, of his own culture" with "no private beliefs, no beliefs that could not reasonably be inferred from the text plus background"(1990: 79).

To make sense of impossible fictions, the Fictional Belief View requires that we look to the inferred beliefs of a fictional author. Since we can infer that individuals believe contradictions without thereby requiring that the contradictions obtain, we can accommodate the fact that according to certain fictions, some claims are both true and false. Neither case is a problem, though, since belief—unlike knowledge—doesn't require truth and it is the beliefs of the fictional author that settle what is true according to the fiction. And it's all too easy to image people believing contradictions. Think, for example, about someone offering mixed up directions across town who, upon reflection, realizes that they believe a street is somehow west of itself; or of the resolute mystic who thinks that their preferred deity is in some (unbeknownst to them) impossible and inconsistent condition.

The upside of the Fictional Belief View is that it seems to accommodate the possibility of incomplete as well as inconsistent fictions. The downside is that, in doing so, it ties our account of truth in fiction to this notion of a *fictional author*—distinct from the actual author. As Alex Byrne (1993) argues, if this view is correct, whenever we encounter a fiction, we are obliged to pretend (a) that there is an individual who believes the claims that make up a given fiction, (b) that this character is distinct from the actual author, (c) that they somehow inhabit the world of the story, and (d) that they believe all the things true according to it. This commitment comes with peculiar and unpalatable consequences. How, for example, can we make sense of fictions according to which, say, there is no intelligent life or there are no agents capable of forming the beliefs attributed to the fictional author? As Byrne suggests, if such a view is correct, then when presented with fictions describing characters' inner mental lives,

> either someone would have had supernatural epistemological powers, or else an incredibly detailed investigation would have taken place. And Currie's fictional author would presumably believe this. But, in the fiction, there was plainly no investigation, and no one in the fiction has supernatural epistemological powers, or at any rate not the kind of supernatural powers needed to tell the story. (1993: 29)

The gist of Byrne's complaint is that in making sense of truth in fiction, we must avoid accidentally requiring that all fictional worlds include an omniscient (or nearly omniscient) fictional author who believes all that's true according to the fiction. But that's just what the Fictional Belief View seems to require.

This prompts Byrne to argue that the claims true in a fiction are just those claims that the author of the fiction "invites the reader to make-believe" (32). Or, more precisely:

> **Authorial Invitation View**: *p* is true according to fiction *f* if and only if the Reader could infer that the Author of *f* is inviting the Reader to make-believe that *p*.

While there is no invitation to make-believe that Holmes has exactly five moles on his arm, we have every invitation to make-believe that Holmes has two nostrils. This is because of the explicit claims about his appearance and the clear invitation to believe that in the world portrayed in the Holmes stories, humans are much as they were in the England of our world in the late nineteenth century. We seem similarly invited to make-believe that Holmes has all manner of properties typical of humans, like being smaller than Buckingham Palace, being incapable of turning invisible, and drinking liquids as a child. Additionally, there's a fairly straightforward way in which the Authorial Invitation View addresses the case of unreliable narrators, since textual hints and storytelling techniques are often used to signal unreliability and, in turn, consequences for what we ought to make-believe about what's true in the story. Put roughly, certain features of the story are invitations to make-believe that what we're "being told" by the narrator isn't how things *really* are according to the fiction.

Despite these desirable features—for example, the ability to address both incomplete and inconsistent fictions and to avoid positing Currie's fictional author—is the Authorial Invitation View without problems? We don't think so, but, before assessing its ultimate merits, it'll be useful to turn our attention from fiction in general to fiction in comics. In the next section we consider how, if at all, we can answer the following question about comics:

> **The Truth-in-Comics Question**: Under what conditions is a claim true according to a fiction told through comics?

2. Truth in Comics

Much like the philosophical work on fictional characters, discussions of truth in fiction have overwhelmingly focused on a certain kind of "standard case"—namely, stand-alone, single-authored, non-serial, text-based works. As far as we know, no one has attempted to explicitly pose, much less answer, the Truth-in-Comics Question. And in considering our prospects for answering this question, it's important to see why a certain general approach won't work. According to the "divide and conquer" strategy, we should focus our efforts on developing a theory of truth in fiction suitable for the "standard case" of text-based fictional storytelling like a novel and also work to develop a parallel theory of accurate depiction—roughly, what it means for a picture to accurately represent its subject matter. Since comics are typically complexes of text and image, this "divide and conquer" strategy assumes that we can simply conjoin the two accounts and end up with a theory of truth in comics that cleanly divides into a theory of truth according to text-based fictions and a theory of accurate depiction.

No view of truth in comics that compartmentalizes text and image in this way can enjoy any serious plausibility. We cannot treat the text in comics like an independent fiction and the pictures as similarly independent depictions. This is because apart from being enormously complicated, the interaction of text and image in comics is itself an apparatus for conveying truths in the fiction—for example, when a character comically understates the seriousness of a depicted situation, we move between text and imagine to extract truths about them. Nor can we compartmentalize the distinctive visual technology of comics as merely textual or pictorial. In a world of comics, characters don't have floating speech balloons above their head when they speak nor do black curly lines actually float upward from freshly baked pies.[3] For these reasons, a theory of depictive accuracy will not provide us with the means for understanding *emanata* like motion lines and other conventions like speech balloons that are often distinctive to comics storytelling.

A more promising approach seeks to adapt the Known Fact View to the comics medium. Recall that this view takes truth in fiction to be settled by what would be true in worlds where fictions are told as known fact. Lewis's term "told" is, however, ambiguous. If pictures and complexes of text and image "tell," then it's already intended as a theory of truth in fiction that encompasses comics. But, if his sense of "tell" is limited to textual or verbal reports, we need to explicitly extend the account to fictions conveyed through image and complexes of text and image. Rather than engage in Lewis interpretation, we'll assume Lewis intends "tell" in the narrow sense. So understood, we can still adapt his account to the medium of comics as follows:

> **Accurate Representation View**: *p* is true according to a fiction *f* told through comics if and only if *p* would have been true had *f* been an accurate comics-based representation of known fact.

Intuitively, this view takes truth in fiction to be settled by what's true in those worlds where a comic is presented as a nonfictional report like, say, a work of comics journalism. In the relevant possible worlds, the narrative text of such comics would be a factual description, the pictures in the comic would be accurate depictions, and the comics-specific conventions regarding the interaction of text and image would also truly and accurately represent matters.

As it turns out, there are certain comics according to which comics creators really are journalists reporting upon the amazing deeds of fictional characters. In John Byrne's *Fantastic Four* comics (most notably, *Fantastic Four* #262 (1984)), he inserts a fictional analogue of himself who follows the exploits of the Fantastic Four and communicates them to readers as nonfiction in comic book form. But, even if this metafictional treatment of superhero comics is coherent, it doesn't mean the Accurate Representation View is a plausible theory of truth in comics. Indeed, it faces a problem that should now be familiar: comics fictions frequently involve impossibilities and contradictions. Just as we saw with the Known Fact View, there is no *possible* world in which anyone can accurately represent what happens in such fictions, since any world where contradictions obtain is, by its very nature, an *impossible* world.

There's a second worry that arises if we try to make sense of truth in comics by invoking the notion of accurate representation. In many depictions of the Joker, perhaps most notably in Jeph Loeb and Tim Sale's *The Long Halloween* (1997), the iconic villain possesses incredibly long teeth. As Cook (2015a) suggests, this is most likely not to be taken literally, in the sense that we should infer from this that in the Batman fiction, Joker has six-inch-long teeth. Instead, it's a visual metaphor, a stylistic representation (or mis-representation) that sacrifices realism for the purposes of giving us more information about the character. The same might be said about the consistent visual metaphor in Art Spiegelman's *Maus* in which the characters are represented as various animals or the way in which the characters are represented as various monsters throughout Emil Ferris's *My Favorite Thing Is Monsters* (2017). This ubiquitous feature of comics—the deployment of style and cartooning techniques like exaggeration, abstraction, and caricature—poses a direct challenge for the Accurate Representation View. After all, if it *were* true, someone in the story would most likely comment on it, given that humans—especially non-superpowered humans like the Joker—don't typically have six-inch-long teeth. But, given the Accurate Representation View, it's not clear how we could deny—much less question—the verdict that according to *The Long Halloween*, the Joker has teeth massively larger than other humans.[4]

The failures of the Accurate Representation View are instructive: they show that accounts of truth in fiction that rely upon accuracy won't help us make sense of inconsistent or contradictory fictions, and they are also poorly positioned to accommodate the complexities of style, cartooning, and visual metaphor within the comics medium. A more promising approach is suggested by the Authorial Invitation View. That said, this view relies upon a notion that fits oddly with the comics medium: authorship. If we tie our theory of truth in comics to the concept of an author, it better be the case that comics have them. But, as we noted back in Chapter 3, this is a matter of no small controversy.[5] While some philosophers have argued that the notion of authorship is a general one that applies to comics just as it does to novels, others (one of us, in fact) hold that comics practice has no plausible place for the notion of an author (though, of course, ample room for writers, artists, etc.), and we are best served to avoid deploying that notion in key ways when it comes to the philosophy of comics.

Rather than try to settle this issue about authorship in comics, we can settle for a plausible compromise: in adapting the Authorial Invitation View to the case of comics, we can appeal to the notion of a *creative team* rather than author.[6] Once we do so, we end up with the following answer to the Truth in Comics Question:

> **Invitation View***: p* is true according to a fiction *f* told through comics if and only if the reader could reasonably infer that the creative team of *c* are inviting the reader to make-believe that *p*.

Here's a pressing question for the Invitation View: What does it mean to be *invited* to make-believe something? As Stacie Friend (2017) argues, when we engage with a fiction, we need not make-believe everything that is true according to it. For example, if you read the Holmes stories, you likely never explicitly engaged in the make-believe that Holmes is smaller than Buckingham Palace. Perhaps because when reading the story, your make-believe never involved Buckingham Palace. But that's no barrier to holding it to be true according to the Holmes stories that Holmes is smaller than Buckingham Palace: no one ever promised that we explicitly make-believe each and every truth in the fictions we engage with. All that matters for the Invitation View is that one could (reasonably) infer that the creative invited them to engage in such make-believe.

Even so, the complexity of our imaginative engagement with fictions told through comics leaves us with other difficult questions that the Invitation View needs to answer. Consider the following page from Sloane Leong's *A Map to the Sun* (2020), which captures a moment in a game of pick-basketball (Figure 5.1).

Like many other moments in the comic, Leong subtly captures the feel and intuitive rhythm of a basketball game. But notice that you can successfully read this comic without at any point engaging in make-believe that Ren's shot was, say, from the free-throw line rather than the corner. At the same time, that *could* be something that you imagine while you read the strip. It is, in some intuitive sense, up to you. In contrast, you will—if you've read the strip properly—imagine that Luna is wearing sandals and palm trees sway in the distance. So, while some imaginative activities seem optional, others do not. What does the Invitation View have to say about the different kinds of "invitations" for make-believe we find in comics and other fictions?

Figure 5.1 *A Map to the Sun* (2020), Sloane Leong. Ren makes a bucket in a pick-up game of basketball with Luna.

The lurking problem here is that the Invitation View implies a homogenous relation between the creative team and the imaginative activities of the reader—namely, that for any given claim, readers of a comic are either invited to believe or they are not invited. But, as Friend (2017: 30) notes, the practice of fiction requires us to distinguish three importantly different relations that the creator of a fiction and, by extension, the fictional work might bear to the imaginative activity of the reader:

(i)   "a work *mandates* imagining that *p* if failure to imagine *p* would mean falling below a minimum threshold for comprehension";

(ii) "a work *prescribes* imagining *that p* if we should imagine that *p* to have a full appreciation of the story";

(iii) "a work *invites* imagining that *p* on the following condition: if the question arises and we must choose between imagining that *p* and imagining that not-*p*, we are required to imagine the former."

The worry for the Invitation View is that there is no way to specify what a reader is invited to make-believe without relying upon the distinction between what's imaginatively required for "a minimum threshold of comprehension" (in Friend's terminology, *mandated*) and what's needed for "a full appreciation of the story" (again, in Friend's terminology, *prescribed*). Moreover, we are regularly invited to make-believe things that are evidently not true according to the fiction, for, as Friend points out,

> [W]e may, compatibly with the content of a story, imagine a great deal that [is not true according to the fiction]. I might imagine Gulliver with brown eyes and you might imagine him with blue, and someone else might not imagine his eye colour at all. That Gulliver's eyes are blue is not [true according to the fiction], because, if the question arose, we would be obliged to imagine neither that his eyes are blue nor that they are not. Given that (as far as I know) Swift leaves Gulliver's eye colour indeterminate, we are *authorized* or *permitted* to fill in this aspect of the fictional world as we desire. (2017: 30)

Friend's remarks suggest that the Invitation View (and, by extension, the Authorial Invitation View) either over-generates truths in fiction (e.g., it forces us into accepting determinate truths about Gulliver's eye color) or it requires a novel and likely peculiar notion of invitation. Neither option leaves us with much hope for the Invitation View.

Despite the failure of the Invitation View, we think that Friend's observations about the difference between mandated and prescribed make-believe make a crucial point—one that suggests a more promising direction. Notice that the difference between minimum comprehension and full appreciation is a fundamentally normative one. The latter is richer and standardly better. That's because engaging with fiction in general and comics reading in particular is a normative practice. Like any skill, the picture-reading distinctive to comics is a thing that can be done better or worse, and how well it goes involves being sensitive to the imaginative requirements, invitations, and opportunities afforded by the creators.

As Hick (2016) shows, this point marks a divide in two different conceptions of picture-reading. Those like David Carrier (2000: 85) take it to be a kind of unreflective disposition of humans, claiming that "You don't need to know anything, apart from that shared knowledge we all possess about contemporary life, to interpret comics." In contrast, Roger Sabin (1993: 6) argues that "Like anything else, reading a comic is an acquired skill. It takes an amazing number of eye-movements to understand a panel." On this conception, picture-reading is more craft than innate competency and viewed in this light, it becomes clear it can be done better or worse. For instance, as David Elkins remarks in his introduction to *How to Read Nancy* (2017: 12): "when I do read comics, I am an awful, irresponsible reader." Here, we side squarely with Sabin, Elkins, and Hick: picture-reading is an acquired and sometimes delicately practiced skill.

As we noted in Chapter 3, there are ways of looking at comics that fall short of picture-reading them. Suppose, for example, that someone scans through a comic to see if it contains product placements or studies it solely to see if it includes any profanity. Consider, for example, Clifford McBride's

Figure 5.2 *Napoleon* from *Famous Funnies* #36 (1937), Clifford McBride. A dog, Napoleon, accidentally causes a house fire.

Napoleon comic strip in Figure 5.2. Suppose, instead of picture-reading *Napoleon* as you would normally, you imagined it not as a series of events involving a single dog but as nine separate look-alike dogs in nine different houses. Such an activity would fail to make clear numerous things that are true according to the comic—namely, that there's a single dog involved and that his hijinks prompted the fire department to visit. Individuals who do this have done *something* with comics, but, in a fairly standard sense, they've done the *wrong thing* if their interest is in using it as it was intended.

The aforementioned cases are fairly obvious examples, but there are acts of picture-reading that would less clearly violate what's mandated of readers. The inattentive reader might fail to make-believe that it is a wayward bone that causes Napoleon's owner, Uncle Elby, to trip and tumble. They might, instead, merely imagine that he has fallen out of clumsiness. This inattentive reader will arguably have imagined what was mandated by the work but will also have failed to imagine all that was prescribed by the creators. In a similar way, readers can often lose the comics *forest* for the comics *trees*. A superhero comics reader who delights in violent conflagration might imagine the blow-by-blow of conflict with rapt attention but disregard the creators' prescription to imagine the hero as overly enthusiastic about engaging in grotesque violence. Such readers only selectively take up invitations to make-believe and, in certain ways, fall short of their readerly duties—namely, their prescription to imagine a character's frequent reliance on violence as raising serious questions about their moral fiber.

Just as there's nothing morally concerning about pushing on a door that only opens when pulled, reading a comic inattentively or incorrectly isn't (usually) any kind of moral failing. And, of course, for inexperienced readers certain features of comics can pose readerly challenges in the form of complicated layouts or nuanced interweavings of text and image. What's more, regular readers of Western comics might well find themselves initially struggling with the differing conventions of manga, and vice versa. These facts indicate that picture-reading is a distinctive practice, one dependent upon a certain measure of skill and thoughtfulness. And, while readerly error isn't usually any kind of ethical misconduct, certain kinds of uncharitable picture-reading—namely, those that actively misread and refuse invitations to imagine—are potential objects of moral criticism. Indeed, Wertham's *Seduction of the Innocent* is rife with descriptions of comics where the banal is transformed into the sinister by picture-reading with an ulterior motive.

Reading comics is a norm-governed activity. It involves negotiating between certain imaginative options. Like riding a bike, it can be done better or worse. If that's correct, then there's no way to get away from normative concepts in uncovering what's true according to comics. It's also clear that picture-reading isn't *just* about invitations to make-believe but about navigating a range of imaginative opportunities and obligations. As Friend shows, some of these are invitations, others are mandates, and yet others are mere permissions.

An alternative approach to truth in comics steers into this inherently normative status and follows on the heels of moral theories that rely upon the idea of an ideal agent—an individual who is both fully rational and fully informed.[7] For our purposes, we can focus on the notion of an *ideal reader*: the reader who reads comics carefully, charitably, and with an eye toward the intentions (outright stated or best-guessed) of the relevant creators. Drawing upon this notion, we get the following proposal:

> **Ideal Reader View**: *p* is true according to a fiction *f* told through comics if and only if the ideal reader would imagine *p* in the course of reading the comic that tells *f*.

Appealing to the notion of an ideal reader provides us a helpful way to reframe a lot of debates about what is true within comics: what we are really doing is arguing about the best way, all things considered, for us to read them. If the ideal reader, upon reading *The Long Halloween*, assents to the claim that *The Long Halloween* establishes that the Joker has six-inch teeth, then according to *The Long Halloween*, the Joker has six-inch teeth. But the ideal reader would be sensitive to Tim Sale's pictorial style and Jeph Loeb's characterizations, as well as the tendency toward visual metaphor in the comics medium as a whole. So, quite plausibly, rather than imagining that the Joker has six-inch teeth, the ideal reader would, upon being pressed to answer the question of how long the Joker's teeth are, express a kind of ambivalence in this regard. They would note that while we can readily imagine that he seems to have six-inch teeth, there's no mandatory or prescribed imagining that his teeth are really *that* long.

We take the Ideal Reader View to be a useful tool for thinking through the kinds of imaginative obligations that arise when we're reading comics. Even so, there's a clear sense in which the Ideal Reader View gets truth in fiction wrong. Look again to our *Napoleon* comic and the second and third panels as Uncle Elby turns to walk back into the house. In turning around, did he turn to his left or to his right? The comic is perfectly silent on this matter, but in reading this comic, you likely imagined that he turned in one of these directions (though perhaps you didn't even notice what you imagined). This is readerly work that requires us to move beyond what's mandated, prescribed, or invited. Importantly, however, the ideal reader isn't a weirdly fastidious reader who avoids closure and seeks to avoid imagining what's *merely* permitted. They are permitted to imagine that Uncle Elby turned to—let's suppose—his left. In this and similar cases, the ideal reader will engage in a considerable amount of merely permissible imagining to deepen their engagement with a comic. We should therefore grant that the ideal reader imagines that Uncle Elby turns in a specific direction—again, let's suppose it's left. But, if that's correct, then it looks like we must—quite implausibly—claim that it's true according to this comic that Uncle Elby turns left. And it gets even worse: we can make exactly the same kind of argument to establish that it is true that he turns right, leading us squarely into a contradiction.

The natural fix is to give up, not on the notion of the ideal reader but on the assumption that the ideal reader is unique. A reader who is careful, charitable, attentive, and reflective in their engagement with *Napoleon* might imagine Uncle Elby turning left, but they might also imagine Uncle Elby turning right. There are, it seems, a plurality of ways to be an ideal reader of a comic. Truth according to this comic isn't therefore a matter of what *the* ideal reader imagines but, instead, what *every* ideal reader imagines. All ideal readers will imagine a coat on fire, but, since only some will imagine that there are more than two firefighters, it's indeterminate whether there are more than two firefighters on the scene. And, while all ideal readers will imagine that Uncle Elby turned around, it's indeterminate which direction he turned, since different ideal readers will fill out the details of his motion in different ways. So, by giving up on the frankly implausible notion that there's a uniquely ideal way to read a comic, but upholding the idea that there are normative standards against which readings might be assessed, we can recover the right kind of indeterminacy in comics. Here, then, seems to be the best version of the ideal reader approach:

> **Every Ideal Reader View**: p is true according to a fiction f told through comics c if and only if every ideal reader would imagine p in the course of reading c.

In Chapter 2, we saw that a potential vice of analyses is that they were unclear or uninformative. The Every Ideal Reader View will face objections on precisely these fronts. That's because the view is adequate only to the extent we can, in turn, explicate the concept of an ideal reader. What kinds of things does an ideal reader do or avoid doing in their readerly work? How much contextual information do they require? How many times will they reread a work to appreciate the structure of what surprised them on their first reading? And so on. This is a serious concern with the view. (It's a concern for the regular Ideal Reader View, too.) It makes clear that any account of what's true according to comics crucially depends upon the norms that govern comics readings—for example, Where do mandatory imaginings differ from the permitted ones and what does it mean to be a charitable reader? Without answers to these questions, it's probably fair to claim that we don't yet have an account of what it means to be an ideal reader. For this reason, the ultimate fate of the Every Ideal Reader View hangs on whether or not these questions can be answered. And, on that front, the jury remains out until we have what we've argued should be a central aim in the philosophy of comics: a full-fledged theory of picture-reading.

We've explored a range of approaches to the question of what's true according to comics. While we find remarkable agreement among readers on this front (as well as some notable and interesting disagreements), it seems that any viable approach must take seriously the diverse ways that we, as readers, negotiate our obligation to imagine what we're reading. We favor an approach along the lines of an Ideal Reader View in part because unlike certain other accounts, it makes clear the fundamentally normative nature of picture-reading. But, at this point, you might (understandably) be skeptical that this is right account of truth in comics or, indeed, whether any tidy account can be given. In this respect, your sentiment is shared by philosopher Kendall Walton (and, to be honest, at least one of us):

> Is there a relatively simple and systematic way of understanding how fictional truths are generated, a limited number of very general principles that implicitly govern the practice of artists and critics? I doubt that any experienced critic will consider this a live possibility. I do not think it is a live possibility. . . . Our examination of these suggestions will reinforce the suspicion that the search is in vain, and will foster a healthy respect for the complexity and subtlety of the means by which fictional truths are generated. (1990: 139)

Importantly, though, even if there's no simple and systematic analysis of truth in comics in the cards, that doesn't mean the notion can't be illuminated through careful examination. We think it points toward a crucial and underexplored task of uncovering the aesthetic norms of picture-reading. And, as we'll see, the notion of truth in comics is crucial for making sense of other features of comics, which we'll turn to in the remainder of this chapter as we explore the notion of canon in comics.

3. Canon in Comics

Inquiry into truth in comics can focus on the "small scale," like non-serial strips, but any comprehensive account must extend out to make sense of what's true within serialized comics. We also need to address the further problem of how to make sense of truth in comics that, as fictions, stretch across large numbers of issues, installments, and series. In the case of what Cook (2012) describes as MSCFs—again, massive, serialized, collaborative fictions—we face numerous puzzles that, roughly put, concern not only truth *in* comics but truth *across* comics—that is, truth in the fictions generated across numerous comics. The interpretive challenges that come with engaging with MSCFs aren't just for philosophers: they're acutely felt by readers, too. Readerly concerns with what's true within MSCFs are, for this reason, the source of many contemporary discussions about canon and canonicity.

Within a shared comics universe, like those produced by Marvel or DC Comics, individual fictions stop being individual fictions and instead become parts of a much larger, emergent whole. Each Batman fiction becomes part of *the* overarching Batman fiction, and that fiction, in turn, becomes a part of the overarching DC Universe fiction. The same goes for the fictions featuring Superman, Wonder Woman, the Flash, Green Lantern, Aquaman, and so on. Just focusing on comics put out by DC Comics, we can count many thousands of fictions, by different creative teams, all going together to arguably form a single MSCF: the DC-MSCF.

This phenomenon is probably quite familiar, but the way we described it isn't quite right. It's not true, after all, that *each* Batman story becomes a part of the DC-MSCF. Some of them—the *canonical* ones—do, while others—the *noncanonical* ones—don't. Perhaps most famously, DC's "Imaginary Stories" veer in wild directions that editors made clear weren't "in continuity." DC's subsequent *Elseworlds* designation functions to the same effect. (Marvel's *What If?* series are in the same spirit albeit slightly different, since they arguably capture in-continuity alternative possibilities.) And when we ascertain the truths within the DC-MSCF, we look at the collection of canonical stories, leaving the noncanonical ones to the side. In this way, the *canon versus non-canon* debate matters. In effect, it asks us to provide an account of the conditions under which a proposition is true across a *canon* or an MSCF. It therefore plays into the determination of what is relevant to the truths within larger fictions—an activity which is, again, a precondition for our interpretation and evaluation of those comics. (It's important to note, however, that noncanonical stories can still inform our take on canonical stories, such as when they shed light on characters by showing readers how they would act in various out-of-the-ordinary scenarios.)[8]

According to Cook, considerations of canon are *political, commercial, dynamic, negotiable,* and *participatory*: that is, what counts as canon can change over time based on changes in political climate, commercial viability, and the creators' relationship with a fan base, including negotiation with and petitioning (formally or informally) by those fans. Craig Derksen and Darren Hudson Hick (2017) point out, however, even if the decision between canon and non-canon status is negotiable and participatory, it is still ultimately up to the discretion of the copyright holder. The fans might *influence* DC to make this-or-that Batman story canonical or noncanonical, but the decision is, at the end of the day, DC's.

Canonicity is interesting not just insofar as it helps us circumscribe particular MSCFs for the purposes of interpretation and evaluation, but also because it leads us into the potentially murky questions of change in fictional truth over time. Some such changes come in the form of the accumulation of new information. When Batman was introduced in *Detective Comics* #27 (1939), his origin was unspecified. In later issues, it was revealed that he donned the cape and cowl as a way to avenge the murder of his parents. The establishment of this truth then retroactively alters *Detective Comics* #27, at least insofar as it is a piece of the larger, emergent fiction. Other such changes come in the form of retcons (short for "retroactive continuity"): in the early issues, Batman had no qualms killing the bad guys, with his characteristic moral code developing only later but being retroactively applied to the entirety of the emergent fiction.[9]

How do we understand this change in fictional truth over time? Given the Every Ideal Reader View, it turns out to be surprisingly simple. Say we read just *Detective Comics* #27. Would an ideal reader of *just that one comic* take it to establish that Bruce Wayne's parents were murdered, spurring his decision to become a bat? No. So, as an isolated story, it is not true in *Detective Comics* #27 that Bruce Wayne's parents had been murdered. But, when read as part of, or as a chapter of, an emergent fiction, it *is* true in *Detective Comics* #27 that Bruce Wayne's parents had been murdered, since it is established as being the case elsewhere in the canonical parts or chapters of that emergent fiction. One wouldn't, after all, expect every truth of a serialized fiction to be established in the first chapter of that fiction. This means, then, that there are two ways of critically engaging with *Detective Comics* #27: either as a stand-alone fiction or as a chapter in a larger, emergent fiction. What is true within the fiction will vary depending on our mode of engagement, and as such, so will our interpretation and evaluation of the comic.

Of course, the case just examined is a case of change by addition, in which nothing was established about Bruce Wayne's parents until later in the series. Other changes—like the aforementioned retcons—do involve changing established truths. An ideal reader of early Batman comics would assent to the claim that those comics establish that Batman is fine with killing criminals (or, at least, letting them die), since he is clearly depicted on the page as doing so. Later, however, it became a major theme in the emergent fiction that Batman categorically does not resort to lethal means, and ideal readers of that later emergent Batman fiction would note that the larger fiction establishes that Batman does not kill criminals. So, perhaps perplexingly, it seems to be true in the overall fiction that Batman never crosses a particular line but true in a part of that overall fiction that he does.

How do we resolve this and other logical tensions that emerge from the size, complexity, and structure of MSCFs? One way—perhaps the easiest—would be to just accept the Batman MSCF as inconsistent, as per our earlier discussion of the frequency with which fictions violate the Law of Non-Contradiction. After all, any MSCF is bound to have some contradictions, so we can surely overlook a few. Those with a strong preference for genuine *continuity*, however, will likely scoff at this solution. Thankfully, for their sake, there are alternatives. Remember that ideal readers will be *charitable* readers: that is, they will read the story in the way that puts it in the best light. If the bulk of the Batman MSCF reads better if Batman is categorically nonlethal, then such readers could simply negotiate and petition (in Cook's sense) toward any story depicting a lethal Batman to be disqualified from the emergent story and relegated to noncanonical status.[10] Suppose, however, that such negotiations or petitions don't convince the copyright holders or that the continuity junkies want to somehow retain those recalcitrant stories as part of the emergent story. What options might they have then?

Their best bet, we think, would be to rely on the idea, discussed earlier, that sometimes images misrepresent that which they depict, for expressive or stylistic purposes. On this approach, an ideal reader would no longer read those early issues as actually depicting Batman killing criminals but would instead read them as using some kind of visual metaphor, just as with Joker's six-inch teeth. Is this a stretch? It is. And we're pretty sure that in many instances, it will be a bit too much of one. But if we take the charitable ideal reader to strive exceptionally hard to avoid positing fictional contradictions and unwilling to part with recalcitrant segments, it might be the only option left. In cases of this sort, we can see, again, why the norm-governed flavor of comics reading is so rich and so important, especially when it comes to the often monumental task of engaging with large swathes of MSCFs. And, as Cook (2013) notes, the participatory character of canon is such that audiences, as readers and fans, have an often unacknowledged role in shaping truth in comics when we step back from individual comics and turn to strips and books as small parts of sprawling, serialized wholes. In the next section, we'll consider an example of this phenomenon and explore the interface of internal and external claims regarding comics.

4. Can Thor be a Woman?

A frequent occurrence stemming from the recent diversification of superhero comics has been the emergence of outcries against changes in characters—perhaps most notably, race- or gender-swapping characters. Viewed one way, such complaints aren't new: there's a long-standing tradition of audiences objecting to what happens to characters in comics. And, if we're correct about canon, they constitute the kinds of negotiations and petitions involved in its formation. Importantly, our interest in this chapter isn't in a political diagnosis of what's happening in such cases but, instead, a philosophical account of what audiences likely intend when they voice certain kinds of objections to changes in characters. In particular, we're interested in claims like the one made by anonymous messageboard commentator "rossatease," who says, "Thor a Woman? It just couldn't be."[11] Similar remarks abound: Captain America can't be black, Spider-Man can't be biracial, Iceman can't be gay, and so on. Now, in some of these cases, careful attention to details reveals all manner of subtle confusions (and gratuitous complexities). Sometimes the relevant stories involve a character taking up the name or title (or "mantle") of another character. But, in certain kinds of reboots or retcons, the central properties ascribed to characters do seem to change in substantial ways. So, what do these audiences mean when they claim that the character *can't* be that way? As we'll see, this hinges on how we understand modal notions like *could* and *must* and, in particular, the notion of characters having certain essential features.

Before diving in, let's first step back. In 1966, Charlton Comics published *Thunderbolt*, featuring the titular character, Peter Cannon. Created by Pete Morisi—an NYPD officer writing under the enigmatic, anonymizing handle "PA|||"—Peter Cannon is something of a throwback to the Golden Age. Blonde, wealthy, and conventionally handsome, he relies upon training received in a Himalayan lamasery to "harness the unused portions of his brain." The handful of early appearances of Thunderbolt are distinctive for Morisi's frozen, deco style which gives the feeling that its mod-ish characters are somehow stuck in transparent amber, as well as for Thunderbolt's anthemic proclamation "I can . . . I must . . . I will" that standardly marks the climax of the issue's action. After a brief run of appearances in Charlton comics, Thunderbolt was sold to DC in the mid-1980s, along with other Charlton characters like the Blue Beetle and Captain Atom, appearing briefly in *Crisis on Infinite Earths*. Although several Thunderbolt series have followed, Cannon is perhaps most familiar as the inspiration for Ozymandias in Moore and Gibbons's *Watchmen*. Indeed, early discussions of what turned into the story of *Watchmen* featured the stable of Charlton heroes rather than their corresponding homages (e.g., Blue Beetle was replaced by a very similar Nite Owl).

Here's a question left unanswered by this description: What is the *essence* of Thunderbolt? Put differently, what are the features that a character has to have to *be* Thunderbolt? Or: What changes to Thunderbolt would actually generate an entirely different character? A new name? Probably not. A new costume? Definitely not. A different origin? Perhaps. What about a different creator? Tough to say. Notice, though, that our line of questioning quickly crossed the divide between internal claims regarding the properties Thunderbolt is *ascribed* and external claims which Thunderbolt *instantiates*. (We set out this distinction in Chapter 4.)

Let's be explicit in distinguishing two kinds of questions we might pose about Thunderbolt's essence, then:

The Internal Essence Question: What properties are essentially ascribed to Thunderbolt? Roughly, what must be true according to a story for a character to be Thunderbolt?

The External Essence Question: What properties does Thunderbolt essentially instantiate? Roughly, what must be true of a fictional character in order for that character to be Thunderbolt?

For philosophers, the External Essence Question is akin to what we ask when we ask about the essence of people like Socrates or objects like the Eiffel Tower. While there is ample reason to be skeptical of many essentialist theses—most notably, invidious ones about race and gender—some are perfectly plausible. Squares essentially have four sides. Water is essentially part hydrogen. In this sense, the External Essence Question seeks information about the nature of fictional characters. How different could the abstract artifact, Thunderbolt, have been? We won't focus on the External Essence Question here, though it raises any number of issues about fictional characters—for example, whether they could have different creators or otherwise different histories.[12]

The Internal Essence Question is one which philosophers have paid far less attention to. It asks which, if any, of the properties ascribed to a character are such that any character not ascribed those properties would be a distinct character. Roughly speaking, an answer to the Internal Essence Question will tell us what the space of story possibilities are for the character in question.[13]

Here's a quick argument that there are no properties that characters like Thunderbolt are essentially ascribed: Morisi created a comic in which Thunderbolt went to the Himalayas, wore a domino mask, and could activate superstrength. But, if Morisi wanted to, he could have written Thunderbolt to have been raised on the moon, to wear a full helmet or no mask at all, and to transform into a bolt of thunder. And, if Morisi could have done those things, then surely he could have done even more radical things—for example, having Thunderbolt be the spirit of the Himalayas made incarnate and, upon completion of his objectives, transform back into a mountain peak. Things in comics, and fiction more generally, can get wild and there are no meaningful limits to creative possibility—not even logical consistency. Indeed, even if you had been initially inclined to think that Superman is essentially Kryptonian or essentially morally excellent, over the trajectory of eighty years of serialization, Superman has been turned into a balloon, shrunk to microscopic size, turned invisible, and many other things besides. At one point, he was even physically and psychologically split into two persons! (And that's not even including the still weirder "Imaginary Stories" in DC Comics history.) So, given enough time and creative freedom, serialization seems to open up the possibility that origins can be upended, previously stable characteristics abandoned, and so on. It looks, then, like the internal essences of characters are exceedingly narrow. So, if Thunderbolt is a typical example, there is no reason to think, at least in the case of superheroes featured in serialized comics, that they have any substantial essential properties. Pretty much anything can happen in superhero comics, given, again, enough time and creativity.

What does this mean for claims like "Thor can't be a woman"? Taken as an external claim, this is trivially true but entirely beside the point: Thor can't be a woman. Or a man. Or a god. That's because Thor, on the account offered in the previous chapter, is an abstract artifact. Obviously, the claim seems to be intended instead as an internal one to the effect that Thor must essentially be ascribed the property of *being a man*. But, given some modest reflection on how wild serial superhero comics get, this is surely false. Thinking through the ontological status of characters therefore suggests that these sorts of protests over characters, if taken as claims about what can and can't be the case, are simply mistaken.

Is there a different way to interpret claims like "Thor can't be a woman"? Sure. "Can" sometimes expresses what's called deontic modality—roughly, moral obligations or permissions like when we say "you can't hurt the innocent." Interpreted this way, such a claim would attribute a kind of moral wrongdoing to those who create stories in which it's true that Thor is a woman. Perhaps some people intend to communicate this sort of claim, but notice that when audiences make these sorts of claims, they typically seek to convey that there's something defective or incoherent about the stories, not merely that they're morally wrong. This suggests a different interpretation. As we noted in previous sections, engagement with fiction requires myriad acts of pretense or make-believe. Some of these vary in their cognitive ease or difficulty. It is, for example, easy to imagine a cat on a mat and hard to imagine a character correctly squaring the circle. In this vein, we might take the claim that "Thor can't be a woman" to mean that comics in which this claim is true are invitations to make-believe that are impossible to accept. *That* would be an interesting and significant claim. But, unless someone has exceptionally limited cognitive abilities, there's just no reason to believe that they can't succeed in this act of make-believe, especially given the frequently baroque and bizarre events in superhero comics.

Where do we now stand in our effort to make sense of the claim "Thor can't be a woman"? Well, there seems to be no way to interpret such a claim as true or even especially plausible, at least not without attributing limited cognitive abilities to those who make such claims. But we're still without a general diagnosis of what's going on when these claims are made. Here, then, is what we take to be a promising account. Our tastes, habits, and commitments shape what we engage with as readers. And, when we read comics and other fictions, what we imagine similarly reflects these and other facts about us. We might imaginatively embellish certain details in romance comics or, out of certain squeamishness, elide various details in horror comics. It would be naïve to think that our moral and political commitments play no role in shaping the imaginings involved in engaging with comics. In those cases where someone insists that "Thor can't be a woman," it is quite likely that while they might purport to claim this is somehow contrary to Thor's essence, this is a roundabout way of expressing a refusal to undertake the imaginings mandatory for reading certain comics—namely, those wherein Thor is a woman. As we've noted earlier, reading comics is a fundamentally normative behavior. When someone marks a refusal to undertake the imaginings mandatory to a comic, they are, in effect, violating readerly norms. Under certain circumstances, this is probably morally commendable and in other circumstances, it is probably morally blameworthy. We suspect, for example, that imaginative refusals bound up with claims like "Thor can't be a woman" stem from objectionable misogyny.[14] This stands in apparent contrast with possible engagement with comics like Frank Miller's *Holy Terror* (2011). In such cases, imaginative refusal to make-believe that the central character engages in racially discriminatory violence and is, in virtue of this, a hero seems to be an apt reflection of antiracist commitments. It might, under the right circumstances, make moral sense to be a less than ideal reader.[15]

We are by no means asserting that one ought to avoid each and every imaginative invitation that is morally questionable. For moral or aesthetic reasons, we can perfectly well imagine that certain distasteful imaginings ought to be undertaken. There is, after all, much to learn from thinking through fictional worlds from a diversity of conflicting perspectives. But what we have seen is that comics practices that audiences engage in can be usefully illuminated via the apparatus of truth in fiction, especially when understood through the lens of invitations, permissions, and mandates to imagine.

5. Recommended Readings

The literature spawned from Lewis's "Truth in Fiction" (1978) is impressively large and, for various reasons, we've carved off a rather selective portion of it. Other important contributions include Matravers (2014), Walton (1990), and Woodward (2011). On the puzzles that arise in making sense of inconsistent fictions, see Priest (1997) and Nolan (2007). On some limit cases of fictional truth, see Xhignesse (2021) and (forthcoming). This body of literature is dwarfed, however, but work on the nature of pictures and, in particular, depiction has tended to focus on the case of depictions of nonfictional characters. An excellent introduction to this literature is Kulvicki (2014). The philosophical work of mapping the conventions for depiction within comics gets underway in Cook's "Does the Joker Have Six-Inch Teeth?" as well as Cook (2012) and (2015b).

6

Genre in Comics

1. Introduction

There are myriad ways to categorize and carve up the world of comics. A chronological survey might divide comics by year or "ages." An investigation into editorial contributions might single out only the comics that a specific editor—say, Karen Berger or Dick Giordano—was involved with. We might focus our attention on the DC horror comics penciled or inked by Filipino creators during the 1980s or when investigating the career of Ogden Whitney divide his Herbie stories from the rest of his work. Simply put: given different practical and theoretical aims, different categories prove relevant. But certain categories play an especially distinctive role in the creation and reception of comics: some categories—romance, western, and science fiction, among many others—are *genres*.

Genre categorization is clearly not unique to comics. Its significance extends across artistic mediums. And, while some have claimed that genre categories pervade all facets of life, partitioning events and objects like gestures and street signs, our interest in this chapter is squarely on comics and the role that genre plays within comics practice.[1] On this front, the most repeated claim about genre is the cautionary disclaimer that the medium of comics should not be conflated with the genre of superhero comics. That's undoubtedly true, but the fact that this claim is made so regularly (and so often seems worth saying) betrays the outsized impact of the superhero genre on the history of comics in North America and other parts of the world. In Section 5, we'll examine the question of what exactly the superhero genre is, but we should emphasize that across the comics medium we are presented with a dizzying range of genres and subgenres that have little or nothing to do with superheroes. So, if we hope to make sense of their categorization as well as their creation and reception, we need a general understanding of what genres are and how they work.

2. Genre in General

Two kinds of questions are central to the project of understanding genre in comics. The first, which we'll call the *Genre Question*, is concerned with which categories count as genres in comics.

Genre Question: When is a category of comics a *genre* category?

This question is concerned with what distinguishes a genre category like western, kung-fu, or romance from non-genre categories like comics from 1982, comics drawn by a left-handed artist, or comics with stories about windmills. As we consider potential answers to this question, it's worth considering how we ought to assess them. Pretty clearly, an answer to the Genre Question that denies the existence of familiar genres (e.g., horror, romance) or proliferates genre categories that we don't recognize (e.g., comics about windmills) will fail to adequately represent comics practice. But there are also some more nuanced facts about genre and genre classification that a suitable answer ought to accommodate.

Notice, for instance, that genres can be nested within one another, yielding subgenres and, in some cases, *sub*subgenres. For example, the mystery genre is broader in scope than the murder mystery genre, since there are mysteries—for example, regarding theft or kidnapping—that are not centered around murder. And, within the comedy genre, we find subgenres like slapstick comedies, buddy comedies, mockumentaries, and so on. Any account of genre ought to accommodate this sort of nested structure. Additionally, genres frequently overlap one another to yield works that are properly included in distinct genres. There is, for example, a seemingly unlimited stream of television programs and films that are rightly classified as both romances and comedies.

It's important to note, however, that many comics defy ready categorization into a single genre or, in some cases, seem aptly categorized into hybrid genres that are distinct from those they're compounded out of. Genre-bending comics like *Space Western* (1952) might, for instance, emerge from science fiction and western genres without being properly categorized as subgenres of either. Taken together, these features of genre suggest a remarkably complex system of classification that resists any easy summary, but also one that has no unqualified universal principles of categorization, as well as ample amounts of indeterminacy. Some specific genre questions—for example, whether to classify *Space Western* #41 as western, science fiction, or both—might therefore rightly be left unanswered.

Since the Genre Question concerns comics in particular, it allows us to sidestep an open question about genre and medium—namely, whether genre categories are medium-specific or somehow transcend specific mediums. One might think that genre categories in film are importantly distinct from those in comics, since, for example, it makes no sense to apply genre categories like *musical* to the genre landscape of comics. How exactly to characterize this disagreement about the medium-specificity of genres is controversial, but, roughly speaking, it asks whether we should think of a genre like horror or romance as a single category that is *realized* via different mediums or, instead, view medium-specific categories like horror films, horror comics, and so on as *distinct categories* that are interestingly related.[2]

Regardless of one's views about the medium-specificity of genre, there is clearly *some* sense in which categories like science fiction and romance cut across comics, film, and other mediums. But, insofar as they do so, it's also important to note how features that are relevant for genre classification vary from medium to medium. As a silent medium, comics have no score or music. So, although the score or music might figure into classifying a film as noir, it plays no similar role in the case of comics. Similarly, comics-specific features like coloring, layout, and lettering can, in principle, bear upon the categorization of works as comedic or horrific, but novels are categorized into genre without attention to these features. This complex interaction between genre and medium is reason to believe that whether or not genre categories are identical across mediums, the mechanisms for determining genre clearly require medium-specific attention.

If genre weren't already complicated enough, there's a further nuance that requires discussion. If we think about genres as categories in which different comics fall, we face a puzzle when we start to think about the often serialized nature of the comics medium. Comics are regularly serialized and therefore published, initially or exclusively, in the form of component installments. So, when we ascribe genres to comics, should we ascribe them to entire series, to specific issues, or to individual stories within an issue? Consider, for example, a long-running series like *Journey into Mystery* (ranging in various forms from the 1950s to the 2010s) or *Strange Adventures* (originally running from 1950 to 1973), which have included horror, science fiction, superhero, and other kinds of stories. Similar examples suggest that seriality and genre exhibit a complicated relationship that likely prohibits us from rightly ascribing genres to series and issues that feature stories which crosscut genres. Notice, however, that this problem can arise even in the case of non-anthology comics like Dave Sim's *Cerebus* (1977–2004) and Colleen Doran's *A Distant Soil* (published in various formats since the 1980s), which comprise stories, arcs, and periods in which features of the comic defy any simple or singular ascription of a genre category. In these cases, different parts of the series arguably occupy different genre categories and so we ought to deny that the entire series is rightly ascribed a single genre. This is evidence that, among other things, a theory of the interaction between seriality and genre is a philosophical project that still needs to be undertaken.

Let's now turn to the second question crucial for understanding the relationship between comics and genre:

> **Membership Question**: What does it take for a comic to be included in a specific comics genre—for example, western or science fiction comics?

This question is concerned with the limits of particular genres and the criteria comics must meet to be correctly included in them. Importantly, the Membership Question is silent on what makes a category a genre category in the first place. Instead, it is concerned with finding a kind of recipe for determining which comics fall within specific genres. In effect, each genre generates its own instance of the overall question. If our interest is in, say, romance comics or superhero comics, we will want to address the *Romance* Membership Question or the *Superhero* Membership Question, respectively.

We'll explore two of these genre-specific questions shortly, but it's important to consider the broader Membership Question for a moment. That's because genre categorization is remarkably heterogeneous: very different features can be relevant to genre classification. In cases like horror and comedy, the relevant features likely include intended affect among audiences—such as fear or amusement. In cases like romance and kung-fu comics, plot structure proves critical. Similarly, setting is essential in the categorization of war, jungle, and western comics. Complex coordination between these and other features often drives genre categorization. Remarking on genre's role in film, Laetz and Lopes (2008: 156) note that "[s]ome [genres] are partly defined by setting (western), some by subject (war), others by affect (comedy), some by format (musicals), and still others by style (film noir)." The same is plainly true of comics, where features relevant to membership in one genre might be largely irrelevant to membership in another (e.g., setting matters greatly for being classified as a western but little, if at all, for counting as a comedy).

The hetereogeneity of genre in comics means that satisfactory accounts of what it takes to be a superhero comic or a romance comic might look very different. It also has consequences for the earlier-posed Genre Question, which asked what made categories into genre categories. A natural strategy for tackling that question is to rely upon our familiar judgments of similarity or resemblance. After all, genre categories do seem to be unified by how much their members are alike one another. Perhaps, then, genres are categories that are defined in virtue of the similarity of their members to one another.

If we aim to define genre categories in terms of similarity alone and provide a general answer that applies to all genres, we cannot rely on any specific kind of similarity (e.g., similarity with regard to setting or story). Instead, we have to invoke the concept of "total" or "overall" similarity. We might therefore posit that genre categories are those categories in which each member is more similar to each other member than any non-member. On such a view, every horror comic must be more similar to every other horror comic than it is to any comedy or romance comic. This delivers what we can call the *Total Similarity View* of genre categories:

Total Similarity View: A category of comics c is a genre if and only if every comic in that category is more similar to every other comic in that category than it is to any comic not in that category.

Take the case of western comics. The Total Similarity View says that there is a genre of western comics if and only if each western more closely resembles any other western than it resembles any horror, war, or superhero comic. It also says that there's a genre of comics from 1984 just in case every comic from 1984 is more similar to each other than any comic from another a year. And, since that's clearly false, the Total Similarity View rightly denies *comics from 1984* is a genre category. So far, so good.

Deeper consideration suggests, however, that the Total Similarity View yields some philosophical worries and some peculiar verdicts. First, we face serious challenges when pressed to assess comics for their total similarity to one another. Should similarity in visual style count for more or less than production techniques or time and place of origin? Does the pattern of publication count for more or less than the plotline? The general worry here is that the notion of *total similarity* between comics is actually far from familiar. In keeping with the sentiments of Nelson Goodman and other critics of total similarity, our coherent talk about similarity might actually be limited to similarity *in specific respects*—for example, being more or less similar in size or in color.[3] According to some philosophers, we can, at best, talk about similarity in specific respects because the notion of total similarity is either incoherent or without any useful application.

Second, the Total Similarity View simply delivers weird results. It seems by most standards that Jean-Michel Charlier and Jean Giraud's western comic *Blueberry* is more similar to Huge Pratt's adventure comic *Corto Maltese* than it is to a Marvel Comics western like *Rawhide Kid*. Fletcher Hanks's superhero comics featuring Stardust the Super Wizard are far more similar to his lumberjack-adventure comics featuring Big Red McClane, King of the Northwoods, than they are to Jack Kirby's superhero comic *New Gods* (1971–2). In these and other cases, there's a criss-crossing network of similarity that shapes audience engagement, but, on its own, total similarity simply turns out to be a poor guide to which categories are actually genres.

The inadequacy of the Total Similarity View is no reason to think that considerations of similarity don't figure into a theory of genre. Quite obviously, comics within the same genre are often very similar to one another. What we've seen, however, is that genre isn't *just* a matter of similarity. With that in mind, let's now turn to what philosophers have said about genre in their efforts to tackle the Genre Question.

3. Philosophies of Genre

Philosophical inquiry into genre has focused largely on the roles that genre plays in our engagement with fiction, whether as audiences, critics, or creators. Among these roles is the scarcely deniable impact genre has upon audience expectations. When a comic falls within a given genre, audience engagement with that comic is shaped by the audience's awareness of genre conventions. When reading a noir detective comic, one expects a murder to take place and some manner of tragic betrayal to follow on its heels. In contrast, when reading a romance comic, audiences would be shocked if the two star-crossed lovers simply got over their breakup with absolutely minimal drama. In this sense, the coordinated features of genres give rise to a "horizon of expectations" that shape readers' experiences.[4]

Genre also plays a substantial interpretive role, shaping what we are invited or prescribed to imagine. Within an apparent superhero comic, costume-clad individuals can reasonably be expected to have superpowers and, even if we witness no display of their powers within an issue, we seem within our rights to imagine that they are exceptionally likely to have some. When reading a western, however, a character wearing a remarkable outfit isn't plausibly assumed to have superpowers—apart, of course, from incredible marksmanship. Similarly, it can be assumed by a reader that when a character is shot multiple times in a western comic, they aren't likely to return. But, in a slapstick funny animal comic, physical harm has only the vaguest of medical consequences, so we might be unsurprised by the return of a shot, exploded, or steamrolled critter later on in a story. As Shen-Yi Liao (2016: 9) puts it, "[g]enre influences the propositions that are warranted to be fictional in a narrative and the ways that one ought to, and actually does, engage with a narrative." In short, genre shapes how we behave as audiences, not only with regard to expectations about what *will happen* but also with regard to what we take *to be happening*. In this way, genre helps guide the imaginings we use to "fill out" fictional worlds.

Along with its interpretative role, genre plays a substantial and far-reaching role in aesthetic evaluation. We often unthinkingly evaluate the merits of comics against the backdrop of a specific genre. Not only is the comparison of works within genres especially natural, the critical reception of works often hinges on how they stand in comparison to the broader norms of the genre in which they fall. We might bemoan a comic as hackneyed, formulaic, or predictable for its extreme conformity with genre norms or, instead, praise it as unconventional, inventive, and unpredictable for violating them. Conversely, comics are often praised for creatively upholding these norms or condemned for awkwardly departing from them. And, given the heterogeneity of genre, the manner in which genre shapes evaluation can differ significantly. Horror comics are praised when they realize their intended fearful affect in the audience, but western comics are rarely praised merely for being set in an unambiguously western locale. For this reason, when creators produce comics with the intention that they fall within a given genre, awareness of these norms shapes how they envision the interpretation and reception of a comic.

The evaluative effects of genre are tremendously complex. It is, for instance, easy to feel flummoxed when asked to compare the merits of a superhero comic with a romance comic or to weigh a horror comic against a funny animal comic. In part, this is because the ways we evaluate comics are so tightly bound up with the apparent genres of the comics at hand. As a consequence, reading lists like "1000 Greatest Comics Ever" can seem a disorienting experience. How, for instance, do we transpose our evaluative judgments across each and every genre in order to determine whether, say, Kuniko Tsurita's *The Sky Is Blue with a Single Cloud* (2020) is better or worse than Fábio Moon and Gabriel Bá's *Daytripper* (2010), or how they both square up to John Stanley's *Little Lulu* (1945–59)?

Here's another way to make the evaluative importance of genre clear: if we were pressed to think of Bill Watterson's *Calvin & Hobbes* (1985–95) as a horror comic, documenting a young child's descent into madness, it would seem confusing, not especially scary, and tonally peculiar. But, read as Watterson intended—namely, as a work of comedy—it's a graceful, rollicking tribute to childhood imagination. Parallel remarks apply to other works which we might forcibly and mistakenly drag into other genres in order to generate odd reading experiences and, in turn, peculiar aesthetic appraisals. In this way, aesthetic evaluations of comics almost always happen against a backdrop of apparent genre.

This last point about evaluation and genre is important in part because it allows us to clarify a potential misunderstanding and get a bit clearer about what genre does and does not explain. As Gregory Currie (2004) notes, although the fact that a work falls within a given genre explains why we *expect* it to have features associated with that genre, or the fact that its creators might *intend* it to have certain features, there are limits to what facts about genre membership can explain. For example, a horror comic isn't scary *because* it is a horror comic nor is a comedy funny *because* it is a comedy: they are scary or funny (if at all) because of their specific features. This observation about genre and explanation in turn raises a broader philosophical worry: if it is specific features of individual comics that explain their effects on audiences like horror or amusement, what exactly do we need facts about genre membership to explain? We do not, for example, explain the haunting air of Bernard

Krigstein and Al Feldstein's "Master Race" (1955) by appealing to its status as a horror comic but, instead, by the eerie, high contrast style and elusive, haunting narrative. Put differently, if we did away with any and all talk about genres and instead talked only about specific comics, what would happen? Are there certain things that we could no longer explain or make sense of? Toward the end of this chapter, we'll argue that without genre, we would be left without explanations of some puzzling features of comics practice.

We've sketched some of the roles that genre plays in our engagement with comics. And, with these roles in mind, we're now in a position to consider some potential answers to the Genre Question. A useful place to start is with the account offered by Simon Evnine according to which genre categories are traditions organized around the production and reception of artworks. He summarizes this account of genre as follows:

> Genres are traditions that are organized, in a certain way, around the production of artworks. A genre such as science fiction has many parts— readers, writers, works, practices of reading and interpreting, publishing houses, fan organizations, conferences, and so on. In this respect, it is similar to traditions that are religions. Unlike religions, in the case of genres, these elements are organized around the production of artistic works. Specifically, authors produce works in the knowledge, and under the influence, of works previously produced as parts of the tradition; the works are read by readers in the ways developed by previously produced works; the publishing houses publish such works, the conventions invite the authors, who may produce new works in the light of interactions. (2015: 5)

If Evnine is correct, genres are to be understood not as merely collections or clusters of works with common features but as historically specific events that comprise works, fans, practices, and other phenomena. Formulated as an answer to the Genre Question, Evnine's view can be summarized as follows:

Tradition View: A category of comics c is a genre if and only if there is a tradition organized, in a certain way, around the production of comics in c.

Notice that this way of summarizing Evnine's view relies upon the clause that traditions must be organized "in a certain way" to count as genres. This means that such an account isn't fully spelled out, but, even so, it is worth carefully considering.

Among other consequences, Evnine's view entails that genres are fundamentally historical in nature. Indeed, the Tradition View is, in effect, a historicist view that precludes the possibility of genres whose members transcend or crosscut organized traditions. So, for example, two stories produced in entirely disconnected contexts cannot be assimilated into the same genre even if they exhibited uncanny narrative similarities. In parallel with historicist accounts of the comics medium that we considered in Chapter 2, if genres are organized traditions with distinctive histories, works can only be included within the same genre if there is some appropriate causal-historical connection between them and the tradition in question.

The plausibility of this historicist constraint is highly controversial. It will, for example, crucially depend upon the plausibility of viewing familiar genres as historically specific and likely denying that when editors assemble collections like *Horror Stories from Around the World* or *Mystery Tales from Across the Centuries,* these collections include works of unified genres. Against this sort of objection, historicists and proponents of the Tradition View can argue that although these stories are apt *to be treated* as belonging to the same genre, this doesn't require that they are, in fact, all members of the same genre. Regardless of whether the historicist constraint on genre is accepted, it is undeniable that genres have histories and that these histories inform how genres serve their interpretative and evaluative roles.

Other approaches to the philosophy of genre like the one developed in Currie (2004) focus not on historical traditions but on the role of genre categories in shaping expectations. According to Currie, genre categories (or at least the relevant ones) are just those categories in which the features of works generate an audience expectation of further shared features associated with the genre. Instead of exploring such expectation-based approaches as general approaches to genre, we'll turn to the role of expectation as it shows up in a theory specifically about genre in comics.

4. Genre versus Style

The Tradition View is a "top-down" approach to genre. It is intended as an account of genre across narrative mediums and should therefore apply automatically to the case of comics. In this section, our interest is in a "bottom-up" philosophical account of genre that is specific to comics: the one given in Catharine Abell's "Comics and Genre" (2012). There, Abell defends an account of genre categories within comics as sets of conventions aimed at meeting certain interpretive and evaluative aims of the sort noted earlier. She describes her view of genres within comics as follows:

> [G]enres are sets of conventions that have developed as means of addressing particular interpretative and/or evaluative problems and have a history of co-instantiation within a community, such that a work's belonging to some genre generates interpretative and evaluative expectations among the members of that community. (2012: 77)

Abell's account is explicit that for a set of conventions to distinguish a genre, they need to generate interpretive and evaluative expectations. So, for example, the superhero convention of including fanciful costumes should, among other things, lead readers to expect that the individuals have remarkable abilities and, in evaluating the comic, the portrayal of violent action rather than, say, arousing a sense of mystery will figure prominently in a reader's assessment of the comic. More simply, for the relevant conventions to carve out a genre, they need to substantially and distinctively shape how readers read and think about comics. In addition, Abell stipulates that the set of conventions must have a "history of co-instantiation" and therefore co-occur with sufficient frequency or memorability to activate readers' expectations. These conventions must also be present in works for a specific reason, addressing what Abell (2012) calls "interpretative and/or evaluative problems." Taken together, we might frame Abell's view as the following sort of answer to the Genre Question:

> **Convention View**: A category of comics c is a genre if and only if comics in c exhibit a set of conventions (i) that are intended to address particular interpretive or evaluative problems, (ii) that have a history of co-occurrence within a community, and (iii) that generate interpretive and evaluative expectations within that community.

It is a virtue of Abell's account that it explicitly incorporates the interpretative and evaluative role of genre categories. At the same time, as an account of genre in comics, there are some reasons to be unsatisfied. Here, we'll focus on two.

The first issue flows from Abell's claim that genres are conventions intended to address specific interpretative or evaluative problems. If we limit our attention to just certain genres—most notably, those like comedy and horror which are crucially tied to audience affect—it might seem plausible that genres are essentially tied to conventions for solving problems. In the case of comedy, the broadest sort of problem is how to engender audience amusement, and, in the case of horror, the broadest problem concerns inducing fear in an audience. But, given the heterogeneity of genre, it's not plausible that there are *distinctive* problems that correspond to each and every genre category that is recognized within comics practice. In the case of war, jungle, and western comics, the setting of the story, broadly construed, seems to ensure that a comic falls within that genre, but it's far from clear that there's a distinctive set of conventions in these comics that aim to solve any *specific* interpretative or evaluative problem. To be sure, western comics include mesas, horses, and cowboys, while jungle comics feature vines, villagers, and quicksand, but there are no *distinctive* problems, whether interpretive or evaluative, that the inclusion of these features address in such cases.

Abell might respond that in the case of war, western, and jungle comics, the appearance of these features is in accord with conventions that creators rely upon to generate a sense of adventure or action. That's surely true, but notice that this response is not sufficient to show that war, western, and jungle comics are each a comics genre. It can, at best, show that adventure or action counts as a genre and therefore leaves us without an explanation of the genre status of these specific categories. And, if that's correct, Abell's account can't quite do justice to the diversity of genres within comics.

A second issue with Abell's account arises when we explore the role of style in comics. The nature of style in the comics medium has been largely ignored by philosophers, so it is to Abell's credit that it figures importantly into her discussion. Specifically, Abell says, "[t]he fact that genres are sets of conventions distinguishes them from categories based solely on works' histories of production. . . . It also distinguishes genres from styles. Genre categories are distinct from style categories because style categories are not comprised of conventions" (2012: 79). There is, however, a problem with such a proposal. Within comics, there are myriad styles that are indeed sets of conventions and, like genres, these styles also have histories of co-instantiation and generate evaluative expectations.

Take the case of *ligne claire*, most famously associated with Belgian cartoonist Hergé. Comics in this style embrace a cluster of visual conventions: they are drawn with closed figures, a paucity of cross-hatching, a bare minimum of shadow, and with flat colors permeating the entire visual field. *Ligne claire* has a robust history of its own and, while commonly tied to Hergé, is by no means purely a matter of *Tintin* homage but instead a robust and distinctive style tradition in comics as evidenced by the following excerpt from Rich Tommaso's *Spy Seal* #3 (2017) (Figure 6.1).

Figure 6.1 *Spy Seal* #3 (2017), Rich Tommaso. Spy Seal observes a variety of anthropomorphic ex-spy characters, drawn in *ligne claire* style.

To read comics in *ligne claire* style is, in part, to evaluate them for their clarity, simplicity, and elegance and to appreciate, among other things, the significance of the work of colorists.[5] Additionally, one would be surprised to discover *ligne claire* style in, say, stories of Lovecraftian existential horror, given the brightness and clarity typical of the style. (For precisely this reason, Murray Groat's *Tintin* parodies featuring Lovecraftian lore are so amusing.) With this in mind, we see that the *ligne claire* style does indeed generate interpretive and evaluative expectations while also being a cluster of historically co-occurring conventions. It looks, then, like Abell's account fails to do justice to the role of style in comics and, perhaps more importantly, the distinction between style and genre. Similarly, on the Tradition View, where genres are conceived as historical traditions, it is unclear how to offer a principled way to exclude *ligne claire* as a genre and thereby respect the divide between genre and style in comics.

Still, there is much that seems right with the Convention View—in particular, its explicit incorporation of genre's distinctive roles. But, in light of these problems, as well as those arising for the Tradition View, it is still unclear how to answer the Genre Question. Even so, our project in the next two sections is to dive into two specific genres—superhero and horror comics—with an eye toward how we might answer certain specific instances of the Membership Question.

5. Case Study: What Are Superhero Comics?

Recall that the Membership Question can be posed as a question specific to each genre. So, when we turn our attention to superhero comics, it becomes the following:

> **Superhero Membership Question**: What does it take for a comic to be included in the superhero genre?

A knee-jerk answer is that a comic is a superhero comic just in case it features superheroes. After all, Superman comics are superhero comics in virtue of including, well, Superman. This suggests the following answer to the Superhero Membership Question:

> **Superheroes Included View**: A comic x is properly included in the superhero genre if and only if x features superheroes. [6]

There is an obvious sense in which superheroes are the focal elements of superhero comics. Interestingly, this seems to be further evidence of the heterogeneity of genre, since superheroes are not settings, plots, intended audience affect, or themes. On the face of it, they are characters and, if the Superheroes Included View is correct, they are the characters whose presence determines what is and isn't a superhero comic. But, if the Superheroes Included View is to shed any real light on the Superhero Membership Question, the next question is an obvious one: What exactly is a superhero?

Recent work in comics studies has thoughtfully explored various aspects of the superhero genre with an eye toward its history and its representation, but there remains no canonical or widely accepted analysis of what it is to be a superhero. Among proposed accounts, the most influential owes to Peter Coogan (2013: 3):

> A heroic character with a universal, self-less, prosocial mission; who possesses superpowers—extraordinary abilities, advanced technology, or highly developed physical and/or mental skills (including mystical abilities); who has a superhero identity embodied in a code name and iconic costume, which

typically express his biography or character, powers, and origin (transformation from ordinary person to superhero); and is generically distinct, i.e., can be distinguished from characters of related genres (fantasy, science fiction, detective, etc.) by a preponderance of genre conventions. Often superheroes have dual identities, the ordinary one of which is usually a closely guarded secret.

If this account is correct, then, granted the Superheroes Included View, any comic which features a character that satisfies these conditions is rightly viewed as a superhero comic. But how plausible is Coogan's proposal?

As a tool for answering the Superhero Membership Question, it has a notable defect. If our ambition is to analyze the concept of a superhero, we cannot appeal to the concept in our explanation or analysis and, at several points, Coogan's remarks are plainly circular. Along with explaining superheroes partly in terms of "superhero identity" and "superpowers," Coogan's reference to a "preponderance of genre conventions" is a clear barrier to informative analysis. We cannot presuppose an account of the superhero genre in defining superheroes if we hope to go on to define the genre in terms of superheroes. That would be obviously circular.

We should be careful, however, not to throw out Coogan's useful insights if we can help it. We can, for example, draw upon Coogan's observation that "three elements—mission, powers, and identity—establish the core of the genre" (2013: 7) to develop a tripartite analysis of what it is to be a superhero. The resulting analysis avoids any obvious circularity:

> **Tripartite View**: x is a superhero if and only if x is a character with (i) a universal, self-less, prosocial mission, (ii) extraordinary abilities, advanced technology, or highly developed physical and/or mental skills (including mystical abilities), and (iii) a code name and iconic costume, which typically express their biography or character, powers, and origin.

When we consider the case of historically popular superheroes, the Tripartite View seems to do a rather good job. It is an apt description of characters like Superman, Wonder Woman, Spider-Man, Daredevil, and many, many others. As we expand the range of characters under consideration and focus on each of the three necessary conditions, though, its extensional adequacy becomes less clear.[7]

Take the case of the first and explicitly normative requirement that characters adopt "a universal, self-less, prosocial mission." Interestingly, this necessary condition is, at the same time, both too demanding and too weak. The demand for *universal* moral concern squares poorly with characters like

Namor and Aquaman, compelled to defend a specific community like Atlantis at the expense of others. More generally, we regularly find superheroes invested in saving the human race with a near-complete indifference to the well-being of nonhuman sentient beings—most notably, alien civilizations. Similarly, the requirement that characters be "self-less" seems regularly flouted by those superheroes interested in, say, vengeance (e.g., Deadman) or fame (e.g., Booster Gold). The normative commitments of heroes extend beyond the moral to the psychological. This is because it is not enough to merely have a mission. A superhero must be sufficiently resolute and, in particular, brave enough to undertake it. While cowardly characters do appear in superhero comics, there are almost no superheroes that are anything other than exceptionally brave (often to the point of being foolhardy).[8]

Similar challenges arise for the other requirements, since notions like "extraordinary abilities," "code name," and "iconic costume" are either obviously unsatisfied (e.g., Jessica Jones) or too vague to help us settle open classificatory questions. Obviously, Coogan is aware of potential challenges to these conditions, noting that "specific superheroes can exist who do not fully demonstrate all three of these elements" (2013: 7). But this results in an awkward theoretical position. We could revise the Tripartite View to require, say, two out of three of the conditions be met, but this generates even more counterexamples, since many supervillains satisfy (ii) and (iii) but not (i). There is, then, little reason to think that a weaker version of the Tripartite View is going to be any more plausible.

The simple fact is that the category *superhero* is a vague one. There are characters that seem correctly described neither as superheroes nor as non-superheroes. We might chalk this up to the fact that the concepts deployed in specifying the three necessary conditions are vague and so the entire analysis inherits this vagueness. But this lets the Tripartite View off too lightly. If there are characters that are clearly superheroes but also fail to satisfy proposed necessary conditions, regardless of whether the concept *superhero* is vague, this is still evidence that the Tripartite View is mistaken. In addition, there is a problem that besets the Tripartite View from the "opposite" direction, which Coogan's remarks about "genre trappings" aim to address: there are clear cases of characters that seem improperly categorized as superheroes but apparently satisfy all three conditions, like, say, Gandalf the White.

There is an alternative to Coogan's approach, which offers a solution to the problems we've encountered with the Tripartite View. Rather than seeking to provide nonhistorical necessary conditions that are jointly sufficient, we might take our inspiration from historicist treatments of genre and argue that superheroes are a kind of historical artifact. While some other kinds of characters precede them and share certain features, this historicist approach claims that with the creation of Superman and other characters in the late 1930s, a distinctive historical tradition began. What it means to be a superhero is, in effect, to be a character created with the intention of participating in this specific historical tradition. Characters that fail to satisfy Coogan's criteria could, in principle, still count as superheroes so long as they are intended as responses to, or variations upon, this tradition. And characters, like Gandalf the White, that satisfy Coogan's criteria but that are not superheroes are to be explained by the fact that they are *not* intended to be a part of the superhero tradition.

> **Superhero Tradition View**: A character x is a superhero if and only if x was created or repurposed in a way suitably historically connected to the story-telling tradition popularized in the 1930s with the publication of *Action Comics* #1 featuring Superman and similar comics.

If the Superhero Tradition View is correct, then a perennial concern of superhero fans and scholars emerges as especially urgent: When did the tradition of superheroes begin? On one view, superheroes precede comics, tracing back to costumed pulp characters like the Shadow and Doc Savage, and then emerge in the medium with masked comic strip avengers like The Phantom, which preceded Superman. On other views, the lineage of superhero stretches back even further to literary figures like the Scarlet Pimpernel. (See Gavaler (2017) for a recent and wide-ranging overview.)

When we focus our attention on superheroes *within comic books*, a recurring organizational tool is the "metallurgic" chronology, developed by comics creators and fans, which partitions mainstream North American comics. The dawn of the Golden Age—and so the critical ascendance of superheroes—comes with Superman's first appearance in *Action Comics* #1 (1939) and includes the emergence of characters like Batman, Wonder Woman, and Captain America. The Silver Age, which runs from the mid-1950s to the early 1970s, was dominated by the popularity of superheroes with richer psychological characterization like Lee and Ditko's Spider-Man and Lee and Kirby's Fantastic Four and the X-Men. The Bronze Age, spanning the 1970s to the mid-1980s, is often characterized as a period in which accumulated continuity of preceding decades piled up while creators increasingly engaged with social concerns like racism and drug abuse. The

Bronze Age was also marked by the emergence of "grittier" superhero comics that signaled a tonal about-face from the Golden Age. Frank Miller's *Daredevil* (1979–83) and *Dark Knight Returns* (1986) and Alan Moore and Dave Gibbon's *Watchmen* (1986) were palpably dark and violent hits which ran roughshod over the stark moral divides between good and evil that were typical in the Golden and Silver Ages.

However we carve up its history, if the Superhero Tradition View is correct, it's only in virtue of participating in this lineage that a character is properly counted as a superhero—regardless of whatever remarkable powers, moral code, or spiffy costume they might possess. And, while the Superhero Tradition View is vague in its own respects—for example, with regard to what a "suitable historical connection" is—we take it fare better than the Tripartite View when it comes to including characters which that view mistakenly leaves out like Jessica Jones and excluding characters which that view mistakenly includes like Gandalf the White.

With the Superhero Tradition View in hand, let's return to the Superhero Membership Question and the prospects for the Superheroes Included View. Now that we have an account of superheroes, can we simply use their inclusion to define superhero comics? We think not. Superman and Spider-Man (or parodic proxies) regularly appear in comedy comics like *Mad* or *What The--?!*. Neil Gaiman's sprawling epic *The Sandman* (1989–96) is hardly a superhero comic but contains cameos by Batman, Superman, and others. We can readily imagine horror comics in which superheroes briefly appear only to be slaughtered by monsters. These and other examples show that the boundaries of the superhero genre aren't fixed solely by which stories superheroes appear in but upon the appearance of superheroes in certain kinds of stories. This doesn't mean that we don't require an analysis of what it is to be a superhero. Instead, it means that along with an understanding of what superheroes are, we need an understanding of how they are *used* to create superhero comics. There is, then, good reason to reject the Superheroes Included View. But, if we can't straightforwardly define superhero comics in terms of superheroes, what *else* do we need to distinguish superhero comics?

Suppose, for a moment, that the superhero genre is a subgenre of the adventure genre and therefore sits alongside other subgenres like jungle or pirate comics. On this view, the narrative requirements for inclusion in the adventure genre—most notably, peril, stakes, risk, and action—just need to be coupled with the presence of superheroes as the focal elements of the narrative in order to distinguish the superhero genre. Roughly speaking, superhero comics are just adventure comics primarily featuring superheroes.

Similarly, pirate comics are adventure comics primarily featuring pirates, jungle comics are adventure comics primarily set in a jungle, and so on. Although this view enjoys some plausibility, there is reason to suspect that superhero comics are not simply definable as adventure comics with superheroes. Superhero comics, we submit, are more closely tied to their setting than this proposal acknowledges.

Despite the presence of fantastic powers, technology, aliens, magic, and other oddities in superhero comics, there is a prevailing trend within superhero comics: they are (characteristically) set in the present in a story-world that departs from actuality only minimally and in ways that primarily accommodate the existence of superheroes.[9] Overwhelmingly, the world of superhero comics diverges from reality in this very distinctive way: it normalizes the possession of fantastic powers and the use of costumes and code names. There are not, for example, widespread and grotesque physical mutations of the populace nor are there typically weird culinary or non-story-relevant historical departures from the actual world. Superhero worlds are tinkered with just enough to permit superheroes and supervillains. And, given the countless ways they could in principle differ, they are conspicuously anchored to reality. Stories that feature remarkable characters but that are set in the distant past, far future, or wildly different worlds are, at best, awkwardly included in the genre. Such stories are far more usually treated as instances of, say, science fiction or fantasy.

While different superhero stories account for the existence of superheroes in different ways (postulating fictional technology, science, magic, etc.), we take it that stories with settings that exhibit this distinctive, targeted divergence are nonetheless "anchored in actuality." Given this feature of superhero comics, we are inclined toward the following proposal for analyzing the superhero genre:

> **Anchored Superhero Adventure View**: A comic x is properly included in the superhero genre if and only if x is an adventure comic, anchored in actuality, with superheroes as focal characters.

Importantly, this account is noncircular only when paired with an independent account of what it is to be superhero, which is precisely what the Superhero Tradition View supplies. It is, however, a vice of the Anchored Superhero Adventure View that it simply assumes that we can use the category of "adventure comic" to define the superhero genre. Obviously, this means that if this definition is to be informative, an account of the adventure genre is also needed.[10] We won't take up that challenge here, but we will note that unlike alternatives approaches, this account makes clear that superhero stories emerge from a broader adventure storytelling tradition rather than as some kind of sui generis, incomparable genre category.

The Anchored Superhero Adventure View, when paired with the Superhero Tradition View, means that superhero comics are historically specific. That doesn't entail, however, that all genres are historically specific. In fact, in the next section, we'll explore an approach to defining the horror genre which seeks to avoid a historical specificity requirement.

6. Another Case Study: What Are Horror Comics?

Let's now take up the case of horror comics. Philosophical investigations into horror stem, in large part, from an abiding interest in a puzzle at the heart of the genre. This puzzle, often called "the paradox of horror," is typically presented as a trilemma, which consists of three plausible claims that stand in apparent tension. Here's the first claim:

FEAR: The experience of fear is intrinsically unpleasant.

FEAR is a broadly psychological claim. Humans dislike the experience of fear or terror, and, in some harrowing cases, individual's experiences of fear are robust enough to cause long-term psychological harm. Like sorrow or anxiety, there are contexts in which the experience of fear can be managed or stomached, and, in truly exceptionally cases like skydiving, humans can arguably disregard or overcome it. But, in marked contrast with oft-pursued feelings like joy, delight, or happiness, human aversion to fearful experiences suggests that fear is, by its very nature, unpleasant.

Here's the second claim:

GENERATE: Works of fiction within the horror genre reliably generate the experience of fear in audiences and audiences are aware that works within the horror genre do this.

We've all encountered works of horror that fail miserably in their efforts to induce fear in their audience. These tend to be memorable precisely because of the extent of their failure—for example, poorly conceived horror movies that induce howls of laughter for their errant judgments about what is and isn't scary. Unlike these outliers, most works of horror succeed in generating experiences of fear ranging from mere startles to searing existential dread. And, while we can easily imagine a clueless customer having no idea what they're in for when they purchase Junji Ito's *Uzumaki* (1998–99), this is a fairly rare occurrence: individuals typically know that the work their engaging with is an instance of the horror genre and that works of horror typically induce experiences of fear.

And now for our third claim:

CONSUMPTION: Many people actively or willingly serve as audiences to works of fiction within the horror genre.

CONSUMPTION is a sociological claim. A fondness for horror fiction, whether on the page or the screen, is by no means universal. And, while most of us know someone who steadfastly avoids engaging with horror fictions, we also probably all know someone who actively seeks out the newest horror films, novels, or comics. In the middle of this spectrum are consumers who occasionally, but willingly, engage with horror fictions.

To see why these three claims together yield a philosophical puzzle, suppose for a moment that you didn't know anything about the patterns regarding how humans consume fiction (e.g., what and how much of various genres they engage with). Suppose, however, that you do know that *FEAR* and *GENERATE* are true. Given this knowledge, it would be exceptionally reasonable to predict that since fear is intrinsically unpleasant and people know that horror fictions generate fear, people will never (or almost never) consume horror fictions. After all, in most other domains, people actively avoid unpleasant things! Imagine your surprise, then, upon learning that people bought *Tales from the Crypt* (1950–5) by the hundreds of thousands or that millions of people have watched William Friedkin's *The Exorcist* (1973).

The philosophical project surrounding the paradox of horror is, in effect, to explain how *CONSUMPTION, FEAR,* and *GENERATE* can be reconciled with one another. Or, put as a question: Why do people actively or willingly seek out fiction-induced experiences that they know are exceptionally likely to be unpleasant and, indeed, aversive? Importantly, this puzzle is different from, say, individuals seeking out pleasant experiences that are likely to harm them in the long term (e.g., unsafe or unhealthy activities). It's also importantly different from the question of why experiences like skydiving are somewhat popular despite being riddled with fear, since that fear is generated not by fictions but by nonfictional experiences.

There are a range of philosophical proposals for addressing the paradox of horror.[11] But the one on which we'll focus—discussed by Noël Carroll in *Philosophy of Horror* (1990)—doubles as a theory of the horror genre itself. As Carroll observes, fear and horror are inextricably linked. For, just as works of comedy aim to induce humorous amusement, works of horror intend to generate fear. This appeal to intentions is crucial. Notice that we feel no pressure, for example, to categorize as horror those works of fiction from which fear is generated unintentionally or accidentally. Suppose, for example, that you read a romance comic in which the protagonist dies of a tragic illness and, as a result, you are stricken with fear that you yourself are ill. Alternatively, you might, for instance, find the vile political humor in an old comedy so disturbing that you're horrified at its creators. Even so, there is no reason to think these works are horror comics. They are, instead, rightly described as unintentionally horrifying.

Furthermore, works of horror must intend not just to cause fear but to cause fear *in a distinctive way*. Consider so-called educational films that present stories about teen pregnancy, drug use, or speeding in hopes of terrifying their audiences into avoiding certain behaviors. If successful, such fictions are explicitly invested in generating fear in their audiences. But, despite their intentional fear-mongering, there's no temptation to categorize them as horror films. While they invite audiences to direct their fear toward actual behaviors, depicted in wildly exaggerated ways, works of horror invite their audiences to direct their fear toward entities, behaviors, or events that importantly diverge from our expectations of the actual world. The most familiar narrative device—the inclusion of which Carroll claims is essential to horror fiction—is what likely sprang to mind as soon as we mentioned horror: *monsters*.

According to Carroll, fictions fall within the horror genre when they are intended to generate in their audience feelings of fear and disgust toward monsters. As he summarizes his view:

[T]he objects of art-horror are such that they are both disgusting and fascinating, both disturbing and interesting, because they are classificatory misfits. [. . .] Fascination is not remote from art-horror, but is related to it as a probable recurring concomitant. Moreover, it is a recurring concomitant because the genre specializes in impossible, and, in principle, unknowable beings. This is the attraction of the genre.[. . .] We seek out horror fictions because the specific fascination they afford is bound up with the fact that it is animated by the same type of object that gives rise to art-horror. (191)

Carroll's accounts of intention, the nature of fear and disgust, and the concept of a monster are sophisticated and deserve elaborate attention. Here, however, we'll simply isolate three central commitments of the theory: (i) works of horror include monsters, (ii) works of horror intend to generate fear and disgust, and (iii) the "targets" of fear and disgust in works of horror are monsters. Carroll's defense of this theory proceeds, in part, by observing the common structures that emerge in typical and formative works within the horror genre—most notably, literary works like Bram Stoker's *Dracula* (1897) and Mary Shelley's *Frankenstein* (1818) and contemporary horror films like *The Exorcist*. Carroll's account does, of course, face numerous challenges, several of which draw upon apparent counterexamples in film, which are useful for getting a clearer sense of how his theory functions.

Here is the first challenge. A potentially surprising feature of Carroll's account is the essential role of disgust, alongside fear, as an intended audience affect. In defense of this claim, Carroll notes that throughout the literary history of horror, we find characters drawing back, recoiling, and aghast at monsters and, given this emotional valence, fear alone seems insufficient to characterize *horror*. He notes that "[i]n film and onstage, the characters shrink from the monsters, contracting themselves in order to avoid the grip of the creature but also to avert an accidental brush against this unclean being"(1990: 17). To assess this disgust requirement, suppose that someone produced a film, *Attack of the Killer Tornado*, about a sentient tornado, hell-bent on destruction. The tornado whirls about, by design, moving from town to town. People are scared out of their wits. While this story features a monster in the form of sentient tornado and the audience experiences fear toward it, Carroll's account would exclude this work from the horror genre insofar as this cyclonic wind creature induces no feelings of disgust. For Carroll, this story and others featuring impossible natural disasters aren't works of horror since audiences evince fear in the absence of disgust.

On to the second challenge: suppose someone produced a comic, *Suburbs of Frankenstein*, about an ugly but well-intentioned creature sadistically hounded by townspeople in increasingly terrible ways. As the townspeople descend into their perverse torturing of the monster, readers find their hostile and cruel behavior a continuing source of fear and disgust, but feel only sympathy for the forlorn monster. Provided that we never feel fear and disgust directed toward the monster, Carroll's account entails that in spite of having all of the "raw ingredients" of horror—namely, fear, disgust, and a monster—*Suburbs of Frankenstein* is put together in such a way that it falls outside of the horror genre. This is because of the requirement that fear and disgust be experienced *toward a monster* and the observation that while their behavior is despicable, the townspeople are not monsters (in the relevant sense).

This challenge makes clear that on Carroll's account, horror has a distinctive affective structure regarding who and what our attitudes are directed toward. But it also shows that we need to be able to distinguish the monstrous from the non-monstrous. According to Carroll, monsters are "beings that do not exist according to the lights of contemporary science" (1990: 40). They could not exist according to our familiar understanding of the world. As Carroll points out, there are myriad ways to "make a monster." We can stitch together concepts that are logically incompatible (e.g., the living dead) or physically impossible (e.g., spectral beings that move through walls) or contrary to what we know about nature (e.g., swarms of ants that move together with astounding intellect and purpose). For Carroll, monsters "are beings or creatures that specialize in formlessness, incompleteness, categorical interstitiality, and categorical contradictoriness" (1990: 32). Rather strikingly, this means that Superman is, by Carroll's lights, a monster—an issue we'll return to shortly.

Finally, the third challenge: Carroll's theory of monsters entails that monsters must be impossible (outside of fictional contexts). It therefore excludes a range of familiar films and novels from the horror genre. Since Steven Spielberg's 1975 film *Jaws* (unlike its sequels) features an odd but by no means impossible great white shark, it is a film (and source novel) without a monster and therefore not a work of horror. Similarly, while films like Alfred Hitchcock's *Psycho* (1960) and Ari Aster's *Midsommar* (2019) involve remarkable circumstances and induce experiences of fear and disgust, the phenomena of violent psychopathy and cultish, ritualized violence are, sadly, by no means impossible. So, according to Carroll, these are also not properly included in the horror genre.[12]

Carroll's account of horror yields some controversial verdicts, but it does justice to some manifest features of the genre. And, if Carroll is correct, it's also the key to addressing the paradox of horror. Roughly speaking, Carroll's claims holds that audiences' fascination and interest with monsters, given their impossible nature, entices them to endure fear in their pursuit of understanding. For Carroll, "the horror story is driven explicitly by curiosity" (1990: 182). So, while monsters are liable to generate fear and disgust, audiences will stomach these unpleasant experiences on account of their curiosity. As Carroll puts it:

[W]orks of horror are those designed to function in such a way as to promote art-horror in audiences. . . . [T]he emotion of art-horror quintessentially involves a combination of fear and repulsion with respect to the thought of monsters like Dracula such that these cognitive states generate some sort of physical agitation, which might be as overt as tremblings and stomach churnings or as muted as tingling sensations or a heightened physical sense of apprehension, alertness, or foreboding. (1990: 52)

Evaluating the adequacy of Carroll's response to the paradox of horror is an ongoing philosophical enterprise, but our interest is whether it supplies us with a plausible account of the horror genre within the comics medium.

We can begin by presenting an answer to the Horror Membership Question that draws directly from Carroll's theory:

> **Feared Monsters View**: A comic *x* is properly included in the horror genre if and only if *x* is a fiction intended to generate feelings of fear and disgust, toward monsters, in its readers.

There's ample disagreement about which was the first horror comic book—perhaps it was Avon Comics' *Eerie #1* (1947) or *Classics Illustrated*'s adaptation of *Dr. Jekyll and Mr. Hyde* (1943) or some other potential candidate. But it is uncontroversial which horror comic books are the most influential: the horror comic anthologies published by EC Comics from 1950 through 1955. Although EC Comics was responsible for only 10 percent of the horror comics produced during this heyday of comics horror, they were consistently of high quality, featuring exemplary artists like Krigstein, Harvey Kurtzman, Wally Wood, and Reed Crandall. They were also unified by a common writing style that traced back to William Gaines's contribution alongside editor and scripter Al Feldstein, and the forceful work of colorist Marie Severin. The five years of EC Comics' success with horror ended rather abruptly with the emergence of the Comics Code Authority and an increasingly unfavorable public reception of comics. Somewhat infamously, this was exacerbated by Gaines's generally unsuccessful efforts to defend the industry's practices while testifying to a senate subcommittee egged on by Wertham's condemnation of comics.

As a historical episode in comics history, the intrigue and significance of the 1950s is unparalleled. In no small part, this is because these senate hearings prompted the Comics Code: a set of guidelines of what was effectively self-censorship by comics publishers.[13] These guidelines placed strict constraints on the narrative possibilities within readily available comic books. In doing so, they stifled the creative dimensions of mainstream

American comics for over thirty years and are chief culprits in manufacturing the sentiment that the comics medium is somehow intrinsically juvenile or unsophisticated. But, prior to this interregnum in horror comics (on the newsstand, at least), EC Comics imprinted its influence on all horror comics that followed.[14] In fact, it's difficult to find a discussion of horror comics that doesn't look backwards to the three horror anthology series *Tales from the Crypt*, *Vault of Horror*, and *Tomb of Terror* as something like founding documents of the genre. Not only are these comics frequently cited as the apogee of horror comics, they are categorized as such without qualification. In light of their formative and abiding influence, they are exemplars within horror comics, and, given their general notoriety, no view that excludes them from the horror genre is adequate. Indeed, any view that leaves their status as horror comics uncertain ought to be rejected.

What does the Feared Monsters View have to say about EC Comics contribution to horror? While fear and disgust are present in ample measure, there's a striking paucity of monsters, at least as Carroll's account characterizes them. In *Tales from the Crypt*, which typically featured four comics stories per issue, over the course of thirty issues and 120 stories, monsters appear in slightly less than half of the features. (Only 58, by our count.) Although each issue includes at least one story with a monster, only one issue (#35) includes four stories featuring what Carroll would recognize as monsters. There's no reason, however, to think *Tales from the Crypt* was a horror comic solely in virtue of its monster-featuring stories, especially given that the critical reception of the series is unqualified in its treatment of the entire series, its various issues, and their stories as horror. We find, for example, no evidence that *Tales from the Crypt* had only a smattering of horror features, much less that over half of it was somehow outside of horror.

Contrary to the Feared Monsters View, clear instances of horror abound even in the absence of monsters. A man, confused after meeting his new wife at a costume party, pries off her face believing it to be a mask (#38). A husband, trapped in his wife's grave, eats her body only to be poisoned by the substance he used to murder her (#23). A mortician mutilates dead bodies until, on account of his misdeeds, his body is strewn across various graves (#36). These tales are without monsters and, in other cases, the role of monsters is minimal or atypical. In several stories, a monster appears in the final panel as a kind of shocking turn but might just as well have been replaced by a sadistic human. In still others, there's no monster but, instead, a human pretending to be a monster or merely a delusion or hallucination of a monster. To be sure, Carroll's discussion of horror reflects the diverse ways in which monsters might figure into horror stories, but, in scrutinizing *Tales from the Crypt* and the other EC Comics horror series, a substantial discrepancy between what counts as a horror comic and the Feared Monsters View emerges.

We've just presented—*ahem*—the Case of the Missing Monsters, so, in seeking to understanding horror comics, what are our options? We might, first of all, hope to repair the Feared Monsters View by revising it in such a way that at least in its application to comics, it delivers the correct verdict and unambiguously counts *Tales from the Crypt* stories as horror comics. One approach might be to liberalize Carroll's account of monsters by holding that insofar as the world seems to contrive fearsome and revolting events, there's a lurking monster that's gone unnoticed—namely, the vile fabric of reality itself.

Another approach, which Carroll himself seems to adopt, distinguishes between works of horror and "tales of dread," where the latter are narrative fantasies about an event in which a character is punished in a fitting, mordantly humorous way (1990: 224). While this is a perfectly apt description of some stories in *Tales from the Crypt*, Carroll explicitly distinguishes between tales of dread and works of horror. He says: "horror stories have a feature that Tales of Dread lack, namely monsters including supernatural ones like vampires, aliens from outer space, spiders larger than houses due to their exposure to radiation, and so on." But, however good a theory of tales of dread might be, the point stands: a theory of horror that excludes *Tales from the Crypt* is surely an unsatisfactory theory of horror comics.[15]

Another option for addressing the Case of the Missing Monsters is to simply reject Carroll's proposal. Other philosophical treatments of horror warrant consideration, perhaps most notably Cynthia Freeland's theory of horror in film, which foregrounds the role of the horror genre as an examination of evil. According to Freeland (2004: 190), "[p]eople enjoy the way good horror stories depict human encounters with evil—whether to understand and defeat it, or to succumb to its power and temptations." Adapting this account to answer the Horror Membership Question would, however, require substantial efforts to explain why superhero comics, with their often intense focus on supervillains and the evil that persons do, fall outside the horror genre. It's important to note, too, that Freeland is explicit that her account is of our *interest* in the horror genre and is not intended as an analysis of the genre itself.

A final option for tackling the Case of the Missing Monsters returns us to an issue with which we began our inquiry into the philosophy of genre: whether we can define a genre like horror without explicit reference to its history. In our efforts to understand horror comics, the claims in which we ought to have the greatest confidence are largely historical and stem from comics practice—for example, that *Tales from the Crypt* is a horror comic. As we've seen, theories of genre that fail to respect such claims simply prove inadequate. Why not, then, simply opt for a historicist treatment of genre like the Tradition View, which abandons the efforts of Carroll and others to somehow extract the conceptual essence of a specific genre? While the appeal of adopting such a position is considerable, in the next section, we'll argue that views like Carroll's are attractive, not only because they further our understanding of the internal structure of genres but also because they underwrite the kinds of explanations that make genres worth thinking and talking about in the first place.

7. The Indispensability of Genre

Science, philosophy, and almost any area of inquiry or communication rely upon cognitive "shortcuts" like simplification, abbreviation, and idealization. In some cases, this is because of preventable errors or outright mistakes, but there are myriad instances of simplification, abbreviation, and idealization that are unobjectionable and downright necessary for practical purposes. Humans are, after all, cognitively limited. We have finite mental capacities that constrain our memories, our ability to appreciate complexity, and our efforts to make sense of quantities both large and small. We abbreviate numerical constants and evolutionary histories to ease computational strain. And we simplify in communicating and arguing for and against theories. These shortcuts are part and parcel of our efforts to make sense of the world. We know that π doesn't terminate at its thirtieth decimal place and that planes aren't frictionless, but, for various purposes, we are justified in acting *as if* these things are true. Were we infinitely powerful thinkers, such idealizations and simplifications would be unnecessary, but, sadly, our intellectual limits are all too apparent.

On one view about genre categories, which we'll call *genre skepticism*, they are rightly viewed in parallel to these cognitive shortcuts. As with idealizing about complex systems, genre categories afford us a powerful organizational tool for talking about sprawling, unruly domains. But, ultimately, they are intellectual or aesthetic fabrications used only to simplify and facilitate our interaction with a vast number of individual works. So, although we act as though there's a meaningful category of "horror" or "western" and we use these categories to explain facts about reception and evaluation, genre categories are like frictionless planes or π with a terminating decimal expansion: useful simplifications that when taken to accurately describe the world ultimately distort our understanding.

But why should we think that genre categories are ultimately eliminable, like idealizations or simplifications? One argument proceeds by insisting that genre categories are eliminable because they don't *really* explain what we think they explain. Suppose, for example, that Steve gets a case of the heebie-jeebies while reading Julia Gfrörer's haunting comic *Laid Waste* (2016), about burial and plague. If we ask for an explanation of why Steve was scared, we might remark offhand that *Laid Waste* is a horror comic. Crucially, however, *Laid Waste* gave Steve the creeps, not because it is in a specific genre category—after all, some horror comics aren't scary—but because of its individual features like Gfrörer's brittle, sparse style and understated, haunting dialogue.

According to this line of argument, whenever we ask about the effects of a comic upon its audience, our best explanation of those effects will be in terms of *that very comic's* individual features. In contrast, facts about which genre categories it does or doesn't fall into are irrelevant. So, when we try to explain the impact of various comic as with Steve's reading of *Laid Waste*, our best explanations—not just the simplest or easiest to state—are explanations that make reference to the individual features of the specific comic at hand. Genres are, on this view, an impediment to a genuine understanding of a medium like comics, since the deepest account ought to somehow strip away all these idealizations and simplifications and involve only discussion of specific comics and their interrelations.

This argument for genre skepticism raises some difficult questions, not only about genre but about explanation and the limits of idealization. (We're also not the first to take up these issues about explanation and genre; see Liao (2016).) While each of the premises in the earlier argument can (and should) be challenged, we'll now argue that even if genre categories don't show up in our best explanation of audience responses, they do show up in different comics-related explanations—for example, regarding the broader structure of comics production. We take this to be reason to think that while genre categories are initially borne out of idealization and simplification, they are not eliminable, not even in principle. For this reason, believing in the horror genre isn't like believing that π has only thirty decimal places. While they're both useful beliefs under the right conditions, the former belief is one we should retain even if we had all the time, knowledge, and computational power in the world. Put differently, even an infinitely powerful thinker would need to posit genre categories in trying to make sense of comics. We also think that the case study we'll offer is a helpful illustration of how genre categories often explain phenomena through their interaction with each other.

Here, then, is an exceptionally strange fact: there are remarkably few scary comics that feature superheroes.[16] To be clear, there are *some* (e.g., Batman's *Arkham Asylum* (1989) or *Red Rain* (1991)). But, not only is this number conspicuously small, there's ample reason to think it should be quite large. After all, audiences invested in superhero comics overlap significantly with horror comics audiences. Artists and writers that work in one genre often work in the other. And, perhaps most obviously, there are myriad characters that appear in the superhero genre that would, were they to appear in the horror genre, serve perfectly well as monstrous objects of fear and disgust. Sociologically, it is a striking feature of contemporary comics that despite their affinities in production and reception, scary comics featuring superheroes are oddly limited in number. (Somewhat famously, Mignola's various *Hellboy* stories have been cast as Lovecraft meets Kirby, but, for all its horror genre trappings, *Hellboy* is conspicuously short on scares.) This is a fact about comics that cries out for explanation and, while we've stated that fact without reference to any genre categories, we contend that the best explanation of this fact requires that we draw upon exactly these kinds of categories.

In the previous section, we set out Carroll's account of horror and noted some potential objections to it. When it comes to comics, however, we think it's a virtue of his account that it provides the raw material for a plausible explanation of this lack of scary superhero comics. To see why, two key points about Carroll's account warrant comment. First, according to Carroll, monsters abound in comics and, perhaps surprisingly, include characters like Superman, the Invisible Woman, and Krypto the Superdog. That's because Carroll takes monsters to be characters that are impossible and unreconcilable with our understanding of the actual world and, quite clearly, Krypto and others fit the bill. That said, Carroll would deny that (almost all) Superman comics are horror comics. That's because the intended attitudes of audiences toward Superman are entirely different than the feelings of terror and revulsion characteristic of the horror genre. Second, recall that the feeling of fear, anxiety, or an excited sense of peril is importantly different, as Carroll argues, from that paired sense of dread and disgust that marks our engagement with the horror genre. We're not merely afraid that Dracula will kill Renfield. We're also revulsed by what Dracula is and what he's likely to do to Renfield. For this reason, a reader's fear (limited though it may be) that Gorilla Grodd will destroy Central City in a Flash comic is importantly different than, say, fear and disgust at Grodd's mere presence in the world.

So how should we explain the comparative lack of scary superhero comics? Here's our best proposal. According to Carroll, a horror comic must generate fear and disgust in its audience and that fear and disgust needs to be directed toward a monster. The story needs to manipulate the audience to attend to and carefully consider the prospects of harm. The art needs to magnify the revulsion felt toward the monster. An absolutely crucial technique for accomplishing this is to foreground a character that can serve as a proxy for the audience.[17] Our sympathetic engagement with this character—feeling what the story suggests they feel—is therefore a critical cue that shapes our affective responses to monsters and events in the story. For instance, to see a character bemoan the hideous visage of a creature while drawing back in terror is to understand and entertain the appropriateness of fearing and being disgusted by that creature. Indeed, it proves somewhat difficult to induce the requisite fear and disgust via a story that contains no characters with affective responses that can inform our own responses.

Now, consider an obvious feature of superhero comics: they most prominently feature superheroes. While supporting characters and supervillains also appear, our affective engagement with superhero comics is driven by our attention to the focal superheroes. More often than not, we think and care about what Batman feels, not what helpless bystanders, Robin, Commissioner Gordon, or Killer Moth feel. And here's a remarkable psychological fact that sets superheroes apart from the rest of us: they're almost never afraid. They are psychologically alien to the rest of us, since, when faced with a sentient pile of slime or mutated crocodile-human hybrid, they're not paralyzed by revulsion but are instead concerned with how to swiftly incapacitate such a creature. As focal characters, the affect of superheroes shapes the affect of the audience and, given the extremely rare event of felt disgust and fear in superheroes, it proves all but impossible to generate the requisite amount needed to turn a superhero comic into a horror comic. Case in point: the fact that Hellboy is almost never scared partly explains why *Hellboy* is almost never scary.

So why are there strikingly few scary comics with superheroes? Because the narrative elements of the superhero genre are in practical conflict with the affective aims of the horror genre. When you have superheroes around, it proves exceptionally difficult to induce the monster-directed fear and disgust characteristic of horror. For example, upon reading "Moon of the Wolf" in Len Wein and Neal Adams's *Batman* #255 (1974), which features a werewolf, there is no temptation to deem the comic a horror comic. It's merely a superhero comic with a werewolf in it. In large measure, that's because Batman evinces not the slightest fear or disgust at the creature and, in turn, readers are left similarly unafraid and undisgusted.

When comics with superheroes do turn scary, it usually requires exceptional narrative deviation. Consider the exceptionally rare case in which Superman is depicted as substantially afraid—importantly, not merely worried or concerned but outright terrified. To induce genuine terror in a being like Superman, we require narrative machinations that, as in Dan Jurgens and Chuck Dixon's *Superman/Aliens* (1995), strip away his exceptional physical powers, place him in an entirely foreign setting, and pepper his circumstances with death and gore. Only under those remarkable circumstances do we find Superman fearful and disgusted and, in turn, capable of producing the necessary affect in readers. The difficulty in overcoming these hurdles is the culprit that explains the "hole" in the comics medium where "scary comics featuring superheroes" should be. And, if Carroll's View is correct, this hole is due to a subtle incompatibility between the genre categories of superhero and horror comics. Without relying upon these genre categories as analytic tools, we're simply not in a position to provide our best understanding of comics practice and, in particular, the paucity of scary superhero comics.

We've sketched one argument for the essential role of genre in making sense of comics. But there's a further moral here for the philosophy of genre in comics and other mediums. Notice that the explanation we just offered draws upon substantial claims about the internal structure of genres like horror and superhero comics. If, instead, genres are understood exclusively and exhaustively as historical traditions with no defining features or essential internal structure, we would be unable to offer such an explanation. That's because traditions can veer off in all manner of different directions or take any of a variety of paths, but categories distinguished by essential internal structure like narrative, character, or setting requirements have no comparable freedom. It's only once we view genre categories as having characteristic elements—perhaps their settings, intended audience affects, or narrative themes—that we can offer explanations of the sort just provided. So, while historicist accounts of genres have obvious appeal and might be apt for making sense of specific genres, it is only when genres are defined by something more than a mere tradition—for example, in the way that Carroll seeks to define the horror genre—that we gain the power to explain certain kinds of phenomena.

8. Recommended Readings

Our focus in this chapter has been squarely on philosophical treatments of genre, which are tiny in comparison with inquiries into the notion from other disciplines—most notably, literature. Duff (2000) is a helpful anthology for approaches outside philosophy.

Philosophical inquiry into the nature of horror has sprung up mostly in response to Carroll (1990). For a range of challenges to Carroll's approach, see Windsor (2019), Gaut (2008), and Carroll (2009). For a related but distinct approach, see Freeland (2002). On horror comics specifically, see Jones (2016).

The literature within comics studies on superheroes is vast and expanding rapidly as licit areas of scholarly focus seem to widen. Coogan (2013) is a useful starting point for attempts to define the genre and includes a number of creator perspectives. Hatfield, Heer, and Worcester (2013) is a carefully assembled anthology of broader and influential discussions of the genre. See also Smith (2016). Ndalianis (2009) includes a wealth of essays focused on relatively recent superhero comics. The best available large-scale overview of the genre is Gavaler (2017). Singer (2020) is a useful starting point for comics studies perspectives on the genre. For a series of takes on psychology and superhero comics, see Rosenberg's *Our Superheroes, Ourselves* (2013).

For overviews of various other genres, see Cremins (2016) on funny animal comics, Grady (2016) on westerns, and Rifas (2016) on war comics.

7

Representing Social Categories in Comics

1. The Significance of Social Representation

While we were in the process of writing this book, the world said a sad goodbye to a real-life hero: Georgia Representative John Lewis, who not only served in the US House of Representatives for over thirty years but also played key leadership roles in the struggle for civil rights in the United States. Lewis helped lead the first march from Selma to Montgomery and famously spoke as a representative of the Student Nonviolent Coordinating Committee prior to the delivery of Rev. Martin Luther King Jr.'s iconic "I Have a Dream" speech. He memorably encouraged young activists to get into "good trouble:" the sort of social and political disruption instrumental to the advancement of equity and human rights. And even with his busy and productive political life, Lewis managed to leave his mark on comics: his three-volume comic memoir, *March*—cowritten with Andrew Aydin and illustrated by Nate

Powell—was released from 2013 to 2015. These volumes received numerous awards, ranging from Eisner Awards to the National Book Award for Young People's Literature and the Robert F. Kennedy Book Award, the latter two of which had never previously been awarded to a comic.[1]

A major source of inspiration leading to Lewis's choice to tell his story in comic form was his early exposure to *Martin Luther King and the Montgomery Story*, a comic pamphlet published in 1957 with a script by Alfred Hassler and Benton Resnik (Figure 7.1). (Some detective work by comics historians suggests that Sy Barry handled art duties.) Lewis discovered this comic as a teenager, finding its presentation of the philosophies of nonviolent protest through civil disobedience deeply affecting. This discovery is a testament to the potential power of representation in comics: in a culture violently oppressive toward Black Americans, a young John Lewis had the rare opportunity of seeing himself and his interests represented in *Montgomery Story*.

To be clear, the presentation of King in *Montgomery Story* is simplified and idealized, especially when compared with more grounded and nuanced biographical comics like Ho Che Anderson's three-volume comic biography,

Figure 7.1 *Martin Luther King and the Montgomery Story* (1957), Alfred Hassler and Benton Resnik (script), Sy Barry (art). Rev. Martin Luther King speaks to an audience regarding protest and justice. © Fellowship of Reconciliation, www.forusa.org. Reprinted by permission.

King: A Comics Biography of Martin Luther King, Jr. (1993, 2002, 2003). Regardless, Lewis internalized the message of the comic as a call to further action. Indeed, without resorting to hyperbole, it is possible that had Lewis not encountered *Montgomery Story*, his involvement in the Civil Rights Movement—and, hence, the Civil Rights Movement itself—might have looked quite different. It is partly for this reason that Lewis went on to create *March*, saying, "I read the *Montgomery Story* and it was moving. I followed the drawings and it made it all real and explained the philosophy of nonviolence. I talk to thousands of kids every year, and I think the graphic novel I'm doing can be used to get that message out to people."[2] Lewis hoped to make the philosophy of nonviolence "real" to his target audience and did so by presenting an honest narrative of his experiences that might serve as an alternative to white-washed, sanitized (or simply false) depictions of the Civil Rights Movement many young Americans learn about in schools.

There are no shortage of worthwhile historical, political, and philosophical questions that emerge upon reflection on comics like *March* and *Montgomery Story*. But our interest in this chapter is an especially general one, prompted by attention to some evident facts about these comics: Lewis was inspired by *Montgomery Story* in part because it represents Martin Luther King as Black. More generally, *Montgomery Story* was a remarkable departure from most other depictions of Black characters in the comics medium up to that point. Similarly, *March* is a critically successful and historically significant comic because it faithfully represents a range of Black characters combatting oppression and anti-Black racism. In fact, if it failed to represent Martin Luther King as Black, *March* would be a highly distorted nonfiction account—distorted to the point that, indeed, even calling it "nonfiction" would feel quite inappropriate.

In some ways, the representation of race in comics might seem somewhat remarkable. That's because among the central insights of the philosophy of race is the fact that the construction of racial categories and the process of racialization—roughly, the ascription of "membership" in these categories— are astonishing in their complexity.[3] The social construction of racial categories is irreducibly connected with numerous and diverse factors including superficial physical characteristics, political power, geographic location, population genetics, historically inherited social taxonomies, and economic marginalization, among many others. An exhaustive explanation of why a given individual, at a specific time, among a specific group, in a particular place is racialized within a particular category therefore presupposes a staggering array of complexities.

But, if race is such an enormously complicated matter and is sensitive to such a vast range of considerations, why do readers seem to have so little challenge in racializing characters? How, in the face of this complexity, can readers so regularly and pervasively ascribe racial categories to characters? Remarkably, this projection of racial categories seems unhindered even when fictions involve strange counterfactual scenarios, alternative world histories, or manifest scientific impossibilities. Given the profound complexity of racial categories and the incredibility of fictional worlds, the persistent and vivid projection of race onto characters, across genres, stands out as a striking phenomenon that requires explanation.

Consider the case of the EC Comics story "Judgment Day" (*Incredible Science Fiction* #33, 1956), written by Al Feldstein and William Gaines, drawn by Joe Orlando, and carefully explored in Qiana Whitted's book *EC Comics: Race, Shock, and Social Protest* (2019). The story details a representative of the Galactic Republic assessing the achievements of a robot civilization, which is marked by the social division of robots into two categories with manifestly unequal treatments. Ultimately, the robot civilization is barred from membership in the Galactic Republic until this inequality is redressed. While the analogy for race is obvious, the most controversial feature of the story—the one which led to resistance from the Comics Code Authority—is the reveal in the last panel when the representative removes his helmet.[4] Despite a fantastic, incredibly far-flung future with robot civilizations, spaceships, and who knows how much social and technological change, the single panel succeeds in racializing the character according to the racial categories operative in the context of the comic's creation and reception—specifically, as a Black man. That such a story exists and prompted the controversy it did is evidence enough that comics readers have little resistance to situating comics characters, fictional or nonfictional, with respect to racial categories.

Philosopher Johnathan Flowers (2020) argues that the racialization of characters within comics is irreducibly tied to the orientation of particular readers and to the individual contexts of the reception and the production of said comics. In discussing McCloud's *Understanding Comics*, Flowers explores McCloud's effort to, at one point, present his own cartoon avatar in a way that he describes as being without race or gender—as truly "universal." In contrast to McCloud's intention, however, Flowers argues that "McCloud . . . fails to recognize that it is his own whiteness that is amplified through simplification of his avatar" (2020: 210). More generally, Flowers emphasizes the significance of the audience's contributions in social representation, arguing that "what McCloud misses is the ways in which readers possess an initial orientation, an initial starting point that places the simplified character 'in reach' so that they may fill it with their identity"(2020: 222).

On one way of developing this sort of view, social representation is irreducibly subjective: the process of racializing characters is done by particular readers and allows for potentially radical subjective variation. But, for our part, it's difficult to view any reader for the *Montgomery Story* who fails to take MLK to be Black as anything short of an incompetent reader. For this reason, accepting the subjectivity of social representation shouldn't involve a radical relativism about the representation of social categories. While there are many axes of interpretable social representations in general, the inherently normative nature of picture-reading places limits on interpretive options regarding particular instances of social representation in comics.

Obviously, the capacity for comics to represent socially constructed categories is not limited to just racial categories. Characters are regularly represented with respect to other socially constructed categories: gender, ethnicity, sexual identity, disability, economic status, and many, many others. Just as the actual construction of social categories differs enormously, so too do the mechanisms of their social representation in comics. But, despite their considerable variation, a unifying feature of social categories is the remarkable complexity in their respective mechanisms of construction. There is nothing simple about the ascription of and identification with social categories like gender, ethnicity, disability, and sexual identity. Nonetheless, comics still tend to overwhelmingly succeed in efforts to present characters in relation to these categories. In fact, the dispositions of audiences to apply social categories afford comics creators various remarkable storytelling possibilities. Think, for example, of Marvel Comics regular but, upon reflection, deeply strange presentation of Death itself as a woman and a fitting object of lust by characters like Thanos. (Death is similarly personified and portrayed as a woman in Neil Gaiman's *The Sandman* series, though characterized in a quite different manner than the portrayal in Marvel's comics.)

As these sorts of cases make clear, when audiences engage with comics they are able to not merely relate characters to social categories but interpretively eager to do so. It is, in a loose sense, interpretively instinctual. Notice, however, that even if superficial characteristics might account for gendering Death as a woman or racializing the astronaut as Black in "Judgment Day," social representation is not a purely depictive matter. Not only is the connection between mere physical appearances and membership in social categories highly problematic, we see in many cases that social representation can be accomplished entirely in the absence of depiction—for example, through text or the interaction of text and other images besides those that might directly depict the character in question. Of course, this phenomenon isn't unique to comics: it's pervasive in narrative—as well as some nonnarrative—mediums. Given that, why focus on social representation within comics?

First, no comprehensive philosophical account of the comics medium is possible without making sense of its manifest features, one of which is, indeed, the representation of social categories. Readers can seek out and relate to racially diverse casts of characters. Critics can assess comics by noting that characters typify or undermine gender-based stereotypes. Historians can examine trends in the appearance and prominence of characters of different ethnicities. Social kinds are therefore an undeniable component of almost any engagement with comics, and this significance owes to our ingrained and seemingly irresistible practice of socially categorizing characters. The phenomenon of social representation as well as the norms surrounding it are therefore part and parcel of comics practice.

Second, comics can represent a lot of things—arguably, *any* things. In some cases, how they do so is of modest interest (e.g., How do comics represent tables?). In other cases, how comics creators meet representational challenges is of enormous formal and practical interest. How, for example, do comics represent motion, musical performance, or the moments before the creation of the universe? Inquiry into the representation of social categories sheds light not only on the nature of readerly activities (e.g., readers' persistent tendency to apply social categories) but also on the interaction of text with image, of history with intention, and of culture with power. Comics studies has, for this and other reasons, focused substantial energies on exactly these kinds of questions.

This chapter doesn't aim at anything like a comprehensive theory of social representation. Such an account wouldn't just be a theory of, say, when characters are represented as falling within a category—for example, being represented as Asian or being represented as heterosexual—but also a theory of when characters are represented as standing in any number of complicated categorial relationships— for example, being represented as nonwhite or being represented as straight-albeit-questioning. Viewed from the highest level of generality, then, our ambition might be to give an account of the conditions under which specific characters are represented as standing in a certain relation to given social categories. In other words, we might aim to answer:

> **Social Representation Question:** Under what conditions is a character depicted in a comic also depicted as a member of a particular social category?

In part for the reasons Flowers raised earlier, though, there is little hope for a theory that could both shed useful light on the distinctive kinds of social representation and, at the same time, apply comprehensively to all manner of social categories.

Suppose, for a moment, that we could answer the Social Representation Question by, say, simply claiming that characters are represented as being members of a social category just in case every ideal reader of a comic would imagine them as being members. Even so, this would tell us nothing at all about the comics-specific mechanisms that induce readers to racialize the astronaut in "Judgment Day" as Black or take Death to be a woman in various Marvel stories. For this reason, the prevailing practice within comics studies of focusing on the specific and heterogeneous mechanisms involved in the presentation of social categories seems the best approach available to us. As works by authors like Adilifu Nama (2011), Sheena Howard (2013), Leonard Rifas (2004), Rebecca Wanzo (2020), and others make clear, an account of how characters are racialized requires careful attention to the norms of genre, the presentation of speech, and the broader history of racial caricature.[5] The depth of this work is evidence that even if a one-size-fits-all theory of the representation of social categories were possible, it is unlikely to further our understanding of comics unless deeply grounded in the intricate specificities of the medium.

Where philosophy can play a potential clarificatory role in understanding social representation, however, is in helping us to think through the moral dimensions of social representation and especially its interaction with aesthetic and epistemic value. The inevitable difficulty of this task, though, is partly due to social representation being inherently normative in at least two ways. First, success in social representation in the *intentional* sense concerns the presentation of a character as read by audiences to stand in the proper relations to the social categories that the creator(s) of the comics intend(s). For instance, Jim Starlin, somewhat remarkably, succeeds in representing Death as a woman in *Captain Marvel*. In contrast, if Feldstein, Gaines, and Orlando had intended to represent the astronaut in "Judgment Day" as a woman, they were evidently unsuccessful. (Though, of course, they didn't.) Second, success in social representation in the *evaluative* sense concerns a character's presentation evaluated against a complex array of aesthetic and moral standards. Is the presentation in question nuanced and insightful with regard to the complex heterogeneity of the relevant category? Does it imply— overtly or covertly— unprincipled moral judgments about the relevant category?

Importantly, considerations of these senses of social representation—the intentional and the evaluative—often overlap. For instance, is the representational intention successful only because of the exploitation of stereotypes? A comprehensive ethics of social representation should, for example, help us explain why the dehumanizing presentation of Japanese characters in the Second World War-era superhero comics are indeed representations of Japanese people while, at the same time, explaining why these representations are so morally heinous. As is apparent, then, while we can conceptually distinguish intentional and evaluative issues, in practice, the assessment of either will typically involve considerations of both.

2. The Perils of Social Representation

In evaluating instances of social representation, a useful distinction among potential vices singles out three species: aesthetic viciousness, moral viciousness, and epistemic viciousness. (Importantly, these are "vicious" in the sense of being *vices*, not in the sense of being, say, actively nasty— though, doubtless, the latter are regularly the former.) As we discuss them, it is important to keep in mind that these species of viciousness frequently overlap or compound one another.

First, *aesthetic* vices pertain to aesthetic evaluation and manifest as detriments to a work's aesthetic value. For example, lettering a comic with serifs on the letter 'I' throughout or placing the first speaker on the right side of a panel usually constitutes aesthetic vices, as do needlessly convoluted page layouts or other formal misfires. Such features diminish the overall aesthetic value of the work, but, at the same time, they are in themselves neither immoral nor plausibly seen as a means of fostering ignorance or unwarranted belief.

Next, *moral* vices pertain to moral evaluation and manifest as detriments to a work's moral value. We hope that many would join us in taking to it to be a moral vice of a comic if it promotes vile moral beliefs or intentionally distorts facts to prompt wrongful action. For instance, a familiar moral condemnation of Robert Crumb's comics revolves around their regressive and violent depictions of women. No less common, of course, is praise for Crumb's cartooning as—independent of these moral issues—nonetheless aesthetically valuable. It is, in this sort of case, conceptually possible to extoll the aesthetic value of a work while still bemoaning its moral value (or vice versa).

Finally, *epistemic* vices pertain to epistemic evaluation and manifest as detriments to a work's epistemic value. A nonfiction memoir riddled with excusable errors (but errors nonetheless) is epistemically vicious insofar as it promotes false beliefs. But, if the story remains engaging and insightful, it might nevertheless be properly evaluated as aesthetically rich. And, provided that the errors are blameless and no one is harmed—rather than the errors being the result of culpable negligence or even intentional distortions—the epistemic viciousness occurs without any apparent moral harm or wrongdoing.

Just as social representation does not take place in a moral vacuum, it does not take place in an aesthetic or epistemic vacuum either. Good storytelling (in the aesthetic sense) might feature wrongful social representation and, conversely, virtuous social representation might find itself mired in bad storytelling. Either could present strict fidelity or thematic embellishments on the truth. There is, it seems, no straightforward way to infer from the presence or absence of morally vicious representations either the epistemic, aesthetic, or even ultimate moral value of a work. Consider, for example, the deft employment of heinous stereotypes by an artist who aims to pointedly and thoughtfully critique structural racism. It's important, for this reason, to note that the moral approbation or condemnation of specific social representation within a comic almost always leaves open what we ought to say about the comic on balance, either aesthetically, epistemically, or morally. As we'll argue later, however, this doesn't mean that the ethics of social representation can't exert certain kinds of significant—and in particular aesthetic—pressure on comics.

With these different species of viciousness in mind, our focus in the remainder of this section will be on morally vicious social representation: roughly, the wrongful presentation of characters in relation to social categories. We'll say more about how to explain or distinguish morally vicious social representation in the next section. Throughout, we'll also leave aside discussion of *nondistinctive* reasons we might find morally vicious social representation in comics—that is, reasons shared by many other non-comics mediums. Most notable among such nondistinctive reasons is the enormous discrepancy in the distribution of power and resources across social categories with regard to comics production and consumption, just as with other non-comics mediums. Indeed, we think that the fact that comics creators have disproportionately been cis-gender, heterosexual white men has done more to negatively impact social representation in comics than either of the two considerations we'll discuss here.

2.1. Vicious Cartoons

As we noted in Chapter 2, comics and cartooning are closely intertwined. While comics need not be cartoons, cartooning remains a dominant mode of comics creation and it is doubtless the most influential one. We won't try to offer anything like a philosophy of cartooning, but we can follow Molotiu (2020a) in noting that simplification, exaggeration, and abstraction are focal strategies of cartooning.

The relationship between cartooning and, in turn, comics and social representation is a tense one. If comics are disposed to be works of cartooning and works of cartooning are disposed to simplify, exaggerate, and abstract, there's reason to believe that comics are disposed toward morally vicious social representation. If, for instance, a cartoonist aims to offer commentary on members of a social category, the default strategy for singling out that social category will be to exaggerate putatively distinctive features, simplify their complex interaction with other factors (e.g., social context), and abstract away extraneous matters (e.g., diversity among members of a social category). This disposition is compounded by the historical trend of comics being compressed, portable, short-form works, sometimes limited to a single panel, and therefore disposed to engage in social representation in terms of only superficial depictions or immediately identifiable associations. Moreover, while certain cinematic portrayals of, for example, indigenous peoples warrant serious moral criticism, by virtue of being a photographic medium those portrayals are (at least typically) of nonetheless evidently human characters. Any survey of cartooning will, in contrast, turn up social representations of indigenous peoples as seemingly nonhuman, since the representational constraints guiding photographic representation are not present in cartooning. For these reasons, there is likely no medium in which stereotypes and caricature exert more gravity than in comics. This, in turn, makes the medium especially susceptible to instances of vicious social representation.

The history of cartooning is replete with evidence of the previous claim. Enormous swathes of cartooning involve distortive and stereotypical presentations of women, BIPOC characters, and non-European characters. Indeed, even Winsor McCay's *Little Nemo in Slumberland* (1905–27), which is lauded as a remarkable achievement in comics on account of its inventive formal contributions, features a morally vicious social representation in the form of an African "imp" character depicted in blackface. Such examples are all too easy to come by in the history of comics and again serve as a reminder that aesthetic value stands in a fraught relationship to moral value. *Little Nemo* is an aesthetically significant work and worthy of attention and appreciation, even in spite of its participation in offensive racial caricature. But such attention or appreciation comes with a positive duty to acknowledge and condemn its racist depictions of certain characters.

Perhaps the least appreciated sort of viciousness in cartooning or—more specifically, caricature—is epistemic in nature. After defending the "essentially distortive nature of caricature" and pointing out the affinity between the editorial cartoon and caricature, Christy Mag Uidhir (2013: 147) argues,

> Even though the editorial cartoon purports to inform its audience about the world, given its employ of caricature, the editorial cartoon requires for its uptake an audience less than ideally rational . . . editorial cartoons traffic substantially, if not exclusively, in radical over-simplifications of often extremely complex and nuanced positions, persons, events, and gross exaggerations of the relevance, importance, and scope of certain features or aspects salient to those positions, persons, events, yet via the illicit work of caricature, the editorial cartoon can nonetheless provide a comparatively far more expedient, simple, and widely accessible manner of delivering for uptake true and false propositions alike. This, taken together with the chief putative subject matter being the eminently profound subject matter of the moral, provides ample reason to consider the misuse and abuse of pictorial caricature something that even the honest have reason to fear.[6]

Mag Uidhir's argument strikes us as highly plausible. And, if he is correct, then the comics medium is disposed toward morally vicious social representation and, it seems, toward epistemically vicious representation as well. Notice, however, that being disposed toward vicious social representation is not an excuse for producing vicious social representation any more than being disposed to lie is an excuse for doing so.

That said, the presence of this disposition arguably makes those cases in which comics engage in positive representation even more worthy of attention and often also admiration. This is especially true, it seems, of those moments in comics history where we find trenchant political commentary that eschews or criticizes vicious social representation. So, while the hackneyed recapitulation of racial, ethnic, or sexual stereotypes for comedic purposes is as cheap as it is odious, the artful dissection of the moral inconsistency of dominant ideologies or the illuminating presentation of moral analogies are moments when social representation in comics is conspicuously virtuous. This distinction is, we think, what divides intellectually flaccid moral outrage porn—like, in our estimation, the work of figures such as Ben Garrison—with the reflective social commentary encountered in the best political cartooning.[7]

2.2. Superheroes and the Social Order

Cartooning is a practice that cuts across the comics medium and, if we're right, works of cartooning are disposed toward vicious social representation. (Again, that doesn't mean they *must* include instances of vicious social representations any more than every fragile glass must be shattered.) As we'll now suggest, there's at least one additional reason that comics—or at least *many* comics—are disposed toward morally vicious social representation: the particular prevalence of the superhero genre. While a disposition toward morally vicious social representation isn't unique to superhero comics (e.g., western comics are no less fraught), given the outsized popularity of superhero comics in North American markets, it is a pervasive one. Before setting out why the genre is disposed in this way, it's important to note a separate but no less significant moral critique sometimes levied against the genre.

A common and influential moral criticism of the superhero genre, premised upon attention to its patterns of social representation, holds the genre itself to be a moral hazard in virtue of the identity and nature of superheroes. Roughly speaking, the genre valorizes social inequities on account of the fact that who gets held up as superheroes are overwhelmingly able-bodied, affluent, cisgender, heterosexual, white men. Throughout *The Content of Our Caricature* (2020), Rebecca Wanzo offers nuanced discussion of the idea that the superhero typically represents some variety of "ideal" citizen. Since superhero comics are typically written in a cultural context in which the prototypical image of such a citizen is uncritically assumed to be an able-bodied, affluent, cisgender, heterosexual, white man, this trend is far from surprising. Even Alan Moore, writer of many landmark works within the superhero genre, acknowledges that "save for a smattering of non-white characters (and non-white creators) these books and these iconic characters are still very much white supremacist dreams of the master race."[8]

When it comes to the occasional superhero of color that has appeared throughout the history of comics, however, it seems that this prototypical image remains at center stage. We tend to be presented either with (i) minoritized characters who "safely" approximate the dominant perspective of the ideal citizen, either by sharing that perspective or by otherwise conforming to it; (ii) characters who operate outside of the default, assumed cultural context and norms, such as Marvel's T'Challa; or (iii) characters who operate *within* that culture and those norms but in a nonnormative manner—such as Luke Cage, a hero who operates only, as it were, "for hire."[9] The resulting trilemma, then, is that superheroes of color are often depicted as either outside of cultural norms, in violation of cultural norms, or adhering to cultural norms strictly in the manner insisted upon by the dominant perspective. This leaves little room for depictions of such superheroes living virtuously and authentically, within the assumed cultural context, in accordance with *their* perspective on that context. Given these tendencies, this criticism maintains that the genre serves—intentionally or otherwise—to reinforce complex and insidious structures of oppression.

Indeed, as P. L. Cunningham (2013: 57) argues, this tendency to write from the dominant perspective can even help explain why there are so few Black supervillains:

> Of course, the vengeful (even if justifiably so) black man is such a popular trope in mainstream comics largely because writers seemingly have very little else upon which to draw. The most prominent black men in American culture were, for quite some time, the beleaguered, defeated black worker and the hoodlum.

Elsewhere in the same article, Cunningham (2013: 56–7) illuminates further:

> Beyond limiting their goals to organized or street crime, the situating of black villains in the ghetto has had two other effects that prevent them from being major supervillains. First, it has vastly limited the powers and abilities of these villains. . . . Beyond greatly limiting the powers of black villains, situating

them in urban locales has also, in many regards, made many of them redeemable figures. Many black villains do not stay villains, and even those who remain so have their villainy seemingly justified.

Ultimately, Cunningham suggests that these tendencies are "[u]ndoubtedly the product of white liberal guilt and the comic industry's sudden interest in addressing social issues in the 1970s" (2013: 57). We see, again, the industry at large operating from the dominant perspective.

A different moral criticism—and the one of particular interest here— asserts that the moral viciousness of superhero comics stems from the genre's narrative structure. This objection holds that regardless of the identity of superheroes (or their creators or writers), the very nature of superhero stories themselves perpetuates social injustice insofar as superheroes essentially function to keep society at, or restore it to, its present status quo. In so doing, works within the superhero genre affirm the moral acceptability of a society marked by a variety of inequities and injustices. Consider, for example, a typical Batman story schema in which Bruce Wayne "saves" Gotham by "making it safe" from some grave internal or external threat and how exceptionally rare it is for that threat to be explicitly (or even implicitly) named as poverty, racism, or some other variety of structural inequity. This typical story schema depicts Batman acting just as the prototypical superhero would. As per this objection, the problem lies not with the social identities of the characters nor those of creators but with the inherent narrative trajectory of superhero comics itself.

Here's another example. We often find Superman striving to save Earth from destruction or struggling to save the universe from collapsing into alternative possibilities. But, insofar as Superman aims to restore the status quo, he is complicit in sustaining a social order that seems rightly criticized for any number of injustices. This moral perplexity is notably singled out by Umberto Eco (1972: 21), who observes that

> Superman could exercise good on a cosmic level, or a galactic level. . . . Instead, Superman carries on his activity on the level of the small community where he lives . . . [H]e practically ignores, not exactly the dimension of the "world," but that of the "United States." . . . He is by preference, not against blackmarketing drugs, nor, obviously, against corrupting administrators or politicians, but against bank and mail-truck robbers . . .[W]here each authority is fundamentally pure and good and each wicked man is rotten to the core without hope of redemption.

As Eco makes clear: Superman could do much more to prevent structural oppression and injustice, but he chooses not to. Why? His interests simply lie elsewhere.

Since this worry is about the nature of stories told within the superhero genre, a proper assessment of it hinges on how we view the genre. Remember that in Chapter 6, we proposed the following view of the superhero genre:

> **Anchored Superhero Adventure View**: A comic x is properly included in the superhero genre if and only if x is an adventure comic, anchored in actuality, with superheroes as focal characters.

Again, to say that a comic is *anchored in actuality* is—roughly—to say that it presents a fictional world that holds all aspects of our own world fixed *except* those that are required to make the superhero narrative seem possible.[10] If we accept the Anchored Superhero Adventure View, then given that superheroes typically aim to preserve the status quo from potential disruptions, we might take them to be morally accountable for sanctioning whatever injustices that status quo involves. If we assume that the status quo is an unjust social order, then superhero comics appear to glorify the perpetuation—or at least preservation—of injustice.

If this criticism is sound, how exactly does it relate to the viciousness of social representation? Well, consider what it means for the generic representation of the social categories within such stories: since the superhero has brought about a return to a just and fair normalcy within society, social categories are implicitly represented in a bizarrely utopian way. Among other things, such categories will not be constructed—not even in part—by structures of oppression. Race, gender, class, and other such categories would instead be constructed in accordance with just and fair norms.

This line of criticism echoes worries about superhero comics promoting fascism, authoritarianism, communism, and most any morally suspect ideology with which critics take issue.[11] But there's a false premise that's important to mark before we might hastily infer that all superhero comics are morally heinous. While the preservation of normalcy and the status quo is exceptionally familiar in superhero comics, it is *not* an essential feature of superhero comics that the status quo and the moral good coincide. That they do is merely (and unfortunately) an assumption of certain—perhaps even typical—superhero comics. There is nothing in the Anchored Superhero Adventure View, however, that precludes distinguishing between a status quo and the genuine moral good: superhero comics in which superheroes actively work against objectionable features of a prevailing social order are somewhat rare but certainly available.

On account of its long-standing and systematic neglect of certain identities and its silencing of diverse creative voices, the history of the superhero genre and its proximity to depictions of vigilantism should leave us with significant moral concern. But, even in the face of the criticisms raised, there is no compelling reason to believe that morally vicious social representation is unavoidable within the superhero genre. That said, the genre remains disposed to offer a moral sanction of the status quo and, in turn, remains similarly disposed to a generically vicious, large-scale social representation: one that glorifies *actual* structures of power over the pursuit of a genuinely equitable social order.

3. Respect, Intimacy, and Representation

We've noted some elements of the comics medium that are disposed toward morally vicious representations. But, in exploring the disposition of comics toward this particular variety of moral vice, we said nothing about what the moral viciousness of odious social representation involves. Put differently: we said that certain social representations are morally wrong but without also offering a plausible account of *why* they're wrong, we're engaged in mere moralizing rather than philosophy.

While debates over the nature of moral value are at heart of much philosophical inquiry, we think it's important to note that negative consequences can, at best, serve as a rough diagnostic for identifying instances of morally vicious social representation. After all, a vile and homophobic cartoon might ultimately spur meaningful social action that, on balance, yields positive consequences. Partly for this reason, the most plausible explanation of the moral viciousness of certain kinds of social representation—notably, the principal wrongdoing associated with, say, a homophobic cartoon—consists in what its creator intends to represent (or can reasonably be taken to intend) rather than the actual effects of that content upon its audience. Accordingly, we take it that in attempting to make sense of morally virtuous and morally vicious representations of social categories, an apt way to proceed is in terms of whether their production is undertaken with a suitable moral respect for persons. And, while that's easy enough to say, it leaves us with a vexing, open-ended question: What does suitable moral respect for persons require for creators engaged in social representation in their works? While we have no swift and straightforward answer to this question, we can learn a lot by considering how failures to afford suitable moral respect can lead to morally vicious social representations. In working through such considerations, we'll keep our focus on social representation within the superhero genre on account of its now-familiar status as an ethical backdrop.

One variety of disrespectful representation concerns what is often referred to as *tokenism*: the inclusion of a character from a traditionally marginalized or oppressed group simply for the purposes of, as it were, "diversifying." Consider a character such as John Proudstar, also known as Thunderbird, who made his debut in *Giant Size X-Men* #1 in 1975, by creators Len Wein and Dave Cockrum. Part of the aim of this reboot of the *X-Men* series was to diversify the team of mutants into a genuinely global phenomenon: Nightcrawler from Germany, Storm from Kenya, Colossus from Russia, and Wolverine from Canada, with Thunderbird presented as a Native American of the Apache tribe. As can be seen on Gil Kane's cover for the issue in which he first appeared, Thunderbird is presented as a generic "Native American," stereotyped through a design seemingly driven not by genuine cultural research but only by the reductive depictions of Native Americans across popular culture. While a character such as Wolverine is presented as a superhero who is also Canadian, Thunderbird unfortunately functions as little more than the "Native American superhero." The comparably diminutive role that the character plays in the composition of the cover (visible via a quick Google search) indicates the minimal investment Marvel had in the character from the start. His startlingly short "lifespan"—being killed off in *Uncanny X-Men* #95 just a few months later—further illustrates the creators' similarly minimal investment.

Remarking on Thunderbird's distinctively indigenous status in *X-Men,* Ramzi Fawaz (2016: 294) argues:

> For a brief time the team also included the Native American superhero Thunderbird. Thunderbird offered a compelling critique of Xavier's utopian intentions in recruiting a band of global superheroes by invoking the history of elite whites' exploitation of indigenous people and their skills. Thunderbird's death three issues into the revamped series suggested the inability of the new *X-Men* to address the distinct category of indigeneity alongside race and gender.

Thunderbird is a prime example of the phenomenon of tokenism, but why exactly does tokenism deliver morally vicious social representations? Well, if the inclusion of character is a product of an unreflective effort to diversify a cast of characters, this merely instrumental deployment of the social category—in this case, First Nations or Native American—involves no genuine respect whatsoever. It involves turning a social category—in this case, a historically oppressed one—into no more than a tool for comics storytelling (or worse: *marketing*). This moral viciousness distinctive to tokenism is compounded by the nature of its commentary on the social category in question. In presenting Thunderbird in such a clichéd, stereotypical manner, the character itself is essentially reduced to the identity of the racial, ethnic, and cultural group to which he belongs. Simultaneously, given that Thunderbird is *the* instance of Native American representation in the comic, the identity of his racial, ethnic, and cultural group of origin is essentially reduced to the identity of just that one character. This simultaneous, symmetric reduction—of character identity to group identity and of group identity to character identity—effectively erases the significance of both. Respect is offered neither for their character nor for the social category to which the character is given standing. And with no respect offered, the instrumentalized employment of the social category is viciously disrespectful.

Acts of tokenism can occur even with good intentions on the part of creators, and the epistemology of tokenism—as we'll see shortly—involves little in the way of certainty. Fortunately, there's no abiding mystery about how to approach the creation of characters if we aim to avoid tokenism: it requires suitable moral respect for the social category in question, as well as its actual members. Such respect involves approaching the relevant category and its members as deserving of equal regard and dignity. It involves suitable reverence for the construction of the social category in question—for example, being invested in learning enough to appreciate the moral significance of relevant components of the representation. When it comes to creating a character, this respect obviously demands attention to how the character is drawn or designed. For example, how certain conventions for depiction reflect a history of caricature or how the design of the character might accurately convey relevant history and social practices. For obvious reasons, meeting the epistemic demands of suitable moral respect—for example, knowing enough about the practices related to a social category—is usually most readily achieved by persons who claim membership in those groups themselves. And, in turn, this provides a strong reason to value and pursue diversification among creators. Moreover, if you're interested in creating a comic character who, for example, is disabled, respect for the breadth and complexity of disability as a social category would naturally invite significant inquiry into the nature of disability alongside an active interest in seeking diversity with respect to who one creates comics with.

Tokenism involves creating or presenting characters in ways that fail to respect the dignity of members of a social category. But social representations can prove vicious even in the absence of tokenism, as in cases of objectional *appropriation*. In part, this is because social categories are constructed and, in many cases, the construction of these categories involves shared activities, values, and behaviors undertaken among members. Just as suitable moral respect places demands on how the people within a social category are represented, it also places constraints upon how certain activities, values, and behaviors might be represented—and by whom.

Philosophers Thi Nguyen and Matt Strohl (2019) argue that an act of cultural appropriation is morally wrong when the practice appropriated is an *intimate* practice—that is, one that serves as a sort of "glue" that aids in the binding together of a group's shared social identity—and that group has, in one way or another, expressed that they do not want persons outside of the group to appropriate it. Nguyen and Strohl illustrate this point through comparison with the use of pet names by those in partnered relationships: if Una and Edie are in such a relationship and use "gigglebutt" as a term of endearment for each other, others ought not refer to either of them as such without receiving permission from Una and Edie themselves. To do otherwise would be to disrespectfully breach the couple's intimacy. So, if the use of, say, a ceremonial headdress constitutes an intimate practice with a particular group and that group has expressed a desire that non-group members not partake in that practice, then an outsider who takes it upon themselves to do so anyway commits a breach of the group's intimacy. This, then, constitutes an objectionable instance of cultural appropriation.[12]

The case is similar with respect to the stories we tell and the characters we create. If a comics creator wishes to tell a story that involves intimate group practices which the group has requested that outsiders refrain from partaking in, this breach of intimacy would constitute an objectionable form of cultural appropriation. The issue is further complicated, however, by the fact that it is not always clear whether a group has in fact issued such a request or, for certain groups, what it would even mean for them to do so. Groups like various Native American tribes have tribal structures that allow for such institutional claims, but when it comes to groups like, say, transgender or nonbinary persons, a best guess about the issuance of such a request would come down to estimation of approximate group consensus. To complicate further: as Nguyen and Strohl (2019) go on to point out, an outsider attempting to determine whether a group has issued such a request and who in doing so privileges the voices of a vocal minority is, in a sense, stepping in to adjudicate an in-group dispute. This adjudication, however, runs afoul of the same sort of intimacy breach found in objectionable instances of cultural appropriation. Another way to ignore, speak over, or steal a group's voice, after all, is to take it upon yourself to settle their in-group disputes for them.

Just as debate over which representations of characters constitute tokenism admits of no easy resolution, a parallel question that looms large is how we might distinguish intimate practices from non-intimate ones. The cultural history of the kayak is, for instance, bound up with the practices of the Inuit, Yup'ik, and Aleut peoples, but there's something profoundly different about presenting characters using kayaks and depicting them with ersatz First Nations headdresses. Again, this is where respect matters: creators ought to invest in learning enough about a group to appreciate the significance and distinctiveness of intimate practices and remain mindful that this distinction, however murky it might be, *matters* for the ethics of social representation.

4. Snowflake and Safespace

We've argued that the moral assessment of social representation ought to be understood in terms of suitable moral respect. But it would be a mistake to think that once adopted, this way of approaching the ethics of social representation affords us easy answers. To draw out the potentially daunting realities of debates regarding social representation—of which there are *many*—we'll turn to a recent example.

In early 2020, as part of the buildup for a relaunch of the *New Warriors* title, Marvel unveiled their first nonbinary superhero. There is a clear sense in which this is quite admirable: nonbinary persons exist (one of them cowrote this book, in fact) and deserve respectful representation no less than those of binary gender identities. The backlash against Marvel, however, was immediate albeit divided. Some responses were of an unfortunately predictable variety: certain vocal contingents of fans complained about what they saw as nothing more than another instance of a (perceived) trend of injecting politics into comics. Of course, such complaints ignore that superheroes have been consistently fighting for allegorically or explicitly political causes since the inception of the genre. As just one example of this phenomenon and its strange internal logic, Wanzo (2020: 114) draws attention to the fact that "[s]ome people condemned Marvel for allegedly politicizing the always political Captain America when the company announced in 2014 that Sam Wilson [a Black character] would become Captain America."

For this variety of objector, there is no intelligible explanation for the inclusion of a nonbinary character—especially a character of color, as this one was—other than transparent pandering toward the so-called social justice warrior crowd. (Perhaps surprisingly, such critiques do seem to acknowledge the viciousness of purely instrumental, token representation.) The recurring charge was that a protagonist of color, or one who is transgender or gay, is an intrinsically *political* character. Indeed, the joke— offered by games writer Emma Vossen at the expense of those who maintain such a mindset regarding videogames—goes: there are only two genders, just as there are only two races and two sexual orientations: (cisgender) male and *political*, white and *political*, heterosexual and *political*.[13] The intentional emphasis on representing such characters is, according to this way of thinking, a surefire way to tank a franchise, both financially and artistically.

A very different line of response to the *New Warriors* title, however, was that while Marvel's attempt at gender-inclusivity was in principle laudable, it was ultimately and unfortunately a failed attempt. After all, while attempting to be respectful is morally preferable than not attempting (or attempting to be disrespectful), mere *attempts* do not constitute or guarantee success. By analogy, working hard to pronounce someone's name correctly but getting it badly wrong is regrettable even if it might be understandable. And, in this particular case, names are especially important. The codename of Marvel's inaugural nonbinary superhero? *Snowflake*. Their twin brother? *Safespace*.

If our attention is squarely on these names, there's a case to be made that despite generally commendable aims, as an instance of social representation, these characters are morally vicious. Notice that a not uncommon intimate practice for many groups is the reclamation of otherwise abusive language. The phenomenon in which a traditionally oppressed group co-opts a slur or other oppressive terms of abuse, giving it new meaning within the context of the group, is likely familiar enough. What is probably far less familiar— thankfully—is non-group members attempting to reclaim such terms on behalf of another group. Since writer Daniel Kibblesmith presents as a cisgender man, it is a potential breach of the intimacy that serves to bind the nonbinary community for someone outside of that community to attempt to reclaim a term of abuse on that community's behalf. To put the matter simply: that is for them to do, not him.

According to Kibblesmith, who cocreated the characters with artist Luciano Vecchio, the names were chosen based on the "idea that these are terms that get thrown around on the internet that they [the characters] don't see as derogatory. [They] take those words and wear them as badges of honour."[14] Put differently, the names are intended to be "post-ironic" (to use Kibblesmith's term). Perhaps that's coherent. (That said, in the face widespread and sometimes lethal transphobia, the idea that we're beyond somehow beyond actively addressing anti-trans movements and in a position to be ironic—or "post-ironic"—about it seems pretty strange to us.) But a serious pursuit of respect shouldn't hang on a knife's edge of satirical delicacy. And these characters' names seem all too close to a punchline for a joke being told by a writer who—even if well-intentioned—was writing from a place of privilege with respect to gender identity. Respectful social representation involves a measure of care and caution, and titling characters in this way offers no indication of either of these virtues.

So, is the case closed? Is Safeflake a morally vicious representation? Perhaps not. And that's because as discussed several times over the course of previous chapters: the creation of comics is usually a more complicated thing than we might anticipate. Kibblesmith, in working on Snowflake, was presumably attempting an act of allyship, and while philosopher Jeremy Fried (2019) notes that works of allyship are obliged not to crowd out those they intend to support, these characters were indeed cocreated with Vecchio, a queer-identifying artist who (at the time of this writing) lists his pronouns in his Twitter bio as "mostly he/him." This fact about the creation of Snowflake and Safespace should give us pause. Not because creators are incapable of producing vicious social representations of the categories they belong to but because the epistemology of respect is a complicated matter— in this case, one that's further complicated by what we can or should know about the parties involved. To give just one particularly thorny example: What should we make of the counterfactual scenario in which Snowflake was indeed created by a nonbinary person who is not "out," as it were, and for the time being publicly presents as a cisgender person? Should that person be required to "out" themselves in order to earn the right to engage in such artistic endeavors? This is to receive public legitimization as an authentic voice at the expense of incurring significant personal, social, and even physical risk. We have no easy answers to this question. It takes us well beyond the domain of comics and, at the same time, settling it is likely a precondition for conclusively settling the previous question of whether Snowflake is a morally vicious social representation of nonbinary people.

5. The Aesthetics of Non-Representation

We've noted some ways in which instances of social representation can turn out to be morally vicious. Our project in this final section is to consider whether they can similarly turn out to be *aesthetically* vicious, and whether and under what conditions epistemically or morally vicious social representations might render comics worse in purely aesthetic terms. In so doing, we'll turn to one instance in which the aesthetic and moral evaluation of social representation might relate in systematic ways to the broader aesthetic and moral evaluation of a comic.

There are any number of reasons that one might ascribe aesthetic value to superhero comics. There are some like Fletcher Hanks's works featuring Stardust the Super Wizard that are elegantly bizarre. Others like Darwyn Cooke's *The New Frontier* (2004) are boldly nostalgic romps. Still others like Ann Nocenti and Art Adam's *Longshot* (1985–6) are manic and effervescent. An especially interesting strain of aesthetic praise for superhero comics, though, is broadly intellectual in character. According to those who express such sentiments, superhero comics are held up as involving subtle insights, synoptic understanding, or an authorial vision that lays bare the true essence of society. See, for example, the following:

> Praise for Frank Miller's *The Dark Knight Returns* (1986): "This isn't just a graphic novel about a superhero growing old and seeing everything he has spent his life fighting for fall apart. This is a very strong critique about society, apathy and governance. Sounds heavy but Miller manages to weave all of these strands into a complete and captivating narrative."[15]

> Praise for Chris Claremont and Brent Eric Anderson's *X-Men: God Loves, Man Kills* (1982): "Although the story is very much an artifact of its time, the core messages that Claremont and artist Brent Anderson brought to life are just as resonant today as they were 38 years ago. Claremont is a master at using characters to solve and explore real-world problems, and this graphic novel is a prime example of that. . . . Whether it's gender, religion, race, or the wearing of masks, mankind has historically legitimized the oppression of

"the other." Historically, "the other" is treated in three major ways—by distancing the other, making the other more like oneself, or trying to destroy the other. . . . That's the central conflict of GOD LOVES, MAN KILLS."[16]

Praise for Alan Moore and Dave Gibbons's *Watchmen* (1986): "Alan Moore and Dave Gibbons work is largely considered the greatest achievement in the medium ever. Its 12 issues—along with Miller's *The Dark Knight Returns*—showed the world that comics are not just for children, with it tackling complex themes such as fears over nuclear war, moral relativism and if there is even a purpose to life . . . or if it's all just a joke."[17]

Praise for Cullen Bunn, Gabriel Hernandez Walta, and Javier Fernandez's *Magneto* #7 (2014): "[Bunn's] talent shines through, as he effortlessly crafts a dark and brooding picture of a man who has lived through the lowest of lows, and is now vying for a purpose to continue on in a world that fears him. . . . The script pulls you in and before you know it you are on an incredibly insightful ride into the mind of a broken man, and you want to turn it right over and ride again when it's finished. I seriously can't say enough about the weight that Cullen Bunn is throwing around with his prose."[18]

While we suspect that claims like these are standardly overblown, they do seem true of at least some superhero comics. But, given their prevalence and the regularity with which the depth of these works is held up as a redeeming feature, we think it's important to see that absent a suitably respectful approach to social representation, these claims turn out to be demonstrably false or rooted in bizarre incoherence.

The Anchored Superhero Adventure View—and, indeed, any view of any genre that makes use of this notion of being *anchored in reality*—comes with some interesting and perhaps surprising consequences. Presumably, making room for the narrative possibility of superheroes in a fictional world anchored in our own actual world does *not* require substantial, or even slight, revisions to actual social demographics involving actual social categories. This means that unless it is otherwise stated in a particular narrative, the worlds of superhero comics share the same social makeup as our own, at least with respect to nonfictional social categories. We should, for that reason, simply be able to look to our world and successfully make use of what we see to extract a range of truths about society and its composition according to the relevant superhero comics.

For example, how many transgender or nonbinary characters are in the United States in the massive fictional worlds of the DC or Marvel Universes? According to a 2016 study by the Williams Institute at the UCLA School of Law, 0.42 percent of the adult US population identifies as transgender.[19] At the time, that amounted to roughly 1.4 million people. Given various complicating factors that make the accurate collection of such data quite difficult, the numbers almost certainly underrepresent the actual amount of transgender persons living in the United States. (Many potential participants might not feel comfortable responding accurately, for any among a variety of reasons—not the least of which is a culture of both externalized and often internalized transphobia.) Furthermore, because the institute is reporting only on the adult population, the numbers offered do not include the number of transgender children and teenagers in the United States. With these complications noted, however, and for the sake of simplicity, let's operate for now under the assumption that 0.42 percent of the US population is transgender. Given the Anchored Superhero Adventure View, in a typical superhero comic set in a fictionalized version of the contemporary United States, it turns out to be true according to that comic that at least 0.42 percent of fictional persons in the version of the United States portrayed in that comic are also transgender. That's just about one out of approximately every 200 fictional persons.

Even restricting ourselves to adult superheroes who are depicted as residing within those universes' fictionalized versions of the United States, the consequence is clear: it would constitute an active departure from actuality to end up with a fleshed out fictional world without any transgender persons appearing or even mentioned. A superhero comic that presents large numbers of fictional persons—heroes, villains, or otherwise—without acknowledging that some number among them will be transgender or nonbinary is quite straightforwardly misrepresenting reality. It is akin to the bad habit displayed in many old superhero comics of drawings of city crowds made up entirely of white people or to the ubiquitous presentation of superheroes—even those of humble, human origins—as possessing only a very narrow range of hypersexualized (and often anatomically suspect) body types. Such a story doesn't just fail to represent a diverse cast including members of traditionally minoritized groups but fails to accurately represent the aspects of actuality in which the story itself is supposed to be anchored. Even minimally trans-inclusive comics writing would not merely acknowledge that trans people exist in the background of the story, but also acknowledge characters in that story *as* trans characters. This is why Marvel's attempt at inclusivity via Snowflake is, in some sense, mildly admirable: they went beyond merely acknowledging the existence of nonbinary identities but instead made space for a nonbinary *person* in their fictional world. This fictional person comes with a narrative point of view, transforming them from background object to relatable subject capable of agency and self-determination. (The previous worries about objectionable tokenism, of course, still apply.)

But, for anyone who offers aesthetic approbation of superhero comics by holding them up as trenchant social commentary, we see no principled way to reconcile the active omission of transgender characters (and disabled characters, Black characters, Muslim characters, etc.) as anything but an aesthetic vice. After all, how can a superhero comic purport to give insights into some aspect of the world, if it actively and gratuitously elides the very complexities constitutive of that aspect? Perhaps the best solution is to withhold such approbation from superhero comics in the first place. But, if you do think that superhero comics are aesthetically better in virtue of succeeding in the way that the previous quotations imply, lack of apt social representation makes the position all that much more difficult to defend.

It might seem weird that getting things factually wrong could ever be an aesthetic vice, but it shouldn't: it's likely you've experienced it as one. In discussing the film adaptation of Philip Roth's novel *The Human Stain*, philosopher Paisley Livingston (2010: 107) says:

> The protagonist in the film (portrayed by Anthony Hopkins) is Oxford-trained Dean Coleman Silk, professor of Classics at a prestigious university in Massachusetts. . . . At one point in the story, Professor Silk converses with a non-academic friend, the aspiring novelist Nathan Zuckerman, who asks him the following question: "What's the moment called in Greek tragedy, you know the one when the hero learns that everything he knows is wrong?" Without hesitation, the professor replies: "It's called peripetio, or peripeteia, take your pick." This glaring error, which is wholly out of character for a distinguished classicist, can be interpreted in two basic ways. Either the scriptwriter mistakenly believed that he was having the professor answer Zuckerman's question correctly, or the scriptwriter has intentionally slipped the mistake into the professor's dialogue in a subtle effort to undermine his reliability for that part of the audience that knows that the correct answer is anagnorisis (discovery) not peripeteia (reversals).

Another possibility, which Livingston goes on to mention, is that the error is not the scriptwriter's but Roth's, and the film has simply inherited this potential lexical mistake from the novel. For simplicity's sake, let's set aside that possibility and consider just two options: either the "mistake" was intentional and hence, not a mistake but instead a decision of narrative significance, or it really was a genuine mistake. If the former, that's one thing, but if the latter, it constitutes an aesthetic flaw on the part of the work. This is because given that *The Human Stain* (both the novel and the film) is a work of realist drama, this distortion of reality is unjustifiably contrary to the aesthetic norms of the genre. Similar remarks can be made for period pieces with inaccurate sartorial depictions (e.g., anachronisms in films like *Glory* and *Braveheart)* or even certain musical choices, such as when in the first season of HBO's *True Detective*, detective Rust Cohle (played by Matthew McConaughey) goes undercover in a biker bar during a scene set in 1995, with "A History of Bad Men," a song by the Melvins released in 2006, playing over the bar's speaker system. For such works, these breaks from reality—unless purposeful and narratively significant—indicate an inattention to detail and a failure to live up to genre norms and also run the risk of distracting the particularly observant or invested audience member by "pulling them out of the experience." Recall, for instance, our example from Chapter 5 where Gwen Stacy's death in *Amazing Spider-Man* #121 occurs at what looks like the Brooklyn Bridge but at what Spider-Man calls the George Washington Bridge. Works that possess such missteps are, it seems, straightforwardly (though often only slightly) aesthetically worse for it.

We're now in a position to see how the sort of misrepresentation currently under discussion can, in superhero comics, give rise to aesthetic vice: since superhero comics are anchored in actuality, presenting a distorted picture of reality unaccompanied by overriding narrative justification indicates (at least) an inattention to detail and failure to live up to genre norms. It also runs the same risk of pulling observant audience members—perhaps especially those who are members of groups who are erased or misrepresented by the comic—out of the experience. A superhero comic, then, that habitually fails to acknowledge (again, without overriding narrative justification) that transgender and nonbinary persons (or disabled persons, Black persons, Muslim persons, etc.) exist is one that is failing *as a superhero comic*, insofar as it is failing to remain anchored in actuality. And, if one holds that superhero comics wherein transgender characters (etc.) go unrepresented are indeed prescient social commentary or insightful reflections on power and justice, the active omission of these characters leaves such remarks barely plausible. Similarly, if such comics engage in this sort of misrepresentation yet are lauded by fans or critics as offering deep insight into "the" human condition, it is worth pausing to reflect on what very limited (and perhaps even exclusionary) notion of *human* those fans and critics are assuming.

There is no shortage of views about the aesthetics of superhero comics. And we've tried not to prescribe one as uniquely correct. Instead, our point is that if you accept a certain common view about what makes superhero comics aesthetically good, or even a view about what their aesthetic norms are, you should find the distortive non-representation of certain identities to be an aesthetic vice. And, if you were inclined to uphold non-representation as somehow aesthetically virtuous, the resulting aesthetics of superhero comics is an exceptionally strange one and one which is evidently incompatible with some of the putative acclaim the genre often receives. For these reasons, the ethics of social representation serves to show that appreciating superhero comics in a morally, epistemically, and even aesthetically principled way is harder than we might have thought.

6. Recommended Readings

Rebecca Wanzo's *The Content of Our Caricature* (2020) is an excellent and recent contribution to the literature on Black representation in comics. Adilifu Nama's *Super Black* (2011) offers a sustained look at Black superheroes in American comics. For a discussion of race and horror comics, see Whitted's *EC Comics: Race, Shock, and Social Protest* (2019). See also Cowling (2020), Davis (2015), Howard (2013), Kunka (2016), Rifas (2004), and Singer (2002). On multicultural comics, see Aldama's *Multicultural Comics from Zap to Blue Beetle* (2010).

On the representation of women in comics, see Carolyn Cocca's *Superwomen: Gender, Power, and Representation* (2016) and Samantha Langsdale and Elizabeth Rae Coody's edited volume, *Monstrous Women in Comics* (2020), as well as Gibson (2016) and the "Why Girls?" chapter of Hillary Chute's *Why Comics?* (2017). See also Brown (2020), Behm-Morawitz and Pennell. For discussion of the representation of disability in comics, see Chute's (2017) chapter "Why Illness and Disability?," as well as Scott Smith's edited volume, *Uncanny Bodies: Superhero Comics and Disability* (2019). LGBTQ+ representation in comics is discussed in Mance (2016) and Chute's (2017) chapter, "Why Queer?" We also heartily recommend The Nib's *Be Gay, Do Comics* collection (IDW, 2020) and Fantagraphics' *No Straight Lines* (2013). On the need for diversity in representation in children's literature, see Philip Nel's *Was the Cat in the Hat Black?* (2017).

8

Are Comics Literature?

1. So-Called Graphic Novels

Though comics historians would likely point out that the term "graphic novel" seems to have originated in an essay by Richard Kyle in a 1964 issue of the *Capa-Alpha* newsletter, many would identify Will Eisner's *A Contract with God* (1978) as the seminal "graphic novel."[1] Given the term's rather fluid norms of application, it might be extended to earlier works by the likes of Rodolphe Töpffer, Lynd Ward, and Frans Masereel, but the status of Eisner's work as a defining "graphic novel" is largely uncontested. Despite being a collection of loosely connected short stories, *A Contract with God* is often seen as both aiming at and succeeding in displaying significant artistic and literary merit, especially given its time and context of creation. Some readers might even tell you that Eisner's celebrated work and its subsequent ilk—works like Art Spiegelman's *Maus* (1980–91), Alison Bechdel's *Fun Home* (2006), Marjane Satrapi's *Persepolis* (2000,

2004), and Chris Ware's *Jimmy Corrigan, The Smartest Kid on Earth* (2000), among many others—are far beyond being just comics. No, they are not mere comics at all but are instead serious works for serious people: the sort of work that is not read casually for entertainment value but instead read carefully, reread often, and studied.[2] Comics are for kids, the story goes, while these "graphic novels" are more befitting those who are just as likely to spend their time with Austen, Beckett, Blake, or Morrison. (Toni, not Grant.)

You may have noticed that we have more or less avoided using this term—"graphic novel"—throughout the book so far. We draw attention to it now only to highlight why we'll be very quickly setting it back aside. It's worth pointing out first and foremost that the use of the term simply cannot be intended as offering a straightforward and adequate description of works like those already mentioned. *A Contract with God* is a collection of short stories, and *Maus*, *Fun Home*, and *Persepolis* are all nonfictional (even if creative nonfictional) memoirs. Short story collections and nonfictional memoirs, though, are not typically treated as novels within critical and appreciative practices focused on written prose. Of the examples on the table, this leaves *Jimmy Corrigan* as the only representative of the sort of unified, long-form fictional narrative that might rightly qualify as a novel in the sense most commonly invoked. (That said, even *Jimmy Corrigan* first appeared as a serialized strip, only later collected for publication.) So, as fluid as the usage of the term tends to be, so-called graphic novels clearly need not be, or even approximate, novels in any more familiar, conventional sense. Instead, it seems that the term is often used either in a nonliteral *classificatory* sense, to denote any long-form (or long-ish form) comic or comics collection, or in a *commendatory* sense, as a marker of supposed quality and, importantly, status.[3] This latter sense is that which undergirds the tendency to apply the term exclusively to supposedly substantial, mature works—again, the kind that are not just read casually but reread with seriousness and studied. Indeed, in an oft repeated story, a well-meaning publisher once said to Neil Gaiman, upon learning that he was the primary creator behind *The Sandman* series: "my god, man, you don't write *comics*, you write *graphic novels*."[4]

There is much that could be said about whether the use of the term "graphic novel" is, on the whole, beneficial or detrimental to the reception of comics as a medium. See, for example, Alan Moore:

It's a marketing term. I mean, it was one that I never had any sympathy with. The term "comic" does just as well for me. The term "graphic novel" was something that was thought up in the '80s by marketing people. . . . The problem is that "graphic novel" just came to mean "expensive comic book" and so what you'd get is people like DC Comics or Marvel comics—because "graphic novels" were getting some attention, they'd stick six issues of whatever worthless piece of crap they happened to be publishing lately under a glossy cover and call it *The She-Hulk Graphic Novel*, you know? It was that that I think tended to destroy any progress that comics might have made in the mid-'80s. . . . But no, the term "graphic novel" is not one that I'm over-fond of.[5]

We won't take on the task of trying to adjudicate these Moorean issues here. Instead, we'll leave it at this: throughout this book, we have sided with, and will continue to side with, many (though certainly not all) creators in opting to exclusively use the term "comics." *A Contract with God*, *Persepolis*, and works of their kind are, in our vernacular, "long-form comics." And unlike the aforementioned, evaluatively loaded commendatory sense of the term "graphic novel," we aim to use our terms in a purely classificatory manner that is neutral with respect to intended or perceived substance and quality. Comics are comics, whether they are superhero comics, funny animal comics, or deeply introspective long-form comics that reveal, say, the depth and pervasive torment of the ubiquitous existential angst synonymous with the human condition.

That said, there does seem to be *something* that the term "graphic novel" and others like it are trying to get at. It could hardly be denied that we do, in practice, separate comics—long form or otherwise—into those that are (or are worthy of being) reread and studied versus those that are (or should at most be) merely read, perhaps for nothing more than cheap entertainment. We can and do draw some kind of line, fuzzy though it may be, between those comics that might find company alongside serious works (e.g., Dante or the Brontes) versus those that, whether through fault or by design, rightly remain among the merely popular works (e.g., J. K. Rowling or John Grisham) or even pulp (e.g., H. P. Lovecraft or Charlaine Harris).

Looking at comics scholarship, articles like Aaron Meskin's "Comics as Literature?" (2009a) and Hillary Chute's "Comics as Literature? Reading Graphic Narrative" (2008) survey many similarities between comics and serious works of literature. Christopher Pizzino's book *Arresting Development: Comics at the Boundaries of Literature* (2016) is a recent exercise in directly applying the techniques of literary analysis to the works of Alison Bechdel, Charles Burns, Gilbert Hernandez, and Frank Miller in an attempt to show that such works can be understood as critical commentary on the artistic and social standing of comics in relation to literature. In light of all of this, we should invest some time in asking: What is the relation between comics and literature?

2. The Literature Question

Are comics literature? Well, what exactly are we asking? Are all of them literature? Only some of them? If only some: Which, and why? We'll address all of these questions as the chapter progresses, but first we should have something to say to those who are inclined to respond negatively to the very asking of such questions in the first place. This negativity might stem from any number of factors, but here we'll focus on three.

First, some might insist that asking whether some, or even all, comics are literature isn't worthwhile because the answers are too easy to come to by: it's all up to the individual. If someone—say, Ronnie—thinks a particular comic is literature, then that comic is literature *for Ronnie*. Maybe it isn't for you. Maybe you think no comics are literature or that every comic *except for that one over there* is literature. On such a view, you would be right: all comics except for that one over there are literature *for you*. Note, though, that this response to our initial question—whether comics are literature—boldly changes the subject. We started by asking a question about comics and literature, and we instead received an answer that has to do with you, or us, or Ronnie. If Ronnie says that *Persepolis* is literature to him, even if it is not literature to you, he tells you nothing about *Persepolis* or about literature other than the tangential fact that he looks at them one way and that way of looking is brutely different than your way of looking.

At this point, the subjectivist might double down and insist that the only appropriate application of the term "literature" is purely subjective. Saying that *Persepolis* is (or is not) *literature-for-Ronnie* (or you, or whoever) is the best we can do. We think that this strategy of doubling-down fails. For one, it seems to offer the following account of when something qualifies as literature:

Subjectivism: *x* is *literature-for-A* if and only if *A* believes *x* to be literature.

Notice that Subjectivism, as stated, is completely uninformative. It's a vacuous claim that amounts to little more than pointing out that if Ronnie believes that x is literature, then Ronnie believes x is literature. Everyone can probably agree to that, and acknowledging that such a claim is true does not tell us all that much. It tells us nothing about x, nor does it tell us anything about literature. All it tells us is some relatively uninteresting fact about Ronnie.

Other concerns militate against Subjectivism, as well. Suppose Luke and Bima are discussing whether or not *Persepolis* is best thought of as a work of literature. They disagree: Luke says it is, while Bima maintains that it isn't. How might they proceed in settling their dispute should they be so inclined? Ideally, they would offer reasons in favor of their respective positions in an attempt to make their case and convince the other. But if Subjectivism is true, then all Luke's claim amounts to is that *Persepolis* is literature-for-Luke and, likewise, all Bima's claim amounts to is that *Persepolis* is not literature-for-Bima. If that's right, though, then there is no disagreement at all, since there is no shared claim that is in dispute: both parties can perfectly well acknowledge that it is in no way inconsistent for *Persepolis* to be literature-for-Luke while not being literature-for-Bima. So, while Subjectivism might *seem* like a good way to go if we want to acknowledge that people have different views, it does little in terms of making sense of our behavior when we face disagreement about those views. In fact, it looks like it might just dissolve such disagreements into the mere trading of contrasting autobiographies.

Moving on, some might insist that asking whether some, or even all, comics are literature isn't worthwhile because the question has no real answer. After all, any plausible attempt at an answer would depend on what we mean by "comics" and what we mean by "literature" (not to mention, as we'll see, what we mean by "are"). This isn't to retreat to Subjectivism but instead to point out that the question, as asked, simply can't be answered without further specifying—most likely in some artificial manner—the meanings of the terms involved. We have no quarrel with this so far. It's certainly true that any attempt to address whether comics are literature needs to be sensitive to what we might mean by the terms involved—but notice that the same thing applies to literally every question we could ever ask. Universally, the meanings of our questions—and hence, the adequacy of potential answers—depend on the meanings of the terms involved. The problem is that it might be too tempting to simply point out that whether comics are literature depends on what we mean by "comics" and by "literature" and then stop the inquiry there. That's not where the inquiry ends, though, but where it begins.

In Chapters 2 and 3, we addressed what we take comics to be, definitionally and ontologically. What remains to be done, then, is to figure out what "literature" means. With that aim in mind, you might expect that we would devote significant attention to answering the following question:

Literature Question: Under what conditions is a comic a work of literature?

If we were to assume that the Literature Question has an answer, we would be assuming that there is some univocal, privileged explication of the concept in question. We agree with Meskin (2009a, b), however, that this assumption is most likely a bad one to make. Honest investigation of critical and appreciative practices reveal many competing and distinguishable notions of *literature*—in the abstract, one according to which something is *literature*$_1$ just in case it is x, y, and z; another according to which something is *literature*$_2$ just in case it is a, b, and c; yet another according to which something is *literature*$_3$ just in case it is p, q, and r; and so on. So, when we ask whether comics are "literature," we could really be asking any number of questions. That realization is the first step toward progress. The next steps are distinguishing and sorting out these questions, figuring out which ones are interesting and fruitful, and then focusing our attention on those. Upon replacing the more coarse-grained question with those that are more fine-grained, we might find that comics are *literature*$_1$, not *literature*$_2$, and borderline cases of *literature*$_3$. By our lights, that counts as progress, even if we never settle once and for and all whether comics are "literature," full stop.

Finally, some might insist that asking whether any or all comics are literature (even while considering the more fine-grained senses, as discussed earlier) isn't worthwhile because the question is pointless. Nothing of value, the objection goes, comes with answering it: whether we call *A Contract with God* literature or not, it's still an important work of significant value that will continue to be read and studied. In contrast, the latest issue of *The Indiscernible Whateverman* (or whatever) most likely won't be. So, even if we can come up with a principled answer to the Literature Question, it will be of interest only to academics and other pedants. In response, we happily grant that pursuing pointless questions is pointless. We disagree, however, that the Literature Question is a pointless question. Both the answers we might settle upon *and* the very act of investigating the question itself can bear fruit. Let's focus on the fruitfulness of answers, first, which we think are of potential benefit for audiences, scholars, and critics alike.

As discussed in previous chapters, determining which kinds of categories our artifacts belong to is imperative when we aim to engage with and evaluate them. If Karamo bakes Tan a cheesecake, and Tan insists on evaluating it as a quesadilla, there is a clear sense in which Tan is being fair neither to Karamo nor to the cheesecake, and also plausibly denying himself of an enriching aesthetic (in this case, gustatory) experience as a result of mis-categorizing the object of his attention. As we'll discuss later, the category (or *categories*) of literature doesn't seem to be a medium category (like comics) or a genre category (like superhero, romance, or horror), but it does seem to form a category of some sort. If that's right, then an audience interested in engaging robustly with comics and evaluating them in a fully informed way should be interested in whether comics qualify as literature and in which candidate senses.

Some evaluations focus just on entertainment value or individual pleasure. Other evaluations aim for more scholarly and critical insight. And which scholarly and critical tools we employ during our evaluations of certain kinds of artifacts depends, at least in part, on which kinds of artifacts we're focusing on. Narratology is fruitfully applied to narrative; it's much harder (though perhaps not impossible) to make use of when we are critically engaging with, say, fully instrumental orchestral music. Similarly, music theory is fruitfully applied to such music but is not nearly as handy of a tool when we're looking at a medium like painting. Over many decades of scholarly work, literary theorists have developed quite a toolbox for the study of literature. If we can determine that some (or all) comics are literature in at least some senses, that suggests that it would be fruitful to dip into the literary theorist's toolbox when we approach them with a scholarly or critical eye. Indeed, this kind of work constitutes a substantial portion of active research within comics studies. If, on the other hand, we determine that comics are *not* literature in relevant senses, that suggests instead that if the tools in the literary theorist's toolbox are of any use at all, they are useful only analogically or indirectly, in a sense extending beyond their intended use.

All of the above has focused on the value of answering the question (or questions) at hand. But notice, as in our discussion back in Chapter 2 regarding the definition of *comics*, that regardless of how or even if we ultimately answer the question, the very activities of clarifying what we mean by the question and considering various possible answers are themselves fruitful, since such activities prompt us to reflect critically and systematically on what we might mean by "literature" in any of its various senses. If, at the end of inquiry, we say that comics qualify as $literature_1$ but not $literature_2$, that tells us something about $literature_1$ and $literature_2$, and that in turn informs our future conversations about *literature*, full stop. If asking the question requires getting clear on the terms in the question, and such clarity leads to a more nuanced understanding of discourse about literature in general, then we're pretty confident that the question isn't pointless at all. Quite to the contrary: even if we don't settle on an answer, the very act of getting clear on the question does us plenty of favors.

3. Quantification

Before we get to the questions of what we might mean by "literature" and whether and in which senses comics qualify, we'll need to take a detour through the topic of *quantification*. In logic and linguistics, a *quantifier* is a device that specifies, appropriately enough, a notion of *quantity*. In formal logic, the paradigm quantifiers are the *universal quantifier*, often written "∀" and meaning "all" or "every"; and the *existential quantifier*, often written "∃" and meaning "some" (or "at least one"). With this in mind, compare the following two sentences and their logical structure:

(1) All dogs have four legs. [∀x ((x is a dog) ⟶ (x has four legs))]

(2) Some dogs have four legs. [∃x ((x is a dog) & (x has four legs))]

These sentences are obviously very different. (1) is clearly false, since we can verify that there exist plenty of adorable but perhaps unfortunate three-legged dogs. At the same time, (2) is clearly true, since at least one four-legged dog exists. So, getting clear on which quantifier we're using can make the difference between undeniable truth and undeniable falsity.

The problem is that people don't always explicitly pronounce their quantifiers, instead leaving them implicit and unspoken. When this happens, context can sometimes make clear which quantifier is being used, but other times the matter might remain quite unclear—even to the speaker uttering the sentence. Suppose someone were to ask

(3) Do dogs have four legs?

In this case, we'd have to do some interpretive work, as the quantifier in (3) is left unpronounced, leaving it ambiguous what the question is actually asking. Are we in a conversational context in which it is clear that the speaker is asking about what is absolutely essential for doghood, in the same way we might ask whether triangles have three sides? If so, we should interpret them as asking whether (1) is true, and the answer is "no." Is the conversational context instead such that the speaker is casually inquiring about whether, if for some reason pressed to quickly locate a four-legged animal, they might usefully start by looking for a dog? If so, we can interpret them as asking about whether (2) is true, in which case the answer is "yes."

When we ask whether comics are literature, we should aim to avoid interpretive confusion and instead be clear about our usage of quantifiers. To start, then, we can distinguish between two potential questions:

Universal Question: Do all comics qualify as literature?

Existential Question: Does at least one comic qualify as literature?

Just as we noticed when discussing sentences (1) and (2), the answers to these questions might end up being very different. Furthermore, notice the danger of failing to disambiguate the question. Suppose that Malik and Anna are arguing over whether comics are literature. Malik has in mind the Universal Question and says "no." Anna has in mind the Existential Question and says "yes." Neither, however, bothers to explicitly pronounce their quantifiers. On the surface, they seem to be disagreeing and perhaps they invest serious time into the debate—but that time is wasted, since, quite plainly, a negative answer to the Universal Question is logically compatible with a positive answer to the Existential Question. There is no contradiction in granting that some, but not all, comics qualify as literature.

It would be nice if all we had to do for maximal philosophical clarity is carefully distinguish between these two questions. But things are not so easy. Consider the following:

(4) Dogs have four legs.

Understood as (1), a universally quantified sentence, the sentence is false. Understood as (2), an existentially quantified sentence, the sentence is true. But there is danger in taking (4) to be just a run-of-the-mill, existentially quantified sentence. Notice that the following is also true:

(5) At least one dog does not have four legs.

If (4) is just short for (2), then you might think that (5) is another way to say:

(6) Dogs do not have four legs.

If the truth of (5) makes (6) true, then putting (4) and (6) together we get

(7) Dogs have four legs and dogs do not have four legs.

Quite clearly, (7) is a contradiction, which indicates that something must have gone wrong. A plausible explanation of what went wrong is this: the quantifier most likely present in a sentence like (4) is neither a universal quantifier *nor* an existential quantifier but instead something called a *generic* quantifier. Logicians and linguists debate the exact best way to understand generic quantification, but for our purposes, we might best understand (4) as saying something like

(8) Typical dogs have four legs.

Helping ourselves to this notion of generic quantification helps us make best sense of (3), which—as you probably already noticed—reads awkwardly when interpreted as asking about the truth of either (1) or (2) but sounds much more natural when understood to be asking about the truth of (8).

Taking this all back to comics, we find ourselves with another version of our main question:

Generic Question: Do typical comics qualify as literature?

Even with the Generic Question distinguished from the Universal and Existential Questions, however, our work is not done. Despite helping ourselves to the use of generic quantifiers, some sentences still have a quantificational structure that cries out for further explanation. Consider:

(9) Mosquitos carry the West Nile virus.

This sentence seems true. It's not true, however, that all mosquitos carry the West Nile virus (the universal reading) or even that typical mosquitos do so (the generic reading). In fact, very few mosquitos at all carry the virus. On top of that, reading (9) as involving an existential quantifier can be quickly shown to generate a contradiction using the same method that led us to (7), earlier. We also can't understand (9) as saying that *only* mosquitos carry the West Nile virus, since that's not true: birds, bats, squirrels, rabbits, alligators, and humans can carry it, too.[6]

On our understanding, (9) is best read as something like this: "the category of *mosquito* is noteworthy for being among the select group of categories that have members that can carry the West Nile virus." This reading doesn't directly involve any universal, existential, or even generic quantification but instead employs what we might call a *noteworthy feature* quantifier. So, turning back to comics once again, we can ask yet another question:

Noteworthy Feature Question: Is the category of *comics* noteworthy for being among the select group of categories that have members that qualify as literature?

To really see how all of these different questions come apart, consider and contrast the following questions about mosquitos:

Universal Mosquito Question: Do all mosquitos carry the West Nile virus?

Existential Mosquito Question: Does at least one mosquito carry the West Nile virus?

Generic Mosquito Question: Do typical mosquitos carry the West Nile virus?

Noteworthy Feature Mosquito Question: Is the category of *mosquito* noteworthy for being among the select group of categories that have members that carry the West Nile virus?

The answers, respectively, are: no, yes, no again (but for different reasons), and yes again (but for different reasons).

Were our attention focused on the intricate logical and linguistic nuances of quantification, we could probably continue to distinguish even more versions of the Literature Question. By our lights, though, we've done enough distinguishing. We started with what might have been taken as just one question: "Are comics literature?" By now, we've introduced four different questions that we might really be after. It's time to investigate some answers.

4. Literature, Literature, Literature, and Literature

In her discussion of comics and literature, Hannah Miodrag (2016: 390–2) chronicles a debate between two other comics scholars, Bart Beaty and Charles Hatfield.[7] On the surface, their topic seems to be the question of whether comics count as literature, but closer investigation reveals that that is not the real issue. Beaty employs a restricted understanding of "literature," according to which many comics do not qualify, whereas Hatfield employs a much looser understanding, according to which most, perhaps all, do. So, despite surface appearances, these two scholars are *not* really talking about comics but are instead engaged in an activity philosophers sometimes call *meta-linguistic negotiation*: they're really debating how we should use the word "literature." Two parties might agree completely about every formal aspect of comics but diverge over whether comics are literature not because of anything having to do with the comics but instead because of each employing different notions of "literature."

As foreshadowed earlier in this chapter, we absolve ourselves of the task of settling the uniquely "correct" employment of the term "literature" and, for that reason, we set aside the project of undertaking this kind of meta-linguistic negotiation. Instead, we'll proceed by identifying various candidate meanings of the term that plausibly get traction in different conversational contexts and then inquire into whether comics satisfy the conditions laid out in any of those candidate meanings. So, while there might turn out to be some uniquely privileged sense of "literature," we're more interested in the variety of senses in play and what happens when we make explicit the relevant quantifiers.

4.1. The Linguistic Sense

Some might use the term "literature" to simply mean any piece of writing at all, with a "piece of writing" being any work produced within a linguistic medium. This brings us to:

> **Linguistic Sense:** x is *literature*$_{ling}$ if and only if x is produced within a linguistic medium.

A question immediately arises: What counts as a linguistic medium? For simplicity's sake, let's stipulate for now that a *linguistic medium* is any medium the conventions of which include and are at least substantially governed by the use of language—minimally, a set of symbols that can be combined and manipulated in a rule-governed fashion for the purpose of expressing semantic meaning for the sake of communication.

Is the medium of comics a linguistic medium, in this sense? This, it turns out, is a tricky matter to settle. It is somewhat common to talk about the "language of comics," but it is not at all clear that this "language" is really a *language* and not instead just something *language-like* in some relevant respects.[8] Some would call music theory a "language," but this is misleading since, quite plausibly, music theory is only analogically, and not genuinely, a language: it does not come packed with rules for generating semantic meaning (e.g., there is no way through pure music to express propositions like *the cat sat on the mat*). Indeed, we agree with Darren Hudson Hick (2012: 140), who argues that "it is difficult to speak of a 'language of comics' in any truly abstracted way" and that "treating comics as analogous to natural languages presents an array of perhaps intractable difficulties." Hick (2012) finally concludes:

> And although discussing comics *as* a natural language is perhaps a stretch, it seems not unreasonable to talk of them as being language-*like*—as constituting a *pseudo*-language—operation in many ways like a natural language. As such, while perhaps not *entirely* accurate, the notion of a "language of comics" seems nevertheless both illuminating and meaningful, and not merely metaphorical.

Even if we follow this line of thought and deny that the "language of comics" is genuinely linguistic, it is still undeniable that the comics medium makes extensive use of language in narration boxes, speech balloons, onomatopoetic occurrences, and other representations.[9] Does this observation provide any justification for the claim that any comics are literature$_{ling}$?

We argue that it does not—at least, not yet. Note that many other mediums make just as frequent use of language, yet we refrain from counting them as literature. Consider film, for example, or song. The presence of language is in fact constitutive of the very notion of *song*—insofar as song is *lyrical music*—but remember (or look into) the mixed reaction when Bob Dylan was awarded the Nobel Prize in Literature for his songs in 2016. For many, this undeserved award was given on the basis of a simple category mistake: song—including the best of song—just *isn't* literature. And even if the lyrics, considered apart from the music and taken instead as poetry, could indeed qualify as literature, it doesn't follow that the whole qualifies as such any more than it follows that a hotdog is a bun because it has a bun as a part.

Putting this all together: Are comics literature in the Linguistic Sense? Whether we intend to ask this in the form of the Universal Question, the Existential Question, the Generic Question, or the Noteworthy Feature Question, we don't seem to be well positioned to settle it until we make some more progress on what it is to be a language and what it is to be a medium sufficiently governed by language. And those questions, it turns out, are pretty hard. Thankfully, we don't need to distract ourselves with them either, since we think that the Linguistic Sense of "literature" also turns out to be pretty uninteresting. Suppose that there is a genuine "language of comics," or at least that the comics medium does indeed qualify as a sufficiently linguistic medium, such that comics do qualify as literature$_{ling}$. They are now placed alongside E. L. James's *50 Shades of Grey* (2011) and the Taco Bell drive-through menu. In that, it just doesn't seem like the Linguistic Sense does justice to the topic to which this chapter is devoted. After all, we can coherently grant that the Taco Bell drive-through menu is literature$_{ling}$ but still go on to ask whether (and, indeed, almost certainly deny that) it is literature in any more robust, interesting sense—the sense that also applies to works like *Moby Dick* and *Orlando*.

4.2 The Commendatory Sense

In his book *Literary Theory: An Introduction*, Terry Eagleton (1983: 2) characterizes literature as "highly valued writing." Let's assume that the people doing the valuing here are at least minimally competent in this job, so that we may recast this characterization as "highly valuable writing." To avoid the problems regarding the concept of *language* in the previous subsection, let's recast again to "highly valuable works situated in a substantially text-based medium." This gives us the following, evaluative sense of *literature*:

> **Commendatory Sense:** x is *literature$_{comm}$* if and only if x is a highly valuable work situated in a substantially text-based medium.

In adopting this sense of "literature," we take the term to function as a sort of compliment, a commendatory term that picks out a special class of works and does so based on their appropriately received quality. What kind of qualities do we have in mind? Robert Stecker (1996: 694) suggests that works of literature possess "aesthetic, cognitive or interpretation-centered value to a significant degree." *Moby Dick* and *Orlando* are both widely recognized as enjoying these kinds of values: the deft usages of language are of aesthetic value, and the narratives and themes are of both cognitive and interpretation-centered value. Both works thereby qualify as literature$_{comm}$.

And what of the Taco Bell drive-through menu? Though some might claim that the items listed on the menu have aesthetic value, it would be perverse to find true aesthetic value in the menu itself. Its cognitive value is limited to some basic information about food choices, prices, and nutritional information, and its interpretive value is null. After all, imagine the absurd scenario of someone spending time looking at the Taco Bell menu, wondering out loud: "What does it *mean*?" Given the absence of these kinds of values, we can conclude that whereas *Moby Dick* and *Orlando* are rightly included as literature$_{comm}$, the Taco Bell menu is rightly excluded.

Are comics rightly viewed as literature$_{comm}$? Let's start with the Universal Question: Are all comics recognized as possessing aesthetic, cognitive, or interpretation-centered value to a significant degree? Certainly not: some are bad in seemingly every way that a comic can be bad. How about the Existential Question? Is at least one comic recognized as possessing aesthetic, cognitive, or interpretation-centered value to a significant degree? Certainly so: one need look no further than the aforementioned usual suspects: *Maus, Fun Home, Persepolis, Jimmy Corrigan*, and the like.

Moving on to the Generic Question: Is the typical comic recognized as possessing the right kinds of value to a significant degree? Here, we would again say that given the actual state of the comics medium and the surrounding comics practice, the answer is "no." And the Noteworthy Feature Question? Is the category *comics* noteworthy in being among the select categories that have members that possess the right kind of value to a significant degree? Well, given the positive answer offered to the Existential Question, it seems that the answer here is "yes." So, we can rest assured: even though not all comics are literature$_{comm}$ and even though your typical comic isn't literature$_{comm}$, it is still true in at least two robust senses—the Noteworthy Feature and the Existential—that comics are literature$_{comm}$.

These answers might be enough for some, but we aren't fully satisfied. This is because we believe in the possibility of *bad literature*: that is, literature that tries but *fails* to possess significant aesthetic, cognitive, or interpretation-centered value. But the Commendatory Sense entails that bad literature, in the sense just described, turns out to be impossible: anything that tries but fails to possess the relevant varieties of value, or merely possesses them to an insufficient degree, would not so much as qualify as *bad* literature but would instead fail to qualify as literature at all. That strikes us as evidence that the category of literature$_{comm}$ is not an especially pervasive sense of "literature" as some might initially expect.

4.3 The Exclusive List Sense

Perhaps something is literature, whether it is good or not, on account of what *kind of work it is*: if something is a novel, or a short story, or a play, or a poem, etc., then it is literature. Or, more formally:

> **Exclusive List Sense:** x is *literature$_{list}$* if and only if x is properly situated within a medium such as that of the novel, short story, theatre, poetry, etc.[10]

Moby Dick and *Orlando* are literature$_{list}$ in virtue of being rightly classified as novels, Flannery O'Connor's "A Good Man Is Hard to Find" (1953) is literature$_{list}$ in virtue of being a short story, William Shakespeare's *A Midsummer Night's Dream* (1595–6) is literature$_{list}$ in virtue of being a play, and the works in Maya Angelou's *Just Give Me a Cool Drink of Water 'fore I Diiie* (1971) are literature$_{list}$ in virtue of being poems. So far, these might seem like good results, until we notice that the very same justifications can be offered for the claim that *50 Shades of Grey*—a novel, just like *Moby Dick* and *Orlando*—is indeed literature$_{list}$, as well. We can save the intuitive distinction between these works, however, by pointing out that the former works are all *good* literature$_{list}$ insofar as they possess aesthetic, cognitive, or interpretation-centered value to a significant degree, whereas *50 Shades of Grey* is *bad* literature$_{list}$ insofar as it doesn't. The Taco Bell drive-through menu, however, isn't like *50 Shades* in being bad literature$_{list}$, since it isn't literature$_{list}$ at all. Regardless of whether we judge it to be good or bad, it is a member of a category—drive-through menus—that isn't on the exclusive list of mediums that qualify as literature$_{list}$.

By focusing on the Exclusive List Sense, we avoid the problems that come with focusing on "literature" in the senses previously discussed. Furthermore, questions about the Exclusive List Sense do not turn on complicated conclusions about the nature of language and the proper understanding of its status as a linguistic medium, as do questions about the Linguistic Sense. And finally, unlike the Commendatory Sense, the Exclusive List Sense is compatible with the possibility of bad literature. So far, so good. There is, however, a looming problem when we focus on questions about the Exclusive List Sense: no matter the quantificational structure of the question, whether or not comics qualify as literature$_{list}$ depends entirely on how we flesh out the "etc." at the end of the list.

Does the medium of comics make it onto the Exclusive List? If so, then all comics are literature$_{list}$. If not, then no comics are literature$_{list}$. The worry here is, in effect, about *which* Exclusive List we're talking about—one that includes comics or one that excludes comics? Surely each list provides us with a potential candidate meaning. But lists are just that: *lists.* Unless we have reason to think one of the lists is uniquely significant—and nothing about the Exclusive List Sense suggests as much—there's no substantial disagreement possible here. A more interesting sense will, in contrast, afford us a way to potentially determine what falls in or outside of a relevant category. For that reason, the Exclusive List Sense offers little room for the sort of philosophical progress we might hope for. With that in mind, let's keep moving on.

4.4. The Intentional Commendatory Sense

Following Stecker's (1996: 694) characterization, we might modify the Commendatory Sense by requiring a condition according to which "the writer of [the work] intended that it possess aesthetic, cognitive, or interpretation-centered value, and the work is written with sufficient technical skill for it to be possible to take that intention seriously." Along similar lines, Peter Lamarque and Stein Haugom Olsen (1997: 255–6) argue that "[a] text is identified as a literary work by recognizing the author's intentions that the text is produced and meant to be read within a framework of conventions defining the practice (constituting the institution) of literature." Despite potential worries about Lamarque and Stein referring to *literature* in their analysis of "literature," we find ourselves with a great deal of sympathy toward these intention-based accounts.[11]

This leads us to our final sense of "literature":

> **Intentional Commendatory Sense:** x is *literature$_{ic}$* if and only if (i) x is situated in a substantially text-based medium; (ii) x's creator(s) intend that x possess aesthetic, cognitive, or interpretation-centered value grounded in the relation between x's content and the conventions of the medium within which x is situated; and (iii) x is crafted with sufficient artistic and technical skill for it to be possible to take that intention seriously.

Note that the first condition requires that the *medium*, not the work, be substantially text-based, which allows for silent comics to qualify as literature$_{ic}$ since they are situated in a substantially text-based medium despite not being substantially text-based themselves. (This blocks subtitled films from qualifying, as the medium of film is not a substantially text-based medium in the operative sense.) The second condition requires a clear connection between the work's relevant values and the fact that the work is situated within—and hence, appreciated as an instance of—some particular medium. And the third condition retains Stecker's insight that the appropriate creative intentions must not only be present but, in some sense, noticeable and capable of being taken seriously.

While we won't assert that this Intentional Commendatory (IC) Sense is *the* definition of "literature"—since, again, we're not interested in the project of meta-linguistic negotiation—we do think that it is the first sense of the term that we've discussed that succeeds in providing a philosophically interesting and also intuitive characterization. It avoids the problems of the previous senses of "literature," while allowing for bad literature. So, while we acknowledge that this sense is just one among many legitimate senses of "literature" we might adopt, we do think that, out of the senses we've considered throughout this chapter, it best explains the philosophical interest that the Literature Question usually generates.

Armed with the Intentional Commendatory Sense, we can now ask: Are comics literature$_{ic}$? First, we look at the Universal reading of the question: Is every comic situated in a substantially text-based medium, with authors intending that they possess aesthetic, cognitive, or interpretation-centered value grounded in the relation between their content and the conventions of the medium within which they are situated; and crafted with sufficient technical skill for it to be possible to take that intention seriously? Clearly, we think, not—as an admittedly controversial example, we submit Frank Miller's *The Dark Knight Strikes Again* (2001-2002), a narrative, visual, and thematic mess that has left many wondering whether Miller was simply trolling his fan base.

What about the Existential reading of the question? Is at least one comic so situated, created with the right kind of intention, and crafted in the right kind of way? Absolutely. Again, for examples, just look at the works mentioned in the opening paragraph of this chapter. The Generic reading? Are typical comics so situated, created with the right kind of intention, and crafted in the right kind of way? Given the sheer mass of mass-produced, commercial comics, made by committee and rushed in before deadlines, we'd say: unfortunately not. And the Noteworthy Feature reading? Is the category *comics* noteworthy for being among the select categories that have members that are so situated, created with the right kind of authorial, and crafted in the right kind of way? Again: absolutely (an observation which we might take to constitute an argument for including the comics medium on the Exclusive List).

Before moving on, it's worth considering a potential problem with conceiving of literature in the Intentional Commendatory Sense: it might err in ruling out some more or less clear examples of literary comics. George Herriman's *Krazy Kat*, for example, is one of the most celebrated comic strips of all time. The strip, which ran in newspapers from 1913 to 1944, is often held up as an exemplar of the artistic and literary potential of the comics medium. Indeed, in David Carrier's *The Aesthetics of Comics* (2000), *Krazy Kat* receives more attention than perhaps any other work. And elsewhere, when the "comics as literature" debate comes up, Herriman's strip almost always receives a mention.

In *Reinventing Comics* (2000), however, Scott McCloud attributes to Herriman a rather particular and perhaps, given the status now conferred upon *Krazy Kat*, peculiar view: "that comics should *remember its place* and never get too *uppity* (27, italics in original). McCloud presents Herriman's sentiment as of a piece with that of Milton Caniff, who claims that comics "was a communication form rather than an art form. I don't think I ever heard anybody use the phrase 'art form' as such" (2000). Both Caniff and Herriman are juxtaposed with Rube Goldberg, who supposedly, after hearing Will Eisner discuss comics as an art form, exclaimed: "[t]hat's *bullshit,* Kid! We're not artists! We're *vaudevillians*! And don't you *ever forget that*!!" (2000: 26–7, italics in original). Indeed, Herriman himself is quoted as saying: "[i]nspiration! Who ever heard of a comic artist being inspired?" (2000: 27). If McCloud's comic history is to be believed, it looks like it might be quite a stretch to attribute to Herriman the kinds of intentions—for his work to be a source of aesthetic, cognitive, or interpretation-centered value—necessary for *Krazy Kat* to genuinely qualify as literature$_{ic}$.

We take it that in most instances in which people claim that *Krazy Kat* is literature or possesses literary merit, the principle of charity steers us toward interpreting them as having the concept of literature$_{ic}$ in mind. How do we make sense of this attribution, in the face of evidence that Herriman lacked the requisite intention, a lack which would be prohibitive of *Krazy Kat*'s purported literary$_{ic}$ status? Here, we trace two potential ways forward. First, we could just proceed in strict adherence to the Intentional Commendatory View and insist that scholars and critics stop holding *Krazy Kat* up as an exemplar comics' literary potential. This, however, runs the risk of methodological foul play, since it would involve philosophers purporting to correct our very data set, namely comics practice itself. Isolated instances of this revision—such as this one—wouldn't be bad in and of themselves per se, but they are nevertheless a cause for suspicious pause.

Alternatively, we might introduce a new sense of literature, the IC-Courtesy Sense, according to which *x* is *literature*$_{icc}$ if and only if it would be literature$_{ic}$ were the creators to have had the relevant intentions. So, *Krazy Kat* would have been literature$_{ic}$ *had it been the case* that Herriman intended it to possess significant aesthetic, cognitive, or interpretation-centered value. In effect, what makes *Krazy Kat* literature in this sense is whether a certain counterfactual is true. Since literature$_{icc}$ is otherwise indistinguishable from literature$_{ic}$, we are permitted to cautiously treat them as more or less equivalent concepts for the majority of critical and appreciative purposes. While this avoids imputing widespread error in comics practice, it does require accepting yet another notion of "literature" and one that might seem suspiciously artificial in nature.

When considered in light of the Intentional Commendatory View, McCloud's retelling of Herriman's attitude about *Krazy Kat* leads us into a dilemma: ride roughshod over comics practice or posit a weirdly counterfactual concept of literature. While neither approach seems totally

Figure 8.1 *Krazy Kat* (February 4, 1919), George Herriman. Krazy and Ignatz discuss *Hamlet* and Krazy is targeted with an inkwell.

unpalatable, neither seems like particularly sound methodology, either. Weighing the options, however, we are inclined toward the first, if only because isolated instances of critical and appreciative revision strike us as less philosophically damning than the issues plaguing the second. (Another potential option: conclude that Herriman was simply being insincere.) To hedge appropriately, we'll cast our conclusion as a conditional: in a world where McCloud's version of history is correct, *Krazy Kat* would fail to qualify as literature$_{ic}$ (Figure 8.1).

5. "The" Answer(s)

Are comics literature? We can see now that it depends on what sense of "literature" is operative when we ask the question and also on how we understand the quantificational structure of the question itself. Armed with what we take to be the *most interesting* candidate for what we mean by "literature" *in this context*—the Intentional Commendatory Sense—we arrive at the following four questions:

Universal IC Question: Do all comics qualify as literature$_{ic}$?

Existential IC Question: Does at least one comic qualify as literature$_{ic}$?

Generic IC Question: Do typical comics qualify as literature$_{ic}$?

Noteworthy Feature IC Question: Is *comics* noteworthy in being among the select categories that have as members things that qualify as literature$_{ic}$?

Based on what has been said so far, we submit the following answers: no, yes, no (but for different reasons), and yes (but for different reasons), respectively. For fun, you might go back and compare those answers to the answers to our earlier set of similar questions about mosquitos and the West Nile virus. As it turns out, comics are literature in the same sense that mosquitos carry the West Nile virus.

Of the four questions, which is the most philosophically interesting and potentially fruitful? That is, if someone simply asks "Are comics literature?," without further clarification, and we want to interpret them charitably, as asking the most interesting and potentially fruitful question they could be asking, which should we take them to be asking? We think the answer is clearly the Noteworthy Feature IC Question. And if that's right, then the most charitable reading of the "Are comics literature?" question produces a positive answer: the comics medium is noteworthy for having members that qualify as literature$_{ic}$. Or: sure, comics are literature (just like mosquitos carry the West Nile virus).

In arriving at this answer, we have taken much inspiration from Meskin's article, "Comics as Literature?" The connections between our conclusions and his are obvious:

> Suppose we treat the question of whether comics are literature as a straightforward question about the extension of our term "literature" (or the concept LITERATURE). Then we are unlikely to get a clear and unambiguous answer. It is eminently plausible that the linguistic practices that underwrite our use of the term do not determine whether some comics fall into its extension. And there is good evidence that there are a number of distinct LITERATURE concepts in play in ordinary discourse. So if we seek to answer this purely descriptive question, then I suspect that there will be no determinate and univocal answer. (2009a: 238)

Elsewhere, Meskin (2009b: 169) elaborates: "I think the right answer to the question of whether *Watchmen* is literature is that it is probably indeterminate. That is, there is no right or wrong answer to the question of whether the graphic novel fits into the category of literature." Here, he is speaking only of *Watchmen*, but it is clear that his conclusion is intended to generalize. And, despite our claim that certain comics, *Watchmen* included, are indeed literature$_{ic}$, we still concur with Meskin's conclusion that it is indeterminate whether they are literature.

As we've argued, and as is emphasized in Meskin's words, there is some indecision about what our ordinary concept *literature* amounts to. We've traced out several potential meanings, and there are surely others to be found. When someone asks whether a comic is literature, the principle of charity might steer us toward interpreting the question with a particular sense in mind, in which case we can perhaps settle on a determinate answer. But suppose that someone pushes back, insisting that they aren't asking about whether the comic is literature$_{ic}$ or literature$_{list}$ or what-have-you, but instead they are asking: Is it literature, *full stop*? It is to this question that Meskin responds by saying that there is "no determinate and univocal answer." Importantly, this is not to retreat to subjectivism, nor is it to reject the asking of the question. Instead, and paradoxically, it is to offer a determinate and univocal answer: that there is no determinate and univocal answer.

Even granting, though, that it is indeterminate whether comics are literature full stop, we still retain our positive answer to the Noteworthy Feature IC Question. How does this conclusion inform the reasons, offered near the beginning of this chapter, for caring about the topic in the first place? With respect to audiences, we suggested that settling whether comics are literature$_{ic}$ can help readers situate their reading against an appropriate backdrop when it comes to evaluation. Is determining whether a given comic is literature$_{ic}$ relevant to evaluation? Straightforwardly: yes. If something is literature$_{ic}$, then part of its process of creation was the intention to offer aesthetic, cognitive, or interpretative value grounded in the interplay between its content and the conventions of the comics medium. Out of this falls a fairly convenient evaluative theory: the more this intention succeeds, the better the comic. And, of course, if a given comic is clearly not aiming to be literature$_{ic}$, it's not fair to evaluate it as if it was.

With respect to scholars and critics, we suggested that settling whether comics are literature$_{ic}$ can help determine which scholarly and critical tools are appropriate and helpful when it comes to comics scholarship and criticism. If our subject of scholarship or criticism is a comic produced with the intention that it offer aesthetic, cognitive, and interpretive value grounded in the interplay between the comic's content and the conventions of the comic medium, we find ourselves with a helpful guide for which scholarly and critical tools we can reach for. In particular, would want to avail ourselves of those tools that help with establishing authorial intentions; assessing aesthetic, cognitive, and interpretive value; inferring content; and determining the conventions of the medium. Perhaps some of these tools might come from literary theory and others from elsewhere, but regardless of the toolbox of origin, the conclusion that comics are literature$_{ic}$ will help pick among them.[12]

Before moving on, it's worth pausing to note the possibility of pushback by those who would, for any number of reasons, argue that we ought not classify comics as literature. In *Reading Comics*, Douglas Wolk (2007: 14) claims that comics "bear a strong resemblance to literature—they use words, they're printed in books, they have narrative content—but they're no more a literary form than movies or opera are literary forms." Several philosophers writing on literature—Eileen John and Dominic McIver Lopes (2004: 43) and David Davies and Carl Matheson (2008: xii) among them—have asserted that the medium of comics is to be distinguished from the literary mediums (and hence, denied a place on their preferred Exclusive List). We offer two responses to this pushback. First, it is not clear that any of those mentioned have in mind the IC Sense of "literature" when they deny that comics are literature, and if they don't, then their claims are more or less consistent with what we have concluded in this chapter so far.

Second, even forced to concede these philosophers are correct, we can nonetheless hold on to the claim that the comics medium is noteworthy in being among the select categories that have as members things satisfying the conditions set out in the Intentional Commendatory Sense—for example, being situated in a substantially text-based medium, being intended to have certain aesthetic and other values, and being crafted with the right artistic and technical skill. As Meskin (2009a: 239) rightfully points out:

> we may establish the status of comics (and the value of teaching and studying them) by straightforwardly showing that works of great art can be produced in the medium. There is no need to show that they are literature in order to do that. We do not need to show that *Maus* or *Krazy Kat* are works of literature in order to establish that they are worth reading, studying, and taking seriously.

This strikes us as exactly correct. What matters is not that we call comics "literature" but that we recognize the nature and source of their artistic and aesthetic merits. We take ourselves to have established that (some) comics are appropriate subjects for such recognition insofar as they qualify as what we call "literature$_{ic}$." At the same time, we are more than happy to accept that "literature$_{ic}$" is a philosophical term of art. Ultimately, what matters is not what term we use but what concept that term picks out, and we're content to express that concept in a variety of different ways.

6. The Value of Comics (Literary or Otherwise)

Even though we have answered "yes" to the Existential IC Question and the Noteworthy Feature IC Question, we still answered "no" to the Universal IC Question and, perhaps most importantly, the Generic IC Question. This latter set of answers entails that at least some comics—and, in fact, *typical* comics—are *not* literature$_{ic}$. Indeed, most of those typical comics probably qualify as what Thomas J. Roberts (1990) calls *junk fiction*: same-y, formulaic fiction that aims primarily to casually entertain, rather than to offer genuine aesthetic, cognitive, or interpretive rewards. They are comics that are doomed—perhaps by design—to be merely *read*, if more than once then most likely for comfortable entertainment rather than serious study, challenge, or insight. Does that mean, as some seem to imply, that the rest of the comics medium is void of aesthetic opportunities for readers? We don't think so, but seeing why might require some investigation.

If we were to ask why we should read or study comics, the answer would be obvious: because they are potential sources of aesthetic, cognitive, and interpretive value. But what about the other comics, the typical comics, the junk comics? What reason, if any, do we have to read them? Of course, you might immediately think: "because it's fun!" And that, we think, is a legitimate reason that should not be, but unfortunately often is, discounted too quickly.

On the one hand, we suspect that if anyone remains unsatisfied with this justification for engaging with comics, they are likely sticks stuck in mud. On the other hand, lots of things are fun, and our time is woefully finite. We will often find ourselves having to pick and choose among our sources of joy and pleasure, with time spent on one source taking up time that could be spent on others. If we spend an hour reading junk comics, after all, that is an hour not spent playing videogames, contemplating poetry, or engaging in other varieties of the playful generation of value. Out of the vast array of potential sources of such value, then, do we have any substantive reason to settle on spending our time with junk comics?

As a literary theorist, Roberts thinks we do. On his understanding, the activity we engage in when we read junk comics is not the same activity as that which we engage in when we read literary$_{ic}$ comics.[13] When we read, say, *Fun Home*, we read *Fun Home*. We reflect on it and the insights it offers. Perhaps we even study it. But, when we read back issues of *Batman*, we're doing a lot more than reading those issues of *Batman*. We're reading what might be thought of as *the Batman system*: that is, we're situating those issues against a massive backdrop of extant fiction, both internal and external to the comics medium. The more Batman-related content with which we engage— whether comics, novels, films, videogames, theatrical serials, amusement parks, or what-have-you—the more systemic reading we've done. So, even if individual Batman stories are formulaic and same-y, when situated within a system, we can compare and contrast details, themes, character portrayals, and extract and critique trends across dozens or even hundreds of works. We attend to how the very same character is used as a tool to tell certain stories with certain themes in certain decades, to represent certain ideologies in the hands of some writers and others in the hands of others, we appreciate the difficulty of telling certain kinds of stories (such as Mike Mignola, Richard Pace, and Troy Nixey's *Batman: The Doom That Came to Gotham* (2000–1), a notable instance in which the superhero genre does cross over with the horror genre). This sort of systemic engagement allows a reader to appreciate displays of creativity within perhaps strict confines, the novel reinvention of familiar themes, and the Jenga-like collaborative process of building a massive serial fiction across titles and across decades. If there is value in this activity of systemic reading, then there is value in reading junk comics.

In "The Paradox of Junk Fiction" (1994), Noël Carroll argues that even if there is merit to Roberts's explanation, it is not expansive enough to offer a comprehensive account of the value of engaging with junk fiction in general. Surely, *some* readers engage in this activity of systemic reading but not all of them do. In suggesting an alternative but still valuable means of engaging with junk fiction, Carroll argues that such fiction affords us the opportunity to exercise our inferential abilities. That is: works of junk fiction give us the opportunity to reason through puzzles. Characteristic of junk fiction is familiarity with recycled plots. Think of a typical Batman-centric detective story, such as, say, *The Long Halloween*: a crime has been committed, Batman must figure out and capture who did it, there are various clues and false leads, and in the end—surprise!—it's probably not who you expected.

On Carroll's account, our familiarity with these rather typical plot structures offers a framework within which we get to exercise our own detective skills, thereby treating the act of reading as, again, a sort of gameplay. Generalizing from the detective subgenre to a more inclusive sense of junk fiction, we might often know, even at the outset of a junk story, what will unfold: its beginning (e.g., a new threat appears!), middle (e.g., the hero is in high-stakes peril!), and ending (e.g., the hero triumphs!). But, even so, we get a fulfilling opportunity to speculate and problem-solve by anticipating the details of how that beginning will become the middle and how that middle will give way to the ending. Insofar as this activity exercises our imaginative and inferential abilities, it is an activity of value, and hence, a reason to engage with junk fiction of all sorts, including junk comics. (To be sure: literary$_{ic}$ comics afford us the very same activity and often to a much higher and potentially more satisfying degree, but that doesn't constitute an argument for engaging *only* with such works: sometimes you play chess, sometimes you play checkers, and sometimes you play *Mortal Kombat*.)

The reasons offered by Roberts and Carroll are not genuine competitors but distinct and consistent rationales for engaging with junk comics. A second glance at each reveals a common feature: to read systemically or make inferences about the narrative goings-on, the reader needs some degree of knowledge and investment in the world of the story. When one becomes invested in the Batman system, one becomes acquainted with Gotham City and its large cast of characters. A deeper dive into the broader DC Universe takes readers on tours through Metropolis, Themyscira, Apokolips, the Dreaming, and other exotic locales. As James Harold (2010) has argued, we might find aesthetic value not just in narratives but in the worlds in which those narratives take place. Harold concludes:

> the value of fictional worlds cannot always be simply reduced to the value of the originating works. Some works, like *The Lord of the Rings*, fail as literature but succeed as worlds because the literary flaws either do not affect the world's value, or even affect it positively because the work's open-endedness vastly increases the possibilities for value in the imagined world. . . . This is not to say that every world that fans like is thereby valuable: a world is valuable if fans rightly or reasonably value it. Some worlds might be very popular but not worthy of that popularity. Sometimes, however, fans are drawn to certain works because of the real value of the world that these works describe. While

critics may focus on the flaws of the works *qua* artworks, many fans look instead to the enormous richness of the world that lies beyond the particular work.

On this line of thought, even if the comics fail to be literature$_{ic}$, a reader might rightfully appreciate, say, Brian K. Vaughan and Fiona Staples's *Saga* (ongoing since 2012) not for its literary merit but for the aesthetic richness of the worldbuilding. We take it, too, that Harold's claim can generalize not just to the aesthetic appreciation of worlds but of characters as well: junk comics with junk plots might still be appreciated for featuring great characters.[14]

We suspect that Harold would resist our claim that the DC Universe is as worthy of aesthetic appreciation as Middle-earth. In fact, he very nearly says as much: "[o]ther worlds, such as the world of *Superman*, are appropriately criticized for their glaring inconsistencies and their lack of any consistent mood or tone. In *Superman's* world, things can happen in just about any way you like" (2010). Notice, though, that granting Harold's claims about the fictional world of Metropolis and Krypton simply reinforces the fact that fictional words are appropriate targets of aesthetic engagement—it's just that not all aesthetic engagement results in a positive appraisal. Could there still be value in engaging with junk comics with aesthetically impoverished fictional worlds? We suspect so: the act of aesthetically engaging with such worlds gives us an opportunity to exercise our critical and appreciative capacities, calibrate our tastes, and perhaps even gain valuable insight into what simply doesn't work.

Beyond these proposals, we'd like to offer one final reason for making space for junk comics in your life. Make no mistake: it's not *the* final reason for engaging with junk comics but merely one that might go unnoticed. There are, of course, potentially many more. But in *this* final reason, we follow Ted Cohen (1993) in supposing that at least one among the potentially many functions of the arts (construed broadly) is to bring us together under common tastes and values. Some mediums, styles, genres, movements, or even particular works—the more obscure, or underground, or peripheral, or elite—bring together smaller, more similar, and hence more intimate groups. Think about how exciting it is to be wandering down the street and see someone else wearing the same obscure Norwegian black metal t-shirt: you instantly connect over having something rather uncommon in common. And if you have that in common, it is perhaps safe to assume that you probably share other interests, as well. Other arts—the more popular, or accessible, or widely known, or canonical—often bring together larger and more diverse groups. Think about how comforting it can be to sing along with a group of strangers to a well-known song on the jukebox at the bar. Cohen's point is that the arts act as a sort of social glue, as a means of facilitating bonds among people and groups of people. Some arts glue together small groups; some bond large groups. And some works—say, the *especially* obscure—might leave us in groups of effectively just one, in contented solitude with our own little aesthetic secret. In a particularly moving passage, Cohen (1993: 156) writes:

> I need both. Urgently. *Hamlet* and *The Marriage of Figaro* connect me with most of you, I would guess, perhaps all of you. Elaine May's movie *Ishtar*, which I am very fond of, leaves me virtually alone. That's all fine: I need to be with you, and I need to be alone. I need to be like you, and I need to be unlike you. A world in which you and I never connected would be a horror. And so would a world in which we were exactly the same, and therefore connected unfailingly, with every object on every occasion. *The Marriage of Figaro* helps us be us. *Ishtar* helps me be me. Thank God for them both.

We think there is something of deep significance to this observation. Junk comics bind together communities—fandoms—and while these communities can certainly be toxic in many ways (see, e.g., ComicsGate, GamerGate, the Sad Puppies, and unfortunately, others) they can also offer a profound sense of belonging and shared interest, shared agency, and shared humanity. Batman fandom needn't be a game of solitaire: it can be a valuable, intimate, and multifaceted group activity. Insofar as junk comics facilitate such an activity, we have at least some reason to not just engage with them but celebrate them. You need not—and probably ought not—devote your entire life to reading junk comics, but, at the same time, you need not suffer any kind of aesthetic or philosophical embarrassment in making room for them.[15]

7. The Fine Art of Comics?

With the subject of high and low art on the table, we conclude this chapter by turning to a natural follow-up to questions about the relation between comics and literature: What is the relation between comics and so-called *fine art*? While comics is a substantially text-based, often narrative medium, it is also a primarily visual one, making it odd to consider whether a work such as *Watchmen* deserves to be placed alongside *Moby Dick* and *Orlando* without also considering whether it is additionally—or instead—deserving of the same kind of recognition afforded to the works of the great painters and sculptors. But the latter questions rarely get asked. Is this because the answer would look almost universally grim for comics? Or perhaps because of the historical accident of comics studies being steered primarily by scholars of literature and narrative, rather than by art historians? Our suspicion is that bits of both explanations are at play here, but more can be said.

The very concept of "fine art" is not without its detractors, especially among those working in or around comics and popular art forms. Artist and writer John Carlin (2020: 258) has offered a scathing critique:

> Ironically, high art has become overly controlled by the forces it is valued for resisting. All too often blue-chip art reflects the dominant ideology while pop culture chips away at the status quo. Fine art has become too satisfied with its own self-awareness while ignoring the real problems of the society in which it exists. . . . Pop culture is ugly, rude, sexist, racist and politically naïve. Fine art is obscure, elitist, misogynist and has no politics. Obviously they were made for each other.

Similarly, in his short strip "High Art Lowdown" (1990, reprinted in Munson 2020), Art Spiegelman writes that "'high n' low' is a question of class/ economics, not aesthetics" and compares the division of artworks and other cultural artifacts into categories such as "fine art," "high art," and "low art" to a famous and absurd thought experiment by Jorge Luis Borges. Under a subtitle of "Chop Suey," Spiegelman writes:

> Borges imagined a Chinese encyclopedia that divided animals into "A. belonging to the emperor, B. embalmed, C. time, D. suckling pigs, E. sirens, F. fabulous, G. stray dogs, H. included in the present classification, I. frenzied, J. innumerable, K. drawn with a very fine camel hair brush, L. etc, M. having just broken the water pitcher, N. that from a long way off look like fles." The high and low show is organized around similar principles!

Carlin and Spiegelman are united in skepticism toward the world of fine art, insofar as that world seems to be governed by principles that are both ideologically suspect, if not outright oppressive, and ultimately arbitrary when it comes to gatekeeping and assignment of status. Indeed, this view has been shared by many underground comics artists; Bart Beaty (2012: 19) quotes Robert Crumb as expressing that "'ART' is just. A racket! A HOAX perpetuated on the public by so-called 'Artists' who set themselves up on a pedestal, and promoted by pantywaste ivory-tower intellectuals and sob-sister 'critics' who think the world owes them a living!" Perhaps, then, a good bit of comics' typical exclusion from the world of fine art is due to the hostility and antagonism toward that world by many comic artists.

While voices like those of Spiegelman and Crumb are loud and powerful, we won't pretend that they are fully representative of attitudes held by typical cartoonist and comics artists. On that, we can only speculate. Putting aside, however, political, moral, and cultural critique of the concept of "fine art," as well as accidents of history, we can ask: Is there anything about the comics medium itself that can help explain its typical exclusion from the world of fine art? The answer, we, think, is "yes."

Though there are exceptions, it is typically the case that if we want to engage with fine art, we must *go to it*, whereas we can bring the low or popular arts *to us*. We can stream a film and either pick up our own personal copies of various comics at the local shop or pull them up on our home devices, but if we want to see a painting or sculpture, we usually have to go to a gallery or a museum. In a seminal discussion of comics art as aesthetic objects, specifically in gallery or museum contexts, art historian Andrei Molotiu (2020b) explores the atypicalities of such displays. For one, what is most often displayed in a gallery or museum is not the "finalized" or printed object that is the comic itself but instead either a comics artist's original work—a page or series of pages, most usually short of the full set—or a fragment of the published work.[16] This practice is at odds with typical expectations when it comes to observing fine art in fine arts spaces, in which we are perhaps more accustomed to being presented with finished, complete works. How are we to appropriately engage, aesthetically, with an object that is an unfinished work or a mere part of a larger whole? While Molotiu argues that these challenges can be overcome and that artist's pages can be appropriate objects of aesthetic interest and evaluation, the mismatch in norms here certainly helps explain some of the tension between comics art and fine art: the nature of the comics medium makes its works quite difficult to properly display within typical fine arts spaces.

Beyond this mismatch, there is at least one other potential reason for oddity when trying to subsume comics under the auspices of the fine arts. Suppose, as it not uncommon, that we characterize the typical goal of the fine arts as that of inspiring beauty and offering sublime aesthetic experiences to an audience. In the *Critique of Judgement* (1790), Immanuel Kant argued that the real experience of the sublime requires a sort of *disinterested* attention: in other words, an encouragement of free play of imagination, unfettered by connections to and concerns of the real world. Comics, however, as artifacts intended to be picture-read, are much more often than not *narrative* and narrativity—much more often than not—involves a chronological sequence of events governed by a causal structure. This very narrativity can potentially frustrate our ability to approach a work with the right sort of disinterest. Reflecting on the *Comic Book Apocalypse* show at CSU Northridge Art Galleries, featuring original pages by Jack Kirby, Molotiu (2020b: 54) gestures at this frustration:

> When I visited the exhibition I found trying to read the story while standing in the gallery rather awkward. The pages didn't draw me forward through the narrative; one could of course force oneself to progress through the book, yet doing so felt closer to a dutiful scholarly pursuit than to an aesthetically rewarding experience. For me, at least, the sideways, page-to-page impulse to *read* conflicted with, and was defeated by, the simple desire to *see* each image. At the same time, the joy in seeing the art was lessened by the duty one felt . . . to keep reading: the presence of many pages detracted from the presence of each single one.

These remarks highlight the tension between approaching a work with disinterested attention (as, if Kant is correct, we typically do when we attempt to appreciate works aimed at beauty and the sublime) and attending to it as a narrative work designed to be picture-read. A good deal of the difficulty in viewing comics as fine art might, it seems, come from the simultaneous but conflicting pulls both away from and toward the temporal, causally ordered engaged practice of picture-reading.

Of course, none of this is to say that neither the comics medium nor the fine arts establishment are rigid enough to preclude some form of further convergent evolution, but our sentiments largely align with Molotiu's (2020b: 60) concluding quip: "[p]ersonally, I'm holding out for a Kirby retrospective at the Met; when that happens, we will be able to say that our cause has finally won." Given the previously discussed account of why engaging with comics is itself valuable, whether or not they are "literature" or "high art" or "fine art," however, the lingering voice of Spiegelman might haunt us, leaving us to wonder whether this is even a battle worth fighting.

8. Recommended Readings

To say that the field of comics studies contains much in terms of literary analysis of comics would be a hilarious understatement. To orient yourself, we recommend starting with Miodrag (2016), which contains an excellent discussion of comics as literature as well as a thorough bibliography. For recent, book-length discussion, see Christopher Pizzino's *Arresting Development* (2016).

On the philosophy of literature more generally, see David Davies's *Aesthetics and Literature* (2007), D. Davies and Carl Matheson's *Contemporary Readings in the Philosophy of Literature: An Analytic Approach* (2008), Eileen John and Dominic McIver Lopes's *Philosophy of Literature: Contemporary and Classic Readings* (2004), and Peter Lamarque's *The Philosophy of Literature* (2009). On some potential reasons to read comics—in particular, superhero comics—see Geoff Klock's *How to Read Superhero Comics and Why* (2006). On the relation between comics and art, see Molotiu (2016), Salter (2016), Bart Beaty's *Comics Versus Art* (2012), and Kim A. Munson's excellent edited volume, *Comic Art in Museums* (2020).

9

Comics, Obscenity, and Pornography

Chapter Outline

1. Accolades and Protests

As you might have gathered from our mentions of Alison Bechdel's comic memoir *Fun Home: A Family Tragicomic* (2006) throughout this book so far, we hold the work in high esteem. And in that, we are far from alone. The recognition Bechdel's first long-form comic has received is of the sort that many creators—of comics or otherwise—strive for but rarely, if ever, achieve. *The New York Times* ranked it among the best books of 2006 and *Time* magazine rated it as *the* best of the year—better than any other comic or non-comic, whether fiction or nonfiction. More recently, in 2019, *The Guardian* listed the book 33rd on a list of the best books of the twenty-first century (so far). As is perhaps clear enough already, many people agree: Bechdel created a book well worth reading. If anything is near-universally regarded as a contemporary classic of the comics medium, *Fun Home* is. Even that claim is itself a bit of an understatement, given the widespread and positive recognition the work has received outside of the comics world, in the broader literary community.

Depicting Bechdel's experience as a young lesbian and her complicated relationship with her gay father who remained in the closet up until his apparent suicide, *Fun Home* delivers its narrative and reflections with profound depth and nuance. Given its themes and quality, the book was well received among many LGBTQ+ organizations. In the year following its release, *Fun Home* received the GLAAD (Gay and Lesbian Alliance Against Defamation) Media Award for Outstanding Comic Book, the Stonewall Book Award for nonfiction, the Lambda Literary Award in the "Lesbian Memoir and Biography" category, and more. That same year, Bechdel's work received two nominations for Eisner Awards: Best Graphic Album and Best Reality-Based Work, with Bechdel securing the win in the latter category. Bechdel herself was nominated for Best Writer.

For just as long as the book has been receiving accolades, it has also been the recipient of protest. From being targeted for removal from libraries to incurring the ire of small groups of high school and college students and their parents, the work's inclusion on the shelves or in curricula has been contested. Perhaps most notably, *Fun Home* found itself the center of controversy at the College of Charleston in South Carolina in 2013, in which a coalition of American conservative organizations—led by the Palmetto Group, affiliated with Focus on the Family and the Family Research Council—objected to the book being used as a common reading assignment for incoming students. As a result of the attention such objections were able to draw, the South Carolina House of Representatives, led by Republican Representative Gary Smith, retaliated by cutting the College of Charleston's funding by $52,000. This led to the involvement of the American Civil Liberties Union, the National Coalition Against Censorship, the Comic Book Legal Defense Fund, and many other organizations intent on defending the academic freedom of college instructors to assign the text at their discretion. Eventually—and with the approval of South Carolina governor Nikki Haley—the funding to the university was restored, though with strict conditions on its use, alongside a mandate that professors who assign *Fun Home* make exceptions for students with objections to reading it, such that they instead be allowed to work with an alternate text.

Why such a controversy over just one comic? The charge initially raised by the book's detractors in South Carolina was that Bechdel's memoir was *pornographic*, since it depicted (some) nudity and sexual activity. A similar complaint was raised two years later, by then incoming first-year Duke

University student Brian Grasso, when *Fun Home* was recommended to his class as common summer reading. In August 2015, once a small chorus of like-minded students received some media attention, Grasso penned an editorial for the *Washington Post* in which he attempted to offer a reasoned explanation for why he refused to read Bechdel's comic, ultimately citing moral and religious justification: "in the Bible, Jesus forbids his followers from exposing themselves to anything pornographic."[1] Since *Fun Home* depicted nudity and sexual activity, Grasso concluded that his religious and moral commitments required that he abstain from participating in the recommended assignment.

Mindful of Smith's claim that *Fun Home* "promote[s] the gay and lesbian lifestyle," one might assume that most of these protests of *Fun Home* as pornographic are no more than homophobic dog-whistles. And, while this is surely true of *some* protests against *Fun Home*, we suspect that there are at least some who object to *Fun Home* sincerely and specifically on the grounds that it is, in fact, a piece of pornography. Answering these objections is an important project and, in doing so, our primary philosophical concern becomes quite specific: determining whether there is any justification at all for the claim that *Fun Home* is pornography. After all, in Grasso's own words:

> My choice had nothing to do with the ideas presented. I'm not opposed to reading memoirs written by LGBTQ individuals or stories containing suicide. I'm not even opposed to reading Freud, Marx or Darwin. I know that I'll have to grapple with ideas I disagree with, even ideas I find immoral.

These claims suggest that it's not the content of the comic that Grasso takes moral and religious objection to but instead the mode of that content's presentation. So, it certainly matters that *Fun Home* is a comic, as that mode of presentation is particularly relevant to Grasso's concerns:

> I think there is an important distinction between images and written words. If the book explored the same themes without sexual images or erotic language, I would have read it. But viewing pictures of sexual acts, regardless of the genders of the people involved, conflicts with the inherent sacredness of sex. My beliefs extend to pop culture and even Renaissance art depicting sex.

In the end, it is not the LGBTQ+ representation but the "cartoon drawings of a woman masturbating and multiple women engaging in oral sex" to which Grasso morally and religiously objects (again, we use his own words here).

Ultimately, the protests over *Fun Home* are minor footnotes in the work's history, especially given its vast impact on contemporary comics, literature, and LGBTQ+ narratives. At the same time, philosophically speaking, it provides an illuminating case study in how people often think and argue about pornography. Most people—the overwhelming majority, we suspect—would agree that despite containing a handful of panels depicting sexual activity or nudity, *Fun Home* is not properly categorized as pornography. But even if there is a consensus that the book is *not* pornography, reasonable people can still disagree as to *why* it's not—and making philosophical progress on that issue can help us make further progress toward adjudicating other cases that will inevitably arise.

2. Pornographic Comics and Obscene Comics

Even if we'll ultimately argue that *Fun Home* is not properly classified among erotic and pornographic works, there is a lengthy history of such comics. As Justin Hall—both a scholar and a creator of comics, including erotic comics—notes,

> [P]orn comics have a long and illustrious history. In Japan, proto-comic books named *kiboyoshi* (yellow covers), often featuring erotic content, were being produced by the emergent merchant class as early as the late eighteenth century. Tijuana bibles—the eight-page, horizontal, hard-core pornographic comics booklets illegally published in North America by the millions from the 1920s to the 1960s—represent some of the world's first underground comics, and they influenced later generations of cartoonists, from Harvey Kurtzman to Robert Crumb. Tom of Finland began producing his gay erotic comics art in underground European publications as early as the 1940s. (2016: 154)

In their discussion of pornographic comics, Christy Mag Uidhir and Henry Pratt (2012: 143) further characterize these Tijuana bibles as

> Cheaply made pocket-sized comic books popular in the Depression-era United States that depict sexually explicit scenarios (both heterosexual and homosexual) involving celebrities and cartoon characters who were well known at the time (e.g. Popeye, Snow White, Nancy and Sluggo, Clark Gable, John Dillinger, Dorothy Lamour).

Hall goes on to detail how during the American cultural revolution in the 1960s, pornographic comics became even more commonplace, appearing in venues ranging from popular magazines like *Playboy* to independent and renowned comics publishers like Fantagraphics.

As Roy Cook (2016) argues, the underground comics scene that emerged in the 1960s contained much in terms of pornographic content: indeed, such underground comics were (and still are) often referred to as *comix*, "a nod to their often x-rated content" (34). Crucial to the history of this era of American comics is Robert Crumb, a prolific, influential, and highly controversial cartoonist. As Cook (2016: 36) writes,

> Robert Crumb's work is often singled out as particularly worrisome. Crumb's autobiographical comics from the underground period explore his sexual predilections, which tended toward misogyny, sexual domination, and rape fantasies, and come across to many readers as cheap pornographic provocation at best.

Of course, Crumb was far from being the only cartooonist producing sexually explicit comics at this time and was likely not even the most extreme: Cook (2016) suggests that "Crumb's notoriety in this respect might have more to do with his fame within the underground comics scene, and less to do with his comics being particularly objectionable when compared to other comics created (by white males) within the underground," making particular note of artists such as "Spain" Rodriguez, Gilbert Shelton, and S. Clay Wilson.

Pornographic comics are, of course, not limited to the American comics scene, with similar booms of pornographic comics taking place in both Japan and Europe. Of particular note in Japan is the emergence and popularity of *hentai manga*, described by Mag Uidhir and Pratt (2012: 143) as subgenre of comics "primarily aimed at adult consumers due to its preponderance of sexually explicit themes and graphic depictions of a veritable host of sexual orientations, acts, and fetishes (e.g. breasts, transsexuality, incest, bestiality, *alien hentai* or 'tentacle rape')." Out of all comics traditions, *hentai* arguably leads the pack when it comes to bizarre pornographic representations.

Given the long history of erotic and pornographic comics, one might expect that the policing of such content in comic books was a central task of the Comics Code Authority, which emerged in the United States in 1954. As detailed by Amy Kiste Nyberg in her historical study of the Code, however, the regulation of sexual content was, while present, of arguably tertiary importance. As Nyberg (2016: 27) explains:

> The Code was divided into three sections. Part A provided 12 guidelines for comics dealing with crime. Part B addressed horror comics. . . . Part C

provided general standards for all comics and included rules for dialogues and costume, along with guidelines for handling religion, marriage, and sex.

Given the extensive attention they receive in the formulation of the Code, crime and horror comics (discussed in Chapter 6) are its foremost targets, with the regulations of and prohibitions against depictions of sexuality in comics mostly relegated to the grab bag of general restrictions in Part C. This is, of course, not to downplay the effect of the Code on the representation of sexuality in comics but instead to caution against thinking that sexually explicit comics like Tijuana bibles catalyzed the Code when, in reality, the public outcry against crime and horror comics was far more impactful. (Doubtless, this is because Tijuana bibles weren't being sold on every neighborhood newsstand.)

Even if pornographic comics were not among the primary targets of the Comics Code, they have been a near-constant subject of public outcry or even litigation. If—as has happened on more than one occasion—a comic shop employee sells certain comics to young customers, they might find themselves charged with distributing pornographic or obscene material to a minor. This is (almost) exactly what happened to Jesus Castillo, employee of the Dallas, Texas, comic shop Keith's Comics, in 2000. Castillo was subsequently sentenced to 180 days in jail, along with a year of probation and a $4,000 fine, with appeals leading all the way up to the US Supreme Court. The comic that landed Castillo in legal trouble was Volume Two of *Demon Beast Invasion: The Fallen* (1998), a horror *manga* written and illustrated by Toshio Maeda. The person purchasing the comic was not actually a minor but an undercover police officer. Despite selling the comic to an adult, the court ruled that Castillo was nonetheless in violation of the law in virtue of the supposed fact that comics are *for kids*. Scott McCloud, acting on behalf of the Comic Book Legal Defense Fund, argued during Castillo's trial that despite being "sexually potent in some places," *Demon Beast Invasion* possessed artistic and literary merit sufficient for disqualifying it from counting as objectionably pornographic or obscene. The court ultimately disagreed.

It is important to note that the actual charge against Castillo was not that of distributing pornography but instead of distributing *obscene* materials. An earlier, quite similar case—in fact, the very first case in the United States of a comics-related obscenity charge—found creator Mike Diana arrested, charged, and convicted for artistic obscenity, after his *Boiled Angel* #8 (1991) was objected to by Florida Assistant State Attorney Stuart Baggish in 1993.

Based on this conviction, Diana was then sentenced to community service and three years of probation. To appreciate the distinction between these two cases and the different issues they raise, we will need to supplement our understanding of pornography with an appropriately clear understanding of the related topic of obscenity. As is hopefully apparent, these investigations carry some weight: clear answers to philosophical questions about the relation between comics and concepts like *pornography* and *obscenity* are indeed relevant to issues of expression, censorship, and—as the cases of Jesus Castillo, Mike Diana, and others make evident—personal freedom.[2]

3. What Is Pornography?

We've now arrived at two distinct but related philosophical questions:

Pornography Question: Under what conditions does something qualify as *pornography*?

Obscenity Question: Under what conditions does something qualify as *obscene*?

We'll begin with the Pornography Question. Despite the importance of getting this question right, bad answers are easy to come by. For example, one might offer the following knee-jerk response (which seems to be something like what Grasso assumes in his aforementioned editorial):

Depiction View: *x* is a work of *pornography* if and only if *x* depicts nudity or sexual activity.

To see the inadequacy of this answer, consider medical textbooks in which depictions of nudity and sexual activity are standard but are obviously presented in a clinical rather than sexualized manner. Such examples make clear that the mere depiction of nudity or sexual activity is simply not *sufficient* for pornographic status. Further reflection quickly reveals that such depictions are not *necessary* for pornographic status either, given the varieties of fetish pornography involving neither nudity nor anything resembling conventional sexual activity. Examples include some pornography designed to appeal specifically to foot or shoe fetishists or the (morally reprehensible) practice of "candid" pornography, much of which involves recordings of clothed women occupying public spaces, unaware that they are being filmed. Such "candid" pornography—objectionable as it is, given the characteristic lack of consent by the subjects of such recordings—depicts neither nudity nor sexual activity and is a further demonstration that such depictions are not necessary for pornographic status. So much, then, for the Depiction View.

Another inadequate—but nonetheless tempting—answer is perhaps the most famous and likely the one that you've heard parroted: when it comes to pornography, "I know it when I see it." This response originated in 1964, with then Supreme Court justice Potter Stewart, in the case of *Jacobellis v. Ohio*, which was to decide whether the state of Ohio could ban showings of Louis Malle's 1958 film, *The Lovers*. Though this case was largely about the nature of obscenity, Justice Stewart uttered his now-famous line with the category of "hard-core pornography" in mind:

> I shall not today attempt further to define the kinds of material I understand to be embraced within that shorthand description, and perhaps I could never succeed in intelligibly doing so. But I know it when I see it, and the motion picture involved in this case is not that.

Suppose that we apply Stewart's take on "hard-core pornography" to the broader umbrella category of *pornography*, as well. A charitable interpretation of this approach delivers a view according to which, even if we cannot define the concept, we can nonetheless reliably identify instances of pornography given our prior familiarity with clear examples. Or, more formally:

> **Resemblance View:** x is a work of *pornography* if and only if an agent familiar with paradigm cases of pornography would, based on x's relevant similarity to those paradigm cases, judge x to be a work of pornography.

Despite being widely parroted, the Resemblance View doesn't fare much better than the Depiction View as an answer to the Pornography Question. First, it violates our requirement that analyses of concepts must be noncircular: in offering necessary and jointly sufficient conditions for pornographic status, the Resemblance View twice employs the very concept it purports to define. Second, the Resemblance View offers no guidance for how to adjudicate disputes among parties who all enjoy similar levels of familiarity with paradigm cases but arrive at different verdicts about whether something is indeed a work of pornography. One party says, "well, I know it when I see it, and I say *that's* pornography!" while the other says, "and *I* know it when *I* see it, too, and *I* say it's not!" The Resemblance View provides us no information whatsoever about which party we should side with, instead leaving us with an irresolvable stalemate. This is far from ideal, given the fact that there is surely more to say about the features typical to pornography and the fact that important questions—not to mention legal ones—often require us to arrive at an answer.

One might respond that despite these problems, something like the Resemblance View is ultimately the best we're going to be able to do. Support for this sort of pessimism might be sought in the views expressed by philosophers such as Ludwig Wittgenstein (1953: 5), who famously argued that certain concepts simply resist any kind of definition in terms of necessary and jointly sufficient conditions. Perhaps Wittgenstein's most enduring example of this claim comes in his remarks about the futility of attempting to define the concept *game*: try as we might, Wittgenstein argued, we will never come up with a satisfactory set of necessary and jointly sufficient conditions for what it is to be a game, leaving us able to distinguish games only by way of their relevant resemblance with paradigm examples.

This Wittgensteinian view might well be true for certain terms or concepts. We caution, however, against accepting it too quickly or accepting it universally. Suppose that we're attempting to analyze some concept into necessary and jointly sufficient conditions. We look at a few attempts at offering such conditions, notice that those attempts fail, and hastily conclude that the concept simply cannot be defined. We see a few such attempts and conclude that the same applies to other concepts—like *pornography*—as well. This, however, is to systematically conflate the rather strong claim that the concepts in question *can't be defined* with the significantly weaker claim that those terms *just haven't been defined yet*. See, for example, Bernard Suits's classic work *The Grasshopper* (2014), in which Suits, unconvinced by Wittgenstein's treatment of *game*, not only attempts to offer an analysis in terms of necessary and sufficient conditions but is also taken by many to have succeeded in doing so.[3] As Suits (2014: 1–2) quite eloquently puts it:

> I am aware, of course, of the fairly widespread disenchantment with the search for definitions that currently prevails in the philosophical community, and indeed in the intellectual community generally. And Wittgenstein, one of the most forceful spokesmen (and certainly the most exotic) for the anti-definitional attitude, is famous for having singled out the attempt to define games as illustrating *par excellence* the futility of attempting to define anything whatever. "Don't say," Wittgenstein admonishes us, "there must be something common or they would not be called 'games'"—but *look and see* whether there is anything common to all. This is unexceptional advice. Unfortunately, Wittgenstein himself did not follow it. He looked, to be sure, but because he had decided beforehand that games are indefinable, his look was fleeting, and he saw very little.

To draw a moral from this story, then: we shouldn't be too quick to give up on analysis and conclude that we have to settle for something like the Resemblance View, since an adequate definition might just be forthcoming. What Suits says about games, we say about pornography.

Recall our definition of *comics*, from Chapter 2: roughly, something is a comic just in case its creator aptly intends it to be picture-read. Perhaps we can take a similar approach to pornography. There is certainly precedent for doing so: Mari Mikkola (2019) argues that works of pornography are a variety of artifact and, hence, governed in part by creative intentions, while Michael Rea (2001) argues that a work's status as pornography is dependent in part on a particular kind of use. Our own view synthesizes these two, offering an account according to which something is a work of pornography just in case it is intended to be used in a certain way. Or, more specifically:

> **Invitation View:** x is a work of pornography if and only if (i) x is a representational artifact, (ii) x's creator intends it to be used as a tool for sexual arousal, and (iii) x's creator also intends that x's representational content play a substantial role in its use.

The Invitation View begins with the idea that to be pornography is to be a tool intended to be used for the generation of sexual arousal. Condition (i) requires that the tool in question be a representational artifact and hence something like a film, photograph, drawing, or recording that depicts subjects. It therefore disqualifies objects like mere sex toys or certain drugs or supplements that might serve as tools for sexual arousal and which clearly do not qualify as pornography. But—and this is surely a peculiar case— what about a sex toy adorned with an installment of Charles Schulz's famed *Peanuts* strip? Such an (admittedly quite strange) object would indeed be a representational artifact intended to be used as a tool for sexual arousal. But, given condition (iii), it would still fail to qualify as pornography: the depictions of the comic are clearly disconnected from the intended use of the object and are not any kind of sexual stimulus or aid. This example helps demonstrate, then, that to be a work of pornography, the depicted content must be intended to play a substantial role in the use of the artifact for its primary purpose of sexual arousal.

Just as something is a comic, then, if its creator intends it to be met with a certain kind of engagement, so too with pornography—just with a rather different variety of engagement. This seems to get a lot of cases right. Matt Fraction and Chip Zdarsky's series *Sex Criminals* (2013–20) features a cast of characters able to experience literally time-stopping orgasms. It regularly depicts nudity and sexual activity but it is pretty clear that those elements are not intended to be used as a tool for the reader's sexual arousal. Even if some readers do in fact use copies of *Sex Criminals* in that way, what matters on the Invitation View is the intentions of the creators—in this case, Fraction and Zdarsky.

In Justin Green's autobiographical comic *Binky Brown Meets the Holy Virgin Mary* (1972), we see many explicit images of penises—including many oddly placed penises serving in place of various other bodily appendages—but those images appear as part of Green's attempt to illustrate his particular struggles with obsessive-compulsive disorder, rather than to elicit arousal or sexual interest in the reader. (Green's particular disorder manifested as obsessive concern about sinful arousal over certain kinds of religious imagery.) Chester Brown's autobiographical comics *Paying for It* (2011) and *The Playboy* (1992) both depict nudity and sexual activity, but for purposes of offering an argument for the legalization of sex work (in *Paying for It*) and offering a confessional-style retelling of his first explorations into sexuality (in *The Playboy*). Neither topics are presented as "sexy" in the least. And, while Gilbert Hernandez's occasionally sexually explicit content in the revered comics series *Love and Rockets* doesn't constitute pornography due to the lack of relevant intention, the presence of exactly that intention in Hernandez's *Birdland* (2000) results in a different verdict: despite significant stylistic and narrative similarities between the two series, *Love and Rockets* is not pornography while *Birdland* is, due to the respective absence and presence of the relevant creative intention on the part of Hernandez.[4]

So far, the Invitation View seems to get things pretty much right. But there is a complication: as we've discussed previously, our intentions don't always succeed. Suppose Edie sets out to make a work of pornography, and in so doing, creates a representational artifact in which the depicted content is intended to play a significant role in the artifact's intended use, namely the user's sexual arousal. But, suppose further that Edie is, as it turns out, a rather incompetent pornographer and ends up producing a depiction of a goat eating from an overflowing compost bin swarming with flies. Despite the vast variety of kinks in the world, we submit that almost no one would realistically be able to successfully employ Edie's drawing in the manner intended. Edie's drawing, then, isn't even *bad pornography*, because it isn't even pornography at all. Instead, it's merely the product of a failed attempt to create pornography. In light of considerations like these, we propose the following revision to the Invitation View:

> **Reasonable Invitation View:** x is a work of pornography if and only if (i) x is a representational artifact, (ii) x's creator intends it to be used as a tool for sexual arousal, (iii) x's creator also intends that x's representational content play a substantial role in its use, and (iv) it is reasonable to assume that the target audience for x could realistically use x in the manner intended.

The key difference between this view and the previous Invitation View is the inclusion of the fourth condition, which sets out to solve the problem just discussed: if something is so incompetently or ineffectively made that it is unreasonable to assume a target audience could realistically use it for sexual arousal, then that thing wouldn't even be *bad* pornography. Instead, it would be a failed attempt at pornography and so not pornography at all. So, even if we were to discover that Schulz intended *Peanuts* to be pornography, we can safely conclude that despite that intention, he clearly failed. No reasonable reader would take the comic to aim at serving as pornography instead of being, say, an all-ages comedy strip. Here, the Reasonable Invitation View offers what seems to be the correct verdict: *Peanuts* is not pornography, regardless of (hypothetical) Schulz's intentions.

What about the example we started with, Bechdel's *Fun Home*? If we accept the Depiction View as an answer to the Pornography Question, the comic counts as pornography. If we accept the Resemblance View, we are left with an unresolvable stalemate between detractors like Grasso and those of us who deny it is pornography. As we've argued throughout this section, though, neither of those views are satisfactory answers to the Pornography Question.

According to far more plausible views, *Fun Home* is decidedly not pornography. When held up against the Invitation View, condition (ii) is left unsatisfied: Bechdel has publicly clarified that the work wasn't intended to elicit sexual arousal. And while the same failure occurs when *Fun Home* is considered under the Reasonable Invitation View, we take it that the work also likely fails to satisfy condition (iv), as well.

We have offered an answer to the Pornography Question and we've established that *Fun Home* is not pornography. But that doesn't settle the issue of whether it's *obscene*. In the next section, we turn to the task of answering the Obscenity Question.

4. What Is Obscenity?

Megumi Igarashi, a *manga* artist who publishes under the pseudonym Rokudenashiko (Japanese for, roughly, "good-for-nothing girl"), has created a wide range of work involving many attempts at de-sexualizing yonic imagery—that is, imagery resembling the vagina or vulva. In addition to her *manga* work, she has created vulva-styled phone cases, necklaces, and even a cartoon character named Manko-chan ("Miss Pussy") as well as a fully functional yonic kayak. Backlash against this work—specifically, against the distribution of data that would allow duplicates of these artifacts to be 3D-printed by her Kickstarter supporters—resulted in Rokudenashiko being arrested in July 2014 and subsequently spending ten days in a women's detention center.[5] As a means of documenting her experiences and furthering her activism—namely, both destigmatizing one variety of genitalia in a society that quite literally has an elaborate festival dedicated to another variety of genitalia as well as drawing attention to "how Japanese detention centers disregard human rights"[6]—Rokudenashiko went on to produce a book-length *manga* on the subject, published by Koyama Press in 2016. The title of Rokudenashiko's *manga*: *What Is Obscenity?: The Story of a Good for Nothing Artist and Her Pussy* (Figure 9.1).

Rokudenashiko's titular question is a good one and points us back to the Obscenity Question: What are the necessary and jointly sufficient conditions

Figure 9.1 *What Is Obscenity?* (2016), Rokudenashiko. Rokudenashiko recounts her experiences prior to and during her arrest by police for obscenity charges.

that must be satisfied for something to qualify as obscene? Not long after Stewart's (in)famous remarks about "hard-core pornography," Justice Warren Berger, writing the opinion of the court in the case of *Miller v. California* (1973), offered the following test for determining whether a particular object is, in fact, obscene:

> The basic standard for the trier of fact must be: (a) whether the average person, applying contemporary community standards would find that the work, taken as a whole, appeals to the prurient interest, (b) whether the work depicts or describes, in a patently offensive way, sexual conduct specifically defined by the applicable state law; and (c) whether the work, taken as a whole, lacks serious literary, artistic, political, or scientific value.

Anything taken to qualify as obscene under this test would, in the United States, no longer fall under the purview of First Amendment protections of free speech. For lack of a better name, let's call this view the *Community Standards View*, which we can formalize as follows:

> **Community Standards View:** *x* is *obscene* for community *c* if and only if (i) the average person from *c*, applying contemporary community standards would find that *x*, taken as a whole, promotes excessive interest in sexual matters; (ii) *x* depicts or describes, in a patently offensive way, sexual conduct specifically defined by the applicable state law; and (iii) *x*, taken as a whole, lacks serious literary, artistic, political, or scientific value.

This view is noteworthy for many reasons, the most relevant is that the verdicts it delivers, even regarding the same object, can vary across locations and times: condition (i) references both "contemporary community standards" and "the prurient interest," the latter of which is parasitic on the socially variable notion of what constitutes *excessive* interest in sexual matters; condition (ii) references "patently offensive ways" of depiction or description, which will vary alongside operative social mores and norms; while condition (iii) references "applicable state law." So, if we adopt the Community Standards View, what counts as obscene is never a universal matter; it is only settled relative to specific social and legal communities at specific times. Put another way: the Community Standards View offers an analysis only of what it is to be obscene *for a community*, not what it is to be obscene, *full stop*.

The Community Standards View is, of course, a codification of the view of obscenity particular to US legal contexts. What about elsewhere? According to Section 163 of the Canadian Criminal Code, something is *obscene* just in case "a dominant characteristic of the publication is the undue exploitation of sex, or the combination of sex and at least one of crime, horror, cruelty or violence." According to Rokudenashiko's attorney, obscenity is defined in Japan as "anything illiciting [*sic*] sexual desire, excitement or arousal in vain, or that violates a reasonable person's sense of propriety, or principles of righteous and moral sexuality" (2016: 36).[7] In India and the UK, obscene materials are vaguely defined as those likely to "deprave or corrupt." Though less rigorously spelled out, such characterizations of obscenity join the Community Standards View in being largely variable in their application, with different communities and different sets of social norms and mores informing what exactly counts as *undue* exploitation of sex or as *depravity* and *corruption* in the relevant senses. But, in all of these contexts, we find a familiar claim that the redeeming merits of works—literary, artistic, and so on—can potentially disqualify a work from being obscene in much the same way that the Community Standards View is sensitive to certain overriding values.

A potential shortcoming of the Community Standards View, however, is that it renders impossible nonsexual obscenities. We might think, however, that the concept of obscenity can extend beyond the sexual: there are materials that are religiously obscene, or morally obscene, or display obscene levels of violence. To make room for such possibilities, we propose the following expansion of the Community Standards View:

> **Extended Community Standards View:** *x* is *obscene* for a community *c* if and only if (i) the average person from *c*, applying contemporary community standards would find that *x*, taken as a whole, promotes excessive interest in matters contrary to those standards; (ii) *x* depicts or describes, in a patently offensive way, objectionable conduct; and (iii) *x*, taken as a whole, lacks serious literary, artistic, political, or scientific value.

The Extended Community Standards View still counts as obscene all of the materials that the first Community Standards View does, but it does not foreclose the possibility of nonsexual obscenities. And, like the standard Community Standards View, the Extended Community Standards View delivers an analysis only of what it is to be obscene *for a community*.

If we apply the Extended Community Standards View to some cases we've considered, we can see that the final condition, (iii), seems to do most of the heavy lifting. A work like *Fun Home*, taken as a whole, clearly displays serious artistic merit by any reasonable measure and depending on how we settle issues pertaining to the category of *literature*, discussed in the previous

262   Philosophy of Comics

chapter, perhaps specifically literary merit as well. Any community that recognizes this merit, then, would have to conclude that Bechdel's work fails to qualify as obscene. McCloud's expert testimony during Jesus Castillo's trial was to the effect that *Demon Beast Invasion: The Fallen* did in fact display serious artistic value—though the jury, of course, disagreed, perhaps influenced by the case made by the prosecutorial team that comics themselves, as a medium, were not capable of displaying any such value. And whether Rokudenashiko's *What Is Obscenity?* qualifies as obscene depends on two factors. First, it depends on whether its images of yonic artifacts would be taken by typical community members to be contrary to community standard and are presented in a patently offensive way. And second, it depends on whether those community members would rightly conclude that the work lacks any of the relevant values. Interestingly, it seems that the serious political value of Rokudenashiko's artistic project stems precisely from its contrarian stance toward particular community standards. Indeed, the very reason it seems to fail to satisfy condition (iii) is because intentionally it aims to satisfy conditions (i) and (ii). In other words: its status as *nearly* obscene, for reasons rooted in activism and protest, seemingly precludes status as fully obscene.

5. Comics Art and Comics Porn

In 1990, Alan Moore and his spouse, illustrator Melinda Gebbie, began work on *Lost Girls*, a meticulously constructed long-form comic which finally reached publication in 2006. This work found Moore and Gebbie appropriating extant fictional characters from the public domain—Alice, from Lewis Carroll's *Alice's Adventures in Wonderland* (1865), Dorothy from L. Frank Baum's *The Wizard of Oz* (1900), and Wendy from J. M. Barrie's *Peter Pan* (1904)—and depicting them as engaged in various and increasingly graphic sexual exploits. According to comics critic Douglas Wolk, despite being "terribly uncomfortable to read" (2007: 255), "*Lost Girls* is shocking, it's lovely, it's ambitious, it's grandly clever" (254), all presented through "an almost modernist formalism" (252). These descriptions are consonant with Moore's intentions behind the work: according to Wolk, Moore set out "to make dignified pornography rather than 'erotica'—to produce something that was beautiful and well wrought and also overtly, unblushingly about what happens behind bedroom doors" (2007). So, on the conception of pornography we've advanced so far in this chapter, it looks like the verdict is clear: Moore and Gebbie's *Lost Girls* is a work of pornography. Beyond that, it also seems to be a genuine work of art.

That might sound like a rather clear and straightforward conclusion. It turns out, though, that there is a well-established line of thought in the philosophy of art that would call this conclusion—that *Lost Girls* is a work of both art and pornography—into question or at least complicate it substantially. According to a view we can call *exclusivism*, it is impossible for any work to be *both* a work of art *and* a work of pornography. So, if exclusivism is true, then *Lost Girls* can be either pornography *or* an artwork, but it cannot be what Moore intended it to be: both.

Arguments in favor of exclusivism take many forms. Some focus on moral, aesthetic, or content-based distinctions between the categories of art and pornography, while others zero in on differences in the required creative intentions, the mode of transmission, or the prescribed mode of engagement and appreciation.[8] Some philosophers in the exclusivist camp—such as Jerrold Levinson (2005) and Christy Mag Uidhir (2009)—are even fine with the possibility of what we might call *pornographic art*—or, in Mary Mikkola's (2014) case, *art-porn*. Their acceptance of exclusivism, however, requires that they distinguish such works of *art-porn* or *pornographic art* from *pornography* proper (and, in Mikkola's view, from *art* proper as well). That is to say: such "pornographic art" isn't *really* pornography, and if this sounds like a contradiction in terms, consider the perhaps parallel fact that not everyone who is *athletic* is an athlete, or that not everything that is monolithic is, in fact, a monolith. In the same vein, something might very well be *pornographic* without really being *pornography*: something could resemble typical works of pornography in relevant ways— depicting aestheticized nudity and sexual activities, and so forth—without being intended to be used as a tool for sexual arousal.

So why should we accept exclusivism? Objections to the view are numerous.[9] It will be sufficient for present purposes, we think, to show that (what we take to be) the best arguments for exclusivism fail. Here, we focus on two such arguments, starting with Levinson's. According to Levinson, regardless of the medium, the formal features of a work of pornography "should present the object for sexual fantasy vividly, then, as it were, get out of the way" (2005: 385). That's because a work of pornography "should be as transparent as possible" (2005). These remarks are illustrative of Levinson's conception of both art and pornography, according to which the sort of attention typically required for artistic appreciation would frustrate the ability to effectively use the same work as a tool for sexual arousal.

When we attend to artworks, we focus on medium-specific features such as framing, editing, rhythm, lighting, and the like, attending to ways in which they interact with and enrich the artwork's content. Attention to such features in the case of pornography, however, would only serve as a distraction. Pornographic content should ideally be presented as "transparently" as possible, allowing us to forget that we're viewing a representational artifact rather than a real event or having a real experience. When viewed as pornography, attention to a work's formal features—essential for its appreciation as art—would therefore be minimized or ignored. So, the argument concludes, nothing can be both art and pornography, since concurrent status as both requires us to do the impossible: to view the object in two incompatible ways, both attending to and ignoring the formal features of the medium in which the work is situated.

As many have pointed out, even if we accept the reasoning behind the argument, it can, at best, establish that the same object cannot *be seen* simultaneously as both art and pornography. This is not, however, the same as establishing that the same object cannot simultaneously *be* both art and pornography. What the argument leaves open is the possibility that a single artifact is simultaneously pornography and art, although it can function as an instance of only one of those two categories at any given time. By analogy: a given console might function as either a Blu-Ray player or a videogame system but is unable to perform both functions simultaneously. Furthermore, even if the sort of attention typical when engaging with an artifact as an artwork might be different from the sort of attention typical when engaging with it as pornography, the previous considerations do not entail that they are *absolutely incompatible*. Instead, we could settle for the conclusion that focusing on formal features compromises the transparency of the content by "taking us out of" that content, so it merely makes it more difficult to effectively use the artifact for sexual arousal. Viewed this way, art status might make something be less effective as pornography, but that's a far cry from establishing that the two categories are strictly incompatible. Indeed, it seems to be an open possibility that some works of pornography could be so effective and innovative in their presentation that they overcome this obstacle of reduced transparency and can still reasonably be engaged with as art. This, it seems, is precisely the intention behind a work like *Lost Girls*.

Mag Uidhir (2009) offers a refined version of a Levinson-style argument that seeks to uphold exclusivism. According to Mag Uidhir, our appreciation of art is *manner-specific*, whereas our appreciation of pornography is *manner-inspecific*. To appreciate something in a manner-specific way is to appreciate it not just for what it is trying to do but also for how it does it. Conversely, to appreciate something in a manner-inspecific way is to appreciate it based just on whether it gets the job done, without regard for the manner in which it does so. Artworks, according to Mag Uidhir, are artifacts that are created with the intention that they be appreciated in a manner-specific fashion: great cinema or great literature is created not just to communicate themes or insights but also to be appreciated for how such works utilize artistic conventions within their respective mediums to convey those themes and insights. Works of pornography, on the other hand, are artifacts created with the intention that they be appreciated in a manner-inspecific fashion: great pornography is created with the intention that it, again, "gets the job done," without regard for the aesthetic or artistic value that might be found in the medium-specific conventions it utilizes in doing so. The creation of art and the creation of pornography, then, both require different intentions and these intentions are in conflict: if a creator intends their artifact to be appreciated through manner-specific means, they do not intend it to be appreciated through manner-inspecific means, and vice versa. So, no artifact can be created as an artwork and as a work of pornography.

Whether you find Mag Uidhir's argument for exclusivism compelling will likely depend on whether you agree that works of pornography are essentially artifacts created with the intention that they be appreciated through manner-inspecific means. Suppose an ambitious pornographer claimed that they were intending to create sophisticated pornography to be appreciated through manner-specific means, and we respond by claiming that they are confused about the concept of pornography, since pornography requires manner-inspecific appreciation. To our ears, this verges on question-begging. And even if a non-question-begging argument for the claim that pornography is essentially manner-inspecific were found, a response similar to the one offered to Levinson's argument remains available: it seems perfectly consistent to create a single artifact with the intention that it be appreciated as art through manner-specific means while also intending that it be appreciated as pornography through manner-inspecific means. Again, by analogy: a console might be created with the intention that it be manipulated with one remote when operating as a Blu-Ray player and another when operating as a videogame system.

Based on these considerations, we find ourselves on the side of the anti-exclusivists: the same object can be properly categorized as both art and pornography. This is so even if, in many cases, appreciating the object as a representative of one category hinders our ability to simultaneously appreciate it as a representative of the other. We can, however, still learn much from considering the case for exclusivism. Recall, in particular, the earlier comment from Levinson regarding how, in typical pornography, the formal features of a work should "get out of the way" as quickly as possible so as to not compromise the transparency of the arousing content. Features that "take you out of the content" and remind you that you're looking at a representational artifact, then, might sometimes be artistically meritorious while simultaneously constituting pornographic flaws. So, even in taking the categories of art and pornography to be compatible, we should acknowledge the tension between them in the contexts of both appreciation and criticism.

Consider, again, *Lost Girls*, of which Wolk (2007: 257) writes:

> The curious—or curiousest—thing about *Lost Girls* is that while it's enormously powerful and gorgeously executed, it's not actually all that sexy, or likely to inspire many fantasies on its own. The kind of release it offers is a fetishist's release: the sense that a ritual has been completed precisely. If it fails a smut, though, it's a victory as art, which is not a bad condolence prize.

Even if *Lost Girls* is both art and pornography, the very features relevant to its quality as an artwork at the same time undercut its quality as pornography. In our estimation, it is likely that the intensely, obsessively formalistic qualities of *Lost Girls*—its rigid panel structures, insistent narrative symmetry, and the like—in conjunction with its rather frequent and heavy-handed attempts at moral commentary lead to it being quite a stretch to suppose that anyone could actually use *Lost Girls* effectively for sexual arousal. If so, *Lost Girls* wouldn't be bad pornography but instead a failed attempted at making pornography. If among Moore and Gebbie's goals behind the work was to create something that is both art and pornography, then, following this line of thought, the work is a failure, at least in this respect: the art aspect got in the way of, and perhaps fatally compromised, the pornography aspect. And, arguably, this is a crucial moral fact about the work. Given its frequent depiction of sex acts involving children, if *Lost Girls* is pornography, its depiction of children as subjects of pornography would be vile. As art, however, and especially in light of its regular and frequently heavy-handed, self-reflexive commentary on the divide between fact and fiction, this is more plausibly viewed as being in poor taste rather than morally vicious.

There is a more general observation about comics to be made here, discussed at some length by Mag Uidhir and Pratt (2012). Think back to our earlier examples of pornographic comics, such as Tijuana bibles and *hentai manga*, along with distinctive trends in each: depictions of outlandish cartoon characters, exaggerated features, biologically impossible sexual acts, and so on. As categories of comics, each portrays their pornographic narratives through a combination of cartooned images and text presented sequentially via formal devices like panel layouts and *emanata*. As comics, Tijuana bibles and *hentai manga* convey information in a way that is unmistakably *conveyed through comics*. Given the active structure of picture-reading, it is nearly impossible to forget that you're engaging with a comic and so truly "lose yourself" as if you were witnessing or experiencing a real event. So, unlike pornography presented through more transparency-conducive mediums like photography or film, nearly all pornography presented through the comics medium will be nonstandard in the sense that the medium-specific features are far less able to just "get out of the way." The distinctive visual technology of comics—panels, speech balloons, onomatopoetic text, and the like—all resist fading into the background of the comics reading experience. They persistently remind readers that they are, indeed, engaging with a comic. Any pornography in a medium so insistent on making itself known will inevitably be atypical in its reliable, even relentless, reminder to the reader of what and how they are reading.

6. Superheroes and Moral Porn

Earlier in this chapter, we considered the possibility that the concept of *obscenity* might extend beyond sexual contexts. Thi Nguyen and Bekka Williams (2020) have recently argued that this holds true for the concept of *porn*, as well. In an effort to make sense of phenomena such as food porn, poverty porn, nature porn, and so forth, Nguyen and Williams carve out a notion of *generic porn*, reserving the term "pornography" just for sexually tinged porn. Piecing together various bits of Nguyen and William's discussion (156–7), we arrive at the following definition:

> **Generic Porn:** x is an instance of *G-porn* if and only if (i) x is a representation of category or phenomenon G, and (ii) it is reasonable to believe that x will be used—by most of the audience for which it was produced—for immediate gratification, while avoiding the usual costs and consequences of actually engaging with G.

Food porn, then, involves representations of food such that it is reasonable to believe that most of the target audience will use to spark their appetites and tickle their gustatory imaginations, without having to deal with actual calories, cholesterol, and gastrointestinal chaos. Nguyen and Williams's primary focus is on *moral outrage porn*, which amounts to representations of moral outrage such that it is reasonable to believe that most of the target audience will use them for immediate gratification without the costs and consequences of actually engaging with a morally robust, nuanced picture of the world.

What should we say about the relation between comics and varieties of generic porn? It seems that there is little stopping particular comics from being among the instances of any kind of generic porn: a talented artist could, after all, probably produce a rather effective instance of comics food porn. Similarly, many political cartoons likely qualify as moral outrage porn.[10] We might even think that comics, as artifacts, can be fetishized through *collecting porn*, in which would-be collectors stare longingly at glass-encased copies or digital photographs of *Action Comics* #1 (worth approximately $3.2 million) or *Detective Comics* #27 (worth approximately $2.25 million).

Most interestingly, however, is perhaps psychologists David A. Pizarro and Roy Baumeister's claim that superhero comics constitute a form of generic porn, namely *moral pornography* (to be distinguished from the aforementioned moral *outrage* porn). Pizarro and Baumeister claim:

> Much like the appeal of the exaggerated, caricatured sexuality found in pornography, superhero comics offer the appeal of an exaggerated and caricatured morality that satisfies the natural human inclination toward moralization. In short, the modern superhero comic is a form of "moral pornography"—built to satisfy our moralistic urges, but, ultimately unrealistic and, in the end, potentially misleading. (2013: 20)

Given what Pizarro and Baumeister argue is a natural psychological tendency in humans to find some pleasure in issuing moral judgments, superhero comics tend to offer readers a simplified, morally black-and-white world in which such judgments are able to be made frequently and with minimal thought or effort. These judgments do not require careful reflection on the complicated moral nuances of the actual world. Instead, superhero comics offer us a surrogate world in which we can scratch our judgmental itches by morally praising the clearly identifiable hero and morally blaming the clearly identifiable villain.

Whether or not we take this conception of moral porn to be equivalent to Nguyen and Williams's notion of moral outrage porn, or a more inclusive notion that subsumes the latter, the potential harms of either conception are comparable. Such porn risks doing harm at least in the sense that it might cause audiences to, knowingly or not, form moral beliefs for nonmoral reasons, for example, so that they can be gratified by engaging with certain fictions. Perhaps more problematically, there is the worry that such porn "cheapens and undermines the role of moral experience" (Nguyen and Williams 2020: 165), and "invit[es] us to instrumentalize something that ought not be instrumentalized" (2020: 169). If this is all correct, superhero comics—along with all manner of mediums, we should add—face the severe charge of encouraging audiences to misuse their moral sensibilities, and further, blunt those sensibilities in light of a cartoon version of moral reality.

Does this criticism of superhero comics carry any weight? In our estimation, it depends on the quantificational structure of the claim that superhero comics are moral porn. (See our previous chapter for a review of different kinds of quantificational structure.) If we read Pizarro and Baumeister as making a universal claim about all comics, then this criticism surely fails. There are certainly superhero comics that do not unreflectively engage in such cartoonish, idealized moral misrepresentations; consider, for example, Moore and Gibbons's *Watchmen* or Grant Morrison's work on *New X-Men* (2001–4). Understood as an existential claim, however, the criticism surely succeeds: consider, for example, Frank Miller's xenophobic *Holy Terror* (2011), a work which Miller describes as "propaganda" and which prompted Morrison to point out that "cheering on a fictional character as he beats up fictionalized terrorists seems like a decadent indulgence when real terrorists are killing real people in the real world."[11] Moral porn, indeed.

As in our discussion of whether comics are literature, though, we take the most interesting question here to be about noteworthy features: Is the genre *superhero comics* noteworthy for being among the select varieties of storytelling that has instances that constitute moral porn? Here, we suspect the answer is, unfortunately, yes. In fact, we take it that even when understood as a generic claim, according to which typical superhero comics are moral porn, Pizarro and Baumeister's claim rings true. This is, of course, not an essential feature of the superhero genre but instead a contingent reality of the mainstream comics industry based largely on what sells. Porn—including moral porn—is big business.

7. The Ethics of Comics Porn

Aside from our digression into superhero comics as moral porn, our discussion of comics and pornography has thus far remained neutral as to the moral status of the latter. This is not an uncontroversial approach, as some take it that the very concept of pornography is morally corrosive at best and perhaps even directly and tangibly harmful. See, for example, the apparent answer to the Pornography Question offered by feminist philosopher Catharine McKinnon (1987), in conjunction with Andrea Dworkin, who characterize pornography as

> the graphic sexually explicit subordination of women through pictures or words that also includes women dehumanized as sexual objects, things, or commodities; enjoying pain or humiliation or rape; being tied up, cut up, mutilated, bruised, or physically hurt; in postures of sexual submission or servility or display; reduced to body parts, penetrated by objects or animals, or presented in scenarios of degradation, injury, torture; shown as filthy or inferior; bleeding, bruised, or hurt in a context that makes these conditions sexual.

We might recast this view as follows:

> **Subordination View:** x is pornography if and only if (i) x is a representational artifact that (ii) contributes to the subordination of women through means of graphic, sexually explicit words or pictures that involve depictions of women dehumanized as sexual objects.

With something like the Subordination View in mind, Rae Langton (1993) argues that since pornography is protected under US free speech laws, leading to pornography itself being conceived of as a form of speech, we can understand it as a variety of speech act that amounts to real sexual discrimination. If the subordination of women and acts of sexual discrimination are morally objectionable (which they clearly are), then pornography is, in every instance, morally objectionable.

As has often been pointed out in subsequent discussions, however, the Subordination View doesn't seem to be a definition of *pornography* per se but instead of *inegalitarian pornography*, characterized by A. W. Eaton as "sexually explicit representations that as a whole eroticize relations (acts, scenarios, or postures) characterized by gender inequity" (2007: 676). (It should be pointed out that mainstream pornography seems to be largely characterized by racial inequity, as well.) If taken as a supposedly inclusive definition of all varieties of pornography—including *egalitarian* pornography not characterized by gender (or racial) inequity—then the Subordination View seems to fall into extensional inadequacy. After all, the Subordination View offers the verdict that neither gay pornography solely involving men nor pornography solely involving combinations of men and nonbinary or gender-nonconforming persons is *really* pornography, and also renders the idea of truly feminist pornography incoherent. As queer and feminist pornographers will likely attest, however, this is perhaps not the best result.

In her survey of philosophical issues of pornography, Lori Watson (2010) points out that views such as the Subordination View are not best thought of as attempts to define the common concept of *pornography* per se but instead serve as tools in social and legal contexts for the purpose of fighting against the oppression of women. In this sense, we can see views like the Subordination View as being reconcilable with views like the Reasonable Invitation View: the latter is an attempt to define, in morally neutral terms, the full scope of the concept of pornography, whereas the former is an attempt to define, in morally salient terms, what the bulk of actual pornography really is. And, if Eaton (2007) is correct that such routine engagement with inegalitarian pornography probabilistically leads to behavior and attitudes harmful to women—in much the same way that routine engagement with cigarettes probabilistically leads to lung cancer— then we might have good moral reason to push back against the production, distribution, and promotion of inegalitarian pornography. Nguyen and Williams's (2020: 167) suggestion that "insofar as the frequent use of pornography encourages a strictly instrumental attitude toward actual people and sexual encounters, then it helps to undermine our capacity to treat humans and intimate human relationships with the dignity they deserve" simply adds to this case. Where moral porn wrongly and harmfully instrumentalizes our moral sentiments and judgments, inegalitarian pornography wrongly and harmfully instrumentalizes our sexual desires and attitudes toward other persons.

One way to push back against the production and distribution of such material, short of criminalizing it, is to replace it. Given the scope of the global pornography industry and the degree to which it is entrenched in contemporary culture—whether people like to publicly acknowledge it or not—it is unlikely that inegalitarian pornography is going to go away any time soon. As Eaton (2017) argues, we might therefore work toward minimizing the presence of inegalitarian porn and its noxious social effects by actively producing and promoting feminist, egalitarian porn instead. According to Eaton, the goal would be a sort of habituation through exposure to such material in an attempt to "organize our sentimental lives, and in particular our erotic tastes, around gender equality" (2017: 252). If a cultural shift were to prompt consumers to seek out pornography in the sense described by the Reasonable Invitation View but not in the sense described by the Subordination View, the result would shift toward the production and distribution of tools for the exploration of safe and healthy sexual practices, free of and ideally in opposition to oppressive power structures.

What to say, then, about the moral status of comics pornography? For inegalitarian comics pornography, one might worry that some of the aforementioned problems are amplified. On the phenomenon of closure between panels via the gutter, McCloud (1993: 68) claims:

> [C]losure in comics is . . . *anything* but *involuntary*. Every act committed to paper by the artist is *aided* and *abetted* by a *silent accomplice*. An *equal partner in crime* known as *the reader*. I may have drawn an *axe* being *raised* in this example, but I'm not the one who let it *drop* or who decided how *hard* the blow, or *who* screamed, or *why*. *That*, dear reader, was *your special crime*, each of you committing it in your own *style*. All of you *participated* in the murder. All of you *held the axe* and *chose your spot*. (Italics in original)

Minus the stylized hyperbole, the suggestion here is that the imaginative act of closure—essential to the characteristic activity we've called picture-reading—is, in an important sense, participatory. By picture-reading McCloud's axe-murder panels, you are not merely an observer but are complicit in the gruesome imaginary homicide. Likewise, in inegalitarian comics porn, you are complicit in the depicted (albeit imaginary) sex acts. A similar point is emphasized by Mag Uidhir and Pratt (2012: 147), through reference to McCloud's (admittedly controversial) claim that the cartoonish style so common in the comics medium fosters increased reader-character identification: if "pornography is a substitute or surrogate for sex" and "effective pornography enables one to envision more closely that one is actually engaged in or with what is depicted," it might be that comics porn is, at least in this way, potentially more effective than more standard pornography. So, even if pornographic comics will be less transparent than, say, pornographic films (as discussed earlier), they might, on balance, be more *effective* in virtue of their greater facility for audience identification.

Although inegalitarian comics porn might exacerbate certain problematic aspects of such pornography, comics might also be a promising medium for the production and distribution of effective egalitarian pornography. The production of such comics could, given the enormous possibilities within the medium, depict a wide range of sexual activities without requiring the participation in corresponding *actual* sexual activities by any real persons.

And, given that pornographic comics of any sort will invariably be instances of nonstandard pornography, effective egalitarian pornographic comics are likely to require certain artistic, aesthetic, and formal innovations. See, for example, the innovative page layouts and narrative style in Dave McKean's silent erotic comic, *Celluloid* (2011).

Of course, this argument isn't specific to comics but also applies to any illustrated, animated, or virtual representational medium that does not require actual human participants for its creation. If we have moral reasons to produce or promote egalitarian pornographic comics, we might also have moral reasons to produce or promote egalitarian pornography in animated film, videogames, and the like. But there is a further reason to focus on the comics medium over these other representational mediums.

Beyond the subjugation of women in inegalitarian pornography, typical pornography tends to also promote the idea that the default way of being is to be white, cisgender, heterosexual, able-bodied, and within a very narrow and specific range of "socially acceptable" body types. To further demonstrate this point, consider that pornography involving persons who identify outside of these categories tends to be categorized among the various kinds of "fetish" pornography. In doing so, it largely treats such persons as mere sexual objects, rather than full-fledged subjects. A truly egalitarian pornography would, therefore, require a significantly more inclusive sense of the "default" way of being a human person.

Furthermore, in line with what Sherri Irvin (2017) has recently argued, an egalitarian pornography might aim to erode harmful norms regarding which kinds of bodies are "correct" or "preferable" through the act of *aesthetic exploration*: "seeking out positive experiences of the unique aesthetic affordances of all bodies, regardless of whether they are attractive in the standard sense." Given its possibilities for depicting different kinds of bodies, the comics medium is potentially well-suited for such aesthetic exploration; see, for example, the depiction of various body types within Allison Moon and KD Diamond's narrative, queer-inclusive sex education comic, *Girl Sex 101*. Moreover, the medium admits of this potential for broader aesthetic exploration without necessarily objectifying or instrumentalizing any real persons, as we might do if we aesthetically explore, in Irvin's sense, by seeking out the relevant positive experiences from actual, flesh-and-blood people.

We conclude this chapter with one final note on obscenity and egalitarian pornography. Among the varieties of pornography that Eaton (2017) considers to be potentially liberatory are "gay and lesbian pornography" and

"S/M (sadomasochistic) pornography." Given sociological facts about the standards of communities and prevailing sex-relevant prejudices (e.g., homophobia, cisnormativity, heteronormativity), many activities depicted in such works are likely to qualify as obscene under the Extended Community Standards View. That alone does not suffice, however, for any negative moral judgment of those pornographic works. Recall our earlier observations about Rokudenashiko's yonic activism. In actively pushing against regressive community standards, her work incurs legitimate political value. The same might hold true here: a work made within a social context that retains harmful or regressive standards, and which pushes back against those standards through the act of intentionally violating them, can incur some degree of positive political value. This would allow such works both to avoid condemnation as mere obscenity and to function instead as instances of protest or resistance. In that, we find a source of moral reasons for comics creators—and indeed, artists and creators of all sorts—to thoughtfully and carefully approach not just the pornographic but also the obscene.

8. Recommended Readings

Hall (2016) functions as a helpful guide to erotic comics in general, in terms of both scholarship and actual comics. A somewhat dated though still historically interesting study of pornographic comic strips can be found in Palmer (1979). For a recent series of fascinating essays on sexuality and superheroes, see Anna Peppard's edited volume, *Supersex* (2020).

Mari Mikkola's *Pornography* (2019) serves as an excellent introduction to philosophical issues about pornography in general. For a wealth of essays on the relation between pornography and art in general, see Hans Maes's edited volume, *Pornographic Art and the Aesthetics of Pornography* (2013), as well as Maes and Jerrold Levinson's volume, *Art & Pornography* (2012).

Those interested in a general discussion of the ethical dimensions of the comics medium as a whole would do well to look at Robson (2016).

10

Page, Panel, Screen—Comics and Adaptation

1. A Golden Age of Adaptation

Comics have long been a source of inspiration for television, film, theatrical serials, radio dramas, and other narrative mediums. Henry Pratt (2016: 230) identifies the first comics-to-film adaptation as G. W. Blitzer's *Happy Hooligan Interferes* (1903), a one-minute silent short that draws from Frederick Burr Opper's *Happy Hooligan* strip (1900–32). Thierry Groensteen and Benoît Peeters (1994: vii) go even further back, giving the honor to Rodolphe Töppfer's *The Voyages and Adventures of Dr. Festus* (1833), a title shared by both a proto-comic series of sketches and a work of prose, published simultaneously and with the latter being an adaptation (of sorts) of the former. After starting publication in 1903, Winsor McCay's *Little Nemo in Slumberland* quickly found itself on Broadway (1908) and in animated film (1911). Just a few decades later, viewers would gather at the theater to enjoy

John English and William Witney's *Adventures of Captain Marvel* theatrical serial (1941). And, in 1942, Alfred Mazure's *Inbraak* appeared, adapting his own *Dick Bos* (1940–67) strip. And those are just a few examples.

Despite this long history, it would be hard to deny that we are currently living in something like a "Golden Age of Adaptation." Indeed, Pratt (2012: 147) elsewhere writes:

> Recently, films adapted from or based on comics have become commonplace. By my count, including only those in English that have received cinematic release, at least 125 films have been adapted from comic books; similar numbers have been adapted from newspaper strips. Over half of these films were made in the last decade alone, and many more in development. Comics have also provided the basis for some of the highest grossing films of all time (as of this writing, *The Dark Knight* (2008) stands at number six).

Since Pratt published that passage in 2012, the trend has only accelerated, with so-called comic book movies—and the numerous television shows on their periphery—becoming an unavoidable cultural phenomenon. Turning to other mediums, we also see the occasional adaptations of comics into novels (Christa Faust and Gary Phillips's 2018 adaptation of Alan Moore and Brian Bolland's 1989 *Batman: The Killing Joke*), musicals (Lisa Kron and Jeanine Tesori's 2013 adaptation of Alison Bechdel's 2006 memoir, *Fun Home: A Family Tragicomic*), audiobooks (the 2020 adaptation of Neil Gaiman's *The Sandman*, produced by Dirk Maggs), and more. We find ourselves in the era of the Marvel Cinematic Universe (MCU) on the big screen, *The Walking Dead* (ongoing since 2010) on the small screen, and Batman on nearly everything. Sure, it's not a Golden Age in the sense that all of the myriad adaptations these days are *good* but instead in the sense that there are just so many of them. Adaptation is nothing new, but it is undeniable that as source material, comics are drawing more attention than ever. In this final chapter, we turn our attention to comics' relationship with other mediums as it concerns the practice of adaptation.

Look at any thriving comics fandom and you can easily find expressions of hopes and speculation about the transformation of characters, stories, and worlds into Hollywood blockbusters, big-budget serialized television programs, or AAA videogames—perhaps all three. When these happen, it is often taken as a legitimization of the comics at the center of that fandom, lending the fans a newfound sense of aesthetic and social capital. At the same time, it is not uncommon to see the dismissal of such releases by substantial subsections of said fandoms, often for not being "true" to the original. Leaving consideration of such nay-sayers aside for now, though, fans seem to crave adaptations, frequently taking them as a form of validation of their love for— or even the objective merit of—their favorite characters, worlds, and stories. On occasion, fans even jump the gun and start "fan-casting" the film themselves, debating which actor should portray which character and which director should be at the helm. Adaptations, we see, are often an object of interest even when they don't exist yet and perhaps never will.

While they are perhaps less culturally prominent, adaptations from other mediums *into* comics are also rampant. Every *Star Wars* film has received (at least one) official comic adaptation, as have several of the novels and novellas in George R. R. Martin's *A Song of Ice and Fire* series. Horror *mangaka* Junji Ito has adapted Mary Shelley's *Frankenstein* (1823), and William S. Gibson's unused script for *Alien* 3 was adapted into *William Gibson's Alien 3: The Unproduced Screenplay* (2018–19), credited to Gibson, Johnny Christmas, and Tamra Bonvillian. Charles Vess's *The Book of Ballads and Sagas* (2018) collects comics adaptations of several English and Scottish folktales, and several installments of Nintendo's *The Legend of Zelda Series* have been adapted into manga by Akira Himekawa. P. Craig Russell even adapted a cycle of Wagner's musical dramas with *The Ring of the Nibelung* (2014). Worthy of special note is *Classics Illustrated*, a series lasting over thirty years and which focused exclusively on comic adaptations of "classics," including *Don Quixote, Moby Dick, Uncle Tom's Cabin*, and many, many more. We could, of course, go on listing examples. Perhaps you already have in mind several of your favorites which we've unfortunately left out. But the point remains: adaptations, both *from* comics and *into* comics, are legion. And, as we'll argue, examining the phenomenon of adaptation is a useful way to shed further light on the nature of comics.

David Roche, Isabelle Schmitt-Pitiot, and Benoît Mitaine (2018: 9) point out that among the research on *adaptation studies*—primarily the product of scholars working in cultural studies, film studies, media studies, and literature studies—the comics medium hasn't received much attention, especially when compared to adaptations between film and novels. Furthermore, philosophers Paisley Livingston (2010) and James Harold (2018: 90) each emphasize that even in that vast literature on adaptation, startlingly little of it has been written by philosophers. Given these historical and scholarly trends, why think that the phenomenon of adaptation as it pertains to comics is worthy of a particularly *philosophical* closer look? Why not conclude that the issue hasn't drawn much philosophical attention simply because there isn't much of philosophical interest to be found here?

Here are three reasons to think philosophical attention to adaptation might pay dividends. First, the very notion of *adaptation* cries out for clarification regarding its norms of application. What is the difference between, say, an adaptation and a *retelling*? A *reboot*? A *translation*? How can we distinguish an adaptation of some story from the telling of a similar but ultimately distinct story that is nonetheless heavily influenced by the first? At bottom, what we need to address is the following question, on which philosophers, like many others, have much to say:

Adaptation Question: When is a narrative work an adaptation?

A philosophical deep dive into the concept of adaptation allows us to make progress toward such an answer. And—as discussed in previous chapters—even if we can't settle on just one "philosophically acceptable" clarification of the concept, the time spent investigating the various alternatives can help us understand the nuances of the concept and its surrounding topics. So, even if we don't eventually succeed in defining *adaptation*, we still stand to learn a lot about the phenomenon from even just the attempt.

The second reason to devote specifically philosophical attention to the concept of adaptation is one of interest to anyone engaged with stories and storytelling. Whereas many fields of study remain humbly descriptive in their claims, philosophy—especially in value-theoretic contexts like ethics and aesthetics—quite often ventures into the normative. Suppose, for example, we take our friend Gomer to a screening of the Russo Brother's *Avengers: Infinity War* (2018). Following the show, we settle down over drinks to discuss our thoughts about what we just experienced, trading impressions and evaluations. We could just talk about what we personally liked and didn't like, but, if we do so, there is a clear sense in which we'd really be talking more about ourselves than we would be talking about the film itself. Saying "I liked *x*!" when it is obvious to everyone that *x* was indeed an aspect of the film serves mostly as statement of the speaker's preferences. Instead of just preference-sharing, we want to go deeper: we want to talk, not just about *us* but about the *film*. We want to talk about what worked and what didn't work, about the film's aesthetic merits and artistic failures—in short, we want to talk not just about whether we liked it but also about whether it was *good*. In doing so, we don't just trade evaluations but *reasons* for our evaluations. Those evaluations, however, will inevitably rest on how we answer certain fundamental questions. Among these questions, we should ask whether *Infinity War* is best thought of as an adaptation at all, and if so, whether it's an adaptation of any specific comics. Is it, for instance, an adaptation of Jim Starlin and Ron Lim's 1992 limited series, *The Infinity War*? Or of Starlin, Lim, and George Perez's 1991 limited series *The Infinity Gauntlet*? Both? Neither?

Answering these questions—even provisionally—will help us determine which works one might need to be acquainted with before making an informed assessment of the film's quality. Depending on whether we take *Avengers: Infinity War* to be a genuine adaptation or instead a story inspired by those (and perhaps other) comics, different evaluative maneuvers become more or less appropriate. After all, if it's not an adaptation, then it makes little sense to talk about how it adheres to or departs from those comics. On this point, Livingston (2010: 106) seems entirely correct: "[t]o appreciate a work of art is, at least in part, to assess it as an artistic accomplishment" and that "knowledge of the source (which means knowledge that there was a source, as well as knowledge of its identity and relevant features) is necessary to a thorough, apt appreciation of an adaptation."[1]

A robust, fully informed engagement with an adaptation requires that we engage with it *as an adaptation*. This, in turn, requires that we have a sufficient degree of acquaintance with the source material being adapted. So, our hopes for the value of such engagement depend, in part, on settling whether a given work is an adaptation in the first place. And when we take up such questions, we inevitably adopt—explicitly or implicitly, consciously or not—standards for what counts as an adaptation and what it takes for an adaptation to be aesthetically effective, artistically lacking, and so on. We should, then, examine those standards to see whether they hold up to philosophical scrutiny. Better to have explicit and reflective standards rather than standards that are left implicit and unreflective.

Our third and final reason for investigating the philosophical underpinnings of adaptation concerns the structure of the comics medium itself. As we'll see, adaptation is often (and perhaps always) a cross-medium phenomenon. Comics get adapted into films, and films get adapted into comics. That much is familiar. Getting less familiar, perhaps under the influence of Gotthold Lessing's (1766) idea of *medium specificity*, you might think that—at least in principle—a film could be produced that simply cannot be adapted into the comics medium or, alternatively, that some comics might resist adaptation into film. To take a concrete example of the latter, Alan Moore and Dave Gibbons were quite clear (or, at least, Moore was) that *Watchmen* (1986) was intended to be a story that could be told *only* through the comics medium, thereby rendering it unadaptable. What, then, do we say about Zack Snyder's 2009 film *Watchmen*, which attempted to adapt it anyway and seems to have succeeded in at least *some* sense?

To answer this question, we have to take a look at whether there is anything Moore and Gibbons did in the comic that is both *essential* to the work—something such that nothing could really be a telling of the story of *Watchmen* without including those elements—and that is unable to be done in another medium. That investigation will drive which views we go on to develop about the sorts of things comics can and can't do, as well as what sorts of things—if any—*only* comics can do. If it turns out that *Watchmen* really is essentially a comic and therefore unadaptable, knowing *why* can tell us something significant about the narrative or formal limits of the comics medium. The same is true if it turns out to that *Watchmen* is *not* essentially a comic. Either way, we learn about the nature of the comics medium, as well as its relations to other narrative mediums.

To sum up so far: philosophical attention to adaptation comes with at least three benefits. It can help us clarify the general contours of adaptation and related phenomena. It can also inform and explain our practices for critically engaging with and evaluating adaptations. And it can help us understand the capabilities or limitations of the comics medium. So philosophical attention to the phenomenon of adaptation is most certainly called for. Importantly, though, this attention is intended as a philosophical supplement to—rather than as a replacement for—work on adaptation across disciplines.

2. Character Adaptations and Story Adaptations

In 1943, Columbia Pictures released *The Batman*, a fifteen-chapter black-and-white theatrical serial. (For those unfamiliar with the format, a theatrical serial was something like our serialized, big-budget television shows of today, with each episode shown at local theaters.) Directed by Lambert Hillyer, the serial stars Lewis Wilson as Batman and J. Carrol Naish as the villainous Dr. Tito Daka. (The portrayal of the Japanese Daka by Naish, a white American, has aged exceptionally unwell and is just one instance of the clear anti-Japanese racism pervading the serial.) Though Wilson's depiction of the titular character is not nearly as iconic as, say, those of Adam West, Michael Keaton, or Christian Bale, it does have the privileged distinction of being the *first*. Is it fair to say then that Wilson starred in the first ever installment of what has turned into an impressively long line of Batman adaptations?

The answer, frustratingly noncommittal as it is, is: yes and no. At the end of the day, it depends on what we mean by "adaptation." Let's start our process of coming to a better understanding of adaptation by drawing a preliminary distinction between two broad kinds. On the one hand, we have what might be called *story adaptations*, which we can characterize for now as instances in which a story originally told in one narrative medium is later told through another narrative medium. Or, as Pratt (2016: 230, emphasis in original) has put it: "roughly as a story being made to travel from one place (a *source*) to another place (a *target*)."

On this preliminary characterization, paradigm story adaptations would include the adaptation of Bechdel's *Fun Home* into a musical by Kron and Tesori; the 2007 animated film adaptation of Marjane Satrapi's graphic autobiography *Persepolis* (2000–2), directed by Vincent Paronnaud and Satrapi herself; and Jay Olivia's two-part animated film adaptation of Frank Miller's *The Dark Knight Returns* (1986). More examples are readily available, but these three illustrate well enough the basic idea of what it is to be a *story* adaptation. (The first two also illustrate that story adaptations need not adapt a fictional story but can draw from nonfictional sources, as well.)

On the other hand, we have what we will call *character adaptations*: roughly, when a character originating and typically associated with one narrative medium is used as a primary focus in an original story first told through another narrative medium. As with story adaptations, examples of character adaptations are probably easy to think of. The characters of the *Star Wars* franchise have been adapted from film into comics since 1977, with only the first six issues of the original 107-issue run retelling the story of (what has come to be known as) *Star Wars: Episode IV—A New Hope* (1977). Damon Lindelof's 2019 HBO series *Watchmen* adapts many of the characters of Moore and Gibbons's original *Watchmen* universe from comics into serialized television. In a similar vein, Saturday morning children's cartoon shows regularly adapt characters from their source material without adapting any particular story.

It is here that we break from what is perhaps the norm in scholarly discussions of adaptation. On our view, a feature of both species of adaptation—character and story—is that at least two distinct narrative mediums must be involved: one as what Pratt called the "source" and the other the "target." To defend the least controversial part of that claim first: we take a medium to be a *narrative* medium just in case it is possible for a work within that medium to serve as a vehicle for storytelling. To do so, the medium in question must have the minimum formal capabilities to portray (or at least imply) some amount of temporal progression, as well as whatever the minimal elements of story might be: perhaps character, setting, plot, and so on. Completely non-representational mediums such as purely instrumental music would therefore fail to qualify as narrative mediums in our sense. As a result, they are not candidates for the roles of either source or target. And, while this accounts for why story adaptations require narrative mediums, what about character adaptations?

To see why even character adaptations must be situated within narrative mediums, notice that *non-representational* mediums are unable to portray characters and even representational but *non-narrative* mediums can do no more than *depict* characters. These limitations account for a subtle distinction familiar from storytelling practice: that a *depiction* of a character in a medium is conceptually distinct from an *adaptation* of that character into that medium. For example, a sculpture of Mike Mignola's Hellboy is not an instance of the character being "adapted" into sculpture. It's just a depiction of Hellboy through sculpture.

In defending our second requirement, that *distinct* mediums must be involved in adaptation, we appeal to common critical and appreciative practice around storytelling. Gus Van Sant's 1998 film *Psycho*, a near shot-by-shot copy of Alfred Hitchcock's 1960 film of the same title, is most often spoken of as a *remake* rather than an adaptation. Were a critic to refer to and evaluate Van Sant's film as an *adaptation*, readers would likely find the choice jarring at best. Similarly, Superman's origin story has been told and retold across more comics than we care to count, but it would be odd to find a comics critic, creator, or fan discussing those comics as *adaptations* of that origin story. The first page of Grant Morrison and Frank Quitely's *All-Star Superman #1* (2005) doesn't adapt Superman's origin story but instead simply retells it. In contrast, that story was told in films like, say, Richard Donner's *Superman* (1979) or Zack Snyder's *Man of Steel* (2013), it seem correctly described as an adaptation.

Although etymology remains no substitute for philosophy, it can occasionally be a useful aid: just thinking about the term "adaptation" itself can provide us some clarity. Consider the use of "adaptation" in the evolutionary sense: we see gradual change in populations through natural selection in part because successful generations of species *adapt* to changes in environment and circumstance. Similarly, when it comes to storytelling, adaptation is the process—or, alternatively, the result of the process—of taking a story (or character, or world, etc.) and *adapting* it into a new environment or new circumstances. That is: molding it, reshaping it, making it fit into some new narrative medium. In a slogan: we don't just *adapt*, we adapt *from* and *into*. From and into what? From the looks of critical practice in comics and other storytelling: distinct narrative mediums.

As we acknowledged, stories are often retold within the very same medium from which they originated. What are these retellings, if not adaptations? As it turns out, there's no uniform answer. Depending on the context, they might be *reboots* (if part of a larger franchise undergoing a process of streamlining and re-setting continuity) or perhaps *translations* (if interpreted and translated from one language or set of languages to another). Or they might just be simple *remakes* or *retellings*. In a general sense, reboots, translations, and remakes are all species of retellings, as are adaptations. But the important point to remember is that adaptations are to retellings as squares are to rectangles: one of many sub-categories.[2]

Returning to *The Batman* serial and the question we set out to ask about it: Is that original theatrical serial an adaptation? Equipped with our distinction between two varieties of adaptation and our rough characterizations of each, we can divide this question in two. The first: Is the original theatrical serial a *character* adaptation? Very clearly and, we think, uncontroversially, it is. Batman, Robin, and other characters originated in the medium of comics and were then used as primary foci in an original story told throughout the serial. So, *The Batman* serial is a character adaptation, and if character adaptations are adaptations full stop, then *The Batman* is an adaptation full stop.

Now for the second question: Is it also a *story* adaptation? The story told throughout *The Batman* is an original tale of our heroes' struggle against the evil Dr. Daka, a character who originated and has to date appeared only in the serial under discussion (with the exception of a brief appearance in the comics *All-Star Squadron* #42 and #43, in 1985). So, no, it isn't: there is no preexisting story from another medium that it is an adaptation *of*. With these two answers in hand, our original, apparently contradictory answer can be made clear: yes, the serial is a character adaptation, but no, *The Batman* is not a story adaptation.

Why does this distinction between story and character adaptations matter? Suppose that Una and Edie are spending an evening watching movies and TV. First, they watch Jay Olivia's animated version of *The Dark Knight Returns*. Since Olivia's film is a story adaptation of Frank Miller's comic, certain evaluative maneuvers are appropriate while others seem inappropriate. Una and Edie might notice that the film departs from the distinctive visual style of the comic while still retaining the story structure and overall themes. They might lament that the four-act narrative structure of the story doesn't lend itself to presentation as a feature-length film and eventually discuss whether the storytelling technique of including "talking head" news anchors serves the film as well as the comic, and so on. Notice what all of these topics have in common: all presuppose some degree of familiarity with the specific source material. To fully engage with and evaluate Olivia's film in an informed fashion, not just *as a film* but *as an adaptation*, Una and Edie need at least some prior familiarity with Miller's work. To be sure, they can certainly watch and enjoy the film despite having never read the comic, but the lack of prior experience with the source material seems to rule out a thoroughly informed engagement or a comprehensive critical evaluation. So, if Una has read Miller's *Dark Knight Returns* and Edie hasn't, they simply won't be able to engage together in a robust discussion of the merits of Olivia's film both as a film *and* as an adaptation of Miller's work.

What should we say when Una goes on to insist that the aesthetic quality of Olivia's film is diminished by the fact that it is derivative of Miller's comic? Edie should rightly point out the extremely peculiar nature of such criticism: any adaptation will be, to at least some extent, derivative from its source material. So holding that fact against the film is like complaining that a lemon is sour or that a horror movie is scary. Such criticism suggests a misunderstanding of what we're engaging with in the first place. Of course, Una might revise her critique and claim instead that even if it isn't fair to object that Olivia's film is derivative of Miller's comic, it is nonetheless a bad film. That, however, is a very different claim and one that might be true even if the film isn't somehow derivative of Miller's comic. Importantly, something can be good *at being an adaptation* while simultaneously bad *at being a film*. And vice versa. While these facts are often connected, our answers to the question of whether a particular film is a good film and to the separable question of it is a good adaptation can and do vary.

The late-night conversation carries on. Una wants an original story, so the two agree to watch the first few episodes of *The Batman* theatrical serial. Since it is a character adaptation rather than a story adaptation, different evaluative maneuvers seem appropriate. They might ask: Is this story good on its own? Does it make good use of the characters it adapts? How well does it present those characters—Batman, Robin, and the like? Is it too derivative of other similar Batman stories told elsewhere? And so on. Credible answers to these questions do not require antecedent familiarity with any particular story. They require only some general acquaintance with the Batman characters and with Batman stories more generally. In this scenario, being too derivative of any particular story might constitute a serious flaw, prompting the judgment that the serial's story is unoriginal or uninspired. And here, failures of the serial *as a serial* are much harder to separate from its failures *as a character adaptation*. If the serial mishandles its titular character, that's a fault both as a serial and as an adaptation of the Batman character.

Let's step back. We've drawn a distinction between character adaptations and story adaptations. As we've seen, this distinction is evaluatively useful, since it helps us determine which questions we really need to ask (as well as which we shouldn't bother asking) when critically engaging with adaptations. With this in mind, we are now well positioned to make our earlier characterizations of these two kinds of adaptation a bit more precise:

> **Story Adaptation:** For any narrative work *x* and narrative work *y*, *x* is a *story adaptation* of *y* if and only if (1) *x* and *y* are situated in different narrative mediums, and (2) *x* is a telling of the same story as is told in *y*.

> **Character Adaptation:** For any narrative work *x* and character *y*, *x* is a *character adaptation* of *y* if and only if (1) *y* originates outside of the medium within which *x* is situated, and (2) the story of *x* is an original story that (3) prominently focuses on *y*.

Putting these together, we arrive at a potential answer to the Adaptation Question, which we raised at the outset of this chapter:

> **Exhaustive Disjunctive View:** A narrative work *x* is an *adaptation* if and only if *x* is either a character adaptation or a story adaptation.

The Exhaustive Disjunctive View offers a set of necessary and jointly sufficient conditions for being an adaptation—namely, being a story adaptation or a character adaptation. In doing so, it offers a potential answer to the Adaptation Question. But should we accept it?

No. While we take the categories of story adaptation and character adaptation to be mutually exclusive and especially prominent, these categories are not necessarily exhaustive: there might be adaptations that are neither story adaptations or character adaptations. While these two kinds of adaptation are surely the most familiar varieties of adaptation, they are only two among many elements that combine to make up narrative works. Another variety of adaptation—what we might call *world* adaptations—does for fictional worlds what character adaptations do for characters (e.g., extended *Star Wars* universe novels). Since we are in principle open to the possibility of world adaptations, event adaptations, and perhaps other species of adaption, we shouldn't accept the Exhaustive Disjunctive View. And, without a comprehensive account of the different species of adaptation, we're not able to offer an expanded answer to the Adaptation Question by enumerating every possible kind of adaptation. For now, we settle for a partial answer in the forms of just a sufficient condition:

> **Disjunctive (Partial) View:** *x* is an adaptation if it is a character adaptation or it is a story adaptation.

Importantly, that doesn't mean we don't have more to learn about adaptation. And, in seeking to learn further, we'll dive deeper into the nature of story adaptation by focusing on the things they adapt: *stories.* How we should think about *stories*? What it is to tell them and what it is for the same story to be told in distinct works within and outside comics? We'll examine those questions next.

3. Stories and Storytelling

The medium of comics—like that of film, the novel, and others—is a storytelling medium. This is not to say that *all* comics tell stories, but it is typical for them to do so. Those stories might be fiction, as with your average superhero or horror comic, or they might be nonfiction, as with comic memoirs like David B's *Epileptic* (1996) or works of comics journalism like Joe Sacco's *Paying the Land* (2020). Whether fiction or nonfiction, though, we can appropriately ask of almost any comic: Does it succeed in telling the story it is trying to tell? That is, does it tell that story *well*?

Notice that this question carries a presupposition: that we can distinguish between a story and its telling. This is no lightweight presupposition, either. According to Aaron Smuts, "[the] foundational claim underlying nearly all narrative theory is that a distinction can be made between a story and its telling" (2009: 5). Indeed, without this distinction, we wouldn't be able to make sense of either Pratt's rough characterization of adaptation—as a story being made to travel from *source* to *target*—or our more detailed characterizations of story adaptations and character adaptations. So, if we grant this presupposition, when we talk about the case of, say, Moore and

Gibbons's *Watchmen* being adapted into film by Zack Snyder, we actually have three entities on the table: the comic as source, the film as target, and the *story* that moves between the two. Or, to translate the matter into our preferred terms: *Watchmen* (the film) is an adaptation of *Watchmen* (the comic) just in case (1) the two are situated in distinct narrative mediums, and (2) the film tells the same story as the comic. Since comics and film are different narrative mediums, the first condition is clearly satisfied. Whether the second is also satisfied will depend on how we characterize stories in general, as well as how we characterize the story of *Watchmen* and *Watchmen*, in particular.

We suspect that some readers—especially those already embedded in adaptation studies or narratology—might take issue with what we're saying here, for at least two reasons. First, they might caution against believing in the existence of stories as genuine entities, distinct from particular tellings. And second, since the field of adaptation studies has more or less come to consensus on the claim that *fidelity*—that is, the property of "being true" to the source material—is neither a requirement for, nor even a virtue of, adaptations, our claim that source and target must tell the same story will be seen as implausibly stringent.

Against this first potential criticism, recall one of the arguments for fictional realism—the view that fiction characters really do exist—offered in Chapter 4, which involved making sense of various external claims ostensibly about fictional characters. Moore and Gibbons created Rorschach. If this is true, then Moore and Gibbons created *something* and that something is Rorschach. So, Rorschach is *something*. What is he? Well, he (it) is a fictional character, and, hence, according to the view we defended there, an abstract artifact. Here, we can make quite similar moves: Moore and Gibbons's comic tells the same story as Snyder's film. If this is true, then the two works have *something* in common and that something is the story. So, the story is *something*. What is it? Well, we'll return to that question in the next section.

What about the second criticism that our preferred account wrongly assumes fidelity—being "true to" the source—is a necessary condition for adapting a story? We concede that is a widely rejected assumption. As Roche, Schmitt-Pitiot, and Mitaine (2018: 12) point out,

> The notion of fidelity raises several questions, including the matter of what the adapter is supposed to be faithful to. Is it the story, the characters, or the original author's intentions, if it is even possible to know what they were in the first place (Stam [2005: 15])? The canonical text is, then, upheld as a sort of transcendent benchmark (Leitch [2009: 3]), instead of the many criteria

that could enable an assessment of whether or not the adaptation is a "good" film, a "good" comic book or a "good" novel. In the end, analyzing an adaptation with this criterion in mind often leads to confirming the superiority of the literary work over the adaptation—and even that of literature over cinema. (Stam [2005: 4])

We take it, however, that "raising questions" isn't a vice, unless proponents of the view that raises them can't go on to offer answers. And, thankfully, answers here aren't too difficult to conjure up. Writing on the value of fidelity in adaptation, James Harold (2018: 92–4) distinguishes between *story fidelity* and *theme fidelity*. Roughly put, an adaptation enjoys story fidelity when it adequately preserves the story of the source and enjoys theme fidelity when it adequately preserves the source's themes. We might add additional fidelities to our list: an adaptation enjoys *character* fidelity when it adequately preserves the characters of the source, *world* fidelity when it adequately preserves the world, and so on. Approaching the matter in this way, we agree that there is no such thing as *fidelity tout court*. Instead, there are varieties of fidelity, and we can meaningfully ask about each of them. So, when we are faced with the question of whether a particular adaptation achieves fidelity to its source material, we ought not respond by rejecting the question. We are much better off just asking for a more specific version of it: "fidelity in which respect?" Doing so would address the first of Roche, Schmitt-Pitiot, and Mitaine's worries.

What about the second of their worries, according to which a focus on fidelity amounts to treating "the canonical text . . . as a sort of transcendental benchmark" that would encroach on our evaluations of the aesthetic and artistic merit of the adaptation? Here, we again follow Harold (2018: 94–100), who takes the presence of some variety of fidelity in adaptations to amount to an aesthetic merit when that fidelity constitutes a genuine aesthetic achievement of the creators of an adaptation. If the preservation of story from source to target is artistically or aesthetically difficult, then success in doing so is an achievement that deserves to be noticed and appreciated when engaging with the resulting work. Likewise with the preservation of themes, characters, worlds, and so on (Harold himself takes story fidelity—as opposed to theme fidelity—to typically be relatively easy to achieve and hence not very often constituting a relevantly appreciable achievement, and we're inclined to agree as long as we emphasize the "typically.") In the end, then, none among the varieties of fidelities are necessary for status as either a good adaptation or even just as an adaptation, nor are they sufficient. Instead, fidelity of whatever sort is an aesthetic virtue of an adaptation when and only when it is a relevantly appreciable achievement on the part of the creators. And this, we take it, defuses the second of Roche, Schmitt-Pitiot, and Mitaine's worries.

Given what we've said so far, there is still some room to push back: How can we coherently claim that something is a story adaptation only if it tells the same story as the source material, while at the same time denying that story fidelity is a necessary condition for being an adaptation? To tackle this question, it will be useful to take a quick detour through an importantly related issue that arises in the philosophy of music.

As Andrew Kania (2006), Stanley Godlovich (1998), and even one of us (Cray 2019)—among others—have pointed out, there are many similarities between storytelling and the performance of songs. Tom Waits's "I Don't Wanna Grow Up" (from the 1992 album *Bone Machine*) has something important in common with the Ramones's "I Don't Want to Grow Up" (from the 1995 album *¡Adios Amigos!*): despite being distinct tracks (i.e., distinct physical encodings of audio data), they are both recordings of the same song, with the latter being a cover of—and hence derivative of—the former. There is something—some *thing*—that the two tracks have in common: a song, also called "I Don't Wanna Grow Up." It is only by positing this third thing, the song, that we can make sense of and explain the relationship between Waits's track and that of the Ramones.

The same holds of adaptations in narrative mediums. Bechdel's *Fun Home* has something important in common with Kron and Tesori's *Fun Home*: they are both tellings of the same *story*, with the latter being an adaptation of the former. There is literally some *thing* that the two tellings have in common—a story, also called "Fun Home"—and its existence is needed to explain the relationship between Bechdel's comic and Kron and Tesori's adaptation. So, just as we might think of the process of *covering* as the transferring of a song from recording to recording (or performance to performance, or recording to performance, etc.), we can think of the process of adaptation as the transferring of a story from telling to telling (though, as we've noted, the two tellings must be within different narrative mediums).[3]

What is it, then, to perform a song? Not just any song, mind you, but some particular song? Taking inspiration from Stephen Davies (2001) and many others, we can say something like the following:

Song Performance: A sound event *e* generated by an agent *a* is a *performance of* a song *s* just in case (i) *a* intends that *p* is an instance of *s*, and (ii) *a* is sufficiently successful in carrying out that intention.

The first condition blocks accidental performances of songs by placing requirements on the performer's intentions, and the second condition ensures that only those performance attempts that meet at least some minimal threshold really count as performances, rather than, say, failed performance attempts. But what counts as "sufficient success"?

If Bon Jovi generates a sound event intended to be an instance of "I Don't Wanna Grow Up," and the audience—appropriately familiar with the song—can tell just by listening that that is what he is trying to do, then Bon Jovi performs "I Don't Wanna Grow Up." On the other hand, if the audience *cannot* tell just by listening that that is what he is trying to do, then Bon Jovi *attempted* to perform the song but failed to do so. What of the case in which Bon Jovi generates a sound event intended to be an instance of, say, "John the Revelator," but the attentive audience instead infers that he was trying to play "I Don't Wanna Grow Up"? Well, in this case, Bon Jovi has failed to perform either "I Don't Wanna Grow Up" (due to the lack of the relevant intention) or "John the Revelator" (due to failing to meet the minimum threshold of success) and instead simply performs a musical mess—albeit one that sounds like "I Don't Wanna Grow Up."

We claim that what goes for songs holds true for stories—or, at least, that we can adapt Song Performance to the act of storytelling as follows:

> **Storytelling:** A narrative work *n* generated by an agent *a* is a *telling* of a story *s* just in case (i) *a* intends that *n* be an instance of *s*, and (ii) *a* is sufficiently successful in carrying out that intention.

As before, the first condition blocks accidental tellings of stories by requiring that the storyteller have the right intentions and the second condition ensures that only those storytelling attempts that meet at least some minimal threshold rather than being merely failed attempts. And thankfully, here we can simply repurpose what we said about song performance: someone is sufficiently successful in carrying out their intention to tell a given story just in case an informed audience could, and would likely, just by attending to the story determine that the letter intended it to be the story in question.

What does this mean in practice? Well, if Quentin Tarantino directs a film intended to tell the story told in Osamu Tezuka's manga epic *Buddha* (1972–83), and an audience—appropriately familiar with Tezuka's relevant work—could tell just by watching that this is what Tarantino was trying to do, then Tarantino has succeeded in telling Tezuka's story and, hence, adapting *Buddha* into film. If, on the other hand, the audience *cannot* tell just by watching that that is what he is trying to do, then Tarantino *attempted* to tell that story but failed to do so—and hence, failed in adapting *Buddha* into film. What about the case, parallel to our song performance example, in which Tarantino generates a film intended to be an instance of, say, Noelle Stevenson's *Nimona* (2015), but the attentive audience instead infers that he was trying to tell the story of *Buddha*? In this case, Tarantino has failed to tell either the story of *Buddha* (due to the lack of the relevant intention) or the story of *Nimona* (due to failing to meet the minimum threshold of success) and instead simply produces a *narrative mess*—albeit one that might easily and forgivably be confused for an adaptation of *Buddha*.

To recap: What ultimately decides whether a given work is an adaptation of some other work? It's partly determined by facts about the storyteller: in particular, whether or not they intend to tell the same story as some previous work through some narrative medium other than that through which the story was originally told. (Remember: if they intend to tell the story through the very same narrative medium, we're dealing with a mere case of remaking, translating, rebooting, etc., rather than a genuine case of adaptation.) And it is also partly determined by facts about the work: whether it is crafted in such a way that an informed audience could, in principle, infer the relevant intention on behalf of the storyteller just by attending to the work itself.

A consequence of this view is that the conditions for telling a story—much like those for performing a song—are really quite minimal. They certainly don't require complete adherence to the specifications laid out in the song's score or in the original story itself. An informed audience can infer that an agent has intended to generate an instance of a particular song even if there are some missed notes or creative departures, and the same goes for stories. In fact, *too much* fidelity to the song being performed or story being adapted could register as an artistic detriment: if you're going to stick to the original that much, then why bother covering the song or adapting the story at all? So if notes or verses or bridges can be left out, chord progressions or melodies altered while still performing the same song, then, by analogy, characters or events can be left out, themes or plot beats altered while still telling the same story. Turning back to the case of *Watchmen*'s adaptation: we cannot infer from the fact that Snyder's *Watchmen* doesn't contain all and only the narrative elements as Moore and Gibbons's that the film wasn't intended to tell the same story, since some of those elements might have been altered by mistake or through creative departure.

This account of what it takes to tell a specific story takes fidelity and intentions seriously and, in doing so, largely squares with what Livingston (2010: 112) says about fidelity in adaptation:

It may be added that once the unrealistic ideal of numerical identity or perfect equivalence has been set aside, fidelity can be understood as raising not one, but many different possible questions about relations between source and adaptation. Broad theoretical arguments against the cogency of these questions founder when specific examples of perfectly sensible questions about the fidelity of an adaptation are raised.

By our lights, Livingston is 99 percent correct. Our only point of disagreement comes in the first line: we contend that it is perfectly possible and realistic to have numerical identity of story across source and target, even if that numerically identical story is not told in equivalent ways. It's this issue that leads us squarely into our next topic: a discussion of what exactly these things called "stories" *are*.

4. What Are Stories?

Whatever stories are, any plausible ontology of them ought to uphold the following three claims:

TELLABLE: Stories can be told.
CREATABLE: Stories can be created.
CONTENTFUL: Stories are contentful, insofar as they contain specifications about what elements—characters, setting, events, perhaps themes, etc.— are intended to be included in a faithful telling.

The first two claims—*TELLABLE* and *CREATABLE*—are straightforward enough. The third—*CONTENTFUL*—warrants a bit of explanation. Recall the previous analogies between stories and songs. Songs, we might think, have *content*: they contain elements—chord progressions, melodies, lyrics, perhaps instrumentation, and so forth—that are intended to be included in a faithful performance. Some songs (the really structurally "thin" ones) might include very little in terms of these specifications, while others (the comparatively "thicker" ones) might specify very many elements and in detail.[4] To perform a given song, the agent attempting the performance must make manifest enough of these elements so that an informed audience, looking just to the performance, would be able to infer that agent's intention. Mistakes can be made, and creative license taken, but too many and too much will together constitute a deal-breaker.

In just the same way, stories have content: they contain specifications about what elements—characters, setting, events, perhaps themes, and so on—are intended to be included in a faithful telling. Some stories (the really structurally thin ones) might include very little in terms of these specifications, while others (the comparatively thicker ones) might specify very many elements and in detail. To tell a given story, the agent attempting the telling must make manifest enough of these elements so that an informed audience, looking just to the telling, would be able to infer their intention. Mistakes can be made, and creative and interpretive license taken, but too many and too much will together constitute a deal-breaker. In this sense, songs and stories alike are contentful. With that in mind, our question of what stories are can now be made more specific: What kind of *things* are well-suited to satisfy all of *TELLABLE*, *CREATABLE*, and *CONTENTFUL*?

We'll sketch one view we take to be especially promising: stories are ideas. But, rather than taking ideas to be private mental particulars, as we discussed in Chapter 4, this view hangs on a different conception of what ideas are. (The view that results from taking stories to be ideas in the sense of private mental particulars is, we think, as much of a non-starter as the view that fictional characters are such things.) Quite unlike private mental particulars, ideas in *this* sense are taken to be shareable, public artifacts. Ideas are things we come up with, sometimes together. They are things that can be bounced around, so to speak, and can spread to new places over time. We can trace their development throughout history and across cultures. And, despite being dependent on mental activity, they can nonetheless exist independently of the mind of any one particular thinker.[5]

What exactly are these things, ontologically speaking? According to the *idealist* about stories, an idea is a system of particular concrete mental states that all share content. In conceiving of mental states as concrete, the view takes them to be identifiable with literal brain states. In conceiving of these literal brain states as particular, it focuses on *tokens*—Sam's literal brain state, Ley's literal brain state, *your* literal brain state—rather than the *type* of which all of those brain states are tokens. And insofar as these particular brain states share their content, they are all *about* the same thing. If you have a brain state of *belief*, that belief is targeted at something—it is *about* something. Similarly with a brain state of *fear*, or *doubt*, or *hope*, or *desire*: you fear Galactus, doubt that Quicksilver could outrun the Flash, hope that *Atari Force* (Vol. 2, 1984–5) gets reprinted, and so on. To say, then, that these particular physical brain states share the same content is just to say that they are all pointed at the same thing, that is, whatever it is that they are about. So, according to the idealist view: an idea is a bunch of particular, physical brain states that are all about the same thing.

It's not just any bunch, though: again, it's a system of such things. The word "system" can take on many meanings but for now, we'll follow Everett and Schroeder (2015) and others in taking a system to be a causally and historically interrelated cluster of entities. So, a system of particular, physical brain states is a causally and historically interrelated cluster of states that are all about the same thing. On this view, the idea originates when a particular thinker (or some particular thinkers, acting in unison) comes into an appropriately novel mental state. At this point, the system is made up of that one novel mental state. But then, through various acts of communication, other thinkers are caused to come into particular mental states that share content with that original, novel mental state—and in so doing, the system grows.

Communication continues, and as more thinkers come to have mental states with that same content, causally and historically traceable back to that original mental state, the system continues to spread. And that system itself, on this view, *is* the idea. So, crucially, ideas are physical entities, rather than abstract entities, and, furthermore, they are public, shareable artifacts in the sense that, in principle, anyone can enter into an appropriate brain state. Now, one need not accept exactly this account of ideas in order to accept the version of idealism sketched here. As long as you have a satisfying account of ideas as physical, public, shareable artifacts, you'll have what you need.

Building off of this, we can take stories themselves to be *ideas for narrative manifestation*: they are ideas for how to manifest various narrative elements— characters, settings, events, perhaps themes—through some medium, whether it be a television series, film, radio drama, musical, comic, or what-have-you.[6] To tell a story, then, is to make good on an idea for narrative manifestation: that is, to make it narratively manifest. Since stories are ontologically thin (in the sense that they are "thin" structures that are "filled out" through the act of telling them), different manifestations might take different liberties with them. And since the telling of the story allows for some mistakes or creative departures, not all of the details of the manifestation need line up exactly with the details contained in the story. Distinct narrative works are tellings of the same story if they stem from the same idea for narrative manifestation, and one work is an *adaptation* of another when one work, situated in one narrative medium, retells a story originally told in some other narrative medium.

The overall picture can be illustrated as follows. In working on her *Fun Home* comic, Bechdel came up with an idea for narrative manifestation, a story—in this case, a work of largely autobiographical creative nonfiction but a story nonetheless—to be told through that comic. Later, after reading the comic and talking with Bechdel, Kron and Tesori utilized that same idea for narrative manifestation, but manifested the story not through a comic but through the medium of musicals. The (numerically) same story, an idea for narrative manifestation, was literally adapted from source (the comic) to target (the musical).

If this explanation sounds simple and intuitive, we'd like to think that's because it is, and that's not bad. But note, too, that the view captures the three claims we started with: Tellable, Creatable, and Contentful. It also serves as sketch of a kind of ontological alternative to positing abstract artifacts of the sort we outlined in Chapter 4. This is partly because *this* kind of idealism has been offered as a competing way to make sense of fictional characters. According to Everett and Schroeder (2015), a fictional character is an idea, too: it's an idea for stories, a tool for particular kinds of storytelling. The content of the idea—that is, the content shared by all of the particular mental states causally and historically clustered together into the system—is the set of the character's internal properties, constituting what sort of "moves" you can make while using that character as a storytelling device. There is, of course, more to be said on the distinction between stories and characters, but this should make clear how the ontology of these two categories might prove surprisingly hard to pull apart.

5. Is *Watchmen* Really *Watchmen*?

By now, we have a partial account of stories, the varieties of adaptation, and how adaptation can affect our critical and evaluative efforts. And though our flagship examples have been few, our hope is that the framework developed is general enough to help guide us through a wide variety of cases. Many of these cases will be rather straightforward: the adaptation of Satrapi's *Persepolis* comic into Satrapi and Paronnaud's *Persepolis* film, the adaptation of John Wagner and Vince Locke's 1997 comic *A History of Violence* into David Cronenberg's film of the same name, and so on. But this straightforward application is far from universal and offers us little assistance with a thorny question we noted earlier: Are some comics unadaptable?

This question has, perhaps surprisingly, already received quite a bit of attention, mostly focused on our running example of Moore and Gibbons's *Watchmen*. Comics critic Douglas Wolk (2007: 241) writes:

> *Watchmen*, bless its twisted heart, is totally unfilmable—not that people haven't been trying to figure out how to turn it into a movie for twenty years, but it's so heavily invested in *being a comic book* that to take it away from its native medium would be to rip all its bones out.

Moore himself echoes these sentiments, stating that "[t]here are things that we did with *Watchmen* that could only work in a comic, and were indeed designed to show off things that other media can't."[7] He goes on to add that he "increasingly fear[s] that nothing good can come of almost any adaptation, and obviously that's sweeping. There are a couple of adaptations that are perhaps good or better than the original work. But the vast majority of them are pointless."

As Pratt (2012) points out, there are a few ways to understand these comments. On one interpretation, the first line of each of the previous comments is taken literally: some essential features of *Watchmen* make the work simply impossible to adapt. On another interpretation, Wolk and Moore alike are better interpreted as making a weaker, though still rather bold claim: that *Watchmen* is impossible to adapt *well*. One thing is clear, though: both Moore and Wolk made these remarks before the release of Zack Snyder's 2009 film, *Watchmen*. And, all philosophizing aside, doesn't the release of that film pretty clearly prove that adapting *Watchmen* is, indeed, possible? Maybe. Maybe not. At least this much is undeniable: Snyder definitely succeeded in making a film inspired by *Watchmen*, called *Watchmen*, and with characters, events, and a setting straight out of Moore's writing and Gibbons's illustration. The question that remains open, however, is this: Is Snyder's *Watchmen* really an adaptation of Moore and Gibbons's *Watchmen*?

Notice that Wolk claims that *Watchmen* is "totally unfilmable." There is an ambiguity in this statement: since we use "Watchmen" as a name both for the story and for the comic, which of the two is he referring to? On a charitable reading, it can't be the comic, because interpreted in that way, his claim would be trivially true: no comic is filmable. Comics are comics, films are films, and one could no more turn a comic into a film than one could turn an apple into an orange. Wolk's claim, though, doesn't seem to be trivially true but *bold*: it's a strong assertion seemingly written with the awareness that it would invite disagreement. If his intention had been to say something trivially true, he wouldn't spend several pages justifying it afterwards.

A better interpretation, then, is that what Wolk means to call "totally unfilmable" is not the comic itself but the story told through that comic—a story which, again, we would also naturally, though perhaps confusingly, refer to as "Watchmen." Returning to his subsequent remarks, we can understand him best as saying that the *story* "is so heavily invested in *being [told through] a comic book*" that to try to adapt it "would be to rip all its bones out."

With this clarification in mind, the claim at issue now seems to be the following:

> **Strong Unadaptability Thesis:** The story WATCHMEN told in the *Watchmen* comic is strictly unable to be told through any medium other than comics.

When Moore speaks of his work, as aforementioned, is he best understood as advancing the Strong Unadaptability Thesis? It's unclear. Again, stories and their tellings are often referred to by the same titles, and perhaps as a result, are commonly conflated or at least not commonly distinguished. So, when Moore claims that "there are things [he and Gibbons] did in *Watchmen* that could only work in a comic," it matters whether Moore is referring to WATCHMEN—the story told in *Watchmen*—or to the *Watchmen* comic itself. If we adopt the former reading, then Moore does seem to be asserting the Strong Unadaptability Thesis. But, if we adopt the latter reading, then he seems to just be saying that their particular means of telling WATCHMEN couldn't have been pulled off outside of the comics medium. While we might quibble about interpretation, we'll proceed under the assumption that Moore intended to endorse something like the Strong Unadaptability Thesis.

The Strong Unadaptability Thesis is, indeed, pretty strong. In his own discussion of *Watchmen*, Pratt (2012) appears to be sympathetic to something more like the following:

> **Weak Unadaptability Thesis:** The story WATCHMEN told in the *Watchmen* comic is unable to be told through any medium other than comics while also preserving exact same aesthetic and artistic features found in the comic.

According to this claim, WATCHMEN can be told in a narrative medium other than comics (like film), but the end result will invariably end up diverging aesthetically and artistically from the *Watchmen* comic. And if WATCHMEN was written intentionally and explicitly *for* comics, then aesthetic and artistic divergence will likely coincide with aesthetic and artistic defect.

Pratt offers a plethora of reasons in favor of (at least) the Weak Unadaptability Thesis. He notes, for example, several formal aspects of the work: the near-strict adherence to the nine-panel grid, the mirrored and symmetrical panel layouts in *Watchmen*'s Chapter V ("Fearful Symmetry"), the withholding of splash pages until the climax, and others. A careful read-through of *Watchmen* reveals that these formal devices lend a significant dramatic effect and, to the attentive reader, imbue some narrative significance. Indeed, a substantial part of *Watchmen*'s prestige comes from Moore and Gibbons's ability to utilize the formal aspects of the medium to such profound effect. And while each of these formal features can be recreated to some degree in film—not directly, perhaps, but analogously—the odds of such techniques finding as much aesthetic success in a film as they did in the comic are much, much lower. Indeed, a close watch of Snyder's film, which involves various panel-into-shot reconstructions—fortifies this very conclusion. Other formal features, like the inclusion of *The Black Freighter*—a comic-within-comic that runs alongside and comments on the main narrative, working in unison with that narrative to amplify various themes—are significantly harder to pull off in film. They seem, for example, to require that the scenes be either disruptively spliced into the narrative or instead compiled into their own separate, supplementary film. But neither of these approaches yields the same effect as was achieved in the comic.

Aside from these formal considerations, there are also thematic concerns in favor of the Weak Unadaptability Thesis. *Watchmen* (the comic) tells a cynical story about superheroes and so is about—is in response to—popular comic books. In this way, the work is self-reflective in the sense that it is a harsh commentary on the very medium within which it is told. In fact, another part of the explanation for the wild success of Moore and Gibbons's work was the way *Watchmen* stood apart from, even in opposition to, the medium within which it was situated. *Watchmen*, it might be said, was a comic against the (then) state of comics, using a superhero story as a tool against superhero stories. When translated into film, however—and especially at the film's time of release, just prior to the recent explosion in popularity of superhero movies—the story loses most of its bite. No longer is it a commentary on the very medium within which it is told, since it is now being told through film, rather than comics. Since the film industry was not saturated with superheroes in the same manner as the comics industry at the time, the cynical portrayal of superheroes is replaced with what amounts to not much more than a bland nihilism. A story which felt like a scathing indictment of superhero fantasy in comics form becomes a generic action flick on the big screen. (Were the film released at the time of this writing, after the over-saturation of popular culture with superheroes, things might be quite different.)

Given these thematic as well as formal considerations, you might start to find the Weak Unadaptability Thesis plausible. Those considerations are not sufficient, however, for establishing the Strong Unadaptability Thesis. Even if we grant the Weak Unadaptability Thesis, we might still acknowledge that although Snyder's film was doomed to failure with respect to the preservation of all aesthetic and artistic value found in Moore and Gibbons's comic, it is nevertheless an adaptation of *Watchmen*. There is a story, WATCHMEN, that Snyder intended to tell. That story originated in one narrative medium (comics), with Snyder moving it into another (film). And, an informed viewer—one familiar with the comic and perhaps some of the discourse surrounding it—could easily infer from just watching the resulting film that Snyder did indeed have the intention to use that film to tell WATCHMEN. That audience might agree that he didn't tell WATCHMEN particularly well, but that's compatible with acknowledging that he still did tell it: a bad adaptation is still an adaptation, after all.

What, then, could justify the jump from the Weak Unadaptability Thesis to the Strong Unadaptability Thesis? Our proposal—which we are here more entertaining than officially endorsing—is that an argument for the Strong version results not from searching for any additional reasons but by recontextualizing those already offered. Suppose that, as we argued in the previous section, stories are ideas for narrative manifestation. What it is to tell a story is to intend to tell that story and sufficiently succeed in carrying out that intention. What's more, the proposed measure of success was whether an informed audience would likely be able to infer, just by looking to the narrative manifestation, that you had intended to tell *that* story. We should ask again: What makes up the content of an idea for narrative manifestation? Well, perhaps at a minimum: some characters, some setting, some events. Given the variety of storytelling practices and preferences, there is almost certainly a wide range of variation here—but at least some of those elements must be present. Otherwise, it would be impossible to actually employ the idea for narrative manifestation on account of the idea being practically empty. Importantly, however, certain storytellers might further saturate their stories with additional elements: their ideas for narrative manifestation include not just characters, setting, and events but also themes or even narratively relevant formal techniques.

We think it would, for instance, be effectively impossible to tell the story of *Fun Home* without including a thematic focus on the struggles of parent–child relationships or the story of *Maus* without engaging with the Holocaust. Similarly, it might be impossible to tell the story of Chris Ware's *Building Stories* (2014) without employing the formal technique of modular "chapters" manifested through a range of different narrative formats. Or, in the case of *Watchmen*, both:

it may very well be a part of the WATCHMEN story—Moore and Gibbons's idea for narrative manifestation—that there are these characters in this setting doing those things, but also that critical commentary is offered on the current state of the comics medium *and* that this is communicated through these narrative elements through a very particular formal structure. The formal structure of *Watchmen*, in Moore's words, is "a truly kind of crystalline structure, where it's like this kind of jewel with hundreds and hundreds of facets and almost each of the facets is commenting on all of the other facets and you can kind of look at the jewel through any of the facets and still get a coherent reading."[8]

If (and this is a very big "if") these thematic and structural features are as central to the idea for narrative manifestation as are the characters, setting, and plot, and if those thematic and structural features cannot be realized in any medium outside of comics, then no one who understands these facts about the story could rationally intend to adapt the story. Since Snyder clearly tried to do so, informed audiences might infer instead that rather than successfully adapting *Watchmen*, he simply failed to understand what Moore and Gibbons's story was in the first place. Of course, this also carries the consequence that any audience members or critics who took the film to be a genuine adaptation of the comic shared in Snyder's misunderstanding of the story. And this sort of mass error might be a bit uncomfortable to attribute in such a cavalierly philosophical manner.

Given the strength of the Strong Unadaptability Thesis, we're not convinced that the case we attempted to make in its favor here is fully compelling. But even if it turns out to be false, sustained reflection on it forces us to consider what it is that comics can do and what it is that they might be able to do that other narrative mediums cannot—and vice versa. Similarly, reflection on the Weak Unadaptability Thesis leads us to consider not what it is that comics are unique in being able to do but instead what comics are able to do especially *well*. This leads us into the final discussion of this chapter, on the notion of medium specificity.

6. Medium Specificity and Comics-Film Kinship

Earlier in this chapter, we mentioned Lessing's notion of *medium specificity*, which Pratt (2012: 149) characterizes as "the view that different [mediums] carry with them different capacities, and hence that each art form is naturally better at doing some things than at doing others." To take just some examples, we might think that given its formal capacities, the novel is better suited for exploring the inner mental life of a character than, say, sculpture.[9] Film is more readily equipped to examine temporality than is painting. And comics are perhaps a more likely choice of medium than photography or written poetry if your aim is to offer a narrative laced with visual metaphor. It is through reference to this notion of medium specificity that we are able to really make sense of the previous Unadaptability Theses. On the Weak version, the medium-specific features of comics naturally make it a better fit than film, and likely the *best* fit, for telling the story of *Watchmen*. On the Strong version, those features make comics the *only* appropriate medium for telling the story.

While the notion of medium specificity is not without its detractors, we won't take up the project of defending it here. Instead, we'll point out that if either the Weak or Strong Unadaptability Theses even make sense—and the Weak version certainly seems to—then some version of medium specificity must be true. (Importantly, this isn't to say that the *truth* of either thesis entails some version of medium specificity. It's that medium specificity of some sort must be true for these claims to even be intelligible.)

One motivation for looking at adaptations either of comics or into comics is that with medium specificity in mind, we seem able to ask fruitful questions: What was the comics creator able to do that the creator of the other narrative work was not, or vice versa? In what ways was the comics creator able to creatively exploit the limitations or strengths of the medium in order to achieve certain narrative, thematic, or emotive ends? How, if at all, could a filmmaker—or a TV producer, or a videogame designer, or what-have-you—innovate within their own respective medium in an attempt to approximate such results?

Consider the aforementioned modular storytelling techniques in Ware's *Building Stories* and how impressively difficult it would be to satisfyingly replicate them in a dynamic, audio-visual format like a feature-length film. Or consider Emil Ferris's *My Favorite Thing Is Monsters* (2017), which handles the projection of interior thoughts onto the external world in a manner that allows the former to shape the latter in narratively revealing ways. How might literary or cinematic narrative mediums undertake, much less achieve, the same goal? Richard McGuire's *Here* (2014) and its direct ancestor "Here" (1989) each non-chronologically (or maybe "hyper-chronologically") depict a single region of space over a range of disparate times (Figure 10.1). In doing so, McGuire comments on temporality and its relation to narrative in a

Figure 10.1 "Here," p. 1 (1989) in *Raw* Vol 2:1, Richard McGuire. Different temporal events in the same physical location are overlaid in a series of panels.

manner that feels especially poignant in comics form but would probably seem wildly tedious if adapted into most other narrative mediums. And, as Cook (2012) argues, some comics prominently feature blatant exploitations of the medium's conventions—such as the tangible thought balloons manifested by character Max Thunderstone in Grant Morrison, Chris Weston, and Gary Erskine's *The Filth* (2002–3). This peculiar metacomic maneuver simply wouldn't make sense in narrative mediums that lack the same conventions.

The same observations regarding medium specificity serve double-duty: not only are they reasons for looking at adaptations, but they are also reasons for making them. Suppose one wants to push the boundaries of what can be done in film, innovating new formal tricks and storytelling techniques that while still within the medium's limitations make creative use of those limitations in ways previously unexplored. To this end, one might pick a particularly difficult-to-adapt comic, like *Building Stories* or *Here*, or perhaps even a particularly difficult-to-adapt character like Pascal Jousselin's metafictional superhero Mister Invincible and attempt the adaptation anyway. The process of adaptation, then, becomes a site for artistic problem-solving. If the adaptation can be done, we learn about both comics and film; if the adaptation can be done *well*, we learn even more. In similar spirit, we might even have reason to attempt to create unadaptable works in any narrative medium. If the effort is ultimately thwarted by a brilliantly innovative adaptor, the very attempt to make something that is genuinely unadaptable might afford useful insight into the formal capacities, strengths, and weaknesses of the chosen medium. Such was the case with Moore and Gibbon's *Watchmen*, and the assessment can easily be extended to works like *Building Stories*, *Here*, *The Filth*, and *Mister Invincible*.

With comics being so rapidly and extensively mined for film and television adaptations, could the notion of medium specificity help to explain this current trend? Is there anything about the formal features of comics and the formal features of film (and television) that would make this trend of comics adaptation predictable? For example, given that McCloud (1993: 8) has committed himself to saying that filmstrips are just very slow comics and that Cook (2012) has spent an entire book chapter defending the claim that comics are not *just* filmstrips, you might wonder just how closely connected the comics medium is with film and television.

In his discussion of why comics are so often adapted into film, Pratt (2012: 148) first focuses on sociocultural reasons, rather than those stemming from aesthetic, artistic, or philosophical considerations. According to Pratt—who acknowledges that his claims here are not much more than conjecture—a lot of this "Golden Age" of adaptation can be explained by the fact that comics, as a mature medium, "presents a rich trove of resources for an industry— film—that is starved for original ideas" (2012). Additionally, superheroes— especially the widely recognizable ones—tend to make for lucrative ventures, an important consideration in a mainstream film industry largely motivated by capitalist concerns of profit. As the capabilities of CGI continuously advance, it becomes both cheaper and more plausible to recreate explosive, fantastic sequences originally drawn for comics. And finally, as the comics medium continues to accrue cultural capital, the long-standing stigma against making "comic book movies" is finally wearing off. While we join Pratt in finding all of these conjectures to be quite plausible, they admittedly tell only part of the story. The *other* reason Pratt offers for why comics are so often adapted into film is simply that with issues of medium specificity in mind, comics are the *best* medium for the job.

Why is comics the *best* medium for adaptation into film? According to Pratt (2012, 2016), there are four main reasons. First, both mediums tend toward being narrative, presenting a sequence of events and offering progression largely through *mimetic* narration ("acts of showing, with no direct narrator") more often than *diegetic* narration ("acts of telling directly by a narrator") (2016: 236). Second, comics and film are both primarily visual mediums, with comics, unlike prose, being pre-visualized and organized in a manner that makes them ready inspiration for (or potentially even just used as) storyboards for films. Third, both comics and film utilize closure to fill in gaps in both temporal and spatial progression, a feature difficult to reproduce in mediums such as theater, in which "audiences maintain a stable spatial relationship to the actors onstage, and the frequency of temporal gaps between scenes is much lower than the frequency of gaps between panels and shots" (2016). And fourth, both comics and films typically make use of techniques such as *indexing* ("guiding the audience's attention by altering their position with respect to an object"), *bracketing* ("framing images so as to include or exclude objects of various degrees of importance"), and *scaling* ("manipulating perspective so as to alter the amount of space an object takes up in the audience's visual field") (2016: 237).[10] These four reasons, taken together, lead Pratt to his conclusion that comics are so often mined for adaptations into film at least in part because the formal kinship between the mediums makes comics perhaps the most suitable source for such mining.

7. Recommend Readings

For an overview of the history of the interdisciplinary field of adaptation studies—interdisciplinary in the sense of combining fields of cultural studies, media studies, literary studies, and so on—as it applies to comics, see Roche, Schmitt-Pitiot, and Mitaine (2018). Other helpful resources include Thomas Leitch's *Film Adaptations and Its Discontents* (2009) and Stam (2015). The volume in which it appears—*Comics and Adaptation*—also contains many interesting case studies on particular comics adaptations. Related to the phenomenon of adaptation is that of *translation*. For this topic, see S. Davies (2007) and Evans (2016). On the relationship between comics and other narrative media, see Gardner (2012).

A classic source on narrative theory and the distinction between (what we are calling here) *story* and *telling* is Seymour Chatman's *Story and Discourse* (1978). On comics and film, see Fischer (2016). A great starting point for philosophical issues regarding film is *Philosophy of Film and Motion Pictures* (2005), edited by Noël Carroll and Jinhee Choi.

Unsurprisingly, much ink has been spilled on Moore and Gibbons's *Watchmen*. We recommend Annalisa Di Liddo's *Alan Moore: Comics as Performance, Fiction as Scalpel* (2009) and Sara J. Van Ness's *Watchmen as Literature* (2010), as well as the chapter on Moore from Wolk's *Reading Comics* (2007).

Afterword

Throughout the past ten chapters, we've focused on what we take to be the central issues that need to be addressed if we are to even approximate an adequate philosophy of comics. When we've ventured into the more peripheral territory, we've tried to focus on the more interesting and exciting parts of that periphery. We've gone down a lot of rabbit holes and hopefully avoided too many wild goose chases.

What we haven't done is formulate or defend a complete, authoritative philosophy of comics. Nor did we try. Any attempt toward *that* lofty goal will take a bunch of people, working together over a long stretch of time. It will require that philosophers of comics, other comics scholars across various academic disciplines, and comics creators (along with critics, fans, and occupiers of any other node of comics practice) collaboratively engage, to varying degrees, with that which each has to contribute. And we think that philosophy and comics would both be all the better for it. So, we invite you to join us in continuing down those rabbit holes.

That's it. That's the book. Thanks for reading it. Hang in there.

Notes

Chapter 1

1. A topic we won't cover is the broader history of when philosophy and comics have intersected. Among its high points is the letter philosopher David Lewis sent to cartoonist Roz Chast, requesting her permission to use one of her cartoons as the cover for his enormously influential book on possibility, *On the Plurality of Worlds* (1986). As it turns out, Chast had already used it as the cover of her own collection, *Parallel Universes* (1984).

Chapter 2

1. In the debate over how to define art, an influential view is *institutionalism*, according to which artifacts are artworks just in case they're treated as artworks by relevant institutions like museums or magazines. The parallel view about comics would hold that some things are comics just in case relevant institutions treat them as comics. Such a view faces the infallibility problem just noted, but it is also tremendously difficult to formulate without lapsing into circularity—for example, by specifying which institutions are the relevant ones without invoking the concept of *comics*. For some of the additional difficulties that institutionalist views face, see Levinson (1979). For an admirable attempt to tackle those difficulties within the context of comics specifically, see Beaty (2012).
2. See Van Inwagen (1990: 7–8).
3. Another constraint is that a suitable answer cannot simply fill in our definitional blank with a massive list of each and every thing that is a comic. While such an answer might be correct, not only would it be impossible for anyone to write down, it would fail to tell us anything about what the listed items have in common or, more importantly, *why* they are rightly included.
4. For various names of comics from across history and languages, see Groensteen (2014a: 96).
5. For a brief historical overview, see Chute (2017: 6).

6. On the nature, epistemology, and ethics of caricature, see Mag Uidhir (2013). On comics and caricature, Holbo (2016).
7. For discussion of the interplay of comics and photography by a cartoonist who draws heavily upon the latter, see McKean (1995).
8. On the aesthetic significance of lines as the product of drawing, see Gardner (2011).
9. The interaction of drawn elements of comics with photographic ones is a complex matter—for example, Cook (2012a, 2015b) explores the aesthetics of photographic images in superhero comic books. See also Pedri (2015) and Postema (2015).
10. For a sampling of site-specific comics as well digital, multimodal, and interactive comics-related experiments, see Gravett (2013: 122–39).
11. Don't confuse the fact that such contrived artifacts are not comics with the incompatibility of poetry and comics. There is an intriguing but generally underexplored category of *poetry comics*. On poetry comics, see Robertson (2015).
12. As Woo (2020) notes, there is no "orthodox" theory or vocabulary for characterizing layouts. Proposed frameworks are developed in Groensteen (2007), Peeters (2007), Postema (2013), and Witek (2009). Gavaler (2017) is a useful overview of axes of variation among layouts and layout conventions in superhero comics. Lefèvre (2009) surveys the emergence of familiar panel layout techniques via a historical survey.
13. For discussion, see Cook (2012b, 2015d, 2016a).
14. Notice that on such a view, a translated comic, which includes different text, doesn't differ *only* at the level of text; the pictures themselves differ, since what a panel depicts characters doing—namely, uttering this-or-that sentence—changes. Translating comics will, on this view, lead to subtle but profound changes in what's depicted, not just what's said.
15. For a catalogue of *emanata*, see cartoonist Mort Walker's *Lexicon of Comicana* (1980).
16. The development of speech balloons in sequential narrative remains a controversial element of comics history. Smolderen (2007) defends a robust distinction between speech balloons and their precursors—"labels" or "loops"—that traces to the narratives in which they were standardly embedded. Rather than capturing speech in genuine narratives, "labels" were deployed in principally allegorical contexts and are importantly different despite their formal similarities. As Smolderen puts it: "the part played by labels in the allegorical scheme is inherently static and didactic. Allegorical pictures are more akin to hieroglyphs than pictorial narratives, and in satirical prints, labels are part of a deciphering process, not of a storytelling process" (2007: 94). Whether or not this historical distinction between speech balloons and labels is warranted, it has all but

evaporated in contemporary critical practice. On speech balloons, see Forceville, Veale, and Feyaerts (2010).

17. For a case of second-person narration in comics, see Bob Powell's "Colorama" in *Black Cat Mystery* #45 (1953).

18. Comics scholars have pursued definitions along similar lines, perhaps most notably Chute (2008: 452) suggests: "Comics might be defined as a hybrid word-and-image form in which two narrative tracks, one verbal and one visual, register temporality spatially." Challenges we'll encounter below arise for this proposal—most notably, the case of silent comics and the requirement that narratives or "narrative tracks" are essential to comics.

19. On visual techniques for the construction of story-worlds in comics, see Horstkotte (2015).

20. The question of what constitutes a narrative is a daunting topic on its own. For discussion, see Nanay (2009) and Currie (2006). In certain debates in the philosophy of art, some have placed the bar for counting as narrative quite high. At least one of us thinks, for example, that Carroll (2001) is mistaken in denying that the following qualifies as a story: "I woke up; later I dressed; still later I went to class." Regardless, we'll talk more about what stories are in Chapter 10.

21. For an overview of Oubapo comics, see Miller (2007a). On abstract comics, see Groensteen (2011: 9–20) and Baetans (2011).

22. Perhaps the Equal Priority View *is* compatible with the existence of nonnarrative comics since in abstract comics, text and image do have *equal* priority; it's just that they each have *no narrative role whatsoever*. Notice, however, that this is true of many artifacts that are non-comics, like stop signs and cereal boxes. This suggests that equal priority in cases where text and image do not generate a story-world is not enough to ensure that something is a comic. For the Equal Priority View to be plausible, text and image must have equal priority and must be *narratively substantial* rather than *trivial*. So, if abstract comics are comics, then the Equal Priority View still turns out to be false.

23. On the tradition and variety of silent comics, see Gravett (2013), Groensteen (2014a: 107), and Postema (2016).

24. Groensteen (2014b: 71) offers a similar taxonomy in trying to articulate what it would mean to provide the specificity of comics: "In order to define the specificity of comics, we need to ask what the medium **allows** artists to do, what it **forbids** them from doing and what it **demands** of them" (bold from original).

25. On text and image interaction especially within avant-garde comics, see Lambeens and Pint (2015).

26. Cf. Groensteen's proposed account of the comics medium: "If one wishes to provide the basis of a reasonable definition for the totality of

historical manifestations of the medium, and also for all of the other productions unrealized at this time but theoretically conceivable, one must recognize the relational play of a plurality of interdependent images as the unique ontological foundation of comics. The relationship established between these images admits several degrees and combines several operations. . . . But their common denominator and, therefore, the central element of comics, the first criteria in the foundational order, is iconic solidarity. I define this as interdependent images that, participating in a series, present the double characteristic of being separated—this specification dismisses unique enclosed images within a profusion of patterns or anecdotes—and which are plastically and semantically overdetermined by the fact of their coexistence *in praesentia*" (2007: 18). Although he relies crucially upon his notion of "iconic solidary" in providing an account of comics, Groensteen later claims that his "position is very similar to McCloud's" (2012: 113).

27. An importantly related sequence-driven view is suggested by Ann Miller (2007b: 75), though it's unclear whether it is intended as an analysis of comics: "As a visual narrative art, *bande dessineé* produces meaning out of images which are in a sequential relationship, and which co-exist with each other spatially, with or without text."

28. Hayman and Pratt's definition, which Pratt (2011) moves away from, differs from McCloud's in some subtle but significant ways. It requires comics to be narrative, leaves open whether the sequence must be deliberate, and imposes a "discreteness" requirement, which raises questions about the extent to which comics images might overlap one another.

29. See Holbo (2012) for a discussion of McCloud's account and, in particular, the threat of radically over-generating comics.

30. On the ins-and-outs of artwork completion in general, see Hick (2008); Trogdon and Livingston (2014, 2015); Gover (2015a); Rohrbaugh (2017, 2018); Cray (2018); Grafton-Cardwell (2020).

31. Discussions about the nature and significance of comics reading abound in comics studies. For a discussion sensitive to Wertham's critique, see Hatfield (2005: 32–67).

32. Clarifying the notion of function is no small matter. Compare, for example, the claim that comics are to be picture-read with a claim like the one from Lacassin (2014: 39) that "the true mission of comics is to depict specific moments in the life of an imaginary character who is condemned to live eternally in the present." Here and elsewhere, it is crucial to distinguish between claims about what comics are *for* with claims about what, in virtue of being picture-read, they aim to express.

33. A potentially useful proposal, defended in Gavaler and Goldberg (2019), takes comics production to involve a *pluralistic author*—a kind of irreducible plural entity toward which we ought to ascribe attitudes and intentions even if such attitudes or intentions can be reduced to those of the specific individuals involved. For further detailed discussion on this topic, see Mag Uidhir (2012) and Mitchell (2016).

Chapter 3

1. As Cook and Meskin (2015) argue, unlike prints that are artworks, comics that are artworks do not typically have instances that are each distinctive artworks in their own right. To get a sense of the distinction, notice that instances of theatre performances are artworks in their own right, but that while a novel is an artwork, its instances are typically not distinctive artworks—they are objects suitable for affording us engagement with the novel itself. This won't matter crucially for our purposes but is important for charting the divide between comics and printmaking.
2. On the aesthetic appreciation of original comic art, see Molotiu (2020b).
3. This doesn't mean, of course, that there are no illuminating analogies between performance and the activity of printing. For discussion, see Gover (2015b) on printing as performance.
4. In *Art as Performance* (2004), David Davies argues that in fact, *all* artworks are performances. Roughly put, the idea is that artworks are the primary focus of our critical and appreciative attention, and it turns out that such attention is best thought of as directed at the *process* of creation, rather than the *product* of creation. Perhaps that's correct, but we take this issue to be orthogonal to our present interest. Any comic artwork would, on this view, be the artist's or printer's performance in the act of creating the comic. But we are still left with ontological questions about the best way to think of the multiplicity of the comic. For, even if the artwork is a performance, that performance is the *process* rather than the *product*, and our questions here concern that product.
5. Not every instance need be a *perfect* instance—some words might end up misspelled or out of order—or else the very possibility of the *misprint* would be much more ominous, as misprints would no longer be less-than-ideally formed instances but literal non-instances of the works in question.
6. The terms "allographic" and "autographic" are introduced in Nelson Goodman's *Languages of Art* (1976) and have received much subsequent clarifying discussion. See, for example, Levinson's "Autographic and Allographic Art Revisited" (1980).

7. The aesthetic esteem for first printings or editions of books reflects an interest in the causal history of books. Collectors will, for instance, typically prize first editions ahead of later ones. Despite differences of this sort, various editions of a novel are nevertheless instances of the same novel but are collected and valued in a kind of aesthetic analogy with fine art prints.

8. This is quite similar to the ontology of rock music proposed in Gracyk (1996) and Kania (2006).

9. Cited also in Bredenhoft (2014), which discusses textual production across mediums and the case of comics.

10. Printing plates were typically metallic or occasionally plastic engravings of a reverse image pulled from original art to press onto paper. While the material printing practices within comics remain one of the least explored aspects of comics history, there's an enormous diversity of techniques that have been put to use at various points. Since letterpress, offset lithography, screen printing, and digital printing methods differ significantly, our talk of printing plates simplifies matters considerably. When other printing processes are involved in production, we take it that the analogous views of authenticity would require a general term like "original production template."

11. We leave aside investigation of how to secure authenticity in those rare cases of reprinting with the original plates. A range of variations on the Strict View are available some of which might require the same paper, ink, and other features of original production. We suspect that critical practice is largely silent on which of these might be more or less plausible; the central issue is, at least with regard to printed comics, whether authenticity is essentially tied to the original material production means.

12. Notice that reprints also frequently differ in who is credited for them. They standardly inherit the creative credits and aesthetic properties that were instantiated by the originals unless, for example, they have been recolored or uncolored. For example, the credited artist of *Miss Fury* (1941–52), whether in the original or reprints, is Tarpé Mills. But the malleability of the reprinting process regularly permits the addition of credits—for example, Rich Tommaso is credited for his work recoloring various of Carl Barks's *$crooge McDuck* comics.

13. The limits of reprinting techniques that satisfy these norms are obviously subtle and complex. We take it, for example, that *Maximum Fantastic Four*, conceived and orchestrated by Walter Mosley, is a suitable reprint of *Fantastic Four* #1 even while it radically expands the size of the panels and typically places them on distinct pages. It also intersperses essays by Mosley and Mark Evanier, but despite this, still facilitates the recognitional norms of picture-reading. We can well imagine, however, disagreement on

this score and take it that works on the aesthetics of comics reprints are overdue and critical for understanding readerly practices.

14. On competing accounts of reading, see Goodman (2019).

15. On some views about authenticity in printmaking, authenticity also requires a certain kind of sanction or creative certification of each instance. See Gover (2015b) for discussion.

16. On supervaluation, see Lewis (1993). The account we sketch here requires amendments around the margins especially when it comes to more nuanced ontological claims—for example, it is true of each instance of *Eightball* #18 that is an instance but that's incompatible with *Eightball* #18 being a multiple. We take it to be the right general approach but one that requires careful attention in a range of cases.

17. Cook and Meskin (2015: 63) seem to suggest that reprints are typically aesthetic preferable to their cheaply printed originals, saying "reprint volumes present [comics like *Action Comics* #1] on better paper, with higher-quality ink and better overall production values. In short, these reprint volumes present aesthetically *better* instance of the multiple instance artwork *Action Comics* #1." If such a view is correct (whether or not it is Cook and Meskin's), the question of how printing quality relates to aesthetic merit of comics looms especially large.

18. For relevant discussion in the context of painting, see Eaton (2003).

19. While digital technology makes reprint projects possible without damage to originals, some previously popular processes for comics reprinting did involve the destruction of original comics—most notably, "Theakstonizing," which bleached out the colors of originals at an early stage in the reprinting and subsequent recoloring process.

20. On this line of argument, see Saito (1989).

21. The process of producing the plates required for color printing within mainstream comic books typically took place outside of the central production departments of publishers and most usually at companies like Chemical Color Plate, which specialized in the now largely obsolete work of doing color separations by hand.

Chapter 4

1. The diversity of fictional discourse and the ways in which internal and external claims interact are substantial points of philosophical investigation. Consider, for example, a claim like "Ewan believes that his grandfather is smarter than Batman." The proper analysis of such claims and how, if at all, they might reduce to complex conjunctions of internal

and external claims is controversial. For our purposes, we leave aside many of these issues, focusing instead on some paradigmatic cases. See our "Recommended Readings" section for pointers to some accessible and representative discussions.

2. This distinction has been drawn in a few different but closely related ways in the philosophy of fiction with some typically parallel terminology. Where van Inwagen (1977) talks about instantiating and ascribing, Zalta (2003) talks about exemplifying and encoding, and von Solodkoff and Woodward (2017) talk about having and holding.

3. We use "he" loosely here. Strictly speaking, fictional characters don't instantiate gender-relevant properties any more than they instantiate properties like *being round* or *being made of paper*.

4. Distinguishing which kinds of causal relationships abstract entities *can't stand in* is an open challenge for platonists. Platonists typically deny that the number seven can exert gravitational force or refract light, but will grant that someone can, for example, make a wager because their favorite number is seven or get exhausted after a day spent thinking about prime numbers. See Cowling (2017: Chapter Two) for discussion.

5. Thomasson mounts this argument against a possibilist treatment of fiction, which takes fictional characters to be merely possible individuals who really do instantiate the properties we take them to be ascribed. But, as Thomasson notes, the same problem arises for any view that posits a necessarily existing plenitude of homogeneous abstract entities.

6. See Gabilliet (2013: 111–33) and Hajdu (2009: 9–39) for a useful discussion of these shops and their workflow.

7. https://www.marvel.com/articles/comics/louise-simonson-and-june -brigman-reunite-for-power-pack-grow-up-1

8. The concept of a "first" appearance raises complications of its own, since date of publication and date of production often come apart with characters occasionally appearing in comics prior to their intended introduction. We won't explore the nuances here except to note that questions about first appearances are especially salient when engaged in collecting practices.

9. According to Cockrum, the history of Nightcrawler actually runs back to its creation during a typhoon while he was stationed with the navy in Guam (Sanderson (1982: 54)).

10. One of us *does* think that characters are ideas when understood according to the different conception of "idea" to be discussed in Chapter 10.

11. For similar views of characters, see Young (2016, 2020) and Everett and Schroeder (2015).

12. See, for example, Caplan and Muller (2015).

Chapter 5

1. This is far from the only place where Morrison explores metafictional weirdness. For a detailed exploration of some of Morrison's metacomics, see Cook (2015a, 2015c, 2016a). And, for Morrison's own take on the structure of fictional reality, see Morrison (2011).
2. While much philosophical work has been undertaken to carefully distinguish among pretense, make-believe, and imagination, we'll treat them as more or less interchangeable for present purposes. The locus classicus is Walton (1990). Note, too, Lewis follows the convention of talking about preten*c*e; we follow the convention of talking about preten*s*e. The two are equivalent.
3. For some exceptions that prove the rule, see Cook (2012b).
4. One strategy for grappling with this and comparable phenomena would draw upon Chris Gavaler's account of *diegetic erasure* occurring when readers "edit contradictions between drawn content and the perceived diegesis" (2016: 45). We take it that a treatment of such phenomena is sorely needed and Gavaler's treatment is especially promising, but our focus is on the broader matter of truth in comics here.
5. As noted in the previous chapter, debates regarding the nature of authorship, the nature of creation, the distinction between the two, and their respective role in comics are firmly underway in the philosophy of comics. See Mag Uidhir (2012, 2016) and Gavaler and Goldberg (2019).
6. As noted in Chapter 3, Gavaler and Goldberg (2019) take the creative team to give rise to an irreducible entity—a pluralistic author—distinct from each of them and which has intentions in its own right. We're happy to leave open such a view here.
7. On ideal agents and their theoretical role in ethics, see Smith (1994) and Rosati (1995).
8. As Cook understands the notion of canon, it is medium-sensitive: what is canon for the emergent Batman story of the comics is not necessarily canon for the Batman films, television shows, or videogames. This is, of course, not a hard-and-fast rule: the Batman miniseries *Sins of the Father* (2018, by Christos Cage and Raffaele Ienco) is noncanonical with respect to the DC-MSCF but canonical with respect to the series of Batman videogames produced by Telltale. Elsewhere, Marvel's *Star Wars* comics released since their purchase by Disney have all (or mostly) been canonical with respect to the films (and novels, etc.). But, in either case, status as the main source of canonical material—status as the *canon leaders*, if you will—remains medium-sensitive: Batman's primary source material comes from comics, *Star Wars* from films.

9. For a broader theory of retcons in comics, see Gavaler and Goldberg (2019).

10. Among the most extreme cases of canon negotiation are the readers hunting Marvel "No-Prizes," which were "awarded" in letter columns for offering logically consistent albeit ad hoc explanations of goofs, errors, and inconsistences arising in Marvel series.

11. This was prompted by Jason Aaron and Russell Dauterman's run on *Thor* where Thor was a woman, eventually revealed to be Jane Foster. With regard to whether Foster was Thor, Aaron was fairly explicit: "This is not She-Thor. This is not Lady Thor. This is not Thorita. This is THOR. This is *the* THOR of the Marvel Universe. But it's unlike any Thor we've ever seen before" (https://web.archive.org/web/20140911024243/http://marvel.com/news/comics/22875/marvel_proudly_presents_thor#ixzz37YlHmVqi). For critical discussion of Aaron's *Thor*, see Kirtley (2020).

12. For discussion of these issues, thanks to Paul Bass. On the essential properties of characters, internally and externally, see Cowling and Ragg (2008).

13. Here's one particularly delicate complication we'll mostly work around: there's a difference between Thunderbolt being essentially ascribed, say, the property of *being human* and Thunderbolt being ascribed the property of *being essentially human*. The first claim entails that there can be no stories wherein Thunderbolt is ascribed a different property in place of *being human*, such as, say, *being a goat*. The latter claim entails that there are stories according to which Thunderbolt is essentially human, but this leaves open whether, in other stories, he might be ascribed the property of *being essentially Kryptonian*.

14. By way of confirming precisely what you might have suspected earlier, the post from "rossatease" concludes: "And do wimmen even read comics?" (https://singletrackworld.com/forum/topic/pc-or-commercialism-gone-mad/).

15. See Brown (2020) for further discussion of superheroes and issues of race- and gender-swapping.

Chapter 6

1. See Frow (2013: 1–12).

2. On genre and medium-specificity as it concerns comics, see Labarre (2020: 17–28).

3. One way to see how reservations might arise is when we begin to ask whether cars are overall more similar to baseballs or stadiums. Aggregating

and suitably weighting which features are relevant quickly begins to seem like a fool's errand. On similarity, see Goodman (1972).

4. See Jauss (1970).

5. This isn't to say that colorists have received their just recognition. Credits for colorists are frequently omitted in *bande dessinées*.

6. Of course, these superheroes must be included in the story the comic tells and not, for example, merely in advertisements, but let's set aside such complications for the moment.

7. Difficult questions arise, too, about how to address changing characters over time. Obviously, some characters vacillate between heroes and villains and some characters are briefly transformed into superheroes, but we'll set aside these extensive complexities here.

8. On cowardice in superhero comics, see Cowling (forthcoming) on Ditko and Skeates's *The Hawk and the Dove*.

9. Our anchoring principle is similar in spirit though different in envisioned details from what some call a "principle of minimal departure"—see, for example, Thon (2019).

10. What should the Anchored Superhero Adventure View say about examples like *Magnus, Robot Fighter*, and *The Legion of Superheroes* which are set in a distant future, spanning numerous planets and alien races? Despite the title, we're inclined to view the comic as a science fiction comic featuring superheroes that, oddly enough, isn't a superhero comic (or at least, not typically; some issues, especially those featuring Superboy, surely are).

11. Some focus on *GENERATE* and the claim that the psychological experience of horror fictions gives rise not to fear but a psychological state readily mistaken for fear. Those proposals must, however, provide a plausible explanation of why this fictive doppelganger of fear isn't intrinsically unpleasant even though fear is. Other proposals reject *FEAR* and assert that fear is *extrinsically* rather than *intrinsically* unpleasant and so, when induced by engagement with fiction, need not be unpleasant. These proposals face a different challenge: explaining why audience's terror directed toward the possibility of satanic possession or ghosts is so different from their fear of disease or violence, with only the latter experiences being unpleasant.

12. On *Jaws* and *Psycho* and the problems they cause for Carroll's view, see Yanel (2003).

13. The history of precursors to the familiar Comics Code is complex and reflects the scale and complexity of comics publishing and distribution throughout the 1950s. For an accessible overview, see Hadju (2008). For a scholarly study of the Comics Code, see Nyberg (1998). We'll consider it from another direction in Chapter 9.

14. The tradition of horror comics continued in a variety of ways, whether as exceptionally watered-down science fiction monster fare or in the form of magazine format comics like *Creepy* and *Eerie* distributed through different publishers and vendors.

15. Regarding tales of dread, Carroll (1990: 15) says: "[t]his method of proceeding distinguishes horror from what are sometimes called tales of terror such as William Maginn's 'The Man in the Bell,' Poe's 'The Pit and the Pendulum,' and 'The Telltale Heart,' Bloch's *Psycho*, Tryon's *The Other*, Michael Powell's *Peeping Tom*, and Alfred Hitchcock's *Frenzy*, all of which, though eerie and unnerving, achieve their frightening effects by exploring psychological phenomena that are all too human."

16. A bit more precisely: there are relatively few comics that feature superheroes and are also intended to produce both fear and disgust, directed toward a monster, in readers.

17. On the role of characters in generating the affect of horror, see Carroll (1990: 23).

Chapter 7

1. Prior to Lewis's passing, he and Aydin, Powell, and L. Fury collaborated on a sequel to *March*, titled *Run*, the first book of which was released posthumously in 2021.

2. From Lewis's 2020 obituary in *Publishers Weekly*, https://www .publishersweekly.com/pw/by-topic/industry-news/Obituary/article/83900 -john-lewis-heroic-civil-rights-leader-dies-at-80.html.

3. See Glasgow, Haslanger, Jeffers, and Spencer (2019) for an informative overview of the topic.

4. See, for example, Yezbick (2015).

5. See also Gateward and Jennings (2015), Aldama (2010), and Tyree (2013).

6. On editorial cartoons, see also Long and Lamb (2016).

7. We return to this notion of *moral outrage porn*, introduced in Nguyen and Williams (2020), in further detail in Chapter 9.

8. For the remainder of the interview from which this quote is drawn, see https://alanmooreworld.blogspot.com/2019/11/moore-on-jerusalem -eternalism-anarchy.html.

9. For sophisticated and detailed discussion of these topics, see especially Wanzo's (2020) Chapter 3 ("Wearing Hero-Face: Melancholic Patriotism in *Truth: Red, White & Black*") and conclusion ("To Caricature, with Love: A *Black Panther* Code.")

10. We say "*seem* possible" rather than "*be* possible," since many superhero narratives clearly present impossible scenarios—certain time-travel gimmicks, various violations of the laws of physics, and so on that are nonetheless assumed to be possible by agents within the fictional world.
11. For a survey of the moral complaints about superhero comics, see Hajdu (2009).
12. For an alternate account of cultural appropriation, see Young (2010).
13. We're not sure if this joke originates with Vossen (who includes it here: https://twitter.com/emmahvossen/status/1138841342921060354?lang=en), but we give her credit at the very least for bringing it to our attention.
14. https://afropunk.com/2020/03/marvel-misses-the-mark-with-offensive-non-binary-character-reveal/
15. https://www.ninthartdelights.com/the-dark-knight-returns-review/
16. https://www.marvel.com/articles/comics/solving-for-x-god-loves-man-kills-through-the-lens-of-now
17. https://www.hollywoodreporter.com/lists/superhero-comic-books-100-best-934371
18. https://www.comicbookherald.com/magneto-7-review-the-master-of-magnetism-is-seriously-underrated/
19. https://williamsinstitute.law.ucla.edu/publications/trans-adults-united-states/

Chapter 8

1. On the term "graphic novel," see McLaughlin (2017b) and Tuusvuori (2017).
2. On this distinction, see Thomas J. Roberts's (1990: 1–3) discussion of *canonical*, *serious*, *plain*, and *junk* fiction.
3. On the *commendatory* versus *classificatory* distinction, see Carroll (1999: 4).
4. Finding non-anecdotal confirmation of this quotation is difficult, so it very well might be apocryphal.
5. Excerpted from the interview at http://www.blather.net/projects/alan-moore-interview/northhampton-graphic-novel/
6. While members of all of these species can *carry* the virus, it is commonly said that only mosquitos can *spread* the virus. This is true, in a sense, but importantly false in another: West Nile virus can be transmitted through blood transfusions, among other means, so anyone receiving a blood transfusion from an infected person (or squirrel, or alligator, etc.) could be at risk for contracting the virus.

7. Beaty and Hatfield's debate is published as "Let's You and Him Fight: Alternative Comics—An Emerging Literature," in *The Comics Reporter*. 2005. Available at: http://www.comicsreporter.com/indix.php/briefings/commentary/3370/

8. See, for example, Cohn (2018).

9. For further discussion on the supposed "language" of comics, see Bramlett (2016, 2020).

10. Cf. D. Davies (2007) on the nature of literature.

11. And to be fair, Lamarque and Olsen define "literature" in terms of *the practice of literature*, which isn't technically circular if we can characterize such a practice without invoking the term in question.

12. Comics scholars with backgrounds in literature and narratology have self-consciously sought to articulate just what such a toolbox might look like. See, for example, Hatfield (2005) and Kukkonen (2013).

13. Cf. Roberts (1990), particularly Chapter Eight: "Reading in a System."

14. Startlingly little has been written on the aesthetic appreciation of characters, though see Cray (manuscript) for some relevant discussion.

15. On comics and fandom, see Pustz (2016).

16. See also Picone (2013).

Chapter 9

1. "I'm a Duke Freshman. Here's Why I Refused to Read 'Fun Home.'" *Washington Post*. URL = https://www.washingtonpost.com/posteverything/wp/2015/08/25/im-a-duke-freshman-heres-why-i-refused-to-read-fun-home/

2. For more on this case and other related cases, see the Comic Book Legal Defense Fund's History of Comic Book Censorship at http://cbldf.org/resources/history-of-comics-censorship/.

3. It's worth noting that, strictly speaking, Suits offers an analysis of *game play*, but modifying this analysis into an analysis of *game* is a relatively straightforward exercise for the reader.

4. The lack of the relevant intention also explains why even a quite sexually explicit like David Quinn and Tim Vigil's *Faust* (1987–2012)—seemingly intended to be a dark superhero/horror comic, rather than a work of pornography—fails to be pornography even if it is still explicit enough to qualify as *pornographic*. We return to the distinction between *pornography* and the *pornographic* in a later section.

5. She was arrested again in December of the same year, when she managed to avoid a two-year sentence and a ¥2.5 million (approximately US$

23,600) fine and instead received a fine of only ¥400,000 (approximately US$ 3,500).

6. Rokudenashiko, personal correspondence.

7. For those curious about manga that, unlike Rokudenashiko's manko pieces, have avoided comparable legal challenge, we recommend readers consult Ebisu Yoshikazu's *The Pits of Hell* (2019) or Shintaro Kago's *Super-Dimensional Love Gun* (2017).

8. For a helpful survey of such arguments, see Maes (2012).

9. See, for example, D. Davies (2012), Kania (2012); Kieren (2001), Maes (2011a, b, 2012), Patridge (2013), and Vasilaki (2010).

10. See Mag Uidhir (2013) for further discussion of ethical questions surrounding editorial cartoons in particular.

11. http://web.archive.org/web/20070705190553/http%3A//www.newsarama .com/dcnew/Batman/Morrison/Morrison_Batman.html

Chapter 10

1. We take Livingston's remarks to hold true even if we deny that the work in question is an *artwork*, as it is still evaluable as a creative accomplishment in the sense that something was created with such-and-such aim in mind.

2. This marks one distinction between reboots and retcons, each of which involve a kind of narrative revisiting. The precise distinction between the two is, however, a matter of emerging philosophical interest. See Gavaler and Goldberg (2019) on this distinction and its relation to semantic theories.

3. Whether the notion of *cover* might actually extend to the comics medium is an underexamined question. For a case that might be treated along these lines, consider cartoonist Chester Brown's retelling of pre-Code horror story, "The Door" (1954, *Weird Mysteries* #11), in his *Ed the Happy Clown* collection. For discussion, see Levin (2012). For discussion of covers in the context of music, see Magnus, Magnus, and Mag Uidhir (2013), and Rings (2013) and (2014), Brown (2014), and Kania (2006).

4. On the distinction between *thick* and *thin* in this sense, see S. Davies (2001).

5. On this view of ideas, see Cray (2014, 2019), Cray and Schroeder (2015), Everett and Schroeder (2015), and Cray and Matheson (2017).

6. According to Everett and Schroeder, a fictional character is this sort of idea: it's an *idea for stories*, a tool for particular kinds of storytelling. The content of the idea—that is, the content shared by all of the particular

mental states causally and historically clustered together into the system—
is perhaps the set of the character's internal properties, constituting what
sort of "moves" you can make while using that character as a storytelling
device. Pretty clearly, if you like this view about stories, it might be natural
to develop it as an alternative to the view we outlined in Chapter 4. See
also Young (2016, 2021) and Cray (2021).

7. https://ew.com/article/2008/07/21/qa-watchmen-creator-alan-moore/
8. http://www.blather.net/projects/alan-moore-interview/watchmen
   -microcosms-details/
9. Cf. Chute (2017).
10. Cf. Carroll (1985).

Works Cited

Abbott, Lawrence. (1986). "Comic Art: Characteristics and Potentialities of a Narrative Medium." *Journal of Popular Culture* 19 (4): 155–76.

Abel, Jessica and Matt Madden. (2012). *Mastering Comics*. New York: First Second.

Abel, Jessica and Matt Madden. (2011). "Foreword." In Alison Bechdel (ed.), *The Best American Comics*, vii–xii. Boston, MA: Houghton Mifflin.

Abel, Jessica and Matt Madden. (2008). *Drawing Words & Writing Pictures: A Definitive Course from Concept to Comic in 15 Lessons*. New York: First Second.

Abell, Catharine. (2012). "Comics and Genre." In Aaron Meskin and Roy T. Cook (eds.), *The Art of Comics: A Philosophical Approach*, 68–84. London: Wiley-Blackwell.

Aldama, Frederick Luis, ed. (2020). *The Oxford Handbook of Comic Book Studies*. Oxford: Oxford University Press.

Aldama, Frederick Luis, ed. (2010). *Multicultural Comics from Zap to Blue Beetle*. Austin: University of Texas Press.

Baetans, Jan. (2011). "Abstraction in Comics." *SubStance* 40 (1): 94–113.

Baldanzi, Jessica and Hussein Rashid. (2020). *Ms. Marvel's America: No Normal*. Oxford: University Press of Mississippi.

Barry, Lynda. (2019). *Making Comics*. Montreal: Drawn & Quarterly.

Beaty, Bart. (2012). *Comics versus Art*. Toronto: University of Toronto Press.

Beaty, Bart and Benjamin Woo. (2016). *The Greatest Comic Book of All Time: Symbolic Capital and the Field of American Comic Books*. Palgrave.

Bechdel, Allison. (2006). *Fun Home: A Family Tragicomic*. Boston, MA: Houghton Mifflin.

Behm-Morawitz, Elizabeth and Hillary Pennell. (2013). "The Effects of Superhero Sagas on Our Gendered Selves." In Robin Rosenberg (ed.), *Our Superheroes, Ourselves*, 73–94. Oxford: Oxford University Press.

Blackbeard, Bill and Martin Williams. (1977). *The Smithsonian Collection of Newspaper Comics*. Washington, DC: Smithsonian Institution Press.

Bors, Matt. (2020). *Be Gay, Do Comics: Queer History, Memoir, and Satire from the Nib*. San Diego, CA: IDW Publishing.

Bramlett, Frank. (2020). "Why There Is No 'Language of Comics.'" In Frederick Luis Aldama (ed.), *The Oxford Handbook of Comic Book Studies*, 16–35. Oxford: Oxford University Press.

Bramlett, Frank. (2016). "Comics and Linguistics." In Frank Bramlett, Roy T. Cook and Aaron Meskin (eds.), *The Routledge Companion to Comics*, 380–9. London: Routledge.

Bramlett, Frank, Roy T. Cook and Aaron Meskin. (2016). *The Routledge Companion to Comics*. London: Routledge.

Bramlett, Frank. (2012). *Linguistics and the Study of Comics*. London: Palgrave Macmillan.

Bredehoft, Thomas. (2014). *The Visible Text: Textual Production and Reproduction from Beowulf to Maus*. Oxford: Oxford University Press.

Brock, Stuart and Anthony Everett, eds. (2015). *Fictional Objects*. Oxford: Oxford University Press.

Brown, Jeffrey. (2020). "The Replacements: Ethnicity, Gender, and Legacy Heroes in Marvel Comics." In Frederick Luis Aldama (ed.), *The Oxford Handbook of Comic Book Studies*, 387–401. Oxford: Oxford University Press.

Brown, Lee B. (2014). "A Critique of Michael Rings on Covers." *Journal of Aesthetics and Art Criticism* 72 (2): 193–5.

Brunetti, Ivan. (2011). *Cartooning: Philosophy and Practice*. New Haven, CT: Yale University Press.

Brunetti, Ivan. (2006). *An Anthology of Graphic Fiction, Cartoons, & True Stories*, vol. 1. New Haven, CT: Yale University Press.

Byrne, John. (1993). "Truth in Fiction: The Story Continued." *Australasian Journal of Philosophy* 71 (1): 24–35.

Caplan, Ben. (2014). "Serial Fiction, Continued." *British Journal of Aesthetics* 54: 65–76.

Caplan, Ben and Cathleen Muller. (2014). "Against a Defense of Fictional Realism." *Philosophical Quarterly* 64: 211–24.

Carlin, John. (2020). "How Low Can You Go?" In Kim Munson (ed.), *Comic Art in Museums*, 257–8. Oxford: University Press of Mississippi. Originally published in *Paper*, September 1990.

Carrier, David. (2000). *The Aesthetics of Comics*. University Park, PA: Penn State University Press.

Carroll, Noël. (2009). "Tales of Dread in the *Twilight Zone*." In Noël Carroll and Lester Hunt (eds.), *Philosophy in the Twilight Zone*, 26–38. London: Wiley-Blackwell.

Carroll, Noël. (2001). "On the Narrative Connection." In Wille van Peer and Seymour Chatman (eds.), *New Perspectives on Narrative Experience*. Albany, NY: SUNY Press. 21–41.

Carroll, Noël. (1999). *Philosophy of Art: A Contemporary Introduction*. London: Routledge.

Carroll, Noël. (1998). *A Philosophy of Mass Art*. Oxford: Oxford University Press.

Carroll, Noël. (1994). "The Paradox of Junk Fiction." *Philosophy and Literature* 18 (2): 225–41.

Carroll, Noël. (1990). *The Philosophy of Horror: Or, Paradoxes of the Heart.* London: Routledge.

Carroll, Noël. (1985). "The Specificity of Media in the Arts." *Journal of Aesthetic Education* 19 (4): 5–20.

Chatman, Seymour. (1978). *Story and Discourse: Narrative Structure in Fiction and Film.* Ithaca, NY: Cornell University Press.

Chute, Hillary. (2017). *Why Comics? From Underground to Everywhere.* New York: Harper Collins.

Chute, Hillary. (2008). "Comics as Literature? Reading Graphic Narrative." *PMLA* 123 (2): 452–65.

Cocca, Carolyn. (2016). *Superwomen: Gender, Power, and Representation.* London: Bloomsbury.

Coogan, Peter. (2012). "The Hero Defines the Genre, the Genre Defines the Hero." In Robin S. Rosenberg and Peter Coogan (eds.), *What Is a Superhero?*, 3–10. Oxford: Oxford University Press.

Cohen, Ted. (1993). "High and Low Thinking about High and Low Art." *Journal of Aesthetics and Art Criticism* 51 (2): 151–6.

Cohn, Neil. (2018). "Visual Language Theory and the Scientific Study of Comics." In Janina Wildfeur, Alexander Dunst and Jochen Laubrock (eds.), *Empirical Comics Research: Digital, Multimodal, and Cognitive Methods,* 305–28. London: Routledge.

Cohn, Neil. (2014). *The Visual Language of Comics: Introduction to the Structure and Cognition of Sequential Images.* London: Bloomsbury.

Cohn, Neil. (2012). "Comics, Linguistics, and Visual Language." In Frank Bramlett (ed.), *Linguistics and the Study of Comics,* 92–118. Palgrave.

Cook, Roy T. (2016a). "Metacomics." In Frank Bramlett, Roy T. Cook and Aaron Meskin (eds.), *The Routledge Companion to Comics,* 257–66. London: Routledge.

Cook, Roy T. (2016b). "Underground and Alternative Comics." In Frank Bramlett, Roy T. Cook and Aaron Meskin (eds.), *The Routledge Companion to Comics,* 34–43. London: Routledge.

Cook, Roy T. (2015a). "Does the Joker Have Six-Inch Teeth?" In Robert Moses Peaslee and Robert G. Weiner (eds.), *The Joker: A Serious Study of the Clown Prince of Crime,* 19–32. Oxford: University Press of Mississippi.

Cook, Roy T. (2015b). "Judging a Comic Book by Its Cover: Marvel Comics, Photo-Covers, and the Objectivity of Photography." *Image & Narrative* 16 (2): 14–27.

Cook, Roy T. (2015c). "Morrison, Magic, and Visualizing the Word: Text as Image in *Vimanarama*." *ImageTexT* 8 (2): 1–35.

Cook, Roy. (2015d). "The Writer and the Writer: The Death of the Author in Suicide Squad #58." In K. Roddy and D. Green (eds.), *Grant Morrison and the Superhero Renaissance*, 64–81. Jefferson, NC: MacFarland & Co.

Cook, Roy T. (2013). "Canonicity and Normativity in Massive, Serialized, Collaborative Fiction." *Journal of Aesthetics and Art Criticism* 71 (3): 271–6.

Cook, Roy T. (2012a). "Drawings of Photographs in Comics." *Journal of Aesthetics and Art Criticism* 70 (1): 129–38.

Cook, Roy T. (2012b). "Why Comics Are Not Films: Metacomics and Medium-Specific Conventions." In Aaron Meskin and Roy T. Cook (eds.), *The Art of Comics: A Philosophical Approach*, . 165–87. London: Wiley-Blackwell.

Cook, Roy T. (2011). "Do Comics Require Pictures? Or Why *Batman* #663 Is a Comic." *Journal of Aesthetics and Art Criticism* 69 (3): 285–96.

Cook, Roy T. and Aaron Meskin. (2015). "Comics, Prints, and Multiplicity." *Journal of Aesthetics and Art Criticism* 73 (1): 57–67.

Cook, Roy T. and Aaron Meskin. (2012). *The Art of Comics: A Philosophical Approach*. London: Wiley-Blackwell.

Cowling, Sam. (forthcoming) "Self-Defense for Superheroes in *The Hawk and the Dove*." In Jo Davis-McElligat and Jim Coby (eds.), *BOOM! #*@&! Splat: Comics and Violence*. Oxford: University Press of Mississippi.

Cowling, Sam. (2020). "Rethinking Racial Ontology through McDuffie's *Deathlok*." *Inks: The Journal of the Comics Studies Society* 4 (2): 179–98.

Cowling, Sam. (2017). *Abstract Entities*. London: Routledge.

Cowling, Sam and Chris Ragg. (2008). "Could Batman Have Been the Joker?" In Mark D. White and Robert Arp (eds.), *Batman and Philosophy*, 142–55. London: Wiley-Blackwell.

Cray, Wesley D. (Forthcoming). Manuscript. "Batman: A Case Study in Ontology and Appreciation." Bloomsbury Contemporary Aesthetics.

Cray, Wesley D. (2019). "Some Ideas about the Metaphysics of Stories." *British Journal of Aesthetics* 59 (2): 147–60.

Cray, Wesley D. (2018). "Psychologism about Artistic Plans: A Response to Rohrbaugh." *Journal of Aesthetics and Art Criticism* 76 (1): 101–4.

Cray, Wesley D. (2017). "Abstract Generation: A Response to Friedell." *Journal of Aesthetics and Art Criticism* 75 (3): 289–92.

Cray, Wesley D. (2014). "Conceptual Art, Ideas, and Ontology." *Journal of Aesthetics and Art Criticism* 72 (3): 235–45.

Cray, Wesley D. and Carl Matheson. (2017). "A Return to Musical Idealism." *Australasian Journal of Philosophy* 95 (3): 702–15.

Cray, Wesley D. and Timothy Schroeder. (2015). "An Ontology of Ideas." *Journal of the American Philosophical Association* 1 (4): 757–75.

Cremins, Brian. (2016). "Funny Animals." In Frank Bramlett, Roy T. Cook and Aaron Meskin (eds.), *The Routledge Companion to Comics*, 146–53. London: Routledge.

Cunningham, Phillip Lamarr. (2010). "The Absence of Black Supervillains in Mainstream Comics." *Journal of Graphic Novels and Criticism* 1 (1): 51–62.

Currie, Gregory. (2006). "Narrative Representation of Causes." *Journal of Aesthetics and Art Criticism* 65 (3): 309–16.

Currie, Gregory. (2004). *Arts and Minds*. Oxford: Oxford University Press.

Currie, Gregory. (1990). *The Nature of Fiction*. Oxford: Oxford University Press.

Davies, David. (2012). "Pornography, Art, and the Intended Response of the Receiver." In Hans Maes and Jerrold Levinson (eds.), *Art & Pornography: Philosophical Essays*, 61–82. Oxford: Oxford University Press.

Davies, David. (2007). *Aesthetics and Literature*. London: Continuum.

Davies, David. (2004). *Art as Performance*. Blackwell.

Davies, David and Carl Matheson, eds. (2008). *Contemporary Readings in the Philosophy of Literature: An Analytic Approach*. Peterborough, ON: Broadview Press.

Davies, Stephen. (2007). "Versions of Musical Works and Literary Translations." In Kathleen Stock (ed.), *Philosophers on Music: Experience, Meaning, and Work*, 79–92. Oxford: Oxford University Press.

Davies, Stephen. (2003). "Ontology of Art." In Jerrold Levinson (ed.), *The Oxford Handbook of Aesthetics*, 155–80. Oxford: Oxford University Press.

Davies, Stephen. (2001). *Musical Works & Performances: A Philosophical Exploration*. Oxford: Oxford University Press.

Davis, Blair. (2015). "Bare Chests, Silver Tiaras, and Removable Afros: The Visual Design of Black Comic Book Superheroes." In Frances Gateward and John Jennings (eds.), *The Blacker the Ink: Constructions of Black Identity in Comics and Sequential Art*, 193–212. New Brunswick, NJ: Rutgers University Press.

Ditko, Steve. (2002). "An Insider's Part of Comics History: Jack Kirby's Spider-Man." In Robin Snyder and Steve Ditko (ed.), *The Avenging World*, 20–4. Bellingham, WA: SD Publishing.

Doxiadis, Apostolos and Christos Papadimitriou. (2009). *LogicComix: An Epic Search for Truth*. London: Bloomsbury.

Dryden, Jane and Mark D. White (2011). *Green Lantern and Philosophy: No Evil Shall Escape This Book*. London: Wiley.

Duff, David. (2000). *Modern Genre Theory*. London: Routledge.

Eagleton, Terry. (1983). *Literary Theory: An Introduction*. Blackwell.

Eaton, A. W. (2017). "Feminist Pornography." In Mari Mikkola (ed.), *Beyond Speech: Pornography and Analytic Feminist Philosophy*, 243–57. Oxford: Oxford University Press.

Eaton, A. W. (2007). "A Sensible Anti-Porn Feminism." *Ethics* 117 (4): 674–715.

Eaton, A. W. (2003). "Where Ethics and Aesthetics Meet: Titian's *Rape of Europa*." *Hypatia* 18 (4): 159–88.

Eco, Umberto. (1972). "The Myth of Superman." *Diacritics* 2 (1): 14–22.

Elkins, David. (2017). "Introduction." In Paul Karasik and Mark Newgarden (eds.), *How to Read Nancy: The Elements of Comics in Three Easy Panels*, 12–19. Seattle, WA: Fantagraphics.

Eisner, Will. (1985). *Comics & Sequential Art*. Tamarac, FL: Poorhouse Press.

Evans, Jonathan. (2016). "Comics and Translation." In Frank Bramlett, Roy T. Cook and Aaron Meskin (eds.), *The Routledge Companion to Comics*, 319–27. London: Routledge.

Evenson, Brian. (2014). *Ed vs. Yummy Fur, or What Happens When a Serial Comic Becomes a Graphic Novel*. Minneapolis, MN: Uncivilized Books.

Everett, Anthony and Timothy Schroeder. (2015). "Ideas for Stories." In Stuart Brock and Anthony Everett (eds.), *Fictional Objects*, 275–93. Oxford: Oxford University Press.

Everett, Anthony. (2005). "Against Fictional Realism." *Journal of Philosophy* 102 (12): 624–49.

Evnine, Simon. (2015). "'But Is It Science Fiction?': Science Fiction and a Theory of Genre." *Midwest Studies in Philosophy* 39 (1): 1–28.

Fawaz, Ramzi. (2016). *The New Mutants: Superheroes and the Radical Imagination of American Comics*. New York: New York University Press.

Fischer, Craig. (2016). "Comics and Film." In Frank Bramlett, Roy T. Cook and Aaron Meskin (eds.), *The Routledge Companion to Comics*, 339–47. London: Routledge.

Flowers, Johnathan. (2020). "Misunderstanding Comics." In Susan E. Kirtley, Antero Garcia and Peter E. Carlson (eds.), *With Great Powers Comes Great Pedagogy: Teaching, Learning, and Comics*, 207–25. Oxford: University Press of Mississippi.

Forceville, Charles, Tony Veale and Kurt Feyaerts. (2010). "Balloonics: The Visuals of Balloons in Comics." In Joyce Goggin and Dan Hassler-Forest (eds.), *The Rise and Reason of Comics and Graphic Literature*, 56–73. McFarland.

Freeland, Cynthia. (2004). "Horror and Art-Dread." In Stephen Prince (ed.), *The Horror Film*, 189–205. New Brunswick, NJ: Rutgers University Press.

Freeland, Cynthia. (2002). *The Naked and the Undead: Evil and the Appeal of Horror*. Indianapolis, IN: Perseus.

Fried, Jeremy. (2019). "Ally Aesthetics." *Journal of Aesthetics and Art Criticism* 77 (4): 447–59.

Friedel, David. (2016). "Abstract Creationism and Authorial Intention." *Journal of Aesthetics and Art Criticism* 74 (2): 129–37.

Friend, Stacie. (2017). "The Real Foundation of Fictional Worlds." *Australasian Journal of Philosophy* 95 (1): 29–42.

Friend, Stacie. (2007). "Fictional Characters." *Philosophy Compass* 2 (2): 141–56.

Frow, John. (2013). *Genre*. London: Routledge.

Gabilliet, Jean-Paul. (2013). *Of Comics and Men: A Cultural History of American Comic Books*. Oxford: University Press of Mississippi.

Gardner, Jared. (2015). "A History of the Narrative Comic Strip." In Daniel Stein and Jan-Noel Thon (eds.), *From Comic Strips to Graphic Novels*, 241–54. Berlin: De Gruyter.

Gardner, Jared. (2012). *Projections: Comics and the History of Twenty-First-Century Storytelling*. Palo Alto, CA: Stanford University Press.

Gardner, Jared. (2011). "Storylines." *SubStance* 40 (1): 53–69.

Gateward, Frances and John Jennings, eds. (2015). *The Blacker the Ink: Constructions of Black Identity in Comics and Sequential Art*. New Brunswick, NJ: Rutgers University Press.

Gaut, Berys. (2008). "The Paradox of Horror." In Alex Neil and Aaron Ridley (eds.), *Arguing about Art*, 317–29. London: Routledge.

Gavaler, Chris and Nathaniel Goldberg. (2019). *Superhero Thought Experiments: Comic Book Philosophy*. Iowa City: University of Iowa Press.

Gavaler, Chris. (2017). *Superhero Comics*. London: Bloomsbury.

Gavaler, Chris. (2016). "'Something Like This Just Couldn't Happen!': Resolving Naturalistic Tensions in Superhero Comics Art." *Studies in Comics* 7 (1): 29–48.

Gibbons, Dave and Tim Pilcher. (2017). *How Comics Work*. Indianapolis, IN: Wellfleet Press.

Gibson, Mel. (2016). "Comics and Gender." In Frank Bramlett, Roy T. Cook and Aaron Meskin (eds.), *The Routledge Companion to Comics*, 285–93. London: Routledge.

Glasgow, Joshua, Sally Haslanger, Chike Jeffers and Quayshawn Spencer. (2019). *What Is Race? Four Philosophical Views*. Oxford: Oxford University Press.

Godlovich, Stan. (1998). *Musical Performance: A Philosophical Study*. London: Routledge.

Goldberg, Nathaniel and Gavaler Chris. (2021). *Revising Fiction, Fact, and Faith*. London: Routledge.

Goodman, Jeffrey. (2020). "On Reading." *Acta Analytica* 35 (1): 51–9.

Goodman, Nelson. (1976). *Language of Art: An Approach to a Theory of Symbols*. Indianapolis, IN: Hackett.

Goodman, Nelson. (1967). "Seven Strictures on Similarity." In L. Foster and J. W. Swanson (eds.), *Experience and Theory*, 19–32. Indianapolis, IN: Bobbs-Merill.

Gover, K. E. (2015a). "Ambivalent Agency: A Response to Trogdon and Livingston on Artwork Completion." *Journal of Aesthetics and Art Criticism* 73 (4): 457–60.

Gover, K. E. (2015b). "Are All Multiples the Same? The Problematic Nature of the Limited Edition." *Journal of Aesthetics and Art Criticism* 73 (1): 69–80.

Grady, William. (2016). "Western Comics." In Frank Bramlett, Roy T. Cook and Aaron Meskin (eds.), *The Routledge Companion to Comics*, 164–73. London: Routledge.

Grafton-Cardwell, Patrick. (2020). "How to Understand the Completion of Art." *Journal of Aesthetics and Art Criticism* 78 (2): 197–208.

Gracyk, Theodore. (1996). *Rhythm and Noise: An Aesthetics of Rock*. Durham, NC: Duke University Press.

Gravett, Paul. (2013). *Comics Art*. New Haven, CT: Yale University Press.

Groensteen, Thierry. (2014a). "Definitions." In Ann Miller and Barty Beaty (eds.), *The French Comics Theory Reader*, 93–113. Leuven: Leuven University Press.

Groensteen, Thierry. (2014b). "The Elusive Specificity." In Ann Miller and Barty Beaty (eds.), *The French Comics Theory Reader*, 63–74. Leuven: Leuven University Press.

Groensteen, Thierry. (2012). "A Few Words about the System of Comics." *European Comic Art* 1 (1): 87–93.

Groensteen, Thierry. (2011). *Comics and Narration*, trans. Ann Miller. Oxford: University Press of Mississippi.

Groensteen, Thierry. (2007). *The System of Comics*, trans. Bart Beaty and Nick Nguyen. Oxford: University Press of Mississippi.

Groenteen, Thierry and Benoît Peeters, eds. (1994). *Töpffer: L'invention de la bande dessinée*. Hermann.

Hajdu, David. (2009). *The Ten-Cent Plague: The Great Comic-Book Scare and How It Changed America*. London: Picador.

Hall, Justin. (2016). "Erotic Comics." In Frank Bramlett, Roy T. Cook and Aaron Meskin (eds.), *The Routledge Companion to Comics*, 154–63. London: Routledge.

Hall, Justin, ed. (2013). *No Straight Lines: Four Decades of Queer Comics*. Seattle: Fantagraphics Books.

Harold, James. (2018). "The Value of Fidelity in Adaptation." *British Journal of Aesthetics* 58 (1): 89–100.

Harold, James. (2010). "The Value of Fictional Worlds (or Why 'The Lord of the Rings' Is Worth Reading)." *Contemporary Aesthetics* 8.

Harvey, R. C. (2005). "Describing and Discarding 'Comics' as an Impotent Act of Philosophical Rigor." In Jeff McLaughlin (ed.), *Comics as Philosophy*, 14–26. Oxford: University Press of Mississippi.

Harvey, R. C. (1996). *The Art of the Comic Book: An Aesthetic History*. Oxford: University Press of Mississippi.

Harvey, R. C. (1994). *The Art of the Funnies: An Aesthetic History*. Oxford: University Press of Mississippi.

Hatfield, Charles. (2017). "Foreword: Comics Studies, the Anti-Discipline." In Matthew Smith and Randy Duncan (eds.), *The Secret Origins of Comics Studies*, xi–xxii. London: Routledge.

Hatfield, Charles. (2011). *Hand of Fire: The Comics Art of Jack Kirby*. Oxford: University Press of Mississippi.

Hatfield, Charles. (2005). *Alternative Comics: An Emerging Literature*. Oxford: University Press of Mississippi.

Hatfield, Charles and Bart Beaty. (2020). *Comic Studies: A Guidebook*. New Brunswick, NJ: Rutgers University Press.

Hatfield, Charles, Jeet Heer and Kent Worcester. (2013). *The Superhero Reader*. Oxford: University Press of Mississippi.

Hayman, Greg and Henry Pratt. (2005). "What Are Comics?" In David Goldblatt and Lee B. Brown (eds.), *Aesthetics: A Reading in Philosophy*, 2nd ed., 419–24. Pearson: Prentice Hall.

Helms, Jason. (2017). *Rhizcomics: Rhetoric, Technology, and New Media Composition*. Ann Arbor: University of Michigan Press.

Helms, Jason. (2015). "Is This Article a Comic?" *Digital Humanities Quarterly* 9 (4).

Hick, Darren Hudson. (2016). "Comics and Criticism." In Frank Bramlett, Roy T. Cook and Aaron Meskin (eds.), *The Routledge Companion to Comics*, 328–36. London: Routledge.

Hick, Darren Hudson. (2012a). "The Language of Comics." In Aaron Meskin and Roy T. Cook (eds.), *The Art of Comics: A Philosophical Approach*, 125–44. London: Wiley-Blackwell.

Hick, Darren Hudson. (2012b). *Introducing Aesthetics and the Philosophy of Art*. London: Bloomsbury.

Hick, Darren Hudson. (2008). "When Is a Work of Art Finished?" *Journal of Aesthetics and Art Criticism* 66 (1): 67–76.

Holbo, John. (2016). "Caricature and Comics." In Frank Bramlett, Roy T. Cook and Aaron Meskin (eds.), *The Routledge Companion to Comics*, 367–79. London: Routledge.

Holbo, John. (2012). "Redefining Comics." In Aaron Meskin and Roy T. Cook (eds.), *The Art of Comics: A Philosophical Approach*, 3–30. London: Wiley-Blackwell.

Horstkotte, Silke. (2015). "Zooming In and Out: Panels, Frames, Sequences, and the Building of Graphic Storyworlds." In Daniel Stein and Jan-Noel Thon (eds.), *From Comic Strips to Graphic Novels*, 27–48. Berlin: De Gruyter.

Housel, Rebecca and J. Jeremy Wisnewski. (2009). *X-Men and Philosophy: Astonishing Insight and Uncanny Argument in the Mutant X-Verse*. London: Wiley.

Howard, Sheena. (2013). "Brief History of the Black Comic Strip: Past and Present." In Sheena C. Howard and Ronald L. Jackson (eds.), *Black Comics: Politics of Race and Representation*, 11–22. London: Bloomsbury.

Howe, Sean. (2013). *Marvel Comics: The Untold Story*. New York: Harper Collins.

Irvin, Sherri. (2017). "Resisting Body Oppression." *Feminist Philosophy Quarterly* 3 (4): 1–26.

Jauss, Hans Robert. (1970). "Literary History as a Challenge to Literary Theory." *New Literary History* 2 (1): 7–37.

John, Eileen and Dominic McIver Lopes, eds. (2004). *Philosophy of Literature: Contemporary and Classic Readings.* London: Wiley-Blackwell.

Jones, David Annwn. (2016). "Horror Comics." In Frank Bramlett, Roy T. Cook and Aaron Meskin (eds.), *The Routledge Companion to Comics*, 174–82. London: Routledge.

Kania, Andrew. (2012). "Concepts of Pornography: Aesthetics, Feminism, and Methodology." In Hans Maes and Jerrold Levinson (eds.), *Art & Pornography: Philosophical Essays*, 254–76. Oxford: Oxford University Press.

Kania, Andrew. (2006). "Making Tracks: The Ontology of Rock Music." *Journal of Aesthetics and Art Criticism* 64 (4): 401–14.

Kant, Immanuel. (1790/1987). *Critique of Judgement*, trans. Werner Pluhar. Indianapolis, IN: Hackett.

Kashtan, Aaron. (2018). *Between Pen and Pixel: Comics, Materiality, and the Book of the Future.* Columbus: Ohio State University Press.

Kieran, Matthew. (2001). "Pornographic Art." *Philosophy and Literature* 25 (1): 31–45.

Kirtley, Susan. (2020). "Hammer in Hand: Feminist Community Building in Jason Aaron's *Thor*." in Frederick Luis Aldama (ed.), *The Oxford Handbook of Comic Book Studies.* Oxford: Oxford University Press. 419–36.

Kivy, Peter. (2011). *Once-Told Tales: An Essay in Literary Aesthetics.* London: Wiley-Blackwell.

Kivy, Peter. (2006). *The Performance of Reading: An Essay in the Philosophy of Literature.* London: Wiley-Blackwell.

Klock, Geoff. (2006). *How to Read Superhero Comics and Why.* London: Continuum.

Kripke, Saul. (2011). "Vacuous Names and Fictional Entities." In *Philosophical Troubles: Collected Papers, Volume 1*, 52–74. Oxford: Oxford University Press.

Kukkonen, Karin. (2013). *Studying Comics and Graphic Novels.* London: Wiley-Blackwell.

Kulvicki, John. (2014). *Images.* London: Routledge.

Kunka, Andrew. (2017). "Comics, Race, and Ethnicity." In Frank Bramlett, Roy T. Cook and Aaron Meskin (eds.), *The Routledge Companion to Comics*, 275–84. London: Routledge.

Kunzle, David. (1973). *The Early Comic Strip: Narrative Strips and Picture Stories in the European Broadsheet from c. 1450 to 1825.* University of California Press.

Labarre, Nicolas. (2020). *Understanding Genres in Comics.* Palgrave.

Laccasin, Francis. (2014). "Dictionary Definition." In Ann Miller and Barty Beaty (eds. and trans.), *The French Comics Theory Reader*, 39–46. University of Leuven Press.

Laetz, Brian and Dominic McIver Lopes. (2008). "Genre." In Paisley Livingston and Carl Plantinga (eds.), *Routledge Companion to Philosophy and Film*, 152–61. London: Routledge.

Lamarque, Peter. (2009). *The Philosophy of Literature*. Blackwell.

Lamarque, Peter and Stein Haugom Olsen. (1997). *Truth, Fiction, and Literature*. Oxford: Clarendon.

Lambeens, Tom and Kris Pint. (2015). "The Interaction of Image and Text in Modern Comics." In Andre Lardinois et al. (eds.), *Texts, Transmissions, Receptions*, 240–56. Leiden: Brill.

Langsdale, Samantha and Elizabeth Rae Coody. (2020). *Monstrous Women in Comics*. Oxford: University Press of Mississippi.

Langton, Rae. (1993). "Speech Acts and Unspeakable Acts." *Philosophy and Public Affairs* 22 (4): 293–30.

Lefèvre, Pascal. (2009). "The Conquest of Space: Evolution of Panel Arrangements and Page Layouts in Early Comics Published in Belgium (1880–1929)." *European Comic Art* 2 (2): 227–52.

Lefèvre, Pascal and Charles Dierick. (1998). *Forging a New Medium: The Comic Strip in the Nineteenth Century*. Amsterdam: University Press Amsterdam.

Leitch, Thomas. (2009). *Film Adaptation and Its Discontents: From Gone with the Wind to The Passion of the Christ*. Baltimore, MD: Johns Hopkins University Press.

Lessing, Gotthold. (1766/1910). *Laocoön: An Essay upon the Limits of Painting and Poetry*, trans. Ellen Frothingham. New York: Little, Brown, and Company.

Levin, Bob. (2012). "To Hell and Back." *The Comics Journal*. http://www.tcj.com/to-hell-and-back/.

Levinson, Jerrold. (2005). "Erotic Art and Pornographic Pictures." *Philosophy and Literature* 29 (1): 228–40.

Levinson, Jerrold. (1990). "Colourization Ill-Defended." *British Journal of Aesthetics* 30 (1): 62–7.

Levinson, Jerrold. (1984). "Hybrid Art Forms." *Journal of Aesthetic Education* 18 (4): 5–13.

Levinson, Jerrold. (1980). "Autographic and Allographic Art Revisited." *Philosophical Studies* 38 (4): 367–83.

Levinson, Jerrold. (1979). "Defining Art Historically." *British Journal of Aesthetics* 19 (3): 232–50.

Lewis, David. (1993). "Many but Almost One." In Keith Campbell, John Bacon and Lloyd Reinhardt (eds.), *Ontology, Causality, and Mind*, 23–38. Cambridge: Cambridge University Press.

Lewis, David. (1978). "Truth in Fiction." *American Philosophical Quarterly* 15: 37–46.

Liao, Shen-Yi. (2016). "Imaginative Resistance, Narrative Engagement, Genre." *Res Philosophica* 93 (2): 461–82.

Liddo, Annalisa Di. (2009). *Alan Moore: Comics as Performance, Fiction as Scalpel*. Oxford: University Press of Mississippi.

Livingston, Paisley. (2010). "On the Appreciation of Cinematic Adaptations." *Projections* 4 (2): 104–27.

Long, Mark and Chris Lamb. (2016). "Editorial Comics: From 'Boss' Tweed to 'Dubya' Bush." In Frank Bramlett, Roy T. Cook and Aaron Meskin (eds.), *The Routledge Companion to Comics*, 209–18. London: Routledge.

MacKinnon, Catharine. (1987). *Feminism Unmodified: Discourses on Life and Law*. Cambridge, MA: Harvard University Press.

Maes, Hans. (2012). "Who Says Pornography Can't Be Art?" In Hans Maes and Jerrold Levinson (eds.), *Art & Pornography: Philosophical Essays*, 17–47. Oxford: Oxford University Press.

Maes, Hans. (2011a). "Art or Porn: Clear Division or False Dilemma?" *Philosophy and Literature* 35 (1): 51–64.

Maes, Hans. (2011b). "Drawing the Line: Art versus Pornography." *Philosophy Compass* 6 (6). 385–97.

Magnus, P. D., Cristyn Magnus and Christy Mag Uidhir. (2013). "Judging Covers." *Journal of Aesthetics and Art Criticism* 71 (4): 361–70.

Mag Uidhir, Christy. (2016). "Comics and Seriality." In Frank Bramlett, Roy T. Cook and Aaron Meskin (eds.), *The Routledge Companion to Comics*, 248–57. London: Routledge.

Mag Uidhir, Christy. (2013). "Epistemic Misuse and Abuse of Pictorial Caricature." *American Philosophical Quarterly* 50 (2): 137–51.

Mag Uidhir, Christy. (2012). "Comics and Collective Authorship." In Aaron Meskin and Roy T. Cook (eds.), *The Art of Comics: A Philosophical Approach*, 47–67. London: Wiley-Blackwell.

Mag Uidhir, Christy. (2009). "Why Pornography Can't Be Art." *Philosophy and Literature* 33 (1): 193–203.

Mag Uidhir, Christy and Henry Pratt. (2012). "Pornography at the Edge: Depiction, Fiction, and Sexual Predilection." In Hans Maes and Jerrold Levinson (eds.), *Art & Pornography: Philosophical Essays*, 137–57. Oxford: Oxford University Press.

Mance, Ajuan. (2017). "LGBTQ Representation in Comics." In Frank Bramlett, Roy T. Cook and Aaron Meskin (eds.), *The Routledge Companion to Comics*, 294–302. London: Routledge.

Matravers, Derek. (2014). *Fiction and Narrative*. Oxford.

Maynard, Patrick. (2005). *Drawing Distinctions: The Varieties of Graphic Expression*. Ithaca, NY: Cornell University Press.

McCloud, Scott. (2006). *Making Comics: Storytelling Secrets of Comics, Manga, and Graphic Novels*. New York: Harper Collins.

McCloud, Scott. (2000). *Reinventing Comics: How Imagination and Technology Are Revolutionizing an Art Form*. New York: Harper Collins.

McCloud, Scott. (1993). *Understanding Comics: The Invisible Art*. New York: Harper Collins.

McGonigal, Andrew. (2013). "Truth, Relativism, and Serial Fiction." *British Journal of Aesthetics* 53 (2): 165–79.

McKean, Dave. (1995). "Storytelling in the Gutter." *History of Photography* 19 (4): 293–7.

McLaughlin, Jeff, ed. (2017a). *Graphic Novels as Philosophy*. Oxford: University Press of Mississippi.

McLaughlin, Jeff. (2017b). "Introduction: What Is It Like to be a Graphic Novel?" In Jeff McLaughlin (ed.), *Graphic Novels as Philosophy*. Oxford: University Press of Mississippi. 3–16.

McLaughlin, Jeff, ed. (2005). *Comics as Philosophy*. Oxford: University Press of Mississippi.

Meskin, Aaron. (2016). "Defining Comics." In Frank Bramlett, Roy T. Cook and Aaron Meskin (eds.), *The Routledge Companion to Comics*, 221–9. London: Routledge.

Meskin, Aaron. (2013). "Comics." In Berys Gaut and Dominic McIver Lopes (eds.), *The Routledge Companion to Aesthetics*, 575–95. London: Routledge.

Meskin, Aaron. (2012). "The Ontology of Comics." In Aaron Meskin and Roy T. Cook (eds.), *The Art of Comics: A Philosophical Approach*, 31–46. London: Wiley-Blackwell.

Meskin, Aaron. (2011). "The Philosophy of Comics." *Philosophy Compass* 6 (12): 854–64.

Meskin, Aaron. (2009a). "Comics as Literature?" *British Journal of Aesthetics* 49 (3): 219–39.

Meskin, Aaron. (2009b). "'Why Don't You Go Read a Book or Something?': *Watchmen* as Literature." In Mark D. White (ed.), *Watchmen and Philosophy: A Rorschach Test*, 157–72. London: Wiley.

Meskin, Aaron. (2007). "Defining Comics?" *Journal of Aesthetics and Art Criticism* 65 (4): 369–79.

Meskin, Aaron and Roy T. Cook. (2012). *The Art of Comics: A Philosophical Approach*. London: Wiley-Blackwell.

Mikkola, Mari. (2019). *Pornography: A Philosophical Introduction*. Oxford: Oxford University Press.

Mikkola, Mari. (2013). "Pornography, Art, and Porno-Art." In Hans Maes (ed.), *Pornographic Aesthetics and the Aesthetics of Pornography*, 27–42. Palgrave McMillan.

Miller, Ann. (2007a). "Oubapo: A Verbal/Visual Medium Is Subjected to Constraints." *Word & Image* 23 (2): 117–37.

Miller, Ann. (2007b). *Reading Bande Dessinée.* Intellect.

Miodrag, Hannah. (2017). "Comics and Literature." In Frank Bramlett, Roy T. Cook and Aaron Meskin (eds.), *The Routledge Companion to Comics*, 390–8. London: Routledge.

Mitaine, Benoît, Dvaid Roche and Isabelle Schmitt-Pitiot, eds. *Comics and Adaptation*, trans. Aarnoud Rommens and David Roche. Oxford: University Press of Mississippi.

Mitchell, Adrielle. (2017). "Comics and Authorship." In Frank Bramlett, Roy T. Cook and Aaron Meskin (eds.), *The Routledge Companion to Comics*, 239–56. London: Routledge.

Molotiu, Andrei. (2020a). "Cartooning." In Charles Hatfield and Barty Beaty (eds.), *Comics Studies: A Guidebook*, 153–71. New Brunswick, NJ: Rutgers University Press.

Molotiu, Andrei. (2020b). "Permanent Ink: Comic Book and Comic Strip Art as Aesthetic Object." In Kim A. Munson (ed.), *Comic Art in Museums*, 33–61. Oxford: University Press of Mississippi.

Molotiu, Andrei. (2016). "Art Comics." In Frank Bramlett, Roy T. Cook and Aaron Meskin (eds.), *The Routledge Companion to Comics*, 119–27. London: Routledge.

Molotiu, Andrei. (2011). "Abstract Form: Sequential Dynamism and Iconostasis in Abstract Comics and in Steve Ditko's *Amazing Spider-Man*." In Matthew Smith and Randy Duncan (eds.), *Critical Approaches to Comics*, 84–100. London: Routledge.

Morrison, Grant. (2011). *Supergods.* New York: Random House.

Munson, Kim A. (2020). *Comic Art in Museums.* Oxford: University Press of Mississippi.

Nadler, Steven and Ben Nadler. (2017). *Heretics!: The Wondrous (and Dangerous) Beginnings of Modern Philosophy.* Princeton University Press.

Nanay, Bence. (2009). "Narrative Pictures." *Journal of Aesthetics and Art Criticism* 67 (1): 119–29.

Nama, Adilifu. (2011). *Super Black: American Pop Culture and Black Superheroes.* Austin: University of Texas Press.

Ndalianis, Angela, ed. (2009). *The Contemporary Comic Book Superhero.* London: Routledge.

Nel, Philip. (2017). *Was the Cat in the Hat Black?: The Hidden Racism of Children's Literature and the Need for Diverse Books.* Oxford: Oxford University Press.

Nguyen, C. Thi and Matt Strohl. (2019). "Cultural Appropriation and the Intimacy of Groups." *Philosophical Studies* 176 (1): 981–1002.

Nguyen, C. Thi and Bekka Williams. (2020). "Moral Outrage Porn." *Journal of Ethics and Social Philosophy* 18 (2): 147–72.

Nolan, Daniel. (2007). "A Consistent Reading of *Sylvan's Box.*" *Philosophical Quarterly* 57: 667–73.

Nyberg, Amy Kiste. (2016). "The Comics Code." In Frank Bramlett, Roy T. Cook and Aaron Meskin (eds.), *The Routledge Companion to Comics*, 25–33. London: Routledge.

Nyberg, Amy Kiste. (1998). *Seal of Approval: The History of the Comics Code.* Oxford: University Press of Mississippi.

Palmer, C. Eddie. (1979). "Pornographic Comics: A Content Analysis." *Journal of Sex Research* 15 (4): 285–98.

Patridge, Stephanie. (2013). "Exclusivism and Evaluation: Art, Erotica, and Pornography." In Hans Maes (ed.), *Pornographic Art and the Aesthetics of Pornography*, 43–57. London: Palgrave Macmillan.

Patton, Michael F. and Kevin Cannon. (2015). *The Cartoon Introduction to Philosophy.* Hill and Wang.

Peaslee, Robert M. and Robert Weiner. (2015). *The Joker: A Serious Study of the Clown Prince of Crime.* Oxford: University Press of Mississippi.

Peeters, Benoit. (2007). "Four Conceptions of the Page." *ImageTexT* 3 (30): 41–60.

Peppard, Anna, ed. (2020). *Supersex: Sexuality, Fantasy, and the Superhero.* Austin: University of Texas Press.

Pedri, Nancy. (2015). "Thinking about Photography in Comics." *Image and Narrative* 16 (2): 1–13.

Phelps, Donald. (2001). *Reading the Funnies.* Fantagraphics.

Picone, Michael. (2013). "Comic Art in Museums and Museums in Comic Art." *European Comic Art* 6 (2): 40–68.

Pizarro, David and Roy Baumeister. (2013). "Superhero Comics as Moral Pornography." In Robin Rosenberg (ed.), *Our Superheroes, Ourselves*, 19–38. Oxford: Oxford University Press.

Pizzino, Christopher. (2016). *Arresting Development: Comics at the Boundaries of Literature.* Austin: University of Texas Press.

Postema, Barbara. (2016). "Silent Comics." In Frank Bramlett, Roy T. Cook and Aaron Meskin (eds.), *The Routledge Companion to Comics*, 201–8. London: Routledge.

Postema, Barbara. (2015). "Establishing Relations: Photography in Wordless Comics." *Image and Narrative* 16 (2): 84–95.

Postema, Barbara. (2013). *Narrative Structure in Comics: Making Sense of Fragments.* Suffolk: Boydell & Brewer.

Pratt, Henry. (2017). "Comics and Adaptation." In Frank Bramlett, Roy T. Cook and Aaron Meskin (eds.), *The Routledge Companion to Comics*, 230–47. London: Routledge.

Pratt, Henry. (2013). "Why Serials Are Killer." *Journal of Aesthetics and Art Criticism* 71 (3): 266–70.

Pratt, Henry. (2012). "Making Comics into Film." In Aaron Meskin and Roy T. Cook (eds.), *The Art of Comics: A Philosophical Approach*, 147–64. London: Wiley-Blackwell.

Pratt, Henry. (2011). "Relating Comics, Cartoons, and Animations." In David Goldblatt and Lee B. Brown (eds.), *Aesthetics: A Reader in the Philosophy of the Arts*, 3rd ed., 369–73. Hoboken, NJ: Pearson-Prentice Hall.

Pratt, Henry. (2009a). "Narrative in Comics." *Journal of Aesthetics and Criticism* 67 (1): 107–17.

Pratt, Henry John. (2009b). "Medium Specificity and the Ethics of Narrative in Comics." *Storyworlds* 1: 97–113.

Priest, Graham. (1997). "Sylvan's Box: A Short Story and Ten Morals." *Notre Dame Journal of Formal Logic* 38: 573–82.

Pustz, Matthew. (2016). "Comics and Fandom." In Frank Bramlett, Roy T. Cook and Aaron Meskin (eds.), *The Routledge Companion to Comics*, 267–74. London: Routledge.

Rea, Michael. (2001). "What Is Pornography?" *Nous* 35 (1): 118–45.

Reicher, Maria Elisabeth. (2016). "What Is the Object in Which Copyright Can Subsist? An Ontological Analysis." In Darren Hudson Hick and Reinold Schmücker (eds.), *The Aesthetics of Copying*, 61–80. London: Bloomsbury.

Rifas, Leonard. (2016). "War Comics." In Frank Bramlett, Roy T. Cook and Aaron Meskin (eds.), *The Routledge Companion to Comics*, 183–91. London: Routledge.

Rifas, Leonard. (2004). "Racial Imagery, Racism, Individualism, and Underground Comics." *ImageText* 1 (1).

Rings, Michael. (2014). "Covers and (Mere?) Remakes: A Reply to Lee B. Brown." *Journal of Aesthetics and Art Criticism* 72 (2): 195–9.

Rings, Michael. (2013). "Doing It Their Way: Rock Covers, Genre, and Appreciation." *Journal of Aesthetics and Art Criticism* 71 (1): 55–63.

Roberts, Thomas J. (1990). *An Aesthetics of Junk Fiction*. Athens: University of Georgia Press.

Robertson, Derik. (2015). "Justification of Poetry Comics: A Multimodal Theory of an Improbably Genre." *The Comics Grid* 5 (1): 1–6.

Robson, Jon. (2017). "Comics and Ethics." In Frank Bramlett, Roy T. Cook and Aaron Meskin (eds.), *The Routledge Companion to Comics*, 311–18. London: Routledge.

Roche, David, Isabelle Schmitt-Pitiot and Benoît Mitaine. (2018). "Introduction: Adapting Adaptation Studies to Comic Studies." In Benoît Mitaine, David Roche and Isabelle Schmitt-Pitiot (eds.), *Comics and Adaptation*, 3–28. Oxford: University Press of Mississippi.

Rohrbaugh, Guy. (2018). "Psychologism about Artistic Plans: Reply to Cray." *Journal of Aesthetics and Art Criticism* 76 (1): 105–7.

Rohrbaugh, Guy. (2017). "Psychologism and Completeness in the Arts." *Journal of Aesthetics and Art Criticism* 75 (2): 131–41.

Rokudenashiko. (2016). *What Is Obscenity?: The Story of a No Good Artist and Her Pussy*. Toronto, ON: Koyama Press.

Rosati, Connie. (1995). "Persons, Perspectives, and Full Information Accounts of the Good." *Ethics* 105 (2): 297–326.

Rosenberg, Robin. (2013). *Our Superheroes, Ourselves*. Oxford: Oxford University Press.

Sabin, Roger. (1993). *Adult Comics*. London: Routledge.

Saito, Yuriko. (1989). "Contemporary Aesthetic Issue: The Colorization Controversy." *Journal of Aesthetic Education* 23 (2): 21–31.

Sanderson, Peter. (1982). *The X-Men Companion*. Fantagraphics.

Salter, Anastasia. (2016). "Comics and Art." In Frank Bramlett, Roy T. Cook and Aaron Meskin (eds.), *The Routledge Companion to Comics*, 348–57. London: Routledge.

Schwartz, Ben. (2010). *Best American Comics Criticism*. Fantagraphics.

Sellars, Wilfrid. (1962). "Philosophy and the Scientific Image of Man." In Robert Colodny (ed.), *Frontiers of Science and Philosophy*, 35–78. Pittsburgh: University of Pittsburgh Press.

Sider, Theodore. (2001). "Maximality and Intrinsic Properties." *Philosophy and Phenomenological Research* 63 (2): 357–64.

Simon, Joe. (1990). *The Comic Book Makers*. New York: Vanguard.

Singer, Marc. (2018). *Breaking the Frames: Populism and Prestige in Comics Studies*. Austin: University of Texas Press.

Singer, Marc. (2002). "'Black Skins' and White Masks: Comic Books and the Secret of Race." *African American Review* 36 (1): 107–19.

Smith, Matthew and Randy Duncan. (2017). *The Secret Origins of Comics Studies*. London: Routledge.

Smith, Matthew. (2016). "Superhero Comics." In Frank Bramlett, Roy T. Cook and Aaron Meskin (eds.), *The Routledge Companion to Comics*, 128–36. London: Routledge.

Smith, Matthew and Randy Duncan. (2009). *The Power of Comics: History, Form, and Culture*. London: Bloomsbury.

Smith, Michael. (2004). *The Moral Problem*. Oxford.

Smith, Scott, ed. (2019). *Uncanny Bodies: Superhero Comics and Disability*. University Park, PA: Penn State University Press.

Smolderen, Thierry. (2014). *The Origins of Comics: From William Hogarth to Winsor McCay*. Oxford: University Press of Mississippi.

Smolderen, Thierry. (2007). "Of Labels, Loops and Bubbles: Solving the Historical Puzzle of the Speech Balloon." *Comic Art* 8: 90–112.

Smuts, Aaron. (2009). "Story Identity and Story Type." *Journal of Aesthetics and Art Criticism* 67 (1): 5–13.

Sousanis, Nick. (2015). *Unflattening*. Cambridge, MA: Harvard University Press.

Spiegelman, Art. (2020). "'High Art Lowdown': This Review Is Not Sponsored by AT&T." In Kim A. Munson (ed.), *Comic Art in Museums*. Oxford: University Press of Mississippi. 256. Originally published in *Artforum*, December 1990.

Spiegelman, Art. (2008). *Breakdowns: Portrait of the Artist as a Young %@&*!*. New York: Pantheon.

Spiegelman, Art and Kidd, Chip. (2001). *Jack Cole and Plastic Man: Forms Stretched to Their Limits*. San Franciso, CA: Chronicle Books.

Stam, Robert. (2005). "Introduction: The Theory and Practice of Adaptation." In Robert Stam and Alessandra Raengo (eds.), *Literature and Film: A Guide to the Theory and Practice of Film Adaptation*. Blackwell. 1–52.

Stecker, Robert. (1996). "What Is Literature?" *Revue Internationale de Philosophie* 50 (198): 681–94.

Suits, Bernard. (2014). *The Grasshopper: Games, Life, and Utopia*, 3rd ed. Peterborough, ON: Broadview Press.

Thomasson, Amie. (1999). *Fiction and Metaphysics*. Cambridge.

Thon, Jan-Noel. (2019). "Transmedia Characters: Theory and Analysis." *Frontiers of Narrative Studies* 5 (2): 176–99.

Tillman, Chris. (2016). "The Matter of Serial Fiction." *Res Philosophica* 93 (2): 425–39.

Tinker, Emma. (2007). "Manuscript in Print: The Materiality of Alternative Comics." *Literature Compass* 4 (4): 1169–82.

Trogdon, Kelly and Paisley Livingston. (2015). "Artwork Completion: A Response to Gover." *Journal of Aesthetics and Art Criticism* 72 (3): 460–2.

Trogdon, Kelly and Paisley Livingston. (2014). "The Complete Work." *Journal of Aesthetics and Art Criticism* 72 (3): 225–33.

Tuusvouri, Jarkko. (2017). "Philosophy in the Bargain: *A Contract with God* (1978) by Will Eisner." In Jeff McLaughin (ed.), *Graphic Novels as Philosophy*, 17–40. Oxford: University Press of Mississippi.

Tyree, Tia C. M. (2013). "Contemporary Representations of Black Females in Newspaper Comic Strips." In Sheena C. Howard and Ronald L. Jackson II (eds.), *Black Comics: Politics of Race and Representation*. London: Bloomsbury.

Van Camp, Julie. (1995). "The Colorization Controversy." *The Journal of Value Inquiry* 29: 447–68.

Van Inwagen, Peter. (1990). *Material Beings*. Ithaca, NY: Cornell University Press.

Van Inwagen, Peter. (1977). "Creatures of Fiction." *American Philosophical Quarterly* 14 (4): 299–308.

Van Lente, Fred and Ryan Dunlavey. (2017). *The Comic Book History of Comics: Birth of a Medium*. San Diego, CA: IDW Publishing.

Van Ness, Sara J. (2010). *Watchmen as Literature: A Critical Study of the Graphic Novel*. Jefferson, NC: MacFarland & Company.

Vasilaki, Mimi. (2010). "Why Some Pornography May be Art." *Philosophy and Literature* 34 (1): 228–33.

Von Solodkoff, Tatjana and Richard Woodward. (2017). "To Have and to Hold." *Philosophical Issues* 27 (1): 407–27.

Walker, Mort. (1980). *The Lexicon of Comicana*. New York: Museum of Cartoon Art.

Walton, Kendall. (1990). *Mimesis as Make-Believe: On the Foundations of the Representational Arts*. Cambridge, MA: Harvard University Press.

Walton, Kendall. (1970). "Categories of Art." *Philosophical Review* 79 (3): 334–67.

Wanzo, Rebecca. (2020). *The Content of Our Caricature: African American Comic Art and Political Belonging*. New York: New York University Press.

Wartenberg, Thomas. (2012). "Wordy Pictures: Theorizing the Relationship between Image and Text in Comics." In Aaron Meskin and Roy T. Cook (eds.), *The Art of Comics: A Philosophical Approach*, 87–104. London: Wiley-Blackwell.

Watson, Lori. (2010). "Pornography." *Philosophy Compass* 5 (7): 535–50.

Waugh, Colton. (1947). *The Comics*. Macmillan.

Wertham, Fredric. (1954). *The Seduction of the Innocent*. New York: Rinehart and Company.

White, Mark D. (2019). *Batman and Ethics*. London: Wiley-Blackwell.

White, Mark D. (2009). *Watchmen and Philosophy: A Rorschach Test*. London: Wiley.

Whitted, Qiana. (2019). *EC Comics: Race, Shock, and Social Protest*. New Brunswick, NJ: Rutgers University Press.

Windsor, Mark. (2019). "Tales of Dread." *Estetika* 1: 65–86.

Witek, Joseph. (2009). "The Arrow and the Grid." In Jeet Heer and Kent Worcester (eds.), *A Comics Studies Reader*, 149–56. Oxford: University Press of Mississippi.

Wittgenstein, Ludwig. (1953/2009). *Philosophical Investigations*, trans. G. E. M. Anscombe. London: Wiley-Blackwell.

Wolk, Douglas. (2007). *Reading Comics: How Graphic Novels Work and What They Mean*. De Capo Press.

Woo, Benjamin. (2020). "What Kind of Studies Is Comics Studies?" In Frederick Luis Aldama (ed.), *The Oxford Handbook of Comic Book Studies*, 3–15. Oxford: Oxford University Press.

Woodward, Richard. (2011). "Truth in Fiction." *Philosophy Compass* 6 (3): 158–67.

Xhignesse, Michel-Antoine. (forthcoming) "Imagining Fictional Contradictions." *Synthese*.

Xhignesse, Michel-Antoine. (2021). "Exploding Stories and the Limits of Fiction." *Philosophical Studies* 178 (3): 675–92.

Yagisawa, Takashi. (2001). "Against Creationism in Fiction." *Nous* 35: 153–72.

Yanel, Robert. (2003). "Two Monsters in Search of a Concept." *Contemporary Aesthetics* 1.

Yezbick, Daniel F. (2015). "'No Sweat!': EC Comics, Cold War Censorship, and the Troublesome Colors of '*Judgment Day!*'" In Frances Gateward and John Jennings (eds.), *The Blacker the Ink*, 19–44. New Brunswick, NJ: Rutgers University Press.

Young, James. (2020). *Radically Rethinking Copyright in the Arts: A Philosophical Approach*. London: Routledge.

Young, James. (2016). "Appropriating Fictional Characters." In Darren Hudson Hick and Reinhold Schmücker (eds.), *The Aesthetics and Ethics of Copying*, 153–72. London: Bloomsbury.

Young, James. (2010). *Cultural Appropriation and the Arts*. London: Wiley-Blackwell.

Young, James. (1988). "In Defence of Colourization." *British Journal of Aesthetics* 28 (4): 368–72.

Zalta, Edward. (2003). "Referring to Fictional Characters." *Dialectica* 57: 243–54.

Index